Regenerating the
Philosophy of Education

Studies in the
Postmodern Theory of Education

Shirley R. Steinberg
General Editor

Vol. 352

PETER LANG
New York • Washington, D.C./Baltimore • Bern
Frankfurt • Berlin • Brussels • Vienna • Oxford

Regenerating the Philosophy of Education

what happened to soul?

Joe L. Kincheloe *and* Randall Hewitt
EDITORS

INTRODUCTION BY Shirley R. Steinberg

PETER LANG
New York • Washington, D.C./Baltimore • Bern
Frankfurt • Berlin • Brussels • Vienna • Oxford

Library of Congress Cataloging-in-Publication Data
Regenerating the philosophy of education: what happened to soul? /
edited by Joe L. Kincheloe, Randall Hewitt.
p. cm. — (Counterpoints: studies in the postmodern theory of education; v. 352)
Includes bibliographical references.
1. Teachers—Training of—Curricula.
2. Education—Philosophy—Study and teaching (Higher)
3. Postmodernism and education. I. Kincheloe, Joe L. II. Hewitt, Randall.
LB1707.R445 370.1—dc22 2011009387
ISBN 978-1-4331-0430-5 (hardcover)
ISBN 978-1-4331-0431-2 (paperback)
ISSN 1058-1634

Bibliographic information published by **Die Deutsche Nationalbibliothek**.
Die Deutsche Nationalbibliothek lists this publication in the "Deutsche
Nationalbibliografie"; detailed bibliographic data is available
on the Internet at http://dnb.d-nb.de/.

Cover art by Moey Hewitt
Moey Hewitt is an artist living in Daytona Beach, Florida

The paper in this book meets the guidelines for permanence and durability
of the Committee on Production Guidelines for Book Longevity
of the Council of Library Resources.

© 2011 Peter Lang Publishing, Inc., New York
29 Broadway, 18th floor, New York, NY 10006
www.peterlang.com

All rights reserved.
Reprint or reproduction, even partially, in all forms such as microfilm,
xerography, microfiche, microcard, and offset strictly prohibited.

Printed in the United States of America

for our *chilrin*

Althea
Bronwyn
Chaim
Chippy
Christine
Cohen
Hava
Ian
Luna
Maci
Marissa
Meghann
Milo Joe
Moey
Ryan
Sadie
Seth

Contents

A Preface ix
   Randall Hewitt

Part One
What Happened to Soul?

1 The Philosophical Soul: Where Did It Come From? Where Did It Go? 3
   Shirley R. Steinberg

2 Eyes of the Education Faculty: Derrida, Philosophy, and Teacher Education
in the Postmodern University 11
   Dennis Carlson

3 Lost Soul: The Eradication of Philosophy from Colleges of Education 25
   Robert V. Bullough, Jr. and *Craig Kridel*

4 "It's Just the Way Things Are:" The Lamentable Erosion of Philosophy
in Teacher Education 35
   Paul Theobald and *Clifton S. Tanabe*

5 The Practitioner Has No Clothes: Resisting Practice Divorced from
Philosophy in Teacher Education and the Classroom 43
   P. L. Thomas and *Ed Weichel*

6 After Socrates: Community of Philosophical Inquiry and the New World Order 55
   David Kennedy

7 (Re)placing: Foundations in Education: Politics of Survival in Conservative Times 69
   John E. Petrovic and *Aaron M. Kunz*

8 Vocational Education and the Continuing Struggle for Critical Democratic Pedagogy .. 87
   James H. Adams and *Natalie G. Adams*

9 Indigenous Knowledge and the Challege for Rethinking Conventional
Educational Philosophy: A Ghanaian Case Study 97
George J. Sefa Dei and *Marlon Simmons*

Part Two
The Soul: Where Will It Go?

10 No Room for Wonder 115
Clar Doyle and *John Hoben*

11 Philosophy Applied to Education, Revisited 127
Barbara J. Thayer-Bacon

12 Cultivating Unique Potential in Schools: Revisioning Democratic
Teacher Education 141
Craig A. Cunningham

13 Pluralism and Praxis: Philosophy of Education for Teachers 157
David A. Granger and *Jane Fowler Morse*

14 Taking Teacher Education into Alien Terrain: The Future of
Educational Theorizing 173
Susan Schramm-Pate

15 On the Importance of Philosophy to the Study of Teachers 187
Greg Seals

16 Philosophy of Education: Looking Back to the Crossroads and
Forward to the Possibilities 199
Douglas J. Simpson and *Lee S. Duemer*

17 Education, Philosophy, and the Cultivation of Humanity....................209
William B. Stanley

18 A Critical Complex Epistemology of Practice 219
Joe L. Kincheloe

Appendix 1: The Southern Epistemology....................................231
Joe L. Kincheloe

Appendix 2: Soul...237
Joe L. Kincheloe

Contributors 239

A Preface

Randall Hewitt

Cold-ass February, 2008. Graduate Curriculum and Standards Committee. I was simply filling in. Up on the Committee's agenda: A vote on keeping Social Foundations as a core requirement in Ed.D. and Ph.D. Programs in the College.

Coming in cold, I attempted to lay out the kinds of questions social foundations courses ask of students: "What do we mean by 'education'?" "What have we meant by 'education' in the past?" "How should we conceptualize 'education'?" "What psycho-sociological facts about the human experience are necessary in answering these questions?" Everyone present accepted the commonly held assumption that the human organism is both a product and producer of its environment. Thus, I argued that social foundations courses work to illuminate the influence of this environment, the influence of class, race, and gender on human consciousness and conduct. In this sense, then, social foundations bring to attention and deliberation the necessary questions of who we are and who we want to be, all of which require the opportunity for sustained and systematic focus, inquiry, and debate. I even broke out John Dewey. I said, "If we can accept Dewey's statement that 'self-criticism is the road to release of creative activity,' then social foundations courses provide the opportunity for us to take a look at ourselves, an occasion for deep soul searching, as Cornel West likes to say, an existential questioning."

Seriously. I never thought that I would ever have to justify the moral importance of social foundations courses—particularly philosophy of education courses—in Ph.D. and Ed.D. programs to a committee of colleagues, all holding Ph.Ds. The "fucking" situational irony of it all was too much to bear.

"What you say is eloquent, Randy, it really is. But, this is a new day and a new way is in order." Stunned, speechless, I started hearing voices, feelings really, and fragments of voices.

> *Emily (Our Town, Act Three): Good-by, good-by, world. Good-by Grover's Corners. . . .Mama and Papa. Good-by to clocks ticking. . .and Mama's sunflowers. And food and coffee. And new-ironed dresses and hot baths. . .and sleeping and waking up. Oh, earth, you're too wonderful for anybody to realize you. . . .*
>
> *Emily to Stage Manager: Do any human beings ever realize life while they live it?—every, every minute?*
>
> *Stage Manager: No. The saints and poets, maybe—they do some.*

I saw flashes of students' faces, blank like coal-miners' and caked with the standard toxic dust of bureaucratic efficiency. The voices rose again.

> *A rationalized, automated, totally managed world. . . .dependents on the apparatus. . . .appendages of the machine.*
>
> *Educational form, habits bereft of soul, deadening, a form actively producing what Cornel West has referred to in another context as "emaciated souls" and "overinflated egos."*

Dewey—believe it or not—screaming through my brain stereophonically against the Committee's chorus of "nuts and bolts issues," educational programming and delivery systems prattle:

> *Hence we are flooded by impressions forced upon us from without, and the outcome is a stagnant pool that permits all kinds of alien things to be thrown in. When we act, we act spasmodically or violently as if in an effort to throw off the very things that should have nourished us but that are only choking us.*

"Call the question," the Chairperson said. *Troubled brain. Maggot brain.* "The 'yeas' have it. . . . Meeting adjourned."

At the doorway I was stopped by a Committee member who wanted to ensure no hard feelings were felt between him and me. "*The Shame of the Nation* is a touching, instrumental piece in my course. And, while I don't understand what he is saying most of the time, I'm down with McLaren's *Life in Schools*, too." He said a bunch of other stuff but I wasn't hearing it. I was flooded with the words of a former student, an old reporter from the *Orlando Sentinel* whose temperament bore deep scars from the corporate rationalizing of his own craft. Having sensed my frustration with a class for not seeing the commercialization of schooling as a problem for democracy, the old reporter said to me, "You have to sell them a fuller understanding of democracy and democratic education in a way that is simple, concrete, beautiful." Sell them? Beautiful?

Anyway I looked at it, I had failed. I failed to justify the place of social foundations work with beauty such that this committee could feel it and understand it as a necessary part in the process of promoting personal and social growth. I failed partly because I myself didn't know in any concrete way anymore. All of the things that I had been arguing about for the last ten years had become mere abstractions: democracy, justice, coming to consciousness, beauty? Who in the fuck was I kidding?

My philosophic sense had failed me, so I ran. I withdrew into private realms where I felt most natural, most at ease, into surfing and skating, into the mundane yet precious breathes taken at the kitchen sink while listening to my girls cackle away hours at petty parlor games. I tried to create a neat, tidy, cordon little sanctum of intense personal meaningfulness. But, one can pin-up experience into neat, tidy little categories like personal, private/social, or public only for so long. As William James puts it, "In the great boarding-house of nature, the cakes and the butter and the syrup seldom come out so even and leave the plates so clean" (James, 1897/1956, p. 22). For instance, Cole constantly harassed RJ at the skatepark with "Your front-side 50s are so gay a freaking girl could do them." Little Randy, his sister Nina, Elijah and his little brother Dominic, plus Blake, Emma, RJ and Gage were dropped off at the skatepark from the moment it opened until after Matt shut off the lights at 10 p.m. Their parents loved them as best they could but still, there were taxis to drive, lawns to cut, cruise-ships to clean, and shit-hole bars to dance topless in. My refuge of particulars too was shot through with struggle, with the precarious, with race and gender and class. I had been raised up by tough-minded people whose ultimate prayer was not to be delivered from experience but to act gracefully in the light of all that experience brings to bear. And here I was running from experience itself, unfaithful to a blue-collar spirit that had animated me and watched over me all of my life. I felt shame and self-pity at the same time. Looking for someone to blame, I called Joe Kincheloe, the person most responsible for encouraging me into academic work in the first place.

I had taken up council with Joe for almost twenty years. Our bond was existential and familial, in a white-trash, soul-brother sort of way. But, Joe didn't introduce me to "holes-in-the-wall," relatives having sex with each other, and drunken and drugged-out fist-fights over Cheetos. I probably was more intimate than he was with drafty trailers, butchering hogs, and grown-ass men smothering themselves in paper bags of grey paint. I'm pretty sure that my mama and daddy wrote the manual on running from and threatening bill collectors, and while my grandpa on my mama's side may not have set crosses on fire, he expressed great sympathy for those who did. My path to redemption and salvation was opened over in Sunnyside, certainly not on the mill-hill and not by Joe either. It was through the graciousness of the Drummonds, Wallaces, and O'Neils that I was cautiously welcomed into their black space and eloquently taught that I wipe my ass just like everybody else. Their living examples pointed up to me something about race—the human race—and that poverty-stricken Sunnyside and "lint-head" Victor Mill had more in common than upwardly mobile Needmore and lily-white, manicured Victor Heights, regardless of race. No, Joe didn't introduce me to the low-down; I was born into that funk. What Joe did was remind me that at root all funk was the blues and gospel and that my funk was just a particular, shared rhythmic attitude toward the precarious and prophetic in experience. And what Joe was a master at doing was drawing this funk out of me so that I could better understand why I dance and cry, hustle and bump, love and hate, and hope and rage. You see, Joe Kincheloe was a bluesman, a foundations man.

In *Boogie Man: The Adventures of John Lee Hooker in the American Twentieth Century*, Charles Shaar Murray argues that the art of the bluesman is the art of the healer. By telling his story—or variations of it—the bluesman "enables us to face our own. In this sense, the bluesman is our confessor, our shrink; it is his job to forgive us and comfort us, shoulder our burdens as he invites us to help him shoulder his own" (Murray, 2000, pp. 8–9). And as the great Eudora Welty suggests, listening keenly and seeing with range and depth are intuitions necessary to all good story telling (Welty, 2002, p. 31). What the storyteller is listening and looking for is the universal as it reveals itself—as it can only reveal itself—through the local, in downtown Kingsport, for example, or on the outskirts of Greer at 4:20 p.m. So, she listens for "the problems of the human heart in conflict with itself," cast through Papa Drummond's cuss words and reflected in Aunt Effie's prayers. She sees "love and honor and pity and pride and compassion and sacrifice" as these are hunched over in a Tampa sod field or hidden in the back corners of the Sagittarius Lounge (Faulkner, 1950). Her task is to "transfer without distortion" the cadence of this shared life expressed through idiom and embodied in gesture just "this side of chaos" (Welty, 2002, p. 71). And when she hits the mark, the emotions that flow out of everyday life become the flashpoints whereby we not only understand ourselves better as *human* beings but because of this understanding, we feel life more variously, more intensely, rendering us, in turn, more susceptible and tender towards our lives together.

To Joe Kincheloe, our lived stories not only were means to underscore a moral point about the world but primarily were modes of inquiry into and ways to craft ourselves, as curricula connecting soul to soul, melodic variations played over the rhythmic repetition called life. He did this foundations work from the inside out. He drew from the depths of his own experience growing up to Depression-era parents in Southern Appalachia, a place riddled with racism, sexism, class prejudice, and, of course, the holy ghost, to understand and validate other people's felt experience and to pull out the demons and daimons wandering the back channels of their consciousness. Joe's stories and my own always shared the same root note, social class. He was my bigger brother forever reminding me of what Daddy had said about this life before he left it: "You may get beat, you may lose this motherfucker, but goddamn you if you are beaten by your own laziness and timidity. Keep your head down, trust your own sensibilities, and charge it with all you got." So, calling on family in a time of personal and professional crisis made good subconscious sense. Joe gave no shelter to self-pity and saw shame as kindling to fire the soul. I knew he was the person to seek out.

"Joe, you are not going to believe this shit but a committee in my college has just stricken social foundations from the core of our Ph.D. and Ed.D. programs."

"But of course," Joe said. "This is the consequence of a neoliberal, techno-rationalist assault on higher education in general and on colleges of education in particular. This has been going on now for forty years. You shouldn't be surprised. It is the democratic struggle, it's life struggle, it's a struggle over the meaning of life, over the meaning of justice, freedom, education, equality, the good life, happiness, it's all of that and more."

"Ok, but what the fuck am I supposed to do. I'm in an institution that doesn't value critical thought! I don't even want to do this shit anymore."

"But then you are just giving up and these forces win without contest. Your job as a philosopher of education hasn't changed any despite the changes in your immediate conditions. You just keep on keepin' on and we'll have a deeper discussion of the state of things when you come up here in December. Then he gave me a "peace be with you" in his best preacher voice and he hung up the phone.

He and Shirley went to Jamaica that December, but only Shirley came back. We never did get to have that "deeper discussion" and I continue to flounder. It is my hope that this collection of essays serves to bring forth the deeper discussion that Joe and I never did get to have.

References

Faulkner, W. (1950). *Nobel Prize Acceptance Speech.* http://www.rjgeib.com/thoughts/faulkner/faulkner.html
James, W. (1897/1956). *The Will to Believe and Other Essays in Popular Philosophy.* New York: Dover Publications, Inc.
Murray, C. S. (2000). *Boogie Man: The Adventures of John Lee Hooker in the American Twentieth Century.* New York: St. Martin's Press.
Welty, E. (2002). *On Writing.* New York: Random House, Inc.

Part One

What Happened to Soul?

One

The Philosophical Soul: Where Did It Come from? Where Did It Go?

Shirley R. Steinberg

Etymology

Growing up in the California education system of the 1960s privileged me as I could choose my own high school courses. To the dismay of my parents, I opted out of math after the eighth grade to take alternative classes. I convinced mom and dad that I could, indeed, make it to university, and courses like philosophy could possibly enhance my education. The elective courses I took in high school did change my life. . .along with the knowledge that I was empowered by the mere act of making my own decisions about my curriculum. I'm sure this sounds radical to those reading. . .students don't make decisions in the schools of the 21st century; and classes like philosophy are certainly not offered in most garden-variety public high schools.

I loved philosophy class. It was decidedly Greek and the term ended with a splash of the Enlightenment. Loved every single white man we studied; relished quoting them, argued the nuances of thinking, existence, and destiny. Coupled with a superb, sort of crazy English teacher (intent on teaching the Transcendentalists), I finished my final year of high school confident that the depth of my knowledge would amaze everyone, and that I could chose my destiny. 1969 was the era of wearing one's intellect in the back pocket of bellbottom jeans. Copies of *Siddhartha, Stranger in a Strange Land,* and (to my eternal embarrassment, *Jonathan Livingston Seagull*) popped out of those tight jeans, and our teenage discourse took on a seriously earnest tone. As we were *talkin 'bout our generation,* we attempted to contextualize how we fit within both the canonical and the nouveau.

I surfed my wave of brilliance for the first years of my adult life. Played around undergraduate courses, and took a hell of a lot of time to graduate. In the mid-1980s, I attended the University of Leeds for a year while living in Yorkshire. Entering a course of study for women who were considering returning to university, I enrolled in another philosophy class. No Plato, no Locke, no Rousseau, no dominant culture. The lightning bolt that was women's studies had seared into my forehead, I realized I had missed a lot in my earlier course. While I cannot discount the importance of my high school philosophy class, I resented (early feminism did encourage resentment) the fact that philosophy had been fed to me as being a white male and European discourse. I also discovered that philosophy was fluid and that the notion of classic, indeed, meant old. . .and that philosophy wasn't a discipline, but concepts which breathed and informed within other disciplines, other ways of seeing the world. My courses at Leeds introduced female writers, poets, artists, and feminist philosophy. I realized that no *gender* had cornered the knowledge market. . .I found I could think about knowledge, and I could create knowledge. I could be a philosopher.

After returning to Canada in 1984, I entered a program for a graduate degree in Education. Alan Bloom had just decreed that schooling must include philosophical classics, and that the American mind had closed due to the elimination of a specific canon (Bloom, 1989). Uncle Alan's tome was just the push I needed in order to start to. . .to start to. . .to start to formulate my own ways of reading the world, of experiencing knowledge, and to question the traditional paths of theorizing thought, action, and human beings. His unilateral demand that schooling contain a prescribed curriculum of knowledge to be deposited into the heads of students ruffled my newly plumed feminist feathers. Certainly, in Robert (Bob) Anderson's spectacular Philosophy of Education class I read more *classics*. . .Comenius, Rousseau, Whitehead, and Dewey. But Bob pushed these thinkers further and challenged me to challenge the good ole boys, to interrogate them and to re-create philosophy so it contextualized my own notions of teaching and existence. Bob introduced me to current feminist thought, philosophy, and to the book and the notions of *Women's Ways of Knowing* (Belenky et al., 1987). It is only fitting that I mention Bob here, in the introduction to a book intent on keeping the soul within educational philosophy. His mentorship and influence have followed me for the past three decades and I am forever grateful.

My journey within philosophy had really just begun. Possibly the seminal philosophical idea that I discovered in those early days is that philosophy is tentative, elastic, and every changing. The lower case *p* is not declarative in the philosophy I would attempt to employ and adopt, and it wasn't an *it*. I began to see philosophy as a series of notions, set forth by people in order to create a discourse. Naturally, I was aware that the philosophers, themselves, may not have agreed. . .indeed, I am sure many of them didn't seek for discourse, but for validation and confirmation that their thoughts and words, were *the* thoughts and words. But Bob's pedagogy of investigation stayed with me and, coupled with early social theoretical groundings and my generation's natural ability to throw around deconstructionn this formed the zygote of my need to know, employ, and create philosophy.

My second term of graduate school at the University of Lethbridge began with a qualitative research course taught by David G. Smith. I wasn't keen on taking a course on research, indeed the idea of research implied empiricism, triangulation, and a left-brain rigor; I expected it to be unpleasant. David taught research as philosophy, and philosophy as research. After reading Dewey's *My Pedagogic Creed* (1897), we wrote our own philosophical credo of pedagogy. Taking cues from Dewey's ability to accessibly and succinctly articulate what it meant to be an educator, I discovered who I was as a teacher and researcher by my own writing. David introduced a series of articles, which grounded qualitative research within social theory and philosophy. I remember how difficult those articles were, to the point that I spoke to David and asked if I was smart enough to continue the program—that the articles were intimidating and in a difficult "language." David laughed, and told me that he felt the same way: "Shirley, don't you think I find them difficult?" He said that he always read these articles more than once and guided me in an ability to gain access to the language. So it wasn't going to be easy. . .becoming brilliant would take time, it would take effort.

David taught qualitative research as a philosophy and social theory. Methodology was not emphasized, rather the notion that one could situate themselves within their own research, validity, and truth was not the goal of research: asking questions of the questions was the goal. . .making meaning. And so, I was introduced to hermeneutics. David also introduced me to the philosopher/theorist/teacher whose work would underpin the rest of my life, Paulo Freire. By bringing Freire into a research class, we understood that society and contextualization could not be separated from research. We discovered that the research could mean *something*, which could bring about change: research grounded in equity and social justice. Research engaged with philosophy to create a soul.

Phenomenology

The origins of my own philosoph(ies) led me directly to my own destiny as a woman, a mother, a partner, and an educator. By finding my way to Paulo Freire, I understood that it was impossible to separate my teaching, my writing, and my life. If I was going to pursue a teaching career, it would have to be grounded in a specific way of reading the world. Even as a young girl, I had always been aware of power, influences of power, and notions of authority. . .and I had bucked against power. I had an innate suspicion of power in my being for as long as I can remember thinking a thought. I was always told that my feelings about power were unfounded, contrary, and would eventually be destructive in future endeavors. Through Freire, I found critical theory and a critical pedagogy. The Frankfurt School gave me a more contemporary philosophy, one which was grounded in social issues, class, and dynamics of power. Theodor Adorno's F Scale spoke to me as a female, a Jew, as a teacher. Understanding the morphing nature of power, the insidiousness of authority, I became acutely aware of the ability of the powerful to marginalize and silence.

The early 1990s saw the fruition of the postmodern movement within education: a discipline that was a step late to literary theory and other social science discourses. Educators have always come to new paradigms with trepidation. Postmodernism became the leftist theory du jour, and I felt comfortable with its lack of structure and form. Revisiting my own early philosophical history I saw the gaps in the upper case P of "classical philosophy," and its replacement by the Enlightenment. Coincidental with my own philosophical renaissance, I attended a conference in Dayton, Ohio, and met Joe Kincheloe. This is not the venue to revisit our lifelong partnership and love affair. However, along with meeting my life partner in Joe, I read his first book where Joe took up the notion of instrumental rationality and positivism. His work moved Freire to the next level. With Joe's mentorship, I began to read Henry Giroux and Stanley Aronowitz and was able to put my new critical theory into a perspective I could understand.

This section of my philosophical soul train was so dynamic that I began to understand that I knew that I did not know much; but that knowing what I didn't know was as/or more important that what I did know. Joe and I began to explore *what it was like* to be a teacher and how we begin to learn to know. We wanted to understand how research, teaching, and practice could become merged, and avoid the traditional nature of the three to remain separate entities. We wanted to teach our students to become teacher/researchers, philosophically grounded and critically informed. And so we became determined to keep the philosophical within teacher education.

Epistemology

Grounded on the assumption that traditional scientific notions of the relationship between knowledge produced about education and practice have not been sufficiently examined, our work began to call for more research on the complex nature of this relationship. We identified that a culture gap often existed between practitioners and theory/research. Many teachers have come to believe that educational philosophers and theorists have little to say that would be helpful to their everyday lives. In this context philosophy and practice are separate entities—many educational scholars are captives of their epistemologies and their professional cultures' own agenda. They are captives in the sense that they have tended to ask only those questions answerable by the empirical methods of physical science. One discipline or paradigm is not adequate to the task of understanding the network of the intricate and ambiguous human relationships making up a classroom or a school. Scholars need a social theoretical/philosophical set of research strategies to help understand such school/classroom interactions and their relationship to deep social, cultural, and economic structures. In the technical rationality of much educational research, the attempt to translate such intricate relationships into pedagogical knowledge often renders the data gathered meaningless in the eyes of practitioners. Until we gain a deeper understanding of the relationship between knowledge and practice—the epistemology of practice—the gulf between researchers and practitioners will remain. The foundations of education are essential in bridging that gulf.

Ontology

In this context Joe and I engaged in the excitement of attaining new levels of consciousness and "ways of being." Individuals who gain such a critical ontological awareness understand how and why their political opinions, religious beliefs, gender role, racial positions, and sexual orientation have been shaped by dominant cultural perspectives. A critical ontological vision helps us in the effort to gain new understandings and insights as to who we can become. Such a vision helps us move beyond our present state of being—our ontological selves—as we discern the forces that have made us that way. The line between knowledge production and being is blurred, as the epistemological and the ontological converge around questions of identity. As we employ the ontological vision we ask questions about ethics, morality, politics, emotion, and gut feelings, seeking not precise steps to reshape our subjectivity but a framework of principles with which we can negotiate. Thus, we join the quest for new, expanded, more just and interconnected ways of being human.

Joe and I posited that an important dimension of a critical ontology involves freeing ourselves from the machine metaphors of Cartesianism. Such an ontological stance recognizes the reductionism of viewing the universe as a well-oiled machine and the human mind as a computer. Such colonial ways of being subvert an appreciation of the amazing life force that inhabits both the universe and human beings. This machine cosmology has positioned human beings as living in a dead world, a lifeless universe. Ontologically, this Western Cartesianism has separated individuals from their inanimate surroundings, undermining any organic interconnection of the person to the cosmos. The life-giving complexity of the inseparability of human and world has been lost and social/cultural/pedagogical/psychological/philosophical studies of people abstracted—removed from context. Such a removal has exerted disastrous ontological effects. Human beings, in a sense, lost their belongingness to both the world and to other people around them.

. . .ologies Do Matter

For the past 19 years, Joe and I made praxis our goal. We, along with the authors in this book, maintain that without philosophical and social theoretical groundwork in teacher education, young teachers will continue to be decontextualized, deskilled, and deprofessionalized. This book is an attempt to bring attention to the loss of philosophy within faculties of education, and to create a dialogue on how to revive it. . .the soul of our profession.

When Joe and Randy conceptualized this book, they invited specific colleagues to contribute. These scholar/teacher/philosophers are all committed to the notion that a philosophically grounded pedagogy is essential and the realization that the very foundations of education have been eviscerated, and contend that the soul of education, indeed, is grounded in philosophy. As responsible scholars and teachers in schools of education, the authors are examining the current trend to eliminate philosophy within our faculties, and then to explore the possibilities.

Joe Kincheloe, a consummate philosopher and teacher of teachers, was also a musician. Several years ago, he wrote a song, *Soul,* which examined the loss of soul within music, social justice, and in the hearts of many people. *Soul* may have been his best song. Whenever Tony and the Hegemones performed, *Soul* was the type of song which everyone thought they knew and sang along to. . ...the first time they heard it. After Joe died, *Soul* became Joe's anthem. Our son, Ian, had lyrics tattooed on his arm: *What happened to soul?* a memorial to Joe's song, and the fact that our lives had lost our soul in losing Joe. Around the same time, Randy Hewitt phoned me and said he would like to rename this book *What Happened to Soul?* Randy acknowledged that, indeed, much of the soul in education lies in the philosophical and social theoretical underpinnings within the foundations of education and education had lost its soul. This book is structured using Joe's song as a metaphor.

The first section of the book asks the question *What Happened to Soul?* Randy articulates soul in his introduction as he talks about the way that Joe did foundations "from the inside out." That is how philosophy must be approached, with an embedded commitment for knowers to understand the known and the unknown. Randy's background as a 'linthead,' a kid from a Southern mill town qualifies him as a philosopher, like so many from the disenfranchised working towns of North America, Randy was born with an intuitive understanding of what he knew and what he knew he didn't know. Drawing his own scholarship from his lived experiences, and his philosophy from Dewey, Randy's teaching and work articulates the ability of knowledge and theory to surpass class. . .sometimes one just has to have, as they say in the South, "the sight." Randy has this sight, but the consequences coming with the gift make it hard to celebrate. As a philosopher, Randy has seen his field dry up like barren cotton fields from an often drought-worn Carolina summer. As a teacher, he has felt the frustration of the academy's abandonment of the soul of foundations. And as a scholar, he often struggles to write about and discuss his own philosophical take on education, as so many see it as unnecessary to the standards-driven, NCATE-d norms in the field of education. Randy knew that we were losing our philosophical souls and this book is Joe's and his attempt to rally our troops.

In "Derrida, Philosophy, and Teacher Education in the Postmodern University," our dear friend, Dennis Carlson uses a deconstructive approach to interrogate the notion of philosophy and the need to employ a self-reflective construct to how we, as educators/philosophers view philosophy. Creating a meta-view of philosophy and its relationship to the university, Dennis also recognizes the need for philosophers to be conscious of their philosophizing, their positionality, and the colonial/elitist notion of what philosophy traditionally means.

Old friends Robert Bullough and Craig Kridel problematize the relevance of philosophy and present the results of their eight-year research study in which educators and scholars engage in a philosophical conversation. Paul Theobald and Clifton Tanabe trace the rise and fall of the philosophy of education within faculties of education and refuse to be satisfied with the notion that "It's just the way things are." Paul Thomas and Ed Weichel rearticulate the need to create and maintain a praxis, which combines teacher education and philosophy. In the past few years, Paul and Joe Kincheloe had become writing partners and it is an honor to include him in this book.

David Kennedy offers a provocative chapter discussing philosophy of children and the use of post-Socratic and philosophical methods of teaching, interrogation, and research. By CPI (community of philosophical inquiry), Kennedy advocates walking the philosophical walk by the integration of the philosophical talk within school classrooms.

Examining the use or lack of philosophy of education within faculties of education, John Petrovic and Aaron Kuntz look at the context of the foundations of education within programs, the needs and failures of this context. They also consider the interdisciplinary nature of work within faculties and conclude by a re-examination of the placement of educational foundations within the larger venue of the university as a whole.

In Chapter 8, Adams and Adams review how the notions of democracy, social efficiency, and social progress were employed to ground the integration of school and work. Examining Dewey's work on democratic citizenship and Snedden's promotion of efficiency, the authors recognize the tensions and confusions within the past century of vocational curriculum.

George Dei and Marlon Simmons's chapter complete Part One, by relating a Ghanain case study. Noting that philosophy is almost exclusively contextualized within a Western discourse, they make the argument for a philosophy of education born through decolonization and indigenous knowledges. George worked closely with Joe over the years on different publishing projects, and his work has increased and informed the educational dialogue on indigeneity. Marlon is poised to continue work in indigenous knowledges and philosophy as a member of the new generation of critical philosophers and social theorists.

Part Two, *The Soul: Where Will It Go?* creates a pedagogy of hope and optimism through chapters that engage a praxis of educational philosophy. Making a case for *wonder* within the educational curriculum, Clar Doyle and John Hoben's chapter reminded me of Alfred North Whitehead's notion of *romance* within the curriculum. Challenging the validity of regimentation and regulation within the curriculum, Clar and John discuss the alternatives through an educational *lebenswelt* of imagination and creativity. Clar is the quintessential artist/philosopher and models wonder as he negotiates the world.

Philosopher Barbara Thayer-Bacon contextualizes her own journey as a feminist philosopher and the tensions within schools of education. She notes that many who teach in faculties of education can be subject to an elitist notion attitude that teaching teachers is somehow "beneath" the dignity of the professoriate. She cautions about the disconnect that occurs when education faculties are not valued. Craig Cunningham looks to Dewey and the notion of democratic citizenship as at odds with the pressure in creating corporatized/consumer education. He makes a case for a "radical transformation" in philosophy of education. David Granger and Jane Morse argue for an eclectic and pluralist philosophy within education programs. They acknowledge the need to understand and teach earlier philosophies without dismissing them for contemporary theories.

Susan Schramm-Pete insists that teacher education not be reduced to skills without theory and philosophy. She notes teacher educators must not perceive students to be atheoretical and without the ability to synthesize and philosophize. Greg Seals articulates Dewey's vision of a science of education and the necessity of theory to inform practice.

In a retrospective piece, Doug Simpson and Lee Duemer discuss philosophy of education. They juxtapose Dewey's scientific concepts about philosophy and education with what they see as Maxine Greene's moralist perspective. The ensuing discussion allows a breadth of worldviews within philosophy, critiquing and analyzing the very nature and perceptions in including philosophy within a faculty of education.

Bill Stanley looks at the issues behind the lack of support and interest in the philosophy of education and offers practical reasoning and curriculum as *Bildung* to emphasize the deep ties between philosophy and education. He goes on to suggest how faculties might reinvent themselves to include a philosophical grounding in teacher education. Doug Simpson and Bill Stanley are two of our oldest friends, there with Joe from the beginning speaking and writing in regional philosophy conferences. They have both exemplified the fusion of scholar/mentors, and are men of integrity and love.

The book concludes with a chapter that Joe Kincheloe wrote articulating the complexity of theory and practice, along with the inclusion of research as a philosophical act. Focusing on the epistemological dimensions of teacher education, Joe reasons that research creates an informative knowing, which is philosophically grounded. He, as the quintessential teacher as researcher, reminds us that research is philosophical and ideological in nature. Following the last chapter is the text of a speech that Joe gave in 1990 as president of the Southwestern Philosophy of Education Society, it is only fitting that this be included as it exemplifies his identity exploration and discussion of the geographical and ethnic differences that inform philosophy. The text of *Soul* is included as an homage to both Joe and to the passion he maintained within his own ontological voyages through writing, music, and philosophy. This book was a labor of love, but a labor, nonetheless. Conceived by Joe and Randy as the book they were *finally* going to do together, it has been emotionally difficult to continue to prepare for publication.

Sometime in November 2008, about a month before Joe died, we had a conversation about death. He told me that other than being separated from our family, he was ready for the next level. He said that he saw death as a consciousness-raising experience and that he thought he would embrace the opportunity to walk further on the road to understand being human. Certainly, that day neither of us expected that his journey would begin so early. The irony is that it is he who should have been writing this introduction to this book. He would want to publicly celebrate his love, pride, and respect for Randy Hewitt, his little brother from the South. Randy and Joe met in the late 1980s, while Randy was an undergraduate student at Clemson University. Randy and partner, Kelley, became Joe's anchors in the myopic faculty housed in Tillman Hall (named for Pitchfork Ben Tillman, champion of slave owners). I met Kelley and Randy in late 1989, and we knew that we had been destined to be soul mates, the four of us. Our love for Randy, Kelley, and then Sadie, Moey, and Althea (Doris) is the love we never felt with siblings. . .a love grounded on radicality, philosophy, and authenticity. Randy and Kelley initiated our children into young adulthood and have always been there as friends, mentors, and colleagues for us all. As I conclude this chapter, I think back with tears and a smile at the thought of July 9, 1990, Sevierville, Tennessee. . .Randy and 7-months-pregnant Kelley witnessing Joe's and my marriage in the shadow of Dolly Parton's statue. . .the love that was felt that day will last forever in my heart.

Special thanks and love to the contributors of this book, thank you for your time and your expertise. . .for your devotion to encouraging educators to embrace philosophy and social theory as a necessity for a pedagogy of empowerment. I am honored to write this introduction for a book and give special thanks to our son, Ian, who typeset this volume; Joe was immensely proud of "his boy," and you are loved. Completing this note is a heartfelt acknowledgment of friendship and love for Chris Myers, a man who has shared the past 20 years with us, who has supported our vision, our writings, and the commitment and philosophy of social justice and equity in education. It is my hope that this book will serve as a new foundation to foundations.

Two

Eyes of the Education Faculty: Derrida, Philosophy, and Teacher Education in the Postmodern University

Dennis Carlson

If there is a "crisis" in the teaching of philosophy in schools of education these days, it is a crisis that is not really separable from the crisis of teaching of philosophy in the broader university, and the crisis of the university itself to "think" its essence. For all of these crises are, at base, about the university and what we are about—those of us who think we are here in the university, teaching about philosophy and the "foundations" of education in a school of education increasingly organized according to regimes of disciplinary power—both directly through state accreditation (NCATE) and less directly through the restructuring of curriculum and instruction in K–12 public schooling under what is now called (and the irony of this naming cannot escape us) "No Child Left Behind" (NCLB). In such a context, philosophy and social theory—and a connection to knowledge in what is called the liberal arts—is devalued in teacher education and (conversely) knowledge in technical rational domains is highly valued or privileged. This technical knowledge includes: skills in testing, the preparation of individualized educational plans (IEPs), graphing and charting student achievement in designated skill areas, and organizing lessons to efficiently teach predetermined curriculum content. As the dominant discourse in state educational policy has sought to reorganize teacher "training" as K-12 education has been reorganized, to bring them into "alignment" as they say, the role of philosophy, and indeed what still passes for the Foundations of Education in teacher preparation programs, will remain tenuous at best.

I do not mean to defend philosophy in opposition to a narrow technical rationality in teacher education, as if there were something called "philosophy" that represents a true or authentic grounding for a democratic pedagogy or critical reason. Indeed, much of what I have to say is in the way of deconstructing philosophy as such grounding, along with the very idea of a foundational grounding. No, to even begin to reappropriate a space for philosophy in teacher preparation or dare to suggest it should be infused throughout teacher education and practice, it must first be deconstructed. For its history as the cornerstone of a "classic" liberal arts curriculum, is precisely what democratic progressives fought against and sought to transcend early in the 20th century. But deconstruction, as Jacques Derrida reminded us, was always one aspect of a larger project of reconstruction. So my concern, one shared by Derrida, is that in order to save the university as a critical, democratic space, we must save philosophy as central to its task—but a philosophy that has been thoroughly reconstructed and merges into both cultural studies and literary criticism, that takes the form of pedagogical practice within various learning communities, and that is thus what Antonio Gramsci called a "philosophy of praxis."

I approach this question of the role and continued existence of philosophy in teacher preparation programs, and school leadership programs as well, by turning to some of Derrida's thoughts on the crisis of philosophy and the modern or postmodern university, delivered in several lectures to diverse audiences in the 1980s and 1990s, and published in two of his later texts: *Who's Afraid of Philosophy?* (2002), and *Eyes of the University* (2004). In the first of these two texts—which I want to only briefly touch upon—Derrida lays out the case for a performative philosophy that is tied to pedagogy and *paideia*. This suggests that the absence of a language of "pedagogy" in teacher education, and its replacement with a language of teacher "training," is not just a minor semantic difference. It strikes to the core of what we are about in teacher education. In *Eyes of the University*—a text I want to spend more time on—Derrida does a deconstructive reading of Kant's "thinking" of the modern university in his famous 1798 essay, "Conflict of the Faculties." In this text, Kant seeks to found the modern public university upon philosophy as a type of critical reason, yet in doing so he sets up binary oppositions that Derrida finds troubling and ultimately contradictory. There is the border that separates the philosophy faculty (broadly conceived as the liberal arts and sciences faculty) and applied or technical faculty (such as faculty employed in preparing teachers for state licensure). This border between faculties is, in turn, dependent upon another border Kant constructs, between the "inside" and the "outside" of the university, with philosophy faculty located fully within the borders of the university and applied faculty dependent upon relationships with groups and institutions on the "outside" (such as teachers and schools). I argue that Kant's "thinking" of the public university in terms of these borders continues to influence what goes on in teacher education programs. Only by thinking beyond and around these borders can we speak of a larger and different role for philosophy in the professional preparation of teachers.

Deconstructionism and the Decolonization of Philosophy

If the "university" has had any coherent meaning over the centuries, Derrida writes, it is this: "The university is philosophy. A university is always the construction of a philosophy" (2002, p. 73). The very idea of the university is a philosophical construct, an attempt to carve out and delineate a space of "self-critical freedom," a space not determined by power or politics or personal investment in the truth. At the same time, it is a space created by philosophy (here meaning in its broader, earlier sense of the liberal arts and natural sciences) in order to pursue an "onto-encyclopedic project" of ordering and classifying all of human experience, of encompassing everything within its unifying logic (p. 100). Put somewhat differently, philosophy cannot exist without a university to provide it with a space in which to grow and develop, yet the modern university is itself a product of philosophy, "thought" into existence by philosophers like Kant. No wonder then that as philosophy has faced its own crisis in a postmodern era—a crisis that has taken the form of deconstructing the very notions of an autonomous space for reason and truth, and the very idea that all knowledge can be classified and integrated within a unifying discourse—the university is facing its own crisis. On the political Left, Derrida argues, deconstructionism has been synonymous with *decolonization*, in which "Occidental" philosophy is revealed as complicit in both Eurocentrism and phallogocentrism, relegating women and non-European males to a "pre-enlightened" developmental status—like the prisoners of Plato's cave. The projects of deconstructionism and decolonization are also deeply problematic, however, since they cannot offer as an alternative either a simple reappropriation of a precolonized past or a simple counter-narrative of pure opposition. Deconstructionism and decolonization must, Derrida contends, be understood as interminable, ongoing projects within philosophy itself, as ways of turning a critical gaze back at critical reason and questioning philosophy's own commonsense, taken for granted cultural biases and complicity in systems of domination.

Because philosophy is a cultural production, written in a language that is the production of a particular people and cultural heritage, part of what must be questioned is the very notion that there is something unified called philosophy that is in crisis. The differences between "continental" and "Anglo-Saxon" philosophical traditions, for example, are serious enough that minimal conditions of communication and cooperation are absent. Even "continental" philosophy is always philosophy within a language and cultural tradition, so that it might make more sense to speak of French, German, or Italian philosophy, for example—each of which loses something in translation. What would it mean to decolonize philosophy in such a context? It would mean to reject the "colonizing principle" of a unifying language and reveal it as a "manipulated simulacrum"—an image that no longer refers back to anything but itself (p. 105). Essential to the colonial project is the attempt to bring all knowledge and knowing together under one meta-language that (it turns out) is always the language of colonizing or hegemonic groups rather than the universal language that it claims to be. To decolonize philosophy would thus be to re-ground it upon a multiplicity of languages and cultural traditions (including African, Asian, and indigenous people's languages and traditions) brought into a fragile relation with one another but never adding up to some unified whole. Indeed, the fact that there is no universal or unifying philosophical language, that philosophy is always a codification of cultural mythology and epistemologies, means to Derrida that it has "an irreducible connection to a so-called natural (or mother) language." This is in sharp contrast to tendencies in scientific language toward formalization, technical rationality, and detachment from a "natural" or living language (p. 105).

As a language, European philosophy is also grounded in another important construct—what the Greeks called *paideia*. Derrida argues that this term, often translated as "upbringing," implies a personal, embodied relationship between teacher and student, as exemplified by Socrates. *Pedagogy* is the term the Greeks used to refer to the teaching of philosophy, and thus to all teaching organized around dialogue and critical self-reflection. The practice or performance of philosophy has thus never really been separable from what Derrida calls the "dialectico-pedagogical relation." It follows that "the permanent, founding, instituting crisis of philosophy will always have been simultaneously a crisis of the pedagogical" (p. 107). The idea of the university as a pedagogical space organized around dialogue and the reading of texts has given way to the idea of the university as a "techno-scientific" space, where knowledge is codified, dispensed, and employed for narrowly utilitarian ends. The first idea of the university is consistent with the centering of pedagogy, the second with the centering of "instruction," or even more technically, "instructional delivery systems." And behind the reduction of teaching to "instruction" it is possible to reveal forces and interests at work that are hardly neutral, but rather seek to "dominate and master—impose themselves upon—the process of teaching" as part of a project of controlling and predetermining what gets taught and how (p. 69). There is, Derrida concludes, no neutral place in teaching; either one becomes a machine, a cyborg "instructional delivery system," or one holds out for pedagogy, and for the messiness of some form of dialogic encounter between teacher and student, for the freedom inherent to such a relationship, and for self-reflexive practice. Finally, teaching as pedagogy is always embodied, Derrida argues, and never separable from student bodies. That is, we don't bring only our minds to the dialogue; we bring our bodies, with all their feelings, desires, defenses, and openness. Pedagogy thus encourages a reflection on "this teaching body that I call mine," that I bring to the classroom in the specificity of each new encounter. There is irony, of course, in viewing philosophy as an embodied pedagogy since philosophy has constituted itself as pure reason, separated from its binary oppositional "other"—the body and all it represents. So Derrida implies that philosophy at its best never has lived up to its claims of disembodied rationality, but instead has always been an embodied rationality, reasoning within a specific, situated, body, a body marked by class, race, gender, sexual orientation and other markers of difference and identity, and thus a body positioned within power relations that are never merely abstract but rather lived out in embodied human relationships, in the specificity of those relationships.

This deconstruction and reconstruction of philosophy, grounding it in the pedagogic and dialogic relationship, offers at least the possibility of a democratic and progressive response to the postmodern crisis of philosophy and the university, and (we may now say) related crisis in teacher education and public school teaching practice. In *Eyes of the University*, to which I now want to turn, Derrida develops some of these democratic possibilities more fully. But he also makes the point that the democratic potential of philosophy remains severely blocked so long as it continues to constitute itself in terms of certain exclusionary borders.

Conflicts of the Foundations of Education Faculty

> Where are we? Who are we in the university where apparently we are? What do we represent? Whom do we represent? Are we responsible? For what and to whom? Jacques Derrida (2004a, p. 83)

Derrida developed his thoughts on the cultural politics of the university and the responsibility of the faculty most extensively and systematically in "Mochlos: Conflict of the Faculties," originally published in 1992 and republished in a collection of essays titled *Eyes of the University: Right to Philosophy 2* (2004). The Mochlos essays were delivered as lectures at Columbia University in 1980, in receipt of an honorary degree; and they include a defense of leaving his own doctoral thesis uncompleted and undefended until he was 50, as a revolt against the logocentric rhetorical norms of the "standard thesis" in philosophy. At the heart of these essays is Derrida's deconstructive reading of Kant's last great work *The Conflict of the Faculties* (1996) originally published in 1798. Here Derrida finds the great philosopher of the Enlightenment attempting to "think" the ground upon which the modern university might be built, although it is perhaps not coincidental (Derrida suggests) that Kant's rational "thinking" of the university turned out to look remarkably like the state university that had already begun to develop within Prussia, with the University of Berlin where Kant taught the prime example. To what extent are we inheritors of this Kantian grounding of the modern, state university in service to both reason and the public? To what extent should we question this inheritance, given that the Kantian university was designed to be consistent with rule by an enlightened despot? How might we democratically reground the university and the responsibility of the faculty without altogether abandoning this philosophical inheritance?

I want to turn now to address these questions specifically with regard to what has been called for some time now the "foundational" faculty of education—that educational faculty aligned with the liberal arts and grounded in the disciplines of philosophy, sociology, and history, in particular. Philosophy is the most foundational of these and has long held a high status within the field. Kant recognized all liberal arts, natural science, and mathematics faculties as members of a broadly defined philosophy faculty. In this sense the foundations of the education movement traditionally has reproduced the Kantian privileging of philosophy as a founding discipline within the field. Yet Kant would have argued that the foundations of the faculty of education occupy an objectively contradictory location within the university. Is there responsibility to the "applied" education faculty or to the liberal arts faculty? Within Kant's "thinking" of the modern university in terms of these borders, foundations of education faculty are put in the position of having to straddle a border not meant for straddling, and not meant for crossing. To appreciate the difficulty of even imagining a philosophically grounded teacher education program, we have to understand just how much the Kantian thinking of the university in terms of impenetrable borders is still very much with us, although these borders are now being breached in ways that are both disturbing and hopeful, that are consistent with turning the university into a corporation guided by a narrow utilitarianism and the "bottom line," or turning it into a space for the emergence of new democratic learning communities of border crossers.

Kant begins his philosophical mapping of the new, public university in terms of defined and identifiable borders that separate binary oppositions caught in a dialectic—although for Kant this dialectic is understood to produce merely conflict, not transformation or victory by one side. It is a conflict he felt could be managed by an enlightened state through the securing and policing of two kinds of borders: those that separate an "inside" from an "outside" of the university, and those that separate "higher" or applied faculty from "lower" (and thus nonapplied) liberal arts faculty. Kant called the applied faculty "higher" because they were closest to the state, the sovereign, and thus the source of all public power. Conversely, the philosophy faculty was situated within the protective borders of the university and thus "lower" down in the university, removed from direct state power and political influence. Kant recognized that the modern, public university had to serve the public, and this was to be the responsibility of the higher faculty. But it also had to serve the principle of critical reason, and this meant it needed to be governed by norms of academic freedom, of "answering" for reason and "obeying" its call, of "rendering" to reason in the sense of a debt, obligation, and imperative (Kant, p. 255). This was to be the responsibility of the "lower" or philosophical faculty. One might say, to begin with, that as a member of the philosophy faculty, Kant is hardly the spokesperson for an autonomous, disinterested reason—although he will claim to be. His biases against the higher faculty are hardly disguised in the text, and he often refers to them as "merchants" or "businessmen" of learning rather than real academics. Much of Kant's effort is directed to building a case for the philosophy faculty against efforts by members of the applied faculty to claim more power and more "space" within the university. This conflict between the two faculties—one applied and one theoretical—is the central conflict that Kant identifies within the modern university.

The enlightened state, Kant argues, is to curtail its own power over the "lower" faculty and even guarantee its academic freedom because it is in its interests to see that the truth "manifests itself," even if that truth has no direct or immediate application, and even if it is unpopular. One cannot help but be struck, as Derrida is, by the naivete of such a hope, that a philosopher king would emerge upon the historical stage out of the Enlightenment, prepared to take on responsibility for protecting the academic freedom of the philosophy faculty because that was the enlightened thing to do, in the long run best interests of "the people." The Platonic idea of an enlightened despot is, of course, an oxymoron, yet Kant never stopped believing in it, and he used this idea to legitimate the absolute sovereignty of the Bavarian monarchy, believing that the monarchy would protect his academic freedom because it served the public interest in the long run to protect academic freedom. Out of such a space of freedom, knowledge would be generated that at some point might prove useful to solve important social problems. But it would take an enlightened monarch to recognize that and to assume responsibility for safeguarding the freedom of the philosophy faculty, even if the masses would not.

Kant presents himself as the great champion of academic freedom in *Conflict of the Faculties*, and of the need for rigid borders to protect the philosophy faculty from the whim of the public. Yet as Derrida argues, he ends up placing so many restrictions on the freedom of the philosophy faculty that he makes academic freedom fit within a discourse of monarchical sovereignty. Kant in fact begins his text by quoting a letter of censure he received from the Prussian king for something he had published, followed by his own letter in defense of his academic freedom. Because these letters will play such a central role in setting out the terms and conditions of his later argument in support of the academic freedom of the lower faculty, I want to refer to them in some detail. They also suggest that behind Kant's reasoned argument lurked some very personal concerns and interests. His problems began, it seems, when he made some critical comments about the theology faculty, which was a "higher" applied faculty engaged in preparing both ministers licensed by the state church and school teachers licensed by the state education ministry. As an applied faculty, the theological faculty placed a strong emphasis upon a curriculum that taught students the skills of organizing and delivering effective sermons and lectures. Kant had made the mistake of remarking that if the theology faculty prepared teachers the way they prepared ministers, then no students "would let themselves be converted by teachers like that" (Kant, p. 239). Of course, as Michel Foucault (1995) has helped us recognize, the preparation of public school teachers and church pastors and priests has been linked so closely historically because teachers have been invested with a form of pastoral authority borrowed from the clergy. As Michael Apple (1999) has observed, teacher preparation programs also have promoted the "official knowledge" contained in textbooks as the "word of god" and thus not to be questioned. So Kant's point is a good one. The theology faculty would prepare teachers to teach "official knowledge" or dogma, and to assume a priestly authority over their students. Teachers might be better taught by the philosophy faculty, where they would learn to think critically and engage in dialogue. Such teachers would teach their students to question all authority and to reflect upon their own commonsense beliefs (Mueller, 2007; Tozer & Miretzk, 2000).

Kant perhaps knew that his public writings on this topic would get him in trouble. In 1788, King Frederick William II of Prussia, acting under pressure from the theology faculty, issued an edict of censorship that prohibited public teaching or writing in opposition to official church doctrine. Shortly thereafter, Kant published a philosophical treatise titled *Religion within the Boundaries of Mere Reason* in which he had sought to put religious doctrine to the test of reason, to determine what was consistent with universalistic ethical principles and what could be dismissed as mere dogma. It is this treatise which, when brought to the attention of the king by the theology faculty, was made the cause for a royal reprimand in 1794. That reprimand, which says so much in so few words, Kant quotes in its entirety. The king begins:

> Our most high person has long observed with great displeasure how you misuse your philosophy to distort and disparage many of the cardinal and basic teachings of the Holy Scriptures and of Christianity. . ... We expected better things of you, as you yourself must realize how irresponsibly you have acted against your duty as a teacher of youth and against our paternal purpose. . . We demand that. . .in the future, to avoid our highest disfavor, you will be guilty of no such fault, but rather, in keeping with your duty, apply your authority, and your talents to the progressive realization of our paternal purpose. (Kant, p. 240)

Does this letter, from another historical era, written by a despot, still speak to us today, if now in a softer and less obviously "paternal" state voice? And what can we say of Kant's self-defense, if indeed that is what it is? He begins by saying that he intends to "put before your Majesty proof of my obedience."

His argument will rest on the defense that he never really was a disobedient royal subject and that he was wrongly accused of something he would never do. As to the charge that as a teacher of impressionable youth, he needed to censor in his teaching any statement or thread of argument that might lead youth astray, he responds: "As a teacher of youth. . .I never have and never could have mixed any evaluation of the Holy Scriptures and of Christianity into my lectures" (p. 240). He used, after all, the standard texts and "these texts do not and cannot contain a single heading referring to the Bible or Christianity." He has always, he wrote, "censured and warned against the mistake of straying beyond the boundaries of the science at hand, or mixing one science with another" (p. 241). Kant agrees to this restriction, to not bring his thoughts about religious doctrine into his teaching of philosophy, to in effect restrict the teaching of theology to the theology faculty and the teaching of philosophy to the philosophy faculty. Kant goes further to stipulate that within each department in the lower faculty, a core curriculum of canonical texts be established/designed to ensure that the nation's youth are not exposed to anything improper. Faculty members are to stick to an established body of knowledge and not interject their own views into their teaching.

By ceding ground on teaching, Kant then seeks to establish the basis for a more limited academic freedom with regard to research and scholarship, which brings us back to the treatise on religion and reason, for which he had been reprimanded. He asserts in his defense that he has done nothing to harm the established religion of the fatherland because the scholarly publication in question "is not at all suitable for the public" (p. 241). It is, first of all, "unintelligible" to the general public, a "closed book" that the masses would not care to open. It is "only a debate among scholars of the faculty," he pleads, of which the public, in its ignorance, will take no notice. Kant thus establishes academic freedom of scholarship and writing as a freedom only within the borders of the university or the academy, using an esoteric linguistic code that only a few professors and graduate students can decode. It is an academic freedom to be grounded in the presumption that the great bulk of the public is not only illiterate but, in Kant's view, "idiots" as well, not capable of grasping the kind of complex arguments and language that academics use.

The irony of Kant's "defense" of academic freedom is that he transforms an unconditional right into a "right" so constrained and contradictory that in the end it makes its peace with the power of despotism. Derrida observes with irony that the reproductive force of authority gets along quite well with scholarly works whose encoded content presents itself as revolutionary, "provided that they respect the rights of legitimation, the rhetoric and the institutional symbolism that defuses and neutralizes everything that comes from outside the system" (2004a, p. 122). This is, of course, a recurring theme in Derrida, the argument that rhetorical style and voice comes with politics. The general rhetorical style of the academy has been what Derrida called *logocentric*, a reference to Plato's attempt to ground truth upon a formal analytic style, in a dialectical development of an argument that proceeds toward a unified, knowable, truth, or *logos*. Anyone who has ever had their writing and speaking disciplined in such a *logocentric* fashion in their schooling knows that part of speaking and writing in a *logocentric* manner involves taking yourself—the speaker—out of the picture and the argument. Derrida suggests that learning to "bracket" or perform a phenomenological *epoché* on the world being studied is not just an effective way of getting at the truth. It is a way of building a rhetorical argument that is in agreement with the borders, and the border contracts, which circumscribe academic freedom and scholarship. The border between "inside" and "outside" the university is both a result of and a precondition of an epistemology of bracketing. Brackets and borders are thus one and the same thing. They serve to remove the intellectual from the real world of cultural politics going on inside the frame of everyday life, and thus "outside" the university. In such conditions it should hardly be surprising that the idea of a public intellectual still faces much resistance within the liberal arts academy, particularly since, Derrida notes, a lack of attention has been paid in the academy to the "problem of its own phenomenological enunciation," to the necessity of using a language "that could not itself be submitted to the *epoché*," that was not apparently "in the world" (2004a, p. 118).

If that was still the case when Derrida spoke at Columbia University in 1980, it is less so today, thanks in large measure to the cultural studies movement that Derrida championed. The result of not questioning the *epoché*, he argued, was a paradoxical transformation of a supposedly universalistic discourse into a quasi-private, insider's language based on the presumption that "to publish, popularize, or divulge it to the general public. . .would necessarily corrupt it" (p. 99). To speak in public would involve an action, by Kant's definition, and the lower faculties are not to act. They are to think—and thereby to judge between the true and the false, the just and the unjust—but they are not to act upon this thinking in any way that affects the public. Here we see the governing theory-practice binary is also implicated in the regulation and policing of liberal arts discourse, without any apparent recognition that all speaking and writing is an action, a performance, a way of doing something. What, then, is such a "pure" academic language performing? Derrida's answer is that it is performing its own "uselessness," its own non-involvement in the public—which is part of its bargain with the state. In exchange for protecting the philosophy faculty from the public, the philosophy faculty agrees to stay out of public debates and not circulate its discourse in the public.

Somewhat ironically, while newer post-structural and cultural studies theorists, including Derrida, have recognized that the language of theory can never be separated from a social and cultural practice, and thus politics, they have themselves been open to the charge of constructing a very esoteric, insider's language that is inaccessible across the borders of the university (Carlson & Apple, 1998). Certainly, Derrida's writing is often considered almost inaccessible to a non-specialist reader. His response to this criticism has been that while "everything must be done to come close to...accessibility," that academics should "never totally renounce the demands proper to the discipline." The struggle to bring the "specialist reader" and the "non-specialist reader" into dialogue is, for Derrida, a two-way street involving a responsibility on the part of citizens in the public as well as academic scholars (Derrida, 2004b, pp. 414–415). Once more, his response is to seek another option other than having to choose between speaking an esoteric, "bracketed" discourse or the language of everyday life. Derrida called on us to be less naive about the "freedom" of the liberal arts professoriate or by implication the freedom of the foundations of education faculty, since traditionally this freedom has been linked to a presumed detached space from which to speak and an esoteric language in which to speak.

Certainly, the academic freedom of the "lower" faculty is important to defend. But so too is an academic freedom that is more engaged and that crosses borders of "inside" and "outside" the university and applied and theoretical knowledge (Aby, 2007). The academic freedom that Derrida was concerned with preserving is thus quite different from the kind of academic freedom Kant sought to construct for the philosophy faculty. For Derrida, we are all "ex-posed" subjects, constituted by borders that bleed and contaminate both "inside" and "outside," so even when we think we are only speaking only within the university we are not (Kamuf, 1991, pp. xvi–xviii).[1] If nothing else, as I have already said, we are performing the public role of an isolated, "useless" professoriate, which can only lead to a backlash against academic freedom. At the same time, Derrida does not associate a democratic cultural politics with the complete abandonment of borders that have both protected and encapsulated rights to academic freedom. For as I now want to explore in more detail, a university without borders is emerging within the postmodern cultural landscape. But this has not been liberating or transformative in any democratic sense. Instead, it has been associated with the emergence of the corporate university, marketing utilitarian knowledge to consumer students and competing with private providers and online universities. In such an environment, as the very idea of the university as a critical, autonomous space for reason is collapsing, it may make strategic sense to secure the borders that protect us from these forces.

The "Higher Faculty" and the Cultural Politics of Teacher Education

In Kant's thinking of the modern university, the applied or higher faculty is made responsible to the state and various interest groups and social movements in the public. Consequently, the border that separates this applied faculty from the "outside" of the university is represented by Kant as permeable—an open or porous border rather than a closed, policed one. Kant's higher faculties include law, medicine, and theology (charged with educating teachers as well as preachers), although today we could add faculties of business, engineering, social work and other fields and domains of research and teaching that are engaged in preparing professionals of one sort or another, and thus in giving-back to the state and the public a return on its investment. As I noted earlier, Kant recognizes that the state and the public cannot be expected to long support a university that is exclusively about the disinterested pursuit of truth without regard for its utility. Consequently, to secure the autonomy and academic freedom of the lower faculty, he is ready to offer up the higher faculty, to strip it of most vestiges of academic freedom and autonomy, to make it a servant of the state and of other powerful forces in civil society. He is willing to do this because he envisions a higher faculty responsible to a state ruled by an enlightened king, committed to the public good, who will listen to the advice of applied faculties and give them some autonomy to run their own "business," while always insisting that they must be obedient to the state in the last instance and respond to the demands of the people for answers to their problems (Kant, 1996 /1798, p. 256). In such an enlightened modern state, the responsibility of the applied faculty would be a duty, but a duty worth taking on as an ethical responsibility to the public.

It is possible to find echoes of this concern with the "practical" in teacher education among progressives from John Dewey to Joseph Schwab, and it connects with a progressive critique of the liberal arts as being organized around an undemocratic dualism that separates "high" and "low" culture, theory and practice. What Dewey and other social reconstructionist progressives sought to develop at Columbia University Teachers College in the 1930s (with only limited success) was a new kind of teacher education program that integrated the liberal arts disciplines (through "foundations of education" courses) with applied "methods" classes in the service of a student-centered and community-centered curriculum (Tozer, 1993). Unfortunately, the Teachers College model of teacher education, integrating theory and practice, critical reason and applied methods, did not prevail. Instead, the public debate over teacher education was framed in terms of a choice between an elitist liberal arts model of teacher preparation and an applied, technical model of "teacher training" that supposedly served the public better (Cuban, 1993). By the mid-20th century, a compromise of all sorts had been reached in this debate, or perhaps it might be more accurate to say that a peace had been negotiated. The "compromise" that emerged in teacher education in the United States by the mid-20th century was heavily weighted toward applied, technically oriented "methods" courses largely devoid of theory, coupled with a few liberal arts-grounded courses (the "foundations of education") that were given a small, marginalized space in the program. Foundations faculty found themselves both secure and marginalized behind a border that separated them from the applied education faculty and that replicated the Kantian border between higher and lower faculties.

Now, the foundation faculty find that even this marginalized space of autonomy is slipping away as more and more of the teacher preparation program comes under the gaze of NCLB and NCATE. This, in turn, reflects a broader trend. Derrida observed that universities are increasingly responsible to "multinational military-industrial complexes" and "techno-economic networks" that organize through and around the state (2004a, p. 141). The "public" is, in this sense, an imagined public, constructed as a mask behind which new global interests are reshaping the university, "conquering" and "administratively dominating" it in order to secure its participation in the new global relations of power and domination (p. 93). The state, as a partner of global capitalism in this project, is advancing neo-liberal "free" market models of competition and productivity within the academy—carried within the borders of the university through research and development programs, as "parasitic" technologies. The postmodern "public" university is fast becoming the "academic capitalism" university, privileging applied research, corporate sponsorships, global marketing of research and development efforts, and the generation of profits (Readings, 1996; Slaughter & Leslie, 1997).

The new image of the intellectual—which Henry Giroux (2007) has called the "academic entrepreneur" —is taking over teacher education as it is other fields. At the University of Oregon, to cite a more extreme example, the educational faculty has been reorganized and partially reconstituted as a revenue-generating faculty, tied into state funding categories through research that directly (and narrowly) addresses the mandates of NCLB to raise achievement levels. Altogether, ten "outreach" centers connect education faculty to "evidence-based" research and development in area schools, and a strong priority is placed on grant-writing in faculty evaluation and promotion. Because of this, the University of Oregon, College of Education can now boast on its Web page that it ranks first in the nation in faculty "productivity," with each faculty member bringing in, on average, over $700,000 dollars in grant monies per year in 2007. When foundational faculty of education are weighed and assessed according to their "profit"-generating potential within an NCLB discursive economy, they obviously cannot be expected to fare very well. Indeed, they lower the faculty average through their "unproductive" scholarship. If this is the model of the new, postmodern university without borders, then the fate of the "foundations" of education is sealed. At best, foundational faculty face being confined to what Derrida calls "little cells," spaces of a "growing confinement" (2004a, p. 167). It seems foolish to attempt to re-secure traditional borders that protected philosophy and the foundations faculty, yet to abandon these borders is to open the flood gates. In fact, there is no adequate democratic response to the situation we face in teacher education today so long as we stay within the Kantian "thinking" of the university in terms of borders that seek to artificially divide theory and practice.

Conclusion: The University to Come

If the university must be "re-thought" and reconstructed in important ways as part of a democratic cultural politics, we now approach this responsibility with some urgency. First, in post-9/11 America we have witnessed the growth of a new McCarthyism in which politically progressive professors have become the new "enemy within," and with academic freedom under attack now more than it has been in over half a century. Since foundational faculty of education typically employ forms of pedagogy and scholarship that are critical, anti-oppressive, and socially reconstructionist, they are inevitably involved in battles over academic freedom being waged throughout the academy, the state, and civil society. Second, and related to the attack upon academic freedom, we are witnessing an intensification of efforts by the neo-liberal and neo-conservative state to bring the "applied" university faculty, and particularly those in teacher education, under much greater control through accrediting agencies such as the National Council for the Accreditation of Teacher Education (NCATE). By aligning teacher education courses with performance-based certification standards and with new forms of assessing preservice teachers such as PRAXIS, the teacher education faculty is losing control over its own curriculum. At the same time, teacher education faculty are expected to compete for funding dollars from the federal government based on narrowly prescriptive funding categories linked to the test-driven reform discourse of "No Child Left Behind" (NCLB). Not only is NCLB "dumbing down" the education many young people receive to a set of basic skills, tied to a new service-industry and low-skill labor force, it is also having the effect of "dumbing down" teacher education through a narrow emphasis upon technical pedagogical knowledge and performance outcomes (Carlson, 2007).

All of this is related, in turn, to developments impacting throughout the university today and that lead critics such as Bill Readings (1996) to argue that the idea of the modern public university, founded upon the principle of reason and dedicated to public service, is in ruins. Giroux (2007) writes that the university is in "chains," the kind that keeps it captive of elite economic, political, and military interests. For Derrida, the university is losing control of its borders so that "one no longer knows with what concept one can still rule it" (p. 89). It lacks a coherent structure and essential responsibility. Not only is the idea of a public university that serves the public being emptied of democratic meaning; so too is the idea of the university as an institutional space responsible to reason and truth. In Kant's day, and in the late 19th century, it was possible, Derrida writes, "to debate together about the responsibility proper to the university," guided by a system of implicit axiomatics related to an essential calling. One could then "think the ground" on which the responsibility of various faculties was determined (2004a, pp. 89–90).

A university needs grounding; although clearly for Derrida, it does not need an originary, fixed, unshakable "foundation"—that of an autonomous reason. That foundation is crumbling now under our feet and does not represent a sufficient grounding for a democratic university to come. At the same time, to think beyond the Kantian system of limits does not mean to leave it totally behind or dismiss it—as if that were even possible given that this is an inherited tradition. The university must be re-grounded, to be sure, but the alternative to a university grounded on the principle of autonomous reason is not a university grounded on irrationality or on technical rationality and economic utilitarianism. Instead the inherited university tradition must "provide on its own foundational soil support for a leap toward another foundational place" (Derrida, 2004a, p. 110). In *Specters of Marx* (1994), Derrida identifies Marxism—like philosophy—as a great "inheritance," from which much can be learned that has application to contemporary democratic cultural politics. "We are inheritors," he proclaimed; but that should not mean we receive something solid, unified, and already formed as an inheritance (p. 94). The unity of an inheritance, if there is one, "can only consist in the injunction to reaffirm by choosing." To choose an inheritance is to "filter, select, criticize. . .[and] to sort out among several of the possibilities which inhabit the same injunction" (p. 40). Through such a choosing, an inheritance becomes a living memory, open to being worked and reworked and stitched together with other inheritances through a form of "memory work" (Derrida, 2001b).

In *Mochlos*, Derrida calls for the re-thinking of the inheritance of the university and philosophy in terms of overlapping and diverse "communities of thinkers" or "interpretive communities" engaged in the working and re-working of a collective memory. For example, Kant exists as a set of texts in the history of one such interpretive community called "philosophy," which might overlap with another interpretive community called "pedagogy." As I have said, Derrida viewed language as performative, so these interpretive communities are inherently performative. Language is not just a "stating, describing, saying that which is," but also a productive and generative force. This means that there is a "politics of teaching and of knowledge, a political concept of the university community." This politics, Derrida maintained, is deeply embedded in "every sentence of a course or seminar, in every act of writing, reading, or interpretation" (2004a, pp. 100–101). The pedagogical relationship is thus central to the "performance" of philosophy in teacher education. Philosophy is also performed by crossing borders, such as those that separate and divide: the "inside" of the "university" from a public "outside," the foundations of education faculty from applied teacher education faculty, and the teacher education faculty from the liberal arts faculty. Derrida's "community of interpreters" is organized and mobilized around texts rather than borders, and they are simultaneously part of multiple local, national, and global communities engaged in taking positions regarding the institutional structures that constitute us and "regulate our practice, our competences, and our performances." In the age of NCLB and NCATE, Derrida would say that the responsibility of the education faculty is to make the "ethico-political" implications of these structures as explicit as possible within a broadening public dialogue (2004a, p. 102).

Derrida never harbored any illusions about just how difficult it would be to democratically reground the public university in an age in which the memory of both the heritage and the promise of the university risk being forgotten or emptied of meaning. He wrote of a "democracy to come" only as a possibility and one which must be actively willed into existence by those who take responsibility for responding when it would be just as easy not to.[2] Furthermore, Derrida had come to believe that a "democracy to come" only exists as a possibility in the face of its alterity, its Other, which also has been constituted through the modern Enlightenment project from the beginning. That Other was constituted in the modern era on both the political Left and Right in the form of orthodoxy, dogmatism, and the policing of borders. Derrida thus placed some democratic hope in the metaphor and the practice of crossing borders in our own teaching, writing, and speaking. One might say Derrida lived this possibility and hope. As a young Algerian French Jew during the time of the Nazi collaborationist government in WWII, he was denied the right to cross the border into France to pursue his education and escape persecution. Later, he would live his life as a nomadic border crosser, always interested in what happens when the traveler from one land crosses the border and confronts that which is "foreign." Will the traveler see in the foreigner that which he or she already expects to see, that is, the face of an Absolute Other? Or will the border crosser, the traveler, remain open to finding something unexpected, to confront the face of a difference that cannot be easily contained within the binary oppositions that the border claims to separate. It will depend upon the traveler recognizing that borders are not frontiers, that every border is perforated by a multiplicity of openings that render it ultimately ungovernable, uncontrollable, and even impossible (Malabou & Derrida, 2004).

Notes

1. Derrida develops this notion of borders as cuts, marks, incisions, and passwords in *Sovereignties in Question: The Poetics of Paul Celan* (2005). He writes that the Hebrew word *shibboleth*, while its meaning remains open and indeterminate, implies "a password, not a word in passing, but a silent word transmitted like a. . .handclasp, a rallying cipher, a sign of membership and a political watchword" (23). A *shibboleth* makes community possible, but only by exteriorization and exclusion as well as inclusion.
2. Derrida refers to a "democracy to come" in *Rogues: Two Essays on Reason* (2001a). He saw a suicidal possibility inherent in the pursuit of democracy since democracy always exposes itself to the possibility that forces hostile to democracy can be elected by the people, or that anti-democratic movements can have a powerful appeal among people, as in "the rise of an Islam considered to be anti-democratic" (31).

References

Aby, Stephen (ed.) 2007. *The academic Bill of Rights debate: A handbook*. New York: Praeger.
Apple, Michael (1999). *Official knowledge: Democratic education in a conservative age*. New York: Routledge.
Carlson, D. (2007). Are we making progress? The discursive construction of achievement in the age of "No Child Left Behind." In D. Carlson & C. P. Gause (eds.). *Keeping the promise: Essays on leadership, democracy, and education*. New York: Peter Lang, pp. 3–26.
Carlson, D. & Apple, M. (1998). Introduction: critical educational theory in unsettling times. In D. Carlson & M. Apple (eds.). *Power/knowledge/pedagogy: The Meaning of democratic education in unsettling times* (pp. 1–40). Boulder, CO: Westview.
Cuban, L. (1993). *How teachers taught: Constancy and change in American classrooms, 1890–1990*. New York: Teachers College Press.
Derrida, J. (1994). *Specters of Marx: The state of the debt, the work of mourning, and the new international*. (Trans.) Peggy Kamuf. New York: Routledge.

Derrida, J. (2001a). *Rogues: Two essays on reason*. (2001). (Trans.) Pasale–Anne Brault and Michael Naas. Stanford, CA: Stanford University Press.
Derrida, J. (2001b.). *The work of mourning*. (Trans.) Pascale–Anne Brault & Michael Nass. Chicago: University of Chicago Press.
Derrida, J. (2002). *Who's afraid of philosophy?* Palo Alto, CA: Stanford University Press.
Derrida, J. (2004a). *Eyes of the university*. Stanford, CA: Stanford University Press.
Derrida, J. (2004b). "*Honoris Causa*: 'This is extremely funny'" in Points. . .Interviews, 1974–1994, ed. Elisabeth Weber, trans. Peggy Kamuf. Stanford, CA: Stanford University Press, 399–421.
Derrida, J. (2005). *Sovereignties in question: The poetics of Paul Celan*. New York: Fordham University Press.
Foucault, M. (1995). *Discipline and punish: The birth of the prison*. New York: Vintage.
Giroux, H. (2007). *The university in chains: Confronting the military-industrial-academic complex*. Boulder, CO: Paradigm.
Kamuf, P. (1991). Introduction: Reading between the lines. In Kamuf (ed.), *A Derrida reader: Between the lines* (pp. xiii–xlii). New York: Harvester Wheatsheaf.
Kant, I. (1996). The conflict of the faculties (1798). In *Religion and rational theology*. Cambridge, UK: Cambridge University Press, 233–328.
Malabou, C., & Derrida, J. (2004). *Traveling with Jacques Derrida*. (Trans.) D. Wils. Stanford, CA: Stanford University Press.
Mueller, J. (2006). Does talking the talk mean walking the walk? A case for forging closer relationships between teacher education and educational foundations. *Educational Studies, 39*, 146–162.
Readings, B. (1996). *The university in ruins*. Cambridge, MA: Harvard University Press.
Slaughter, S., & Leslie, L. (1999). *Academic capitalism: Politics, policies and the entrepreneurial university*. Baltimore, MD: Johns Hopkins University Press.
Tozer, S. (1993). Toward a new consensus among social foundations educators: Draft Position Paper on the American Educational Studies Association Committee on Academic Standards and Accreditation. *Educational Foundations, 7*(4).
Tozer, S., & Deborah, M. (2000). Professional teaching standards and social foundations of education. *Educational Studies, 31*, 146–162.

Three

Lost Soul: The Eradication of Philosophy from Colleges of Education

Robert V. Bullough, Jr. and Craig Kridel

School Philosophy, Relevance, and the Eight-Year Study

The current state of educational foundations, generally, and the philosophy of education, specifically, has been lamented by faculty who identify themselves with these fields. Issues of significance and worth are raised with an accompanying chorus underscoring the important yet apparently forgotten role of philosophical discourse in education. Those in the field of teacher education, however, mostly have ignored the wails and cries, being consumed by other insistent concerns: pressure from increasingly aggressive accountability and accreditation demands, expanding and endless field responsibilities, and a deepening, politically inspired, disenchantment with public education. Often viewed in colleges of education more as service faculty than serious academics, teacher educators have little sympathy for the plight of their foundations colleagues, even when housed within the same department. Questions of the relevance of educational philosophy and foundations become critical missives tossed among professors, with few satisfying conclusions resulting other than educational foundations now finding themselves on the sidelines and in dire need of a total reconceptualization (Provenzo, 2009).

The eradication of philosophy from colleges of education is not a sudden occurrence (Jerritt, 1979; Bullough, 2008). Charges of irrelevance have been made for decades and addressed in years past. Recently, a special issue of *Educational Studies* examined the vitality of the foundations of education, with the guest editor writing, "my analysis suggests that SFE has minimal visibility, and by implication minimal voice, in contemporary educational policy deliberations" (Butin, 2005a, p. 287). Introducing the issue, two disturbing questions were posed: "Does social foundations of education matter?" "What do prospective teachers gain, if anything, from taking a social foundations course?" (p. 214). Earlier, prompted by Arcilla's (2002) essay, "Why aren't philosophers and educators speaking to each other?," a special issue of *Educational Theory* addressed the relevance question for the philosophy of education (Burbules, 2002a). Not surprisingly, most of the authors, philosophers all, took exception to Arcilla's conclusion that, "By and large, the philosophical community expresses no interest in thinking about education. [In turn, the] educational community does not seem to care about philosophy" (2002, p. 1). Some even criticized Arcilla's argument more than his conclusions. Fenstermacher, for example, asserted Arcilla's claims were hopelessly broad and, calling attention to teacher work conditions, suggested that he was insensitive to the situation befalling educators, however defined: "Absent sufficient sense of agency and autonomy, the educator may perceive little advantage in becoming more engaged with the philosopher in the conceptual, logical, and theoretical aspects of practice" (2002, p. 342). Underlying the essays in both special collections is a sense of urgency and deep concern. Something very important, foundational, relevant, and profoundly philosophical is increasingly missing from teacher education programs.

Rethinking Relevance

Relevance, to use a phrase made famous by Boyd Bode, the distinguished philosopher of education, is "a weasel word." Relevant to what? The status quo . . . and what if, as is usually the case, the status quo is found to be troubling? Under such conditions, how is an educational philosopher to behave? A conundrum follows: Criticism is an important philosophical act, but to offer a systematic critique of the practice of others, those whose identities are in some fashion embedded in their practices, can easily become arrogant as well as irrelevant. What those being criticized most want is assistance and helpful insight, even when their practices may be personally and professionally troubling, as when a teacher feels compelled to work against her better judgment. Teachers, generally, make the best of the situations that confront them—and criticism often does not help but actually hurts (Day, Kington, Stobert & Sammons, 2006).

Considering the potential roads to relevance, several pathways open. One is to engage in what Burbules characterized as "situated philosophy" (2002b, p. 354). By this he means "the work of the philosopher who is involved on site." Philosophy, then, becomes not system-building but problem-solving, and philosophers occupy the "stance of the collaborator," those who seek to make a bargain with teachers: "You help me to see what is philosophically interesting and important about this matter, and I will help you to think more philosophically about it; eventually you may not need me at all" (p. 354). Obviously, if sincere, a relationship like this can only develop with teachers who are predisposed to value what philosophers have to offer. But, we suspect, the good will of the educator increasingly cannot be assumed; it must be earned. Teacher educators face a similar challenge to prove to teachers the worth of their wares. These tensions, among others, appear in our research on the Eight-Year Study (1931–1943) and provide an important example of collaboration among academics and educators where school philosophies and engagement in philosophical discourse proved relevant and significant for improved practice and greatly enhanced the quality of life for students and school staff (Kridel & Bullough, 2007). The work of the philosopher, however, is understood broadly, in the sense suggested by Fenstermacher, as including engagement in "social science (of sorts)" (2002, p. 348). Fenstermacher's point is important, that increasingly the lines separating philosophical inquiry from other kinds of professional activity are blurred and much good philosophy is done by academics who are social scientists first and philosophers second.

The Eight-Year Study and Situated Philosophy

The Eight-Year Study originated from the frustration of Progressive Education Association (PEA) members who objected to the dominance of the colleges over the high school curriculum. College admission standards were set independently of the wishes of high school educators, and progressive elementary school practices necessarily faded during the secondary years as college admission loomed. The view was widely shared within the PEA that curricular experimentation in secondary schools was hindered yet badly needed. In 1931, the PEA formed the Committee (later Commission) on the Relation of School and College with the charge to address the problem (Aikin, 1942). Initially funded by the Carnegie Foundation and later the General Education Board (GEB), plans were made for secondary schools (some were school systems) to be freed for curricular experimentation. Naively, the PEA staff assumed that simply removing barriers to reform would lead to a radical innovation, this despite Dewey's contrary warnings (Dewey, 1931, p. 296). Over 250 colleges agreed to suspend established admissions requirements for five years in favor of alternative forms of documentation provided by the schools. Remarkably, no specific program was set out in advance to guide the Thirty Schools. Instead, each school faculty was expected to engage in curricular experimentation. Differing dramatically—from large public school systems to small, elite, private schools—the school faculties approached reform with very different levels of interest, understanding, and commitment.

The Study quickly evolved in unanticipated ways. Gradually, leaders realized that even under the best of conditions, change would come slowly, if at all. Changing traditions and ways of thinking would not be easy. Distrust of university faculty by teachers and school administrators was another source of difficulty. Although a few of the participating schools made remarkable headway, others dragged well behind. It became apparent that participating school faculties needed help rethinking the curriculum and, to this end, the Commission on Secondary School Curriculum was formed in 1933. This commission published a series of volumes presenting an approach for reorganizing general education in the various disciplines around a social and personal concept of adolescent needs. In 1936, a group of Curriculum Associates began visiting each school to work, as requested, with teachers to develop core curriculum and other programs. Emphatically, they were not to impose their views on teachers.

In addition, both the (Aikin) Commission on the Relation of School and College and the (Thayer) Commission on Secondary School Curriculum formed evaluation committees to gather data for guiding program development within the participating schools as well as for judging the results of the study. At the suggestion of Boyd Bode, a member of the Eight-Year Study Directing Committee, Ralph Tyler was appointed to lead the evaluation effort of the Aikin Commission. At the time Tyler was working as a research associate at the Ohio State University Bureau of Educational Research and was earnestly engaged in developing a new approach to evaluation and testing. Yet, formulating and clarifying educational aims proved central to Tyler's approach to "comprehensive appraisal," where instruments were designed to ascertain student development and not merely to determine the acquisition of factual knowledge. For him, testing was a process by which the *values* of an enterprise—namely, schooling—were articulated and ascertained. In essence, evaluating—or drawing out values—was conceived as first and foremost a philosophical rather than a technical activity. Tests became a way to determine the values of a school and to gather information about students and about the effectiveness of practices. Tyler maintained that evaluation should begin with teachers discussing "what kinds of changes in its pupils the new educational program was expected to facilitate" (Tyler, 1936, p. 79). Here was a social scientist whose work was deeply philosophical.

Effective evaluation, in Tyler's view, required clarity of purposes and agreement about changes in behavior; students' development would be determined in relation to established purposes or objectives. He was not interested in imposing aims. Rather, his desire was to help school faculty clarify what they sought to accomplish and, then, to give them means for gathering data that would be helpful for improving curriculum and instruction. By December 1934, Tyler had statements of the "most important objectives of thirteen schools" and the process of creating instruments then began (Havighurst, 1934, p. 1). For many school faculty members, articulating and clarifying aims proved difficult, and for some the efforts seemed silly, wasteful of time and energy. Not only did the school faculties need help rethinking the curriculum, they needed assistance to think more deeply, clearly, and systematically about the purposes of education.

"Let's give no more time to philosophy"

The schools were slow to accept the challenge of thinking through the social purposes of their work. For the first few years of the project, other matters were of greater importance to the teachers and administrators. Remarks made following an October 1935 session devoted to the "search for the meaning of democracy" nicely capture the feeling of the majority of participants. Aikin reported that several school principals responded by saying, "This has been very interesting, but let's give no more time to philosophy. What we need is discussion of the practical job of curriculum revision" (Aikin, 1942, p. 30). Educational means dominated conversation while ends were accepted as already fixed. Further, those teachers at the elite private schools associated with the Aikin Commission saw little reason to change their long-term commitment to traditional liberal education. Maintaining hard-won reputations of academic excellence proved paramount, and any other educational philosophy or social aim seemed far removed from this dominating concern. Why, when their academic programs were highly respected, would faculties from these renowned institutions want to reconsider their purposes?

The more experimental schools faced a different sort of challenge. As Edmund Day of the GEB observed: "As long as progressive education was largely an attack on existing educational organization, its forces could act effectively with no clear statement of positive purpose . . . . [The] time has come for progressive education to indicate its primary aims much more explicitly and systematically than it has done thus far" (Day, 1936, p. 1). Day argued that progressive educators had to declare explicitly a positive social vision, one which the schools could use to guide decision making, to judge the quality of their programs, and to inspire commitment among teachers, students, and parents. They could no longer be comfortable simply opposing traditional educational practices and representing a "movement of revolt." They needed to stand for something constructive and progressive.

At the 1935 Thousand Island Park Conference, the third and final gathering of the Eight-Year Study participants, PEA staff urged participants to assess their own programs to determine if a common understanding of purposes was being achieved. Clearly, the Aikin Commission staff believed the schools' educational aims were unfocused and that some position on social philosophy was necessary in order to generate discussion and find direction. They proceeded to draft a memorandum as a means for better focusing their experimentation (Alberty, 1937, p. 7). Receiving mixed reviews when released at the headmaster's conference in Briarcliff, New

York, the initial statement reconsidered the aims of secondary education and sought "to make changes in our schools to achieve those objectives more effectively and completely" (Aikin, 1935). What became known as the Briarcliff Memorandum begins with a brief description of "the American tradition" followed by a list of eleven educational statements, each serving as a preliminary standard for evaluating programs. The implications of the memorandum were far reaching, suggesting changes in accepted patterns of school organization; curriculum; teaching practice; and student, teacher, and administrator roles and responsibilities.

For example, one plank redefined the process of educational change by maintaining "that the fundamental purposes can be attained only to the degree that the members of the school staff help to formulate and understand the objectives, desire their achievement, are willing to analyze them into their essential elements, participate in the planning, and cooperate in putting into effect such procedures as contribute to carrying them out." Another standard—"That the students be given the opportunity to make their school an example of successfully working social life, the school and community a laboratory of intelligent citizenship"—urged for a greater degree of involvement from students (Second Memorandum on Central Objectives, 1935, p. 2). Taken seriously by a school faculty, these statements invited wide participation in curriculum decision making, including teacher-pupil planning, and altered traditional teacher and administrator roles to include regular consultation with staff and students. Ongoing discussions about educational aims and their assessment would become a central activity, and citizenship moved to the center of the school program rather than being seen solely as a responsibility of the social studies teachers. These proposals promised dramatic program changes and no doubt were seen by many as threatening long-established and valued practices.

Slightly revised in January of 1936, the Briarcliff Memorandum remained a general orientation, a point of departure for discussion. Initially, some faculties did not appreciate that they would have to work out their own statement of aims and instead criticized the document for lacking specificity and clarity. As discussions of the memo continued, signs of frustration with dawdling school principals arose. One year after the Briarcliff Conference, Edmund Day told the headmasters and Aikin Commission staff that while he was not interested in forcing a particular formulation of social aims on the various schools, he saw no excuses for delay: "[It] does seem to me," he said, "important at this stage. . . for every school that seriously regards its responsibility to American society to undertake some formulation of its own purposes." Determined to press the issue, he posed a heavily loaded question: "To what extent, and under what circumstances, is a school justified in declining to state its educational philosophy?" (Day, 1936, p. 4). In Day's mind, no such justification existed, but for many school staffs, larger educational aims were still being taken for granted. Educators had yet to make a connection between their daily lives in classrooms and any larger social ideal for secondary education.

Articulating Aims and Making Progress

To help with the task, during autumn and winter of 1937, Harold Alberty, serving as part of the curriculum staff, visited all participating schools. Unlike the other Curriculum Associates, his responsibility was to "[assist] all of the teachers in our thirty schools to see the social significance of their work and to help them give it direction" (Aikin, 1936, p. 190). Alberty, a lawyer by training and a former student then colleague of Bode's, assisted the various faculties in their effort to reconsider educational aims and build working social philosophies; his efforts were not in vain. The question of the social aims of education would be considered by the school faculties, and an outgrowth of Alberty's work was the formation of a set of criteria to help participating school faculties assess and think more clearly and critically about their social philosophy. This was not a standard to be enforced but, instead, a series of questions that arose from what he judged to be the best activities and practices taking place in the schools: (1) Is the announced social philosophy of the school the product of group thinking on the part of the entire teacher staff, the pupils, and the parents? (2) Is the social philosophy of the school in the process of continuous reconstruction and revision in the light of changing conditions? (3) Does the social philosophy of the school provide a sense of direction in all areas of school life? (4) Does the social philosophy of the school serve as a basis for integrating school community attitudes and practices? (5) Does the social philosophy of the school aid the pupil in developing standards for determining beliefs, attitudes, and plans of action concerning personal problems of school and community life? (6) Is the effectiveness of the school's social philosophy being systematically tested by available means of evaluation? (Alberty, 1937, pp. 7–10).

These questions represented developing beliefs embraced by the more experimental of the faculties of the thirty schools, as Aikin wrote: A consensus was emerging that "the high school in the United States. . .should be a demonstration, in all phases of its activity on the kind of life in which we as a people believe. . ... Everyone recognized the need of a sound philosophy for the reconstruction of American secondary education" (1942, p. 30). Philosophical discourse was becoming a way of life at some of the participating schools and fulfilled Bode's belief that "social theory must become a part of the bone and tissue of everyday life if it is to be more than an academic showpiece. In other words, education must make provision for the application of social theory to conduct if it is to escape futility and frustration. Teaching democracy in the abstract is on a par with teaching swimming by correspondence" (1937, p. 75). What is done within a school, every phase of life lived, Bode argued, constitutes a way of life that must be public and democratic: "The school must be a place where pupils go, not merely to learn, but to carry on a way of life" (Bode, 1937, p. 77).

Discussion of the social purposes of education intensified throughout 1938. The faculties of many of the Aikin Commission schools became increasingly critical of their own practice and a sense of urgency was evident in the meetings. H. H. Giles, during his 1938 visits to the schools, came away deeply impressed with the "extension of democracy in many—not all—of these schools. It is democratic to attack problems through group thinking rather than to make a solitary game of it—no matter how brilliantly one plays. . . . Democracy is painful, not least because it is the long way of doing things, but it seems to many schools to be worth suffering for. . ... Increasing efforts to create a partnership between pupils, teachers, administrators, and parents, however, testify to the realization that extension of democracy through practice of it is of ultimate importance" (Giles, 1938, p. 238). The PEA philosophy of education conferences, the Eight-Year Study workshops, the efforts of the Curriculum Associates, numerous Commission-sponsored meetings and discussions, and, importantly, events in the world, all converged to alter long-held opinions about the proper aims of education. Unfortunately, while many of the Eight-Year Study sites were engaged in fruitful conversation about school purposes and exploring the educational implications of democratic values, the same could not be said of the PEA. Throughout the 1930s the PEA membership had become increasingly fractious. Two committees had been appointed, one in 1936 and another in 1938, and charged with articulating the aims of the Association. Both failed. The first committee accomplished very little. As best as we can determine, the report of the second committee was never formally adopted (Committee on Philosophy of Education, 1940). By trying to cut a pathway between advocates of extreme child-centeredness, most of whom were concerned exclusively with elementary education, and the social reconstructionist wing of the PEA, the committee only succeeded in alienating both groups.

While the PEA failed to achieve agreement on the purposes of progressive education, the faculties of the Aikin Commission schools made steady headway. According to Aikin, 1937 was a turning point for the Eight-Year Study. By 1938, the task had become concrete and practical, not a venture into meaningless abstractions. Where PEA leaders sought a single and shared statement of purpose, Aikin Commission staff encouraged participating school faculties to vary their programs as necessary. Differences in guiding philosophies were not only inevitable but desirable; no single all-encompassing statement was necessary. A few schools made little headway, a point that would later be of great concern to Bode when the occasion came for reporting final results, but others produced remarkable documents that proved their value in practice.

Democracy itself suggested that differences should follow honest and open deliberation among faculty about educational aims. In fact, from such discourse, understanding of the social purposes of education and the unique challenges of teaching and learning in a democracy evolved among the Eight-Year Study participants. On this view, philosophical work was not tangential to the programs of the schools, but central. Virtually every aspect of teaching raises profoundly philosophical questions, as Dewey argued: "When philosophic issues are approached from the side of the kind of mental disposition to which they correspond, or the differences in educational practice they make when acted upon, the life-situations which they formulate can never be far from view. If a theory makes no difference in educational endeavor, it must be artificial. The educational point of view enables one to envisage the philosophic problems where they arise and thrive, where they are at home, and where acceptance or rejection makes a difference in practice" (Dewey, 1916, p. 383). Gradually, Study participants came to more fully understand the far-reaching and unique claims that democracy, as a social and ethical ideal, a "way of coming at life," makes on educational practice and to appreciate the complexity of the challenge to develop programs that helped better realize these claims (Hullfish & Smith, 1967, p. 259).

The Significance of School Philosophy and the Success of the Eight-Year Study (8YS)

The Eight-Year Study is frequently remembered exclusively by the results of the College Follow-up Study. A mere component from one of three Eight-Year Study commissions for a project that directly influenced the curricula of over forty-two high schools and twenty-six junior high schools and the educational experiences of hundreds of teachers and thousands of students, the Follow-up Study recorded the college success (for the first and second years) of 1475 students from the participating ("experimental") high schools. Academic records and extracurricular activities were then compared with similar data of 1475 college students who attended traditional secondary schools. The Eight-Year Study is often deemed unsuccessful based on the results of the experimental group—1475 students—with their "slightly higher total grade average" and "somewhat better job than the comparison group" (Aikin, 1942, p. 111). Since the college grades were not notably superior than the control group's, critics began to cite the Follow-up Study to show that "progressive education" was no better than the traditional course of study, a view that permitted many to dismiss the project and a belief that is still held by many educators today. Yet, the 1475 "students sample" were drawn from all of the participating schools where some programs clearly did not institute any experimental efforts.

Another more accurate follow-up assessment, the Study within the Study, compared students' college records from the six most experimental schools with data of those graduates who attended traditional high schools as well as others who graduated from the lesser innovative schools of the Eight-Year Study (Chamberlin, et al., 1942, pp. 164–175). This study revealed that students from the more experimental high school programs were substantially more successful in college than their peers, thereby undercutting the claims and conclusions of the Follow-up Study. At these schools, teachers and staff developed a complex conception of adolescent needs and of core curriculum, explored new roles and responsibilities for teachers, developed creative types of student assessment and innovative teaching materials, and clarified the meaning of democracy for themselves and for others. While neophyte historians may criticize any educational experiment—certainly the Eight-Year Study—by selecting examples that do not necessarily represent the intent of the project, any thoughtful consideration would examine the work at these six most experimental schools.

Eight-Year Study participants initiated a wide range of innovations at many of the school sites. They developed free-reading programs and social studies courses based on the scholarly examination of contemporary issues, introduced teacher-pupil planning as a model for curriculum decision making, created revolutionary mathematics programs emphasizing the nature of proof, established social-oriented community study programs that engaged students in the analysis of their own cities and neighborhoods, and even introduced novel uses of Hollywood feature films for the examination of social issues. It is worth noting that these innovations were rooted in the participants' substantial academic backgrounds. Among the staff—Wilford Aikin, Eugene Smith, V.T. Thayer, Alice Keliher, Caroline Zachry, Eirk Erikson, Margaret Mead, Margaret Willis, Ralph Tyler, Boyd Bode, Harold Alberty, Peter Blos, Ruth Benedict, James Michener, Helen Lynd, W. Robert Wunsch, and Edna Albers, among others—were mathematicians, scientists, artists, professors of English, historians, documentary filmmakers, lawyers, philosophers, psychologists, anthropologists, and sociologists.

Developing a deepening commitment among many of the school faculties to the value of an articulated social vision for school reform coupled with a growing understanding among Study staff of the educational implications of taking democracy seriously led to a reconsideration of many accepted school practices. New approaches to professional development were created, including the establishment of six-week summer workshops for teachers where activities focused upon their educational and intellectual needs and interests. New forms of student assessment were created to include performance records and the analysis of classroom practices (obscured by its titling as "human relations") and means for gathering data useful for making more informed and sensitive curriculum decisions. Unique forms of classroom experimentation and approaches to implementative research were also developed. And, significantly, the school curriculum was enriched by inclusion of a much greater range of humor concerns, guided by the staff's assertion: "To be a good teacher one must be first of all a good human being." Seemingly, this issue was addressed by the staff's belief in the importance of "belonging to an adventurous company" and engaging in serious and shared intellectual exploration. (Giles et al., 1942, pp. 231, 208). Through the workshops and with the consistent support of Study staff, over time faculties gained in the confidence needed to confront the most pressing educational issues of the day. Community deepened and competence grew.

Conclusion

The story of the growing appreciation of the importance of school philosophy among Eight-Year Study participants is at first a tale of indifference and resistance, which for most faculty eventually gave way to interest and concern. The Briarcliff Memorandum (1935) begins with the sentence, "Some philosophy of government, of society, and of life inheres in every educational program." Yet, social aims and school purposes are not often discussed by college of education faculty, let alone by school administrators, teachers, and students. For many of the participating schools, an educational philosophy only existed on paper and was in no way connected to their educational practices or to their curriculum programs. The issue was not whether teachers should conceive a new vision for secondary education. Instead, many of the educators merely asked whether they needed to articulate any social vision for their school. Similar to today, educational aims were seldom discussed and, as one staff member recognized, "Democracy was taken for granted" (Aikin, 1942, p. 9). On the surface, the high school faculty and staff acknowledged the schools' important role in strengthening democracy, but there was little agreement on exactly what this meant once platitudes were set aside.

Then, as now, the case had to be made that social philosophy was profoundly important and should infuse virtually all educational practice. Slowly they came to realize that determining educational aims and means led to rich, lengthy discussions about what type of community they wished to build for themselves and for their students. From this effort would emerge a social philosophy—or more accurately, cluster of philosophies—which centered on democracy as a way of life, a way of living determined to be most supportive of human growth and the development of personality. In the process, philosophical discourse became normal, part of every day conversation, and school philosophy documents became touchstones for discussion as well as evolving guides for classroom practice. The educational communities that many of the Eight-Year Study Schools developed, especially the most experimental of the schools, became places where teachers and students wished to belong. In these settings, educational discourse was more thoughtful, actions were more considerate, and democracy became a way of life and not merely an abstraction. "The philosopher," at times the university academic, the foundations of education professor, the teacher educator, school staff, and even students, worked in collaboration and interacted with others as they constructed the sort of learning community in which they wished to live.[1] No other aim would prove more important to the Eight-Year Study, and its lessons remain crucial for contemporary efforts at school reform and renewal and for reconsidering the place of philosophy in schools and colleges of education.

Note

1. The participation of students proved crucial and significant for the success at the Eight-Year Study's most experimental schools. Teacher-pupil planning was a common practice and described in many different accounts. In addition, two graduating classes prepared descriptions of their educational life. See Class of 1941, East High School (1939) and Class of 1938, Ohio State University High School (1938).

References

Aikin, W. M. Personal correspondence to H. Smith, (Oct. 8, 1935); Ethical Culture/Fieldston Schools Archives: RG3 A4; B47, S4, F3a. Tate Library, The Fieldston School, New York.

Aikin, W. M. (1936). Division of high-school and college relations. *Educational Research Bulletin, XV*(7): 189–192.

Aikin, W. M. (1942). *The story of the Eight-Year Study*. New York: Harper.

Alberty, H. B. (1937). The social philosophy of the school. *Thirty Schools Bulletin: An Occasional Publication for the Teachers in the Study of the Relation of the School and College, 1*: 6–11.
Arcilla, R. V. (2002). Why aren't philosophers and educators speaking to each other? *Educational Theory, 52*(1): 1–11.
Bode, B. H. (1937). *Democracy as a way of life*. New York: Macmillan.
Bullough, R. V., Jr. (2008). Teaching and reconsidering the social foundations of education: A self-study. *Study Teaching Education, 4*(1): 5–15.
Bullough, R. V., Jr., Hobbs, S. F., Kauchak, D., Crow, N.A., & Stokes, D. K. (1997). Long-term PDS development in research universities and the clinicalization of teacher education. *Journal of Teacher Education, 48*(2): 85–95.
Burbules, N. C. (2002a). The dilemma of philosophy of education: "Relevance" or critique? Part one. *Educational Theory, 52*(3): 257–261.
Burbules, N. C. (2002b). The dilemma of philosophy of education: "Relevance" or critique? Part two. *Educational Theory, 52*(3): 349–357.
Butin, D. W. (2005a). How social foundations of education matters in teacher preparation: A policy brief. *Educational Studies, 38*, 214–229.
Butin, D. W. (2005b). Is anyone listening? *Educational policy perspectives on the social foundations of education, 38*, 286–297.
Butin, D. W. (2005a). How social foundations of education matters in teacher preparation: A policy brief. *Educational Studies, 38*, 214–229.
Butin, D. W. (2005b). Is anyone listening? *Educational policy perspectives on the social foundations of education, 38*, 286–297.
Chamberlin, D., Chamberlin, E. S., Draught, N. E., & Scott, W. E. (1942). *Did they succeed in college? The follow-up study of the graduates of the Thirty Schools*. New York: Harper.
Committee on Philosophy of Education (1940). *Progressive education: Its philosophy and challenge*. New York: PEA.
Day, C., Kington, A., Stobart, G., & Sammons, P. (2006). The personal and professional selves of teachers: Stable and unstable identities. *British Educational Research Journal, 32*(4): 601–616.
Day, E. E. (1936). Heads of Schools Conference, Columbus, Ohio, October 22; General Education Board Collection, Series 1, Subseries 2, Box 281, Folder 2932. Rockefeller Archive Center, Pocantico Hills, New York.
Dewey, J. (1916). *Democracy and education*. New York: Macmillan.
Dewey, J. (1931). *Philosophy and civilization*. New York: Minton, Balch.
Fenstermacher, G. D. (2002). Should philosophers and educators be speaking to each other? *Educational Theory, 52*(3): 339–348.
Giles, H. H. (1938). Travels of a curriculum associate among the secondary schools. *Educational Research Bulletin, 17*(8): 237–247, 254.
Havighurst, R. J. (1934). Conference with Prof. R.W. Tyler, Bureau of Educational Research. General Education Board Collection, Series 1, Subseries 2, Box 282, Folder 2946. Rockefeller Archive Center, Pocantico Hills, NY.
Hullfish, H. G., & Smith, P. G. (1967). *Reflective thinking: The method of education*. New York: Dodd, Mead.
Kridel, C. & Bullough, R. V., Jr. (2007). *Stories of the Eight-Year Study: Reexamining secondary education in America*. Albany, NY: SUNY Press.
Provenzo, E. F. (2009). Toward a renewed definition of the social foundations of education. In E. F. Provenzo (ed.), *Encyclopedia of the social and cultural foundations of education* (pp. 967–1002). Los Angeles: Sage.
Second Memorandum on Central Objectives (1935): GEB: S 1–2, B 281, F 2932. The Briarcliff Conference of Heads of Schools, Briarcliff Manor, New York (Oct 25–27, 1935); GEB: S 1–2, B 281, F 2936. General Education Board Collection, Series 1, Subseries 2, Box 282, Folder 2946. Rockefeller Archive Center, Pocantico Hills, NY.
Tyler, R. W. (1936). Defining and measuring objectives of progressive education. *The Educational Record, 17*(9): 78–85.

Four

"It's Just the Way Things Are:" The Lamentable Erosion of Philosophy in Teacher Education

Paul Theobald and Clifton S. Tanabe

Over the years, we have each had students in our introductory education foundations courses who question why they were being asked to think about and study philosophy in a course focused on education. After all, we can't wave a magic wand that will make everyone a good learner. Vast achievement discrepancies are dismissed away by the ever-popular student quip, "It's just the ways things are." One particularly concerned student offered, "If I wanted to sit around thinking, I wouldn't be paying to go to college." To some of our students, spending time examining what might be called the "why and ought questions" associated with schooling seems unnecessary and out of sync with the fast-paced, technologically focused character of modern education. And, every once in a while, a student with such concerns will remind us that teacher education programs are supposed to be teaching students how to work in the "real" world. The implication of this reminder is that in the world outside of the university classroom, what counts is knowing how things actually are and what to do about them, rather than sitting around thinking about how things ought to be.

The idea that teacher education courses should be focused on the examination of knowing how things are, rather than on how things ought to be, is not without merit. After all, it is true that there are many things that preservice teachers should be learning that have little to do with careful philosophical investigation, such as learning the techniques, behaviors and attitudes that will allow them to effectively discipline and motivate children on a daily basis. Perhaps this is part of the reason that a serious focus on philosophy seems to be harder and harder to find in teacher education programs across the nation. Yet, philosophers of education (including us) continue to insist that there is a place for philosophy in modern teacher education programs. But why? Or more to the point, why now, given that the standard arguments for teaching philosophy to teacher education students, such as that exposure to philosophy and philosophical thinking helps prospective teachers wield greater clarity of thought, seem to fall on deaf ears?

In this chapter, we begin with a cultural analysis of why educational philosophy has fallen on hard times in 21st-century teacher education in the United States, an analysis that moves us next to consider the need for new and more persuasive arguments supporting student engagement with philosophy in the teacher training process. This is followed by an attempt to offer some direction for such arguments.

American Culture and the Demise of Educational Philosophy

The late Christopher Lasch has referred to the hyper-individualistic cultural milieu in the United States as a "culture of narcissism" (Lasch, 1979). Philosophers of considerable distinction, from John Rawls to Charles Taylor, have spent time and energy trying to sort through the vast array of historical circumstances that have come together to create America's brand of individualism.

These two philosophers, in particular, have identified developments such as these: Augustine's depiction of Christianity as the singular individual's relationship to God, Reformation arguments about individual's choice or autonomy in the embrace of religious belief and practice, Renaissance science that seemed to hold great promise for making individuals the "masters and possessors of nature," Enlightenment arguments about the "state of nature" and the allegedly undeniable impulse of individuals to fend for themselves—arguments contending that humans are therefore, quintessentially "economic beings." Although the general philosophical outlooks of Rawls and Taylor are often at odds, their work nevertheless coheres around these essential "ingredients" to our hyper-individualistic culture.

Sometimes, timing is everything. The gradual translation of these developments into a kind of modern worldview seemed to come to fruition at the very moment of the founding of the United States. If humans are primarily economic beings, then they require a governmental system that will function on their behalf, with their consent, so that they may focus on economic pursuits. Further, by virtue of their status as economic beings, individuals require an educational system that will focus on preparing them for their "evident and probable" occupational destiny (to borrow a phrase from long-time Harvard president, Charles Eliot). These are generalizations, of course, for there have certainly been many arguments for a more participatory governmental system and for an educational system intended to prepare citizens for both a political and an economic dimension to life. But these alternative arguments have never been mainstream. As a result, we still lead, as Michael Sandel has argued, "unencumbered" lives with no political role to play beyond coming out to vote once every couple of years (Sandel, 1998). And, further, we still send our children into school systems designed to deliver the dispositions and skills required by future employers. We still greet first graders with the question: "What do you want to be when you grow up?"

The individualistic assumptions about the human condition that underlie all institutions in American society have yielded that "hyper-individualistic" culture that Walzer and others have described. So what does that have to do with educational philosophy? Well, here's the rub. The essence of philosophy, the quintessential questions about the human condition, questions concerning beauty, goodness, truth, justice, and so forth, are all inevitably tied to the quality of one's relationship with others. Philosophy is the study of the shared aspects of a human's life: governance, economics, and education. Within the American experience, therefore, the study of philosophy offered less utility. In a society where life was seen as a solitary journey chiefly defined by economic struggle, of what use was philosophical inquiry?

This was a dramatic shift in the culture of university life in particular, for down through the centuries, philosophy was deemed to be the very pinnacle of scholarly study. But it has never been so in the United States. That role was usurped by the ascendancy of modern science and the tight connection, so clearly demonstrated by Renè Descartes and especially Francis Bacon, between scientific study and technological advancement. Science gradually became a key ingredient to the Industrial Revolution, and in the process, especially in a society ostensibly built on the separation of church and state, it easily and swiftly moved to the top of the discipline status list in the world of American higher education. Science was a much better fit than philosophy in a society built on the assumption that humans are essentially economic creatures. As the accolades for scientific study grew, the status of philosophy simultaneously fell.

It should be evident that philosophy was not a good cultural fit in the United States. This was to be a country of action, not contemplation. One could certainly make the argument that the twentieth-century response from the discipline of philosophy to this cultural development only augmented a further erosion of its status. Cornel West captured much of this in his first great scholarly contribution *The American Evasion of Philosophy*. In short, the discipline of philosophy suffered from what is often jokingly referred to as "physics envy" for most of the 20th century. Trying to compensate for the perception that philosophy lacked the rigor of science, mainstream philosophers moved away from traditional pursuits to focus on such things as linguistic analysis and logic, areas where one might approach the kind of mathematical precision that defined the sciences. The result was that philosophy simply moved farther down the wrong end of the continuum, that is, between what was deemed to be useful and what was deemed to be useless.

The need for new and better arguments

The field of education was not immune to these developments. With the rise of science and technology in society came the ascendancy of the idea that the field of education, and specifically classroom instruction, would greatly improve with the widespread use of applied science and technology (Cuban, 2003). This point is reflected in the educational policy milieu of the George Bush era, which was defined by No Child Left Behind, a law laced with the modifier "scientifically based" in front of every reference to research—a further contributor to the decline of educational philosophy as a useful component of teacher preparation. But, as Larry Cuban and others have suggested, the technological turn in education may not have produced the results so many had assumed it would.

Writing the *Phaedrus* around 420 B.C., Plato relayed a similar story. When the inventor of the pen came before the ancient Greek King, Thamus, expecting great praise if not a handsome reward, he was deeply disappointed. Thamus chastised the man saying,

> O man full of arts, to one it is given to create the things of art, and to another to judge what measure of harm and of profit they have for all of those that shall employ them. And so it is that you, by reason of your tender regard for the writing that is your offspring, have declared the very opposite of its true effect. If men learn this, it will implant forgetfulness in their souls; they will cease to exercise memory because they will rely on that which is written, calling things to remembrance no longer from within themselves, but by means of external marks. (Hamilton & Cairns, 1961, p. 520)

The loss of memory would be the cost of the pen, at least in the eyes of King Thamus. His reaction to the pen may be the earliest written insight into the unpredictability of technological advancement. Much later, Johann Gutenberg dramatically increased the power of the pen with the invention of the printing press. He was convinced that he had created something that would increase the glory and dominion of the Roman Catholic Church. But what did it do? It became the catalyst to the Protestant Reformation.

Still later, of course, the advent of computers and the Internet stepped up the availability of the printed word many, many times over. Its advocates proclaimed that its development would be a great democratizing force as more and more people would acquire easy access to the world's store of information. But has this happened? What, in fact, is happening, as a result of widespread access to the Internet?

This is a question that is only slowing beginning to receive scholarly attention, but the early results suggest that teacher preparation should indeed require the kind of deep contemplation that comes with philosophical study. Richard Foreman, a playwright of worldwide distinction, claims that the Internet is creating "pancake people," individuals who are intellectually flat and shallow. Whereas generally accepted definitions of an educated person nearly always include the acquisition of a depth and breadth of knowledge that enables the creation of connections between pieces of information, the Internet appears to be moving us in the direction of having those connections made for us, externally, as Thamus warned, only this time through computer links and search engines. In a persuasive essay entitled "Is Google making us stupid?" Richard Carr argues that Internet use is slowly re-wiring our brains (Carr, 2008). He cites evidence of UCLA brain studies that demonstrate markedly different kinds of brain activity between heavy Internet users and those who use the Internet only seldom. Carr Foreman and a growing number of scholars warn that we are slowly creating a society of individuals with a reduced capacity for prolonged concentration on ideas of substance. Instead we are becoming prone to distraction, to fidgeting, to impatiently waiting for another opportunity to click to a new stimulus.

Google and other search engine sites are in business to make money. It is in their financial interest to get us looking at as many advertisements as possible, meaning they do everything in their power to get us to move from one Internet page to another and all over the world wide web as quickly and as much as possible. Carr argues that the Internet is pushing people in a new direction, imposing its own sort of intellectual ethic on its users, making them less able to sit down and immerse themselves in a book or in the kind of deep study that used to be a pivotal part of the definition of an educated person.

The contemplative nature of philosophy served for centuries as a bulwark against the negative consequences of ill-considered ideas. While it is true that a new technology may enable us to do some things better and faster, it is also true that the same technology will impede our performance at other things. This was the lesson Thamus wanted the inventor of the pen to consider, and had he lived at the time, he would have asked for the same consideration from Gutenberg and the creators of the Internet. Thamus, of course, is not here. We are left to our own devices with respect to how we will prepare those responsible for the intellectual life of the nation's youth.

Given the reality that educational technology alone may not be the answer to all of our modern educational questions, the future of American education will depend on additional vigorous fields of study. But, should the philosophy of education be one of those? Can it contribute in ways that it has not done so previously? Is the philosophy of education worth saving? If it is, we must first recognize and acknowledge that it needs to be argued as such. In the past, when it came to the matter of arguing for the importance of educational philosophy, many of us were lazy. We were arrogant. Perhaps we thought that the need for philosophy in teacher education was so evident or so obvious that it did not require a spirited defense. We were wrong. And that has cost everyone.

It is clear, now more than ever, that philosophers of education must employ their skills in the fight to save our field as an integral part of teacher preparation. We are experts trained in the art of the argument. Persuasion is our game. But, how are we to respond to the criticism that the essential questions in the philosophy of education are not conducive to the fast-paced, Internet- and entertainment-based, minute-to-minute nature of modern classrooms?

First and foremost, we assert that in order to save itself, the field of educational philosophy must lead the way in the development of new and more germane theories and principles that help to guide and direct educational policy makers, educational researchers, and teacher education programs. In the current climate of reality television, instant electronic gratification and viral advertising, teachers and students need more from educational philosophy than the proclamation that detached reflection is worthwhile and leads to better understanding (regardless of how true and necessary such reflection is). That is to say that the first step to defending the philosophy of education in teacher preparation is for philosophers of education to more assertively and more effectively focus on arguments that are readily applicable to the "real world" (or at least to the world faced by newly minted teachers). It is not coincidental that in the age of No Child Left Behind, philosophy of education is in danger of being left behind. We can no longer rely on the tired and arrogant justifications for the inclusion of philosophy of education in teacher preparation that were offered in the past. Fostering greater clarity of thought may be important, but it seems less and less persuasive as a reason for keeping the philosophy of education in teacher preparation.

In the following section we argue for a specific direction that the field of philosophy of education might take in order to make it a more relevant and therefore more vital and significant part of the current teacher education process.

Examining Pedagogy and Policy:
Toward a Clear Role for Educational Philosophy

Before the ascendancy of psychology to the status of distinct discipline within American universities—and the subsequent application of psychological theories in what became known as educational psychology—teacher preparation leaned much more heavily on educational philosophy than it currently does. Turn-of-the-century college catalogs reveal such courses as "pedagogical ethics" and "the philosophy of teaching." Recognizing that the teaching act necessarily occurs between teacher and student or most often teacher and students, and, recognizing, further, that philosophy as a discipline focused on the shared aspects of human life, it seemed as if educational philosophy was a natural fit in any teacher preparation program. This represents one of the two critical directions for the reinvigoration, and hopefully, the reinsertion of educational philosophy in the preparation of American teachers.

The other direction we would like to advance is the examination of educational policy. This is not new, of course, for there have been many campaigns for policies that would create a kind of educational justice, for lack of a better term, including desegregation, busing, multicultural education, bilingual education, special education, and so on. But despite the fact that justice is a focal point of philosophical study, educational philosophy side-stepped most of these pressing interests while continuing to focus on the large philosophical approaches generally referred to as the "isms." Essentialism, existentialism, pragmatism, idealism, perennialism, and realism were just some of the approaches that dominated the curriculum of educational philosophy courses throughout the 20th century. Neglecting the controversial policy issues that touched real lives in profound ways, educational philosophy seemed increasingly less relevant to becoming a teacher.

As the 21st century has begun to unfold, the number of policy issues has increased quite dramatically. School prayer, vouchers, charter schools, heavy use of standardized tests, prescribed curricular standards and, in many cases, prescribed instructional approaches—all of these are controversial policies that can only be assessed by the quality of educational justice they produce—an assessment that must rely largely on sophisticated conceptions of what constitutes justice, or, said another way, on educational philosophy, properly focused.

But we will begin with pedagogy. Since the second decade of the 20th century, the view that instruction could be refined through the application of scientific principles has held considerable currency. The ascendancy of behavioral psychology put the focus squarely on instructional actions that yielded desired responses. The reductionism of scientific management in the workplace was translated to the schooling enterprise. Teaching, like manufacturing, could be broken down to step-by-step tasks. Behavioral objectives were linked to the steps teachers needed to take. Critics like John Dewey and George Counts notwithstanding, the popularity of applying science to the world of teaching was overwhelming. With science providing the answers to what teaching behavior should be, what place was there for the study of pedagogical ethics?

For too long, educational philosophers had few answers to this question. Speaking generally, but with fair accuracy, they merely moved aside and created textbook after textbook of curricular material focused on the isms. In the current educational milieu, one defined by an ever greater emphasis on conformity, standardization, and testing, the ethics of curricular and instructional decisions have never been more salient. Direct instruction, as an example, is touted as the answer to minority student underachievement. Its use is mandated in hundreds of school districts—but is the "drill and kill" nature of this approach ethical? Why is it that its use tends to be mandated in central cities, while suburban districts still retain some semblance of instructional freedom? Is this circumstance ethical?

Is there such a thing as teacher authority? Can teachers responsibly make pedagogical decisions on the basis of intimate knowledge of the learners in their charge? Thousands of teachers will tell you that they are denied the ability to do this—is that ethical? Noted educational researchers have argued eloquently for the need for "nurturing pedagogy" (John Goodlad, 1997) or for "caring" as a critical part of pedagogy (Nel Noddings, 1984). Why have these ideas not taken hold? Why are they uncommon in the world of America's schools? Does their absence constitute an injustice? These are critical questions for anyone who intends to become a teacher. They demand sophisticated answers, something educational philosophy can help them create.

What about current educational policy, the second direction for refocusing educational philosophy? What kinds of questions should it pose for prospective students? The professional lives of America's teachers have become increasingly impinged upon, increasingly molded and shaped by non-educators in the policy arena. A kind of tidal wave hit American teachers in 1983 when they found themselves under attack by their own government. The infamous *A Nation at Risk* report, though a deeply flawed document, chastised America's teachers as mediocre—even treasonous, as the oft-quoted line from the report implies: "If an unfriendly power had attempted to impose on America the mediocre educational performance that exists today, we might well have viewed it as an act of war" (National Commission on Excellence in Education, 1983, p. 5).

The report triggered a non-stop barrage of federal policies ostensibly intended to improve American public education. From Goals 2000 (Bush) to America 2000 (Clinton) to the 2002 No Child Left Behind Act, the heat has remained squarely on the backs of America's teachers. With each new federal policy, the range of teacher decision-making has narrowed. There are legitimate questions to be asked about this circumstance. An obvious one is whether or not it is wise to make educational decisions at a level vastly removed from the lives of individual children. Before exploring this question, however, it is worth a short digression to reveal the kinds of specific educational decisions NCLB, in point of fact, mandates.

The bill was some 1200 pages long and included over 500 separate performance measures for schools to meet. In practice, it has been nearly impossible to fully implement. And, indeed, the Bush Education Department continually had to make exceptions and allowances for unexpected developments. Because education is by constitutional default a state-administered burden, some freedom had to be given to the states to determine what might constitute acceptable annual progress toward the ultimate goal. This in turn meant that some states looked very good in the first years of the program, while other states looked very bad. It created a kind of public relations nightmare and an incredible statistical mess for state departments of education. The general consensus of the educational research community is that No Child Left Behind is bad policy at best, and potentially damaging at worst. Gerald Bracey described it this way:

> It has been 20 years . . . since A Nation at Risk appeared. It is clear that it was false then and is false now. Today, the laments are old and tired—and still false. "Test Scores Lag as School Spending Soars" trumpeted the headline of a 2002 press release from the American Legislative Exchange Council. Ho hum. The various special interest groups in education need another treatise to rally around. And now they have one. It's called No Child Left Behind. It's a weapon of mass destruction, and the target is the public school system. Today, our public schools are truly at risk. (Bracey, 2003, p. 620)

There are really so many problems with No Child Left Behind that it is difficult to know where to begin to delineate them, but perhaps the most significant one is the manner and emphasis with which it conflates the definition of an education with a test score. Anyone interested will look in vain throughout the corpus of the best literature the West has to offer for any definition of what constitutes an education—or an educated person—that includes a single reference to performance on a test. And yet we have come to the point in this country where we wholly define education in those meager terms. It is a sad commentary on American culture, to be sure, but it is also pernicious, for the simple truth is that if those students who score in the bottom half nationally move to the top, we would be forced to come up with new tests to give us a new bottom half. Tests may illuminate curricular and instructional issues of concern to educators, but they are not a vehicle on which we can ride en route to a better school system.

While teachers exercised some authority over what and how they would teach, an educational philosophy course focused on the isms, one that stayed away from the policy arena, was perhaps a less egregious omission than it seems to be today. In an age where teacher authority has been reduced by policymakers to the point where it can scarcely be said to exist, a substantive course in educational philosophy seems to be a kind of professional imperative.

Conclusion

We cannot send sophisticated, technically savvy, and jaded young teacher education graduates into the schools and expect them to invest a life's work fighting for a more equitable, more just, and better system of schooling. If we want real change, if we want real educational reform, we need to do a better job of immersing teacher education students in the life-changing experience of philosophical contemplation. We need to open their eyes to the natural, powerful, and inspirational excitement that comes from focusing on ideas like justice, beauty, truth, and happiness.

The future stewards of the intellectual life of our youth should not be "pancake people," well equipped to find an engaging lesson plan on the world wide web, but incapable of creating one on their own. Those individuals who will shape the future most directly, that is, the future teachers in American society, can ill afford to be distracted, fidgety, and incapable of the kind of deep immersion in the world of ideas that was once the hallmark of an educated person. Make no mistake about it, the philosophy of education is needed more now than perhaps ever before. It may be culturally out of step, but few would argue that the United States doesn't stand in dire need of a cultural corrective.

To be sure, if educational philosophy is going to reestablish a foothold as a key component to teacher preparation, it is going to have to be seen as relevant; it's going to have to be grounded in student perceptions of "the way things are," rather than hypothetical attempts to identify the teaching practices of a pragmatist, or an existentialist, or a perennialist. Pedagogical ethics and policy analysis represent two highly fruitful directions for a truly relevant and impactful approach to educational philosophy in the 21st century.

References

Bracey, G. (April 2003). April foolishness: The 20th anniversary of a nation at risk. *Phi Delta Kappa, 84:* 616–621.
Carr, N. (July/August, 2008). Is Google making us stupid? *The Atlantic, 31*(6): 56.
Cuban, L. (2003). *Oversold and underused: Computers in the classroom.* Cambridge, MA: Harvard University Press.
Goodlad, J. I. (1997). *In praise of education.* New York: Teachers College Press.
Hamilton, E., & Cairns, H. (1961). *The collected* Marcuse *dialogues of Plato.* Princeton, NJ: Princeton University Press.
Lasch, C. (1979). *The culture of narcissism: American life in an age of diminishing expectations.* New York: W. W. Norton.
National Commission on Excellence in Education (1983). A nation at risk: The imperative for educational reform. Washington, DC.
Noddings N. (1984). *Caring: A feminine approach to ethics and moral education.* Bereley: University of California Press.
Sandel, M. J. (1998). *Liberalism and the limits of justice* (2d ed.). Cambridge: Cambridge University Press.

Five

The Practitioner Has No Clothes: Resisting Practice Divorced from Philosophy in Teacher Education and the Classroom

P. L. Thomas and Ed Welchel

In Hans Christian Andersen's fairy tale, "The Emperor's New Clothes," an emperor is deceived by swindlers who claim to make for the emperor clothes stitched of fabric no one can see. Of course, the emperor sees nothing, but trapped in the arrogance of power (classically called "pride" or "hubris") he falls prey to the hoax.

The climax of the tale that stays with us as a culture involves a child exposing the emperor as blinded by his own arrogance of power (an arrogance born from the absence of a critical view of reality)—thus, "the emperor has no clothes." In the tale, the adults were unwilling or unable to challenge the flawed authority of the emperor; the adults are paralyzed by a cultural awareness that masks their empowerment. Self-deception is often a powerful and pervasive slavery, the tale implies.

While students are rarely as bold as the child in this tale, one fact of teaching is that often our students do notice that our words and our actions clash in the day-to-day reality of the classroom. Most teachers express in many ways a belief in the dignity of all children, a call for success by all children, and a commitment to the value of learning for learning's sake. Most teachers believe and speak for classrooms that embrace democratic ideals. Yet, what many teachers do for and to students has devolved into what Freire (1998) calls "the bureaucratizing of the mind": "The freedom that moves us, that makes us take risks, is being subjugated to a process of standardization of formulas, models against which we are evaluated" (p. 111). Teachers' words and their actions far too rarely match in the classroom.

In essence, the practitioner who says one thing and practices another, the practitioner who rejected and continues to reject the necessity of exploring her or his philosophy of life and of teaching and learning (and instead calling always for that which is solely "practical"), finds herself or himself standing before students as if professionally clothed, but in fact this practitioner has no clothes—if the practitioner has resisted (or has been denied) a full consideration of educational philosophy. As Freire (1998) argues, "It is in this sense that I say again that it is an error to separate practice from theory, thought and action, language and ideology" (p. 112).

In the real world of daily classrooms and throughout the modern history of education in the United States, a disturbing paradox exists. At any point during the last 100 years, you can find ample evidence of a nationwide disappointment in the effectiveness of schools—low graduation rates lamented, low test scores bemoaned. By mid-twentieth century, this criticism of the education system became intertwined with blaming that failure on progressive education and the philosophy of John Dewey. By the 1980s and during the publicity surrounding the "Nation at Risk" report under Ronald Reagan, that blame included condemning our schools as Leftist, Socialist, and Marxist (consider also the more recent demonizing of William Ayers and Barack Obama during the 2008 presidential campaign with similar pejorative name-calling).

The paradox grows from the simultaneous *belief* that schools are in theory progressive, critical, and left-leaning along with the *reality* that schools are in fact traditional, behavioristic, and mechanistic—thus conservative. Kohn (2008) identifies this exact disequilibrium:

> The rarity of this approach [progressivism], while discouraging to some of us, is also rather significant with respect to the larger debate about education. If progressive schooling is actually quite uncommon, then it's hard to blame our problems (real or alleged) on this model. Indeed, the facts have the effect of turning the argument on its head: If students aren't learning effectively, it may be because of the persistence of traditional beliefs and practices in our nation's schools.

The chasm that exists between how people view education and how education actually is can be directly connected to the lack of a critical lens in many practitioners. Classroom teachers without rigorous and extended considerations of educational philosophy become victims of assumptions that function as norms in the daily teaching of children and in the daily workings of our society. Here, we will argue for such rigorous and extended considerations of educational philosophy, focusing on the progressive and critical philosophies and works of John Dewey and Paulo Freire.

John Dewey and the Progressive Vision Ignored

Think not the torch
Is one of joy and light
Its scattered sparks but scorch
And die in falling night.

No course is lit
By light that former burned
From darkness bit by bit
The present road is learned.
   (John Dewey cited in Jackson, 2002, p. xv)

A full consideration of all teachers' philosophy of education is essential because it helps to clarify the sense of mission that will guide them as they navigate the muddy and often turbulent waters they are bound to find themselves in, regardless of when, what or where they teach. Throughout the 20th century, American educators have generally and traditionally vacillated between essentialism and progressivism. Dewey referred to essentialism as traditional education. Essentialists are more concerned with content than with process. They argue for teacher-centered classrooms and see students as empty receptacles into which fragmented and disjointed facts are poured. Essentialists are concerned with "covering" information and preparing students for the inevitable end-of-course test. True understanding has little meaning to them. Standardized test results mean everything.

Progressives tend to value student-centered classrooms. They are more concerned with teaching students how to think as opposed to what to think. For true progressives, the students' interest will dictate the curriculum as well as affect the instructional methods and strategies to be used. Progressives realize the significance of recognizing that all students are individuals in every sense of the world. They also realize that students don't shed the problems presented by the contexts of their lives at the schoolhouse door, like backpacks. They carry their personal and individual dilemmas and challenges with them as they journey through school each day. Their family and personal problems and situations must be taken into account as teachers plan to teach students as individuals.

Following the publication of "A Nation at Risk" in 1983, the essentialist perspective has dominated American education for it was during the Reagan years that the current standards movement began and now holds full sway in American education. The latest incarnation of essentialism is embodied in the No Child Left Behind Act (NCLB). Issued in 2001, and receiving bipartisan support in the United States Congress, NCLB has pushed the essentialist agenda to the point that American public schools have largely become test-prep factories. Many who once claimed to be progressives have aligned themselves and their classrooms with the essentialist paradigm for effective education. They have felt and have given in to the pressures of NCLB, but privately they are very aware of the precarious position this capitulation has put their own perceptions of effective teaching and learning in; they have sensed the tension between their own beliefs and experiences and that of the essentialists who have endlessly pushed the standardization of education. Ultimately these closeted progressives have become unclothed emperors in their practice. The essentialists have won the battle for control of American educational institutions.

One of the first issues that must be resolved in every effective teacher's philosophy of education mandates an examination and the establishment of an intellectual position concerning the aims of education. In other words, what are the ultimate purposes of the educational enterprise? According to John Dewey, "The need for a philosophy of education is thus fundamentally the need for finding out what education really is" (Archambault, 1964, p. 4). What does it mean, specifically, to become an "educated" man or woman? According to Dewey, education "is a process of development, of growth" and "An educated person is the person who has the power to go on and get more education" (Archambault, p. 4).

This also involves a consideration of the aims or purposes of American education. A casual perusal of the mission statements and stated purposes of educational institutions generally reveal statements of good, but often hollow, intentions. These statements of purpose include the intent to "prepare students for productive lives in our democratic society" along with the notions of "social adjustment" and "literacy" as well as "basic skills," but what does this actually mean for the teacher as practitioner and, more importantly, for students whose futures are largely dependent on these high-sounding but often empty phrases? Again Dewey speaks to us, "The philosophy of education must go beyond any idea of education that is formed by way of contrast, reaction and protest. For it is an attempt to discover what education is and how it takes place" (Archambault, 1964, p. 3). While discussing the nature of the development of aims or purposes in his *Democracy and Education*, Dewey consistently focused on the "futility of trying to establish the aim of education—some one final aim which subordinates all others to itself" (Thayer, 1965, p. 247). According to Dewey, such efforts to find "the aim of education" are useless because statements of aims are matters of emphasis in a given context and at a specific time, in response to situations peculiar to that time. Because of this, they tend to omit factors that require little or no emphasis and to highlight defects and needs.

Dewey did go so far as to describe the characteristics of the "ideal school." In his *The School and Society*, Dewey (1900) confronts us with his description of the "ideal school":

> If we take an example from an ideal home, where the parent is intelligent enough to recognize what is best for the child, and is able to supply what is needed, we find the child learning through the social converse and constitution of the family. . . .Again the child participates in the household occupations, and thereby gets habits of industry, order and regard for the rights and ideas of others, and the fundamental habit of subordinating his activities to the general interest of the household. Participation in these household tasks becomes an opportunity for gaining knowledge. . . .Now if we organize and generalize all of this, we have the ideal school. (pp. 51–52)

Schools and teachers, according to Dewey, should provide an environment in which students can acquire the discipline and the habits of mind that will enable them to adapt to an ever-changing society and the challenges posed by change. Regarding this mission of schools and the teachers who staff them, Dewey (1922) wrote,

> In order that education of the young be efficacious in inducing an improved society, it is not necessary for adults to have a formulated definite ideal of some better state. An educational enterprise conducted in this spirit would probably end merely in substituting one rigidity for another. What is necessary is that habits be formed which are more intelligent, more sensitively percipient, more informed with foresight, more aware of what they are about, more direct and sincere, more flexibly responsive than those now current. Then they will meet their own problems and propose their own improvements. (p. 128)

To reach the progressive goal of using the educational system to foster positive social change, Dewey advocated that schools be concerned with inculcating in all students a deep understanding of reflective thinking and how it is an essential part of coming to grips with the problems posed by the contexts and challenges of their times. Dewey used the term "reflective thinking" to distinguish it from the process of "mere thinking." To Dewey, "mere thinking" was the uncontrolled and random stream of ideas that fill a student's mind. Reflective thinking involved an ambiguous or confusing situation, a difficulty or problematic situation that requires a solution. The process of reflective thinking is an essential part of Dewey's method of intelligence or problem solving.

Briefly reviewed, Dewey's method of intelligence involves five steps. It begins when the student is confronted with a confusing situation begging for a solution. This generally calls for an attempt to locate the difficulty or source of doubt. The second step involves the student calling upon past experience and prior knowledge in order to formulate possible solutions. The third step calls for the application of these possible solutions to the problem in an effort to determine the relevance and appropriateness of each possible solution. This crucial step calls on the student to think reflectively. Such reflective thinking requires the students to be patient and determined as they exhibit an unwillingness to accept a possible solution without the proper proof. They must learn to suspend judgment when appropriate and necessary, as they search for other possible solutions. The fourth step involves further application of all seemingly probable solutions. During the fifth step, students will attempt to verify or confirm the chosen solution. Dewey's method of intelligence may not require that all five steps be applied to all problems. Not all problematic situations require the application of all five steps. Some problems will be solved when the source of confusion is identified. Resolution may be achieved at each succeeding stage. Each step in the method of intelligence may involve long periods of time as hypotheses are formulated, applied and corroborated. "The senses," Dewey (1916) noted, "are avenues of knowledge not because external facts are somehow 'conveyed' to the brain, but because they are used in doing something with a purpose" (p. 165). This requires that students be tasked with relevant and meaningful pursuits that call on them to think reflectively and often, outside the walls of their present classroom. Thinking is thus an activity—the "intentional endeavor to discover *specific* connections between something we do and the consequences which result, so that the two become continuous" (p. 170). Dewey summarized the steps or stages of his method of intelligence:

> . . .first, that the pupil have a genuine situation of experience—that there be a continuous activity in which to be interested for its own sake; second, that a genuine problem develop within this situation as a stimulus to thought; third, that he possess the information and make the observations needed to deal with it; fourth, that suggested solutions occur to him which he shall be responsible for developing in an orderly way; fifth, that he have an opportunity and occasion to test his ideas by application, to make their meaning clear and to discover for himself their validity. (p. 192)

This paradigm for learning and education stands in stark contrast to the essentialist mantra of behaviorism, standardization, and memorization. Dewey did not perceive students as passive and compliant recipients of information, knowledge and skills as defined and imposed by adult curriculum makers. He viewed students as active and social by nature and as voluntary participants in their own learning. The fruitful and profitable learning experience requires students to construct, reconstruct and reorganize their experiences as they encounter cogent problems relevant to their own lives and experiences. As experiences are reconstructed and reorganized, meanings are enhanced and clarified.

Dewey connected his method of intelligence to his inherent faith in democracy as a way of life:

> . . .For what is the faith of democracy in the role of consultation, of conference, of persuasion, of discussion, in formation of public opinion, which in the long run is self-corrective, except faith in the capacity of the intelligence of the common man to respond with common sense to the free play of facts and ideas which are secured by effective guarantees of free inquiry, free assembly, free communication? (Thayer, 1965, p. 267)

According to V.T. Thayer, Eduard Lindeman first called Dewey's method of intelligence the "golden mean" of education (p. 251). As an example, Thayer used Dewey's method of analyzing the principal and recurring issues of education:

> This began by opposing thesis to antithesis, laying bare the partial truth contained in each of two competing theories, together with their limitations, exaggeration, and neglected aspects and concluded with a synthesis so much richer and relevant to the problem that it constituted a new and original contribution. (p. 251)

It was largely because of and through his method of intelligence that Dewey became known as the "father of progressive education." Dewey did much to address the inherent controversies surrounding the clash of traditional versus progressive education.

In his 1902 publication *The Child and the Curriculum*, Dewey attempted to reconcile and understand the perspectives of two opposing groups of educators, the essentialists or traditionalists and the progressives. Traditional educators were intent on passing the cultural heritage to the next generation. Progressives were more concerned with reaching students as they were, regardless of their developmental stage. Traditionalists or essentialists believed specific content or subject matter trumped a student's interests and experience.

Progressives and developmentalists insisted, according to Dewey (1902),

> The child is the starting point, the center and the end. His development, his growth, is the ideal. . . Not knowledge or information, but self-realization is the goal. To possess all the world of knowledge and lose one's won self is as awful a fate in education as in religion. Moreover, subject-matter never can be got into the child from without. Learning is active. It involves reaching out of the mind. It involves organic assimilation starting from within. Literally, we must take our stand with the child and our departure from him. It is he and not the subject matter which determines both quality and quantity of learning. (p. 13)

After summarizing the chief tenets of each position, Dewey (1902) found common ground between the two:

> Abandon the notion of subject-matter as something fixed and ready-made in itself, outside the child's experience; cease thinking of the child's experience as also something hard and fast; see it as something fluent, embryonic, vital; and we realize that the child and the curriculum are simply two limits which define a single process. . . . It is continuous reconstruction, moving from the child's present experience out into that represented by the organized bodies of truth that we call studies. (p. 16)

While Dewey addressed the child versus the curriculum, he also wrote more broadly concerning the competition, in some minds, between those who promoted a more traditional view of education as opposed to those who held a more progressive view. In perhaps his most easily understood book *Experience and Education*, Dewey (1938) held that traditional education was based on the following assumption:

> The subject-matter of education consists of bodies of information and of skills that have been worked out of the past; therefore, the chief business of the school is to transmit them to the new generation. In the past, there have also been developed standards and rules of conduct; moral training consists in forming habits of action in conformity with these rules and standards. Finally, the general pattern of school organization (by which I mean relations of pupils to one another and to the teachers) constitutes the school a kind of institution sharply marked off from other social institutions. Call up in imagination the ordinary school room, its time schedules, schemes of classification, of examination and promotion, of rules of order, and I think you will grasp what is meant by "patterns of organization." Since the subject-matter as well as standards of proper conduct are handed down from the past, the attitude of pupils must, upon the whole, be one of docility, receptivity and obedience. Books, especially textbooks, are the chief representatives of the lore and wisdom of the past, while teachers are the organs through which students are brought into effective connection with the material. Teachers are the agents through which knowledge and skills are communicated and rules of conduct enforced. (pp. 17–18)

Progressives, by the time of the publication of *Experience and Education* (1938), had developed a great deal of dissatisfaction with the more traditional approaches to American education. Dewey summarized their discontent,

> The traditional scheme is, in essence, one of imposition from above and from outside. It imposes adult standards, subject-matter, and methods upon those who are only growing slowly toward maturity. The gap is so great that the required subject-matter, the methods of learning and behaving are foreign to the existing capacities of the young. They are beyond the reach of the experience the young learners already possess. Consequently, they must be imposed; even though good teachers will use devices of art to cover up the imposition so as to relieve it of obviously brutal features. . . .the gulf between the mature or adult products and the experience and abilities of the young is so wide that the very situation forbids much active participation by pupils in the development of what is taught. Theirs is to do—and learn, as it was the part of the six hundred to do and die. Learning here means acquisition of what is already incorporated in books and in the heads of the elders. Moreover, that which is taught is thought of as essentially static. . . . It is to a large extent the cultural product of societies that assumed the future would be much like the past, and yet it is used as educational food in a society where change is the rule, not the exception. (pp. 18–19)

The tenets of the new or progressive education were essentially opposed to those of the traditional or essentialist camp. Again, Dewey (1938) speaks,

> To imposition from above is opposed expression and cultivation of individuality; to external discipline is opposed free activity; to learning from texts and teachers, learning through experience; to acquisition of isolated skills and techniques by drill is opposed acquisition of them as means attaining ends which make direct vital appeal; to preparation for a more or less remote future is opposed making the most of the opportunities of present life; to static aims and materials is opposed acquaintance with a changing world. (pp. 19–20)

Dewey resolved the differences between the traditionalists and the progressives by referring to the nature of experience and its complete implications for education. Traditionalists were mistaken because of indifference to the relationship between the knowledge, skills, inner attitudes and dispositions they would have students acquire. Progressives often ignored the twofold nature of experience: that the quality of experience derives from the interaction between environment and internal conditions. In order to learn through experience, attention must be paid to environmental factors in relation to the personal needs, capacities and purposes of the student.

John Dewey's vision of progressive education has had little impact on the current state of education in the United States. As previously stated, the traditionalists/essentialists have won. They control the educational enterprise, regardless of whether the schools are public or private and also regardless of whether they take the form of charter or magnet schools. Educators such as E.D. Hirsch, in his *What Every Child Needs to Know* series, continue to be seen as the primary fount of educational wisdom.

Paulo Freire and the Critical Challenge Condemned

Thomas Jefferson claimed: "The moment a person forms a theory, his imagination sees, in every object, only the traits which favor that theory." Jefferson here acknowledges our philosophies not just as the lenses through which we see the world, but primarily as the lenses that show us the world we want to see. In short, human nature is such that we are what we believe—or better yet, the world is as we see it. For educators, the question is not whether or not we hold an educational philosophy—beliefs about the nature of teaching, of learning, of being human—but this: Are we aware of the influence of our philosophical groundings as they impact the thousands of decisions and behaviors we conduct each day in the name of teaching?

As we have considered so far, a teacher may call herself "progressive" and may recall having read about Dewey (or on occasion, may have even read some text written by Dewey). That same teacher may still carry with her the affection she felt for those beliefs associated with

Dewey and the label "progressive." Yet, if we sit in this teacher's classroom, we witness daily teacher-centered practices that reinforce the power structures and assumptions in the status quo of the school and the society. For example: "Similarly, Nystrand and Gamoran (1991) found that all the teachers in their study of eight ninth-grade suburban English classrooms believed it was important for their students, in the words of one, to 'discuss, contribute, and offer original ideas.' Observations of the classes, however, documented not even one second of such open-ended discussion" (Anagnostopoulos, Smith, & Nystrand, 2008, p. 5).

When anyone conducts the act of being, she or he is living a belief system; thus, we are bound always by that reality. For living broadly and for conducting the act of teaching, both are made more humane, more full if the person's being is an aware state. As a teacher, I must know what I believe and I must be able to step back from both my beliefs and my practices in order to consider the relative equilibrium or dissonance created by the two. Thus, while we believe that practitioners need to study carefully and richly the traditional and progressive philosophies that have competed in the field of education for more than a century, we also believe that practitioners must move beyond this study into the broader considerations of critical pedagogy, specifically the writings and philosophy of Paulo Freire.

Even if a practitioner commits herself or himself to the rigorous study of educational philosophy, without a critical awareness to guide and check that ever-evolving understanding, the practitioner still has no clothes.

Freire (1998) opens the last text he composed before his passing as follows:

> Two subjects occupy me in the writing of this text. The question of what forms education and becoming a teacher, and a reflection on educative practice from a progressive point of view. By "progressive" I mean a point of view that favors the autonomy of the students. (p. 21)

While there is much to unpack in this initial comment, the "reflection on educative practice from a progressive point of view" must not be ignored. It is through critical pedagogy, a way of being, that the practitioner comes to know the relationship between philosophy and action.

Many practitioners balk at time spent considering mere philosophy, and many also resist a consideration of critical pedagogy, discounting both as impractical and dangerously radical in the traditional contexts of most schools. Yet, when we consider a foundational aspect of critical pedagogy, we can begin to establish that philosophy and critical pedagogy are in fact "practical":

> Thus, proponents of critical pedagogy understand that every dimension of schooling and every form of educational practice are politically contested spaces. Shaped by history and challenged by a wide range of interest groups, educational practice is a fuzzy concept as it takes place in numerous settings, is shaped by a plethora of often-invisible forces, and can operate even in the name of democracy and justice to be totalitarian and oppressive. (Kincheloe, 2004, p. 2)

This "practicality" can be framed as philosophical awareness and critical perspectives empower a teacher to manage the political dynamic that is *teaching*. Without philosophical awareness and critical pedagogy, the teacher joins the student in having education done *to* them, instead of *by* them.

"Critical reflection on practice," Freire (1998) argues, "is a requirement of the relationship between theory and practice. Otherwise theory becomes simply 'blah, blah, blah,' and practice, pure activism" (p. 30). Ironically, in these hyper-conservative times whereby the standard popular condemnation of schools as liberal institutions propagandizing our youth is propagated and believed without a challenge, the reality is that most teachers are *unconsciously* "practice[ing] pure activism" and maintaining the status quo (thus, the activism is *conservative*).

If we return to Jefferson's assertion at the beginning of this section, anyone who *unconsciously* (thus uncritically) imposes her or his philosophy onto the world—and for teachers this would be onto students—that person is being partisan, oppressive. That such uncritical behavior is oppressive supercedes whether or not that oppression is conservative or liberal; the ideology means little when it wields power over those without power. Thus, our call for careful and rigorous considerations of educational philosophies as a nonpartisan act of empowerment.

"My theoretical explanation of such practice ought to be also a concrete and practical demonstration of what I am saying," Freire (1998) explains, thus connecting the philosophical with the practical (p. 49). Without a careful consideration of what we believe about teaching and learning, we are ill equipped to measure what we do with any precision, a precision unlike the traditional view of the term (not mechanistic quantification, but holding the real against the ideal as an act of qualitative validity). Teaching and our classrooms, then, must be "something witnessed, lived" (Freire, p. 49).

The progressive challenge that pushed against the traditional and mechanistic assumptions of teaching and learning offers practitioners a consideration of alternative views of education, but without a critical perspective, practitioners are left vulnerable to a dualistic and thus incomplete understanding of a classroom that creates the conditions necessary for the pursuit of democracy and freedom. Here, we find the necessity for the critical perspective that becomes a way of being, one that is "ethical" as teaching and learning are acts of empowerment—"to 'spiritualize' the world, to make it either beautiful or ugly" (Freire, 1998, p. 53).

The most damning result of either/or thinking is believing, falsely, that classrooms must be either authoritarian or chaotic. Freire (1998) explains the critical alternative:

> It is in this sense that both the authoritarian teacher who suffocates the natural curiosity and freedom on the student as well as the teacher who imposes no standards at all are equally disrespectful of an essential characteristic of our humanness, namely, our radical (and assumed) unfinishedness, out of which emerges the possibility of being ethical. (p. 59)

The empowering classroom is far more complex than any either/or dynamic as such dynamics oversimplify and necessarily distort human endeavors (Kohn, 1993). But it is Freire's recognition "of being ethical" that poses the greatest argument for the need to explore philosophy fully and rigorously.

A wrestling with the ethical implications of teaching and learning exposes "the dilemma arising from the tension between authority and freedom. And we invariably confuse authority and authoritarianism, freedom and license" (Freire, 1998, p. 60). And this, I believe, is the crux of why practitioners balk at any pursuits they deem impractical. They are trapped by the false dichotomy of what a classroom can be, primarily because they themselves have experienced and excelled in those exact settings that critical pedagogy challenges for being mechanistic and oppressive. When practitioners call for "practical" over "philosophical," that call is masking a fear of deconstructing the exact assumptions that housed their own success as students—and often their own physical and psychological safety as professionals.

The practical becomes in effect a perpetuation of the status quo, a fixed thing. A philosophical perspective, one augmented with a critical lens, however, is an embracing of a state of flux: "This permanent movement of searching creates a capacity for learning not only in order to adapt to the world but especially to intervene, to re-create, and to transform it" (Freire, 1998, p. 66). With the practical, we have a sense of security; with the theoretical, a sense of risk. The classroom that seeks and embraces risk is a classroom that confronts authority; thus, the practitioner trapped by dualistic assumptions believes confronting authority can only lead to chaos. Without a critical perspective, the practitioner is left without the possibility of authoritative (instead of authoritarian), without the possibility of freedom (without slipping into license).

Classrooms guided by practitioners who have ignored a careful consideration of philosophy—of progressivism and critical pedagogy—slip into an authoritarian, and thus oppressive, dynamic that contradicts democratic ideals by silencing students. The mechanistic assumptions of these classrooms embrace a traditional view of objectivity as both attainable and preferable to the contextual arguments made by critical pedagogy: Freire (1998) maintains "that the school...cannot abstract itself from the sociocultural and economic conditions of its students, their families, and their communities" (p. 62). Education without a rich philosophical understanding embraces a clinical view of humanity—oppressive in its narrow view of "scientific."

A philosophical pursuit is an act of questioning, an act that doesn't assume a fixed conclusion. As Freire has warned many times, a traditional view of teaching often assumes the teacher as the bearer and depositor of knowledge as capital and the student as the empty and passive receptacle. That assumption imposes a fixed nature of knowledge that is rejected by a philosophical pursuit—ontological, epistemological, and existential ways of knowing. But a critical perspective offers a rejection of static knowledge: "Mere mechanical memorization of the superficial aspects of the object is not true learning" (Freire, 1998, p. 66).

And this argument by Freire applies not only to the behavior of students in our classrooms, but also to the process of learning to teach. Those preservice and inservice teachers who reject philosophy as merely academic, as not practical, are by default accepting learning to teach as "teacher training," a "mechanical memorization of the superficial aspects of the object" in effect. Learning to teach, then, cannot be completed in an undergraduate program of certification or an alternative certification program. For the students in classrooms to those candidates striving to be teachers to those practitioners already teaching—"[t]his permanent movement of searching creates a capacity for learning, not only in order to adapt to the world but especially to intervene, to re-create, and to transform it" (Freire, 1998, p. 66).

In effect, then, we can argue that teaching is an act, as Freire argues in *Pedagogy of the Oppressed*, for the teacher/student and student/teacher. Teaching is necessarily learning to teach; or as Freire (1998) believes:

> Teachers who do not take their own education seriously, who do not study, who make little effort to keep abreast of events have no moral authority to coordinate the activities of the classroom. (p. 85)

This call by Freire confronts the practitioner's complaints about philosophy as "impractical" since the critical perspective values learning for learning's sake.

Studying educational philosophy is practical, we believe, but we are also left with those practitioners who still resist philosophy, especially critical pedagogy, as too radical, too risky. However, "there is no such thing as freedom without risk" (Freire, 1998, p. 87). A rigorous and ongoing consideration of educational philosophy is both practical and *necessarily* risky:

> Genuine freedom, even rebellious freedom, in this context is never seen as a deterioration of order. . . . [T]rue discipline does not exist in the muteness of those who have been silenced but in the stirrings of those who have been challenged, in the doubt of those who have been prodded, and in the hopes of those who have been awakened. (Freire, p. 86)

Two additional forces—the traditional call for teachers to remain neutral or objective and the contemporary call for standardization—make our call for philosophy essential. First, traditional approaches to teacher education—itself prescriptive—warn teachers to remain always neutral, objective. Yet, as Freire (1998) explains, "Education never was, is not, and never can be neutral or indifferent in regard to the reproduction of the dominant ideology or interrogation of it" (p. 91). The hidden reality of neutrality or objectivity is a *subjective* de facto support for the status quo.

The traditional call for neutral or objective teaching carries many assumptions that corrupt teaching if our goals are empowerment and democratic ideals. Knowledge is never value free; thus, the teaching/learning process can never be value free. This is the inherent paradox of objective teaching being subjective. Further, as Freire (1998) acknowledges, adopting the objective stance as the default and preferred scholarly or scientific stance is also an *abdication of being* for both the teacher and the student. It is "fatalistic quietude" (Freire, p. 92).

While the call for neutrality is a tradition within education, a more recent and possibly more insidious reality is the call for standardization: "The freedom that moves us, that makes us take risks, is being subjugated to a process of standardization of formulas and models in relation to which we are evaluated" (Freire, 1998, p. 102). Neutrality and standardization work as hidden givens unless practitioners have sharpened their own philosophical lenses in order to measure what they *believe* against what they *do*—and against what they are *mandated* to do.

Ultimately, the act of teaching must be an act of humility, the teacher as teacher/student facing a room of student/teachers, and "[h]umility is not made of bureaucratic rituals": Teaching "is something that the merely scientific, technical mind cannot accomplish" (Freire, 1998, p. 108). It is for the philosophical mind, the critical mind.

Teaching as a philosophical act recognizes, as Freire (1998) writes, "If education cannot do everything, there is something fundamental that it can do. In other words, if education is not the key to social transformation, neither is it simply meant to reproduce the dominant ideology" (p. 110). The classroom cannot have fixed means or ends if we have committed our classrooms in a free society to the dignity of each student and to the honor of that freedom that insures the education.

Critical pedagogy, then, supports teaching as a philosophical act creating the environments conducive to teachers and students having access to "[t]he knowledge of how to uncover hidden truths and how to demystify farcical ideologies, those seductive traps into which we easily fall" (Freire, 1998, p.123). Without the power of philosophical awareness, teaching that hides behind "neutral" and "standards" becomes an oppressive act that silences students and teachers with the din of dominant ideologies so loud that it drowns out the warning shouted to us by that perceptive child: "The practitioner has no clothes!"

The Practitioner and the (Philosophical) Power Suit

The empowered student necessarily requires the classroom offered by the empowered teacher. Any who teaches must first work through the philosophical evolution that Dewey and Freire represent—as well as continuing beyond the possibilities offered by Dewey's progressivism and

Freire's critical pedagogy. The pursuit of an educational philosophy, then, is a journey that is inseparable from being a practitioner—not something we "finish" in undergraduate courses and then mindlessly build upon.

Choosing between the status quo (norms and traditions) and progressive as well as critical possibilities is a choice between the moribund and the fecund. Norms and traditions are moribund—but the mind requires the fecund classroom that works against norms and traditions (thus progressive and critical) instead of bowing mindlessly to them. Philosophy is not something merely academic, something that wastes a teacher's time better spent on the practical. Again, as Freire (1998) argues, "Critical reflection on practice is a requirement of the relationship between theory and practice. Otherwise theory becomes simply 'blah, bah, blah,' and practice, pure activism" (p. 30). The soul of teaching, then, is an act of the mind and the heart that rises above the limitations falsely separating theory from practice.

References

Anagnostopoulos, D., Smith, E. R., & Nystrand, M. (2008, October). Creating dialogic spaces to support teachers' discussion practices: An introduction. *English Education, 41*(1): 4–12.
Archambault, R. D. (1964). *John Dewey on education: Selected writings*. New York: The Modern Library.
Dewey, J. (1900). *The school and society*. Chicago: University of Chicago Press.
Dewey, J. (1902). *The child and the curriculum*. Chicago: University of Chicago Press.
Dewey, J. (1916). *Democracy and education*. New York: Macmillan.
Dewey, J. (1922). *Human nature and conduct*. New York: Henry Holt.
Dewey, J. (1933). *How we think*. Boston: D.C. Heath.
Dewey, J. (1938). *Experience and education*. New York: Macmillan.
Freire, P. (1998). *Pedagogy of freedom: Ethics, democracy, and civic courage*. (Trans.) P. Clarke. New York: Rowman & Littlefield.
Jackson, P. (2002). *John Dewey and the philosopher's task*. New York: Teachers College Press.
Kincheloe, J. L. (2004). *Critical pedagogy primer*. New York: Peter Lang.
Kohn, A. (1993, September). Choices for children: Why and how to let students decide. *Phi Delta Kappan*. Retrieved from http://www.alfiekohn.org/teaching/cfc.htm.
Kohn, A. (2008, Spring). Progressive education: Why it's hard to beat, but also hard to find. *Independent school*. Retrieved from www.alfiekohn.org.
Nystrand, M., & Gamoran, A. (1991). Instructional discourse, student engagement, and literature achievement. *Research in the Teaching of English, 25*, 261–290.
Ryan, A. (1995). *John Dewey and the high tide of American liberalism*. New York: W.W. Norton.
Thayer, V. T. (1965). *Formative ideas in American education: From the colonial period to the present*. New York: Dodd, Mead.

Six

After Socrates: Community of Philosophical Inquiry and the New World Order

David Kennedy

The gradual silencing of philosophy that has spread through most U.S. colleges of education over the past half-century is not an isolated academic phenomenon. The same process of diminution has been at work in philosophy departments in schools of humanities and social sciences as well since 1980, which saw the ascendancy of globalized corporate capitalism and neoconservative politics and culture, the exhaustion of the political left, and the neutralization of the center. The dramatic and effective assault on progressive educational ideals represented by the No Child Left Behind Act of 2001 did not originate with the right-wing administration of the first decade of the 21st century, but in fact represents the culmination of a trend that began with the advent of the Cold War that included the permanent militarization of the state, the normalization of a state of emergency (Agamben, 2005), and the arrogation of the indoctrinating function of state-funded education to purposes, not just of economy and consumption, but of war and of biopower.

The role of philosophy in a world order characterized by perpetual war, dramatic economic injustice and exploitation, internal and external terror, and a global economic system geared to eventual ecocide can only be prophetically oppositional (Hardt & Negri, 2000, 2004), as it has tended to be in the Continental tradition. In the United States and England, academic philosophy in the form of the analytic movement took the opposite approach and assumed the role of the logic and language specialist in the administration of the epistemology of science, much as scholastic philosophy was a functionary in the administration of the epistemology of religion in the medieval period. From the point of view of the history of philosophy this may be understood as the pinnacle of a process of refinement—such as, for example, the paradigmatic example of philosophical discourse became the exquisite and enigmatic simplicity of

Tarski's "'Snow is white' if and only if snow is white"—but for the lay philosopher, it has all the earmarks of an inside joke delivered in an invented language.

The Socratic Model

For the lay philosopher—and it is the assumption of this paper that philosophy is a kind of thinking and talking that is universal and available to everyone—the paradigmatic example of philosophical discourse is the group of inquirers who used to gather with Socrates in the agora in Athens around 500 B.C. Although these meetings were somewhat hindered by Socrates' domineering preciosity (or Plato's exaggerated representation of it, or both), they are the first historical representations we have of a kind of thinking that not only demonstrates a controlled form of wondering about the world, but is directly connected with everyday life, and that both reflects upon and leads to action. The inquiry into justice in *The Republic*, for example, takes poignant meaning from the perilous political circumstances of the early 4th century B.C. It is also a kind of thinking that assumes the position of ignorance, clearly stated by Socrates, and that accepts and even delights in the aporia as the expression of our fundamental epistemological situation in the world. The aporia values the question over the proposition because it knows that there is no final statement that will end inquiry into the things that are really important to us—only as C.S. Peirce said, a truth that will be discovered by "the unlimited community of inquirers . . . in the long run"—which, of course, will never arrive (Raposa 1989).

The Socratic model is a pedagogical model: it is about teaching and learning in a small group without a clear hierarchy, conducted through conversation in everyday language, and with a ludic element—whether agonic, mimetic, or both. Epistemologically, it is about concept reconstruction as the pivot of teaching and learning and about how student and teacher together labor over that reconstruction. Because they labor together, it is also about the epistemological complexity of the student-teacher relationship. It is—again, Socrates' overbearing talent notwithstanding—a democratic model, in that it assumes an ideal speech community, in which no utterance has more authority than any other except on the grounds of its inherent reasonableness. Developed to its full potential, the community of interlocutors first presented to us by Socrates[1] is directly connected to the Freirean model of dialogue, where the teacher becomes a receiver as a well as donor of new meanings and the student the inverse, thus opening the classroom to multilogical relations of interlocution, and resolving what Freire (1968) called "the student-teacher contradiction." It fulfills the Vygotskian criteria for optimal learning as well: in an intentionally dialogical community, the zone of proximal development for each individual is present in the distributed intelligence of the whole group. In short, on this model, education and philosophy are one and the same thing.

I want to suggest here that the return of philosophy to schools of education, while not possible in its previous form as a distinct sub-discipline, is possible in the form of (post) Socratic pedagogy emerging as a distinctive, honored pedagogical methodology in all classrooms dedicated to teacher preparation. This post-Socratic pedagogy is already present in the theory and practice of what is known as "community of philosophical inquiry," which I will describe below. On this dialectical model, the return of philosophy to schools of education will come, so to speak, from "below," emerging in the classroom itself as a discursive form, a way of talking that problematizes and works to reconstruct common, central, and contestable concepts in education through communal philosophical dialogue, whether the specific classroom focus be curriculum, teaching, or governance. Community of philosophical inquiry (CPI) represents an integration of philosophy and education such that the problematization, deconstruction and reconstruction of concepts become a fundamental aspect of all educational discourse. As such, a methods class will be as concerned with problematizing the concept of "method" itself as cataloging currently available methods, and courses in administration will be concerned to problematize concepts like power, authority, freedom, control, and so on. So positioned, philosophy directly confronts the regimes of truth of the world of educational theory and practice. Rather than isolated in a speculative realm, a realm where its very freedom from the constraints of practice condemns it to triviality, educational philosophy is here thrust into confrontation with the rutted habits of educational theory and practice and is in a position to directly challenge the fatalism and presentism—indeed, the almost active anti-utopianism—that characterizes the public school realm.

Death and Rebirth

We may well ask, especially given the outcome of the historical dialectic of the last half-century, what there was to lose in the demise of a field—philosophy of education—the chief characteristic of which, in the words of one of its more influential recent spokespersons, ". . . has been that from the very first uses of the term the negotiation of what the field itself is has been one of its primary objects of preoccupation"; and in which "a central tension . . . has been between its philosophical, disciplinary aspirations and its relevance to educational policy and practice" (Burbules, 2000). That tension was indeed unpleasant enough in a state bureaucracy like universal compulsory schooling in a country as anti-philosophical as the United States; but it was when even that tension went slack—when the reified discourses of idealism, realism, pragmatism, existentialism, perennialism, essentialism, progressivism, naturalism, and so forth appeared to separate themselves completely from practice—that proponents of a knowledge-commodified, instrumentalist educational model moved in for the kill. As the foundations departments closed down, their moral and intellectual energy was assumed by cultural studies, which was, besides its unsuitably leftist assumptions, too cross-disciplinary and thematically untamed to fit in any teacher training taxonomy and could as easily be housed in a department of philosophy, literature, anthropology, or film studies. Meanwhile, the ideological and cultural lock-down consolidating itself in the public schools as a direct expression of the "Reagan revolution" had its inevitable effect on the schools of education that were supposed, the majority of superintendents of these large systems implicitly believed, to be serving them, not attempting to transform them.

The triumph of the Right in the public schools that was consolidated in the 1990s represented the final discrediting of the idea that teaching was a profession whose success depended on a vital, even risk-taking theory-practice relationship. Teacher as intellectual, inquirer, or "reflective practitioner" is a concept embarrassing or inimical to teacher as deliverer of curriculum packages mandated by the state and the corporate world in the form of aggressively marketed trade textbooks, all kept in place by a proliferating series of obligatory standardized tests. In a teaching profession in which the theory-practice relationship has gone slack, philosophy becomes irrelevant. In the American *fin de siècle* world of philosophy and education the two, rather than being one and the same thing as in the Socratic model, barely met in the first place, and as the Anglophone Western world moved to the Right, eventually the two did not meet at all. All that remains of philosophy in most colleges of education are one or two courses crammed into departments of educational leadership, where they fulfill some sort of survey knowledge—or knowledge about a domain of knowledge—thought necessary to add a bit of sparkle and polish to an administrator's portfolio. Their uneasy, step-child presence is mocked by the very course titles surrounding and vastly outnumbering them—"supervision of instruction," "human resources management," "executive leadership and communication," "administrative aspects of management and supervision," "creating a culture of continuous improvement," and so on. The loss of prestige is emphatic and near-ubiquitous and extends to students as well. Among undergraduates, philosophy of education is the ultimate non-necessity, and graduate students in education, especially those already practicing in schools, often resist it angrily as an academic effrontery perpetrated by a few out-of-touch elitists on an honest, hardworking proletariat who have no need for such a thing, especially since their bosses have no need for it.

Although trends in public education have been known since the advent of progressive education one century ago for their pendulum effect, there is little reason to expect the return of philosophy of education in anything like its current form—especially in a dramatically transformed information environment, the long-term effects of which are not yet clear. As the meanings and purposes of literacy change under the influence of new technologies, our understanding of doing philosophy changes as well. In the heyday of print, the dialogical element that is inherent in philosophical discourse was expressed in individualistic and diachronic terms. Hume responded to Descartes and Locke, Kant responded to Hume, Fichte responded to Kant, and so forth. The new information environment, still unfolding as it is, and unclear as to how it will change the way we think and communicate, promises—indeed, assures—the emergence of new literacies as well as the death or demographic miniaturization of others, and, with the ascendancy of popular culture, new distributions of these various literacies among classes. There is no more "high culture"—which is to say that particular forms of art or communication are no longer marks of class and privilege. A powerful member of the corporate or political, corporate, or criminal elite can as easily be found hosting a rap artist for his gala demonstration of power and wealth as a string quartet. The canon, the demise of which was pronounced in the cultural revolution of the 1960s and 1970s, no longer belongs to anyone.

The dismantling of the traditional hierarchies will have its emancipatory and its oppressive sides. In the realm of philosophy, it means that the discipline will no longer, except for the specialist, have its special connections with science, and it lost theology long ago. Philosophy as clarification of one's own beliefs becomes less important in a non-theological age. Now it is important in the *reconstruction* of belief—of common sense belief—in an age of transvaluation of values, the latter spurred by technological innovations such as genetic engineering that in themselves pose deep philosophical questions, as well as dramatically new world-situations, such as massive weapons proliferation, global warming, environmental degradation, extreme economic inequalities, organized crime, domestic terror perpetrated by random psychotic killers, and criminal governments propped up by state terror and information control. The reconstruction in question, again, is a collective, communal one, in keeping with the interactive quality of the emergent information environment. It is not about great thinkers retiring to their attics and developing grand systems but about collaborative pragmatic reconstruction *in situ*, and *in processu*. For Pragmatic reconstructionists, the Ship of Theseus problem is no longer relevant, for the original ship is so far in the past that one cannot be sure there ever was one.

This brings philosophy closer to the function it served in the Athenian agora and helps to explain the rise and endurance of the philosophy café, which in its theory and methodology could as easily be called Philosophy for the People. It also heralds the reuniting of philosophy and education in the emergence of the theory and practice of community of philosophical inquiry, a model for classroom discourse that has served for forty years as the teaching methodology of Philosophy for Children, a program for promoting philosophical dialogue among school children. Community of philosophical inquiry races genealogically back to Socrates, but with significant influences, not just in Enlightenment salon practices (of which the philosophy café is an offspring), but in Peircean logic and semiology (Dewey, 1938, 1948; Corrington, 1987, 1992), Buberian, Gadamerian, Bohmian, and Freirean dialogue theory (Buber, 1948, 1965, 1970; Gadamer, 1975, 1980 (and see Kennedy, 1990); Bohm, 1990, 1997; Freire, 1968), Habermasian communication theory (Habermas, 1981), group psychodynamics (Schilder, 1950) and Vygotskian and Meadian learning theory (Vygotsky, 1978, Mead, 1934). That is, it is multiple in its origins, but converges in Philosophy for Children's formulation of CPI (Lipman, Sharp & Oscanyan, 1980; Lipman, 1993, 2003; Sharp, 1986, 1992; Splitter & Sharp, 1995; Kennedy, 1999) in a classroom discussion methodology that looks virtually the same whether in kindergarten or graduate school and which is communal, egalitarian, dialogical, and dedicated to an emergent process of problematization, deconstruction, and ongoing reconstruction of concepts like justice, freedom, and education, method, power, or autonomy, for example.

Three Characteristics of Community of Philosophical Inquiry CPI

One way to place CPI historically and to evaluate its prospects as a new—or renewed—discursive form in educational institutions is to understand it as an adaptation—not the only one, certainly—to the emergent information environment of the 21st century. For one thing, it combines the oral and the literate. Socrates' groups did this as well, but from the position of pre rather than post-literacy, and Plato's perfection of the written dialogue may be thought of as an adaptation on that end of the history of literacy. As a form of performative group oracy, CPI is—again it must always be emphasized, in theory if not always in performance—an ideal speech situation, a form of distributed intelligence, and a zone of proximal development. It fulfills all the criteria of the first in that it assumes equal opportunity to challenge, question or assert on the part of every member, and takes equal participation as its regulative ideal—that is, it asserts an egalitarian power structure and resists any form of domination. It is a speech situation deliberately designed as a democratic one, and as such offers an exemplar for a classroom discourse and for a form of education that aspires to democracy—in the sense that Dewey (1916) intended when he spoke of "social democracy" as the necessary and sufficient condition for authentic political democracy. As an ideal democratic speech situation, CPI reconstructs power in the classroom, and by implication, in the school as a whole.

CPI is a distributed intelligence in that it is a structure of more or less coordinated perspectives that form a complex emergent system that functions through the interaction of each individual intelligence that makes it up, and whose goal is the full coordination of the unique perspective represented by each one. As an unfolding conversation in which a structure of concepts is assembled through many twists and turns by the participants' interplay, and as a system whose emergent course is not controlled by any one individual or ideology, CPI is self-organizing, or autopoietic. The argument develops non-linearly, through the interactions of each individual perspective with each other, and with all the others as a whole. The process is also characterized by moments of dislocation and disorganization, by role reversals and polarization, stagnation and chaos, by unpredictable organizers (something that seems irrelevant at first but shifts the whole argument), and by ambiguous control, whereby everyone in the system exercises some measure of control but no one (including the group leader or facilitator) total control, which creates ambiguity (Lushyn, 2002; Lushyn and Kennedy, 2000, 2003). These often labile open-system characteristics, which in communication theory would be referred to as "noise," in fact create the necessity for focused intentionality and voluntary resolve on the part of each member of the group and the affirmation, implicit or otherwise, of group identity as a task-oriented collective, in order to avoid failure through being overcome either by chaos or stagnation.

The coordination of individual perspectives—the implicit and normative goal of CPI—is not the same as a unification of perspectives. The latter would mean entropy and system death. The former implies a permanent element of dissonance and tension, and a system state in which there is always a "fault" or crack, something unresolved. The system develops both because of and in spite of a permanent process of problematization, deconstruction, and reconstruction through self-correction, each instance of which is a change in each individual's intelligence in the system and in the intelligence of the system as a whole. As such, any change of state, any realization and change of belief or self-correction the individual undergoes is the result of a "group action," so to speak.

The zone of proximal development that CPI forms is a result of the fact that in any group there are different levels of articulateness, communicativeness, mental alacrity, self-confidence, and metacognitive grasp or awareness of "the larger picture"; as such, the conversation is, in its meandering way, representing different skills and dispositions. One person may summarize well, another generate examples, another refine categories, and another identify hidden assumptions or contradictions. On the psychodynamic level, one person may tend to act as provocateur, another as coordinator of perspectives, another as a memory and another as a prophet, and another as purveyor of the counterfactual. These roles tend to emerge spontaneously through interaction.[2] If I am told, for example, that all dogs are brown, I (and a kindergarten student, as well) will most likely spontaneously think of a counter example, and that intervention acts as a model behavior, available for assimilation by the other members of the group. This exemplifies the Vygotskian dictum that the interpsychic—what emerges through interaction—is appropriated by the intrapsychic—the individual, and the correlative notion that I can perform at a higher level when interacting with a (sympathetic) person at a higher level (Vygotsky, 1978). In this case, that "person" is the group itself, which forms a large scaffolding apparatus for the practice and internalization of the skills and dispositions of critical and philosophical discourse. And this process is, of course, an oral one; it happens through conversation, and it happens spontaneously. The interventions or "moves" that are made by each interlocutor—generalizing, classifying, making a distinction, identifying a contradiction, giving an example, reasoning analogically, restating for example—emerge as system elements; they are "called forth" by the situation. Certainly they can be evaluated as good or bad for the argument that is being shaped through them, either by the group after they have emerged, or by the person through whom they have emerged before he or she articulates them, and this—the metacognitive dimension of CPI, the imperative to evaluate the conversation as it unfolds—is a critical element of CPI pedagogy.

Following the Argument Where It Leads

As a form of performative group literacy, a CPI—at least in the way it has been construed by philosophy for children—is typically dealing with some stimulus text, to which it is responding and which it is busy problematizing. But even if we consider instances of CPI practice in which the "text" is made up solely of the concepts (e.g., justice or love) being problematized by the participants—such as might happen in a philosophy café, a Bohmian dialogue (Bohm, 1998), or a sans texte philosophy course dedicated to the emergence of group-generated concepts from session to session—a textual element is present to the extent that the argument itself is an artifact in the process of continual reshaping. As in the Socratic dialogues, the argument is the conceptual structure created by the moves of the conversation. It could be thought of as a trace, or a residue, and, if transcribed and actually turned into text, an item for textual analysis. This analysis identifies the argument as a product of the moves, but as is well known, Plato's Socrates in several places suggests that the argument is in fact ahead of its performers, as in his famous admonition, "we must follow the argument wherever, like a wind, it may lead us" (*The Republic of Plato*, 394d).[3]

Perhaps this binary—argument as author and argument as resultant text—is analogous to the dual aspect of the new information environment. The argument as author reflects an orality effect: in primary oral cultures, spoken language is "a mode of action and not just a countersign of thought," as Walter Ong (*Orality and Literacy*, 1981, p. 32) has put it. The word has creative power. This characteristic of oracy, which Ong calls "the word as power and action," together with the fact that the argument is built through communication, results in the fact that the conversation in a CPI is in a very real sense out of the control of its participants, even if just out of control (Lushyn, 2001, has characterized it as "barely predictable"). And in a group situation, with multiple interlocutors, the progenitive, self-organizing character of language is magnified. The argument is like a wind, and the facilitator who attempts to control it completely ends up in a more dictatorial position than a traditional teacher, for he must impose a linear scheme on a complex process of emergence and silence all voices but the two whom he sets in opposition.

Assuming the argument takes its own course—although it is changed by each intervention, however, small—the facilitator in CPI acts, among her other roles, as reconnaissance. She stays slightly separated, her multiple gaze hovering above and around the argument, trying to see its larger shape, and to evaluate the branching and complications it is undergoing, with an eye to its optimal path, its best way forward. She works like a shepherd with her sheep dog to keep it out of dyadic face-offs, cul-de-sacs, wild rabbit chases, and power plays. This means she remains, as the saying goes, procedurally strong and philosophically self-effacing, although in fact these two are difficult to distinguish. Her goal is to preside over the process of distribution of the facilitating moves she herself is modeling—restating, clarifying, connecting ideas, attempting to locate the argument, maintaining equal participation—throughout the group (Kennedy, 2004). In a mature, ideal CPI every member has become a facilitator as well, and when this point is reached, she no longer needs to be philosophically self-effacing because she knows she no longer has any more power than anyone else in the group.

The facilitator also looks backward, at the traces the argument has left in its passing. She acts here as the group memory, or text-keeper, and this particular role is eventually distributed as well. In the primary oral universe, says Ong, "the oral utterance has vanished as soon as it is uttered," but in this post-oral universe of digital literacy it will no doubt soon be possible that the utterance is recorded by a machine, which immediately presents it as a text on a screen. This multiplies the possibilities both for recursion and for metacognition in that the conversation becomes text the moment it is uttered rather than vanishing and becomes available for evaluation and analysis, and the effects of the analysis feed back into the further emergence of the argument.

To summarize, the four characteristics identified here—ideal speech community, distributed intelligence (and, in a mature group, distributed facilitation), zone of proximal development, and argument as ambiguously authored text—are dimensions of CPI that identify it as a form of discourse that is educationally adaptive in relation to the information environment now emerging as a result of a technological transformation as profound as was the invention of the printing press in 1450. The new information environment is post-oral and post-literate. Its literacy is undermined by orality in its emphasis on immediacy and communication (and, it should be added, its integration of images and video with sound and print), and its texts tend to read like the spoken word transcribed. Its orality is in fact skin deep, since everything is potentially (and increasingly actually) recorded and transcribed and thereby rendered as text. CPI as a self-organizing argumentation system that forms through oral interaction and communication, and which aspires to building arguments that have the characteristics of texts—that is, structure, balance, deliberative interconnection of elements—fits the emergent information environment through combining orality and literacy and offers a model for classroom discourse that fits it as well.

Signs and Precursors

Community of philosophical inquiry is a classroom discursive form that does not so much talk about philosophy as do philosophy with the concepts at hand, and thus a form of philosophizing that is appropriate and applicable wherever concepts are recognized as contestable, or as calling for problematization and reconstruction, and wherever concept reconstruction has practical applications—in the design of curriculum for example, or in the way one teaches. I have referred to it as a reuniting of philosophy and education for this very reason. More specifically, it is a return of philosophy from within the material itself, rather than as a separate subject. On this model, a separate course in educational philosophy is no longer necessary (although it is certainly not inappropriate), because each course in education has a philosophical dimension. Nor, if I am planning a curriculum course, do I include a section on "philosophy and curriculum"—rather I approach the phenomenon of "curriculum" philosophically. I ask, what is curriculum? I call for thought experiments that consider the concept of curriculum across multiple contexts—in spiritual growth, in the development of a relationship, in listening to music, in parenting, and so on. I ask whether there are curricula in the natural world, and among other animals; is there an implicit curriculum in an infant's process of learning language? If so, is there such a thing as a self-generated curriculum, and what are the implications for how we do curriculum in school? Is there such a thing as a dialogical curriculum, in which the teacher and the student negotiate a curriculum? In other words, I problematize the concept of curriculum itself, and in the deconstruction of the concept—in identifying implicit assumptions and evaluating them against normative ideals (which are also open to problematization), and considering the possible instances and applications of the concept across multiple contexts—the concept is reconstructed and new applications invented or discovered. This is philosophy as praxis.

At least two precursors or parallel pedagogical movements have prepared the way for the emergence of communal philosophical dialogue from within the curricula of schools of education and cleared a space for CPI as an accepted and growing form of classroom discourse there. One—the critical thinking movement of the late 1980s and early 1990s—has already passed its peak but has left its traces in the normative ideal of public education as responsible for fostering clear and self-aware thinking and what have been called "higher order thinking skills." Whether this ideal is touted as a pre-requisite for white-collar survival skills in the shark-infested waters of late capitalism, as a necessary ingredient for the technological development and proliferation associated with late capitalism, or as a necessary tool for citizen resistance to the now-ubiquitous and deeply engrained state and corporate propaganda that is late capitalism's public voice, in all cases it appears to be a response to what Lyotard called complexification (Lyotard, 1991). CPI as an element of curriculum is in fact another sort of complexification but in the interest of the problematization of what seems obvious and thereby of demystification, difference, transformation, and the multilogical.

CPI as an educational discourse gains credence and prestige from an emphasis on critical thinking not only because the latter shifts the pedagogical focus toward thinking rather than just what is thought about, but more specifically because it trades on thinking *about* thinking—metacognition. Communal philosophical dialogue, because it is distributed thinking and a natural zone of proximal development for all participants, succeeds or fails through the ability to watch itself thinking, to evaluate that thinking, and to grow from the lessons taken. Furthermore, as a discourse, critical thinking is based on the skills and dispositions of informal reasoning, which—along with formal reasoning and what have been referred to as "interpersonal reasoning" and "philosophical reasoning" (Cannon & Weinstein, 1993). These four dimensions provide the basic operational grid for the moves of community of philosophical inquiry. Critical thinking is also closely related to argumentation theory, a field whose application to the complex, systemic emergence of argument in a situation of facilitated but "barely predictable" communal dialogue has not, to my knowledge, been attempted. Because of these connections between CPI and the theory and practice and critical thinking, those schools of education that have embraced the latter are primed for the former.

More recently, the world of teacher preparation has been influenced by the introduction of a theory of curriculum development that takes as its fundamental units of design what are called "big ideas" and their accompanying "essential questions" (Wiggins & McTighe, 2005). Although the fit is not exact, it is clear that an essential question is closer to a philosophical concept than a behavioral objective and that planning curriculum on the armature of a "big idea"—for example, "liberty versus license," or "scarcity"—is more conducive to dialogical thinking than planning it on something like the "ten key facts" that will appear on a test. Even if the "big idea" movement moves in a positivistic direction in the hands of the inherently conservative institution of the public school, the emergence of the discourse itself indicates at least two related possibilities. For one, it would seem to indicate that the power and influence of the authoritarian and dehumanizing trend in education represented by the No Child Left Behind Act of 2001—which, through a naïve and damaging category mistake punishes teachers in the name of "accountability" for the general breakdown of an under-resourced system—is on the wane, or at least being effectively challenged; that, if one can dare hope, the pendulum is swinging.

For another, and concomitantly, the "essential questions" movement represents an impulse to put curriculum planning back in the hands of teachers and challenges them to act as intellectuals through thinking and planning their own curriculum content on a conceptual level. This by implication opens the possibility for the reuniting of philosophy and education that CPI represents, because to identify the common, central, and contestable concepts upon which the science or history curriculum is based is already to put in question the assumptions for which they act as vehicles. The concept of "alive" in the biological sciences is, for example, a historically and culturally mediated concept and like any other concept, vulnerable to a paradigm shift—a vulnerability that is already apparent in the stress on the concept when, in Gaia theory, it is argued that the biosphere is "alive," or by instances of "life" that we might find on other planets that involve different criteria. To identify the major common central and contestable concepts in biology—for example, alive, organism, environment, adaptation—is by implication to problematize them, which is already to embark on their reconstruction.

To make contact with this understructure of assumptions that shape the disciplines is to contact their philosophical dimension, and in this way we can see a direct link between the "essential questions" movement and a way of doing philosophy of the disciplines that leads directly to the theory and practice of CPI. This allows us to imagine a normative ideal in which the school-world corresponded to the university-world—where both pre-teachers and practicing teachers engaged regularly in community of philosophical inquiry as a way of clarifying the philosophical framework of the curriculum they were teaching, and finding the conceptual connections between the disciplines—how, for example is a historical "fact" like or unlike a scientific "fact," and what does their similarity or difference mean for the issue of objectivity in the sciences? Such an approach to curriculum promises to bring philosophy permanently into the curriculum, but—again—not as a separate content area but as a dimension of the subject matter itself.

The Long March

In addition to the critical thinking movement and the "essential questions" movement, both of which are relatively recent phenomena, at least one other influence may be cited as acting over the long run to prepare a place in schools for the theory and practice of community of philosophical inquiry. This may be referred to at least broadly as the "dialogical turn" in pedagogical theory and practice. The turn can be traced, not just to its most obvious champion at the end of the 20th century—(Freire, 1968) but to the effects over the course of the 19th century of Rousseau's *Emile* on transformative educators like Pestalozzi, Froebel, Montessori, Dewey, and no doubt countless other less-publicized theorists and practitioners. The historical thread of dialogical pedagogy can also be traced into and through the 20th century in the rise of constructivist epistemology in Piaget and in Dewey, who had as large an influence on educational thought in the first half of the century as Piaget had in the second.

From the point of view of educational theory, the epistemological changes that are associated with pragmatism and constructivism were also changes in how adults see children, and as such, it could be argued that any change in education that is more than superficial will stem from a perceptual change—which of course is itself dependent on countless social, economic, cultural variables (Kennedy, 2006a, 2006b). The net result of the changes in epistemological theory over the course of the 20th century was to redefine the child as an active inquirer—a "little scientist," which implies "little philosopher" as well. That, in spite of this revolution in the perception of children as knowers and learners, public schooling remained tied in multiple ways to a behavioristic model of learning is testimony to the repressive character of universal compulsory education performed in the technological and military service of the nation state, which has been virtually the only model offered since the massive centralization and ideological takeover in the first decade of the 19th century in Napoleonic France (Gutek, 1995).

The dialogic turn represents, it could be argued, one aspect of a larger movement, a movement that (Plato's politics apparently to the contrary) we associate with the practices of Socrates, and call "democracy," by which is meant democracy as a normative ideal, whatever the distorted or corrupted versions we currently have of it as a form of politics. As a philosophical discourse dedicated to the problematization, deconstruction and reconstruction of concepts, and as a form of classroom discourse, CPI satisfies the criteria for a truly democratic pedagogy—a pedagogy that fulfills the exigency of what de Tocqueville (2002) called "the most continuous, ancient, and permanent tendency known to history," the "democratic revolution," (p. 9) which he characterized as "irresistible . . . advancing century by century over every obstacle and even now going forward amid the ruins it has itself created" (p. 12).

When De Tocqueville called on "those who now direct society" to "educate democracy; to put, if possible, new life into its beliefs; to purify its mores; to control its actions; gradually to substitute . . . knowledge of its true interests for blind instincts" (p. 12), he was implicitly calling for a transformation of educational theory and practice in the interests of what Dewey (1916) later distinguished as social democracy, which he famously described as "more than a form of government; it is primarily a mode of associated living, of conjoint communicated experience" (p. 87). That Tocqueville neither described the schools he found in the United States in the 1830s, nor sketched a system of schooling that he considered worthy of the "irresistible tendency" he was tracing, can be interpreted in various ways. It could be that he considered the real "school" of democracy to be the whole society, and any distinction between what was learned in the school house and what was learned on the street a weak one. Be that as it may, universal compulsory state-provided schooling is still a powerful influence on the formation of social subjectivity among the young, and a key status-determiner in the contemporary state and economy. It still functions to socialize the worker/citizen for a system that in its default form is designed, not to promote social democracy, but to maintain hegemonic class, economic, and political relations. Whereas Tocqueville seemed to be arguing implicitly for the relative unimportance of schooling in "educating democracy," Dewey considered the school as a form of intentional community of adults and children—to be an institution that could play a key role in the reconstruction of deep-seated social habits.

The change that social democracy demands is a change that can only rest, as has already been suggested, on a reconstructed view of the teacher-student relation, and by close association, the adult-child relation. Rousseau was the first well-known voice to call, however inchoately, for this reconstruction, and the seed he planted, nurtured by Pestalozzi and Froebel in the face of a century of reaction, flowered in the Progressive education movement of the early 20th century, but has not yet borne full fruit. The first half of the last century saw the largest global conflicts in recorded history debouching into a state of perpetual ("cold") war, and the National Defense Education Act of 1958, passed one year after Sputnik, froze the American educational establishment on a war footing, even as the right-wing ideologues discredited Dewey as "soft" (Cremin, 1961). Scientific and pre-technical education became a national "security" need, and primary educational emphasis placed on math and science, geared to weapons and product development. The cultural revolution of the 1960s and the period of post-colonialism saw the return of the "irresistible tendency" in the dialogical theory of Freire and many others, but the authoritarian reaction that began with the Nixon administration and reached majority in Reagan, dampened and starved its progress through the 1970s. In the 1980s, reigning right-wing national policy makers called again for educational militarization in the name of global economic competition in the "Nation at Risk" manifesto, and at the turn of the 21st century, in the name of the "war on terror." To all appearances, universal public education has been colonized for purposes of economy and militarism, and the long march stalled indefinitely.

It is a characteristic of historical (as well as psychological) dialectic, however, that the contradictory element, or (to use an antiquarian term) the "antithesis," is not only already and always present—however one-sided the present situation—in the process, but that it in fact gains strength and is empowered by negation. In fact the very concept of "long march" depends on it. Nor should we ignore Tocqueville's invocation of the "ruins" that the irresistible tendency itself has created, and through which it must make its way. Those ruins may be understood to be, at least in part, the very reactions of fear, violent repression, and domination, as well as the depredations of late capitalism, that the irresistible tendency creates. To invoke the irresistible tendency is in fact an act of faith. In keeping with that faith, the idea that philosophy should return to educational theory and practice as a form of deliberative dialogue—return from within, as grass returns to the earth—is here interpreted as a sign of a more global change than would be signaled by philosophy returning in its previous form. Emerging as it is from within, it could be interpreted as evidence of, in Deweyan terms, the reconstruction of habit, of the emergence of one "mode of associated living, of conjoint communicated experience" fundamental to authentic democracy.

As a form of discourse, CPI reaches back to Socrates and before—it would be safe to assume that this form of group deliberative discourse has been in existence from early in human history and is found universally across cultures, whether in the Hopi kiva, the *boule* of Ionian Greek city states, Socrates' *agora*, certain graduate seminars, or certain discussion-based Philosophy 101 classes. It is a genetic form of group discourse with obvious evolutionary value, and, whatever the differences across history and culture, gathered around the common task of creating an ideal speech situation. The ideal speech situation can vary historically according to class and age and sex differences; in the case of the Ionian *boule* or the Hopi kiva, age, sex and public reputation determined who could speak. The ideal speech situation of our era is understood—even, it should be pointed out (and in support of Tocqueville's thesis) by those who flout and abuse it—as a democratic one. It may even be characterized as the centerpiece of social democracy.

As such, CPI reaches *forward* into a form of education that has been theorized by a few prophets—and no doubt practiced in its basic lineaments by many in the relative obscurity of their classrooms—and that follows from the epistemological reconstruction of the last century and the exigency of democracy. CPI is the performative centerpiece of an epistemology that may be described as constructivist, relational, transactional, distributive, fallibilist, reconstructionist, and complex (in the sense of complex systems theory), with pronounced democratic, if not philosophically anarchist, political implications. As such it leads the way in the path of the reconstruction of subjectivity that the irresistible tendency that moves us along requires. And if it grows in use as a pedagogical practice in schools of education, it will not be with fanfare—in fact the word "philosophy" may very well be replaced by one less intimidating to American ears. Be that as it may, for those on the journey, it will be a triumphal return.

Notes

1. Based no doubt in turn on the democratic councils of the Ionian city states, the *boule*, or councils of citizens. But the Socratic boule is a "wild" variety, which in deconstructing concepts like justice, threatens to deconstruct the state. This makes Socrates' murder by the larger *boule* of Athens more understandable, if not more acceptable.
2. Although one can tell the "trained" philosopher by her self-conscious assumption of one role or the other, usually in the service of a studied epistemological caution.
3. CPI as a normative ideal assumes, like Socrates, the existence of an "Argument" that is the construction of the interventions of the assembled interlocutors, and it also assumes that this Argument has some measure of independence or whole identity—some structure that is larger than the sum of its parts—and that it is moving somewhere. Whether we can assume that the Argument moves teleologically or randomly is not made completely clear in Plato. This is complicated by his choice of metaphor: we usually think of the wind as pushing us somewhere rather than leading us. Whether he means that each subsequent step must connect logically with the one before it—as seems to be the case in the *Sophist*, where Theaetetus, when presented by the Stranger with an example that challenges his definition of "sophist," affirms it as a member of the same class, saying "I must do so, for I have to follow where the argument leads"—or whether he means the argument is leading, however circuitously, towards a "truth" whether large or small and we must follow that larger arc, is unclear. CPI theory and practice accepts the aporia that any consideration of a teleological argument implies, but allows itself room by identifying it in the context of emergent complex systems or "chaos" theory. The complex system that CPI represents is the system that forms when the perspective of each person in the group—each interlocutor—is put in interaction with the perspective of every other. This is more in keeping with the Gadamerian notion of play, in which, for example, "The being of all play is always realization, sheer fulfillment, energeia which has its telos within itself" (Gadamer, 1975, p. 101).

References

A nation at risk: The imperative for educational reform (1983). A Report to the Nation and the Secretary of Education, United States Department of Education by the National Commission on Excellence in Education, April 1983. Retrieved May 2009 at http://www.ed.gov/pubs/NatAtRisk/title.html.
Agamben, G. (2005). *State of exception*. Chicago: University of Chicago Press.
Bohm, D. (1990). *On dialogue*. Ojai, CA: David Bohm Seminars, 1990.
Bohm, D. (1997). *Thought as a system*. New York: Routledge, 1997.
Buber, M. (1948). *Between man and man* (R. G. Smith, Trans.). New York: Macmillan.
Buber, M. (1965). *The knowledge of man: A philosophy of the interhuman* (M. Friedman & R. G. Smith, Trans.). New York: Scribner.
Buber, Martin (1970/1922). *I and thou* (Walter Kaufmann, Trans.). New York: Scribner.
Burbules, N. C. (2000). Philosophy of education. In B. Moon, M. Ben-Peretz, & S. Brown (Eds.), *Routledge international companion to education* (pp. 3–18). New York: Routledge.
Cannon, D. & Weinstein, M. (1993). Reasoning skills: An overview. In M. Lipman (Ed.), *Thinking children and education* (pp. 598–604). Dubuque, IA: Kendall Hunt.
Corrington, R. S. (1987). The origins of American hermeneutics: C.S. Peirce and Josiah Royce. In *The community of interpreters* (pp. 1–29). Macon, GA: Mercer University Press.
Corrington, R. S. (1992). The signs of community. In *Nature and spirit: Essays in ecstatic naturalism* (pp. 83–120). New York: Fordham University Press.
Cremin, L. A. (1961). *The transformation of the school: Progressivism in American education, 1876–1957*. New York: Random House.
Dewey, J. (1916). *Democracy and education*. New York: Free Press.
Dewey, J. (1938). The existential matrix of inquiry: Biological (Chapter II) & The pattern of inquiry (Chapter VI). In *Logic: The theory of inquiry* (pp. 23–41 & 101–119). New York: Holt.
Dewey, J. (1948). *Reconstruction in philosophy*. Boston: Beacon Press.
Freire, P. (1968). *Pedagogy of the oppressed*. New York: Seabury, 1968.
Gadamer, H-G. (1975). *Truth and method*. New York: Crossroad.
Gadamer, H-G. (1980). *Dialogue and dialectic: Eight hermeneutical studies on Plato* (P. C. Smith, Trans.). New Haven, CN: Yale University Press.

Gutek, G. L. (1995). *A history of the Western educational experience* (2nd ed.). Prospect Heights, IL: Waveland Press.
Habermas, J. (1984). *The theory of communicative action*. Boston: Beacon Press.
Hardt, M. & Negri, A. (2000). *Empire*. Cambridge, MA: Harvard University Press.
Hardt, M. & Negri, A. (2004). *Multitude: War and democracy in the age of empire*. London: Penguin.
Kennedy, D. (1990). Hans-Georg Gadamer's dialectic of dialogue and the epistemology of the community of inquiry. *Analytic Teaching* 11,1, 43–51.
Kennedy, D. (1999). Philosophy for children and the reconstruction of philosophy. *Metaphilosophy* 30,4, 338–359.
Kennedy, D. (2004). The role of a facilitator in a community of philosophical inquiry. *Metaphilosophy* 35, 4.
Kennedy, D. (2006a). *The well of being: Childhood, subjectivity, and education*. Albany, NY: SUNY Press.
Kennedy, D. (2006b). *Changing conceptions of the child from the Renaissance to post-modernity: A Philosophy of childhood*. Lewiston, NY: Edwin Mellen.
Lipman, M., Sharp, A. M., & Oscanyan, F. (1980). *Philosophy in the classroom*. Philadelphia: Temple University Press.
Lipman, M. (Ed.). (2003). *Thinking children and education*. Dubuque, IA: Kendall Hunt.
Lipman, M. (2003). *Thinking in education* (2nd ed.). Cambridge: Cambridge University Press.
Lushyn, P. & Kennedy, D. (2000). The psychodynamics of community of inquiry and educational reform: A cross-cultural perspective. *Thinking: The Journal of Philosophy for Children*, 15, 3.
Lushyn, P. (2002). The paradoxical nature of ecofacilitation in the community of inquiry. *Thinking: The Journal of Philosophy for Children* 16,1, 12–17.
Lushyn, P. & Kennedy, D. (2003). Power, manipulation, and control in a community of inquiry. *Analytic Teaching* 23,2, 103–110.
Lyotard, J-F. (1991). *The inhuman: Reflections on time* (G. Bennington & R. Bowlby, Trans.). Stanford, CA: Stanford University Press.
Mead, G. H. (1934). *Mind, self and society*. Chicago: University of Chicago Press.
Ong, W. (1982). *Orality and literacy: The technologizing of the word*. London: Methuen.
Piaget, J. (1976). Biology and cognition. In B. Inhelder & H. H. Chipman (Eds.), *Piaget and his school*. New York: Springer Verlag.
Plato (1945). *The Republic of Plato* (F. M. Cornford Trans. & Ed.). London: Oxford University Press.
Plato (1961). *The collected dialogues of Plato* (E. Hamilton & H. Cairns, Eds.) Princeton, NJ: Princeton University Press.
Raposa, M. L.(1989). *Peirce's philosophy of religion*. Bloomington: Indiana University Press.
Rousseau, J-J. (1979 [1763]). *Emile, or on education* (A. Bloom, Trans.). New York: Basic Books.
Schilder, P. (1950). *The image and appearance of the human body: Studies in the constructive energies of the psyche*. New York: International Universities Press.
Sharp, A.M. (1986). Community of inquiry and democracy. *Thinking: The Journal of Philosophy for Children*, 12,4.
Sharp, A.M. (1992). What is a community of inquiry? In W. Oxman, N. Michelli & L. Coia (Eds.), *Critical thinking and learning*. Montclair, NJ: Montclair State University.
Splitter, L. & Sharp, A. M. (1995). *Teaching for better thinking: The classroom community of inquiry*. Melbourne: ACER.
Tocqueville, Alexis de. (2002 [1835–1840]). *Democracy in America* (G. E. Bevin, Trans.). London: Penguin.
Vygotsky, L. (1978). *Mind in society: The development of higher psychological processes*. Cambridge, MA: Harvard University Press.
Wiggins, G. & McTighe, J. (2005). *Understanding by design* (2nd ed.). Alexandria, VA: ASCD 2005.

Seven

(Re)placing Foundations in Education: Politics of Survival in Conservative Times

John E. Petrovic and Aaron M. Kuntz

> *For all these reasons, the goal of teacher preparation cannot properly be defined solely as the production of a good technician – a skillful classroom operator who knows his subject. It is rather the development of an educational statesman able to take his place, as a professional, with his colleagues in the conduct of the educational system of the nation.*
> —William O. Stanley, 1968, p. 230

Introduction

Many critical scholars have commented on the contemporary context in which education is currently immersed, often framing our current educational condition as governed by neoliberal agendas (Giroux, 2005; McLaren, 2005), conservative modernization (Apple, 2006), or methodological conservatism (Lincoln & Cabrella, 2004). These scholars condemn educational formations that privilege individual accountability over collaboration, rigidly standardized mechanisms for defining student and institutional success, economic substantiations for educational meaning, and a definitional conflation of democracy with capitalism. More and more, these are the times in which we find ourselves—the contexts in which we must rationalize our work within the social, historical, and philosophical foundations (henceforth simply "Foundations") as well as the contexts against which we might work for radical change through education.

Though the overarching issues inherent in our current era are certainly historical—an emergent product of socialized interpretations of education—they do present pointed challenges for faculty in Foundations programs throughout the country. Of particular note is the way in which these programs are rhetorically placed within colleges of education and how Foundations' faculty responds to such placement.

The placing of Foundations amidst contemporary contexts is the focus of our chapter. We seek to examine the means by which Foundations are rationalized within educational institutions and the many ways in which Foundations faculty take on, or work against, such rationalizations. Inherent in questions concerning the place of Foundations within education today is the way in which both education generally, and Foundations specifically, are framed. A social frame presents a unique means of interpreting the world, one that entails particular definitions of key terms (such as student, professor, and knowledge) even as it asserts some social practices as legitimate and others as deviant. The way Foundations is placed within education remains a product of the social framing within which such placement occurs.

In elaborating on this claim, the rest of this chapter is organized as follows: (1) We begin with an examination of the current state of Foundations in education, especially as it relates to teacher education. This necessarily includes some historical discussion of the development of the field; (2) Next, we discuss strategies for "replacing" Foundations against a teacher education context; (3) We then discuss the politics of engaging in disciplinary boundary work within interdisciplinary contexts; (4) Finally, we present the intricacies involved in cognitive framing before concluding with a re-examination of particular strategies on and challenges with placing Foundations within larger institutional contexts.

Placing Foundations in Teacher Education

Historically, if one had taken a foundational course in education, it would have been discipline specific as in courses titled Philosophy of Education, History of Education, or Sociology of Education. A major turn from this approach is credited to George Counts' publication in 1934 of "The Social Foundations of Education" (Tozer & Miretzky, 2005). This turn owed to an interdisciplinary discussion group formed at Teachers College wherein, as Kenneth D. Benne described it, the group "came to believe that all teachers should become students of the issues to questions of educational aims, methods, and programs. They also believe that a cross-disciplinary approach was conducive to adequate treatment of these issues" (as cited in Tozer & Miretzky, p. 7). This turn was, of course, not a discreet, totalizing event; indeed, disciplinarily titled courses can still be found in many reputable Foundations programs across the country. In some cases, historically, the new "field" was listed among, but as something different, apparently, than the original triad of studies. Consider the way that Stanley (1968) refers to the coursework: "I refer, of course, to such courses as philosophy of education, history of education, comparative education, sociology of education and the social foundations of education" (p. 228, emphasis added). Foundations as inclusive of or distinct from multiple disciplines within education remains a key element of its placement within the field generally, and within the structures of Colleges of Education more specifically. In this way Foundations exists within multiple and, at times, contradictory frames, representing both interdisciplinary fields of inquiry and more historically defined perspectives and meanings of education.

While Foundations is an eclectic field, some consensus does seem to exist as regards its role in teacher preparation. As Eric Bredo (in Butin 2005b) argues, "our job is to offer perspective" (p. 51) both from the fringe and from the center. Further, as the history of the field suggests, Foundations provides a skill set by engaging students in different kinds (philosophical, historical, sociological, anthropological, etc.) of disciplinary analyses. Offering perspective through various disciplinary lenses seems to be part and parcel of what Harry Broudy called "interpretative knowledge," which he distinguished from the "applicative knowledge" delivered generally within methods courses (cited by Stanley, 1968).

Decrying the "segmentation" of the teaching enterprise and condemning the view that "the task of the teacher may be adequately defined as that of a competent classroom operator," Stanley (1968) argued, ". . .teachers must be able to consider intelligently problems entailing the relationship of the school to the social order and the aims, the organization, the curriculum of the school in a particular society confronting a particular set of social problems" (Stanley, 1968, pp. 228 and 230, respectively). Similarly, Dan Butin (2005) makes the case that ". . .the social Foundations classroom is supposed to help students understand the complex, intertwined, and deep roots of why we do what we do in contemporary schooling" (p. xiv). These discussions of the role of Foundations in teacher preparation are ultimately summed up by the Council for Social Foundations in Education (1996): "The purpose of Foundations study is to bring these disciplinary resources to bear in developing interpretive, normative, and critical perspectives on education, both inside and outside of schools" (n.p.). From these perspectives, the teacher is more than simply a manager of educable bodies, more than a referee in the application of state or federal standards. Instead, teachers represent a critical link between the processes of education and the socio-historical contexts in which schooling is immersed. Thus, Foundations provides a dimensionality to schooling, a critical orientation to the very roots of our educational systems. Contemporary contexts, however, grant little virtue to multidimensionality, preferring instead a flattening out of educational practice that foregrounds issues of efficiency and pre-defined accountability.

"Replacing" Foundations in Teacher Education

While ongoing, Foundations face a particularly stringent challenge in this neoliberal age of standards and accountability. We face a daily obligation to try to replace Foundations. On the one hand, "replacing" can mean "substituting for." Some of the strategies we have engaged in, in fact, resemble this understanding (replacing a systematic study of philosophy with diversity courses, for example). On the other hand, "replacing" can mean "situating again." This is reflected in calls to redefine the purposes of education and, thus, the purposes of and need for Foundations. It involves reframing what it is that we do.

Of course, the multiple and dynamic definition of replacing is anything but distinct and complete. Attempts to replace Foundations in one way (to rearticulate what Foundations means within a larger College of Education, for example) run the risk of enabling the replacement of Foundations in the other sense (the substitution of alternative coursework or programs for a specifically defined Foundations program). Thus, it remains particularly important to maintain an awareness of the consequences of how we rhetorically and materially place Foundations within multiple institutional discourses. How we frame Foundations at the level of both the individual and the institution matters. We return to this in our analysis ("Problematized Framings: Embracing a Politics of Survival") in this chapter. For now, we turn to a review of some arguments as to how to replace Foundations.

Replacing Foundations

Tozer and Miretzky (2005) argue that the challenges to continued inclusion of Foundations in teacher education are twofold: First is "the loss of the protection of Social Foundations courses when state curriculum requirements are reduced or eliminated in favor of outcome assessments." Second is "to show how social foundations preparation actually contributes to success in these outcome assessments" (p. 14).

Following from the increased focus on teacher outcome assessments, Tozer and Miretzky (2005) argue that faculty in Foundations will have to demonstrate that the coursework they offer results in improved teaching performance. Simultaneously, engagement with the standards movement must continue in the form of critiques but within a discourse of improvement. To their minds, passivity will mean elimination and straightforward resistance is futile. Although they might quarrel with our assessment, essentially, the strategy of Tozer and Miretzky is twofold. First, they recommend replacing (in the sense of substituting for) Foundations as multicultural education to prepare teachers to serve "the children left behind." Here they cite Dennis Shirley, chair of the Teacher Education program at Boston College, who argues, that:

> It's important that beginning teachers have at least a rudimentary ability and understanding of how to interact with constituents and parents from different cultural, class, religious, and ethnic backgrounds. There needs to be a facility and joy in cross-cultural encounters, and a lot of creative skills to go along with that. (p. 19)

Of course, Tozer and Miretzky connect this to the more progressive Council of Social Foundations Educators standards. Certainly, we do not want to suggest that Foundations courses should not engage with issues of diversity and multiculturalism. Indeed, we should stake traditional multiculturalism out as terrain to be cultivated through conceptualizations of social justice, radical definitions of democracy, and understandings of oppression through critical pedagogy. Nevertheless, this strategy may prove problematic.

Second, Tozer and Miretzky recommend that Foundations faculty choose from among existing standards and principles within various accrediting bodies (NCATE, ISLLC, etc.) and argue that a particular standard is within the effective purview of Foundations (replacing in the sense of situating again). This includes the necessity to make the case that "dedicated study in Foundations elevates the knowledge of the teacher to a distinctive professional level that is appropriate for teachers who have to make decisions in complex cultural contexts" against those who argue that "such skills [understanding and process, justification and interpretation, and critical reflection] can be and have been integrated throughout teacher preparation programs without distinct social Foundations courses" (p. 22).

In the end, we agree with Tozer and Miretzky that "these are largely standards-based, instrumental arguments that fall short of the oppositional, democratic ethic" expressed by Harold Rugg, George Counts, and Maxine Greene, among others. To what extent, then, will this strategy of survival affect and continue to redefine the field? How will framing Foundations within the language of the standards movement assert particular readings of what Foundations do—enabling and constraining particular practices?

Replacing Teacher Education

While one strategy is to reframe social Foundations as multicultural education so as to serve those current standards to which we might lay claim, another strategy is to replace teacher preparation in the social Foundations disciplines. Kathleen deMarrais (2005) describes such a program developed at the University of Tennessee. This was a fifth-year program with a yearlong internship wherein students, with a faculty team, "examined schooling through sociological analyses of school structures" and "engaged in educational philosophies as they developed their own teaching philosophy (p. 171). deMarrais goes on to explain,

> Although we explored the traditional "methods" of language arts, science, math, and social studies as part of the elementary school curriculum, we framed this work within the politics of knowledge production as well as within the sociocultural contexts of children's lives. The methods portion of our program was grounded in transformative school practices. (p. 171)

An important aspect of this model is team teaching. Not only does this provide a model for interns for how to work collaboratively but it also serves strategically "to disrupt notions of curricular ownership" (p. 183). One of deMarrais' points here is to find ways to work across the false walls that are so often built in colleges of education generally and teacher preparation programs specifically.

Replacing Standards and Accountability within Foundations

In some ways, Eric Bredo's (2005) strategy finds itself between (and among) those offered by Tozer and Miretzky and deMarrais. Bredo agrees that to critique the movement as our sole strategy or to ignore it are both problematic. He argues that the purpose of Foundations generally is to offer students a space for reinterpretation of education. This, then, is something we must be willing to engage in to address the "accountability dilemma." Toward this end, he asks, "Can we reconstrue performance and accountability so that these concepts aid rather than detract from our mission?" (p. 234). Once we have crafted this reinterpretation, we must then ask, "What kinds of effects do we want social foundations courses to have on students? What would constitute a valid indication of our performing well as teachers?" (p. 237). As Petrovic (1998) has argued,

> . . .we can, or should, agree that a purpose of schooling. . .is to promote democratic character. That a prospective teacher demonstrates the critical skills and teaching ability to do this is a reasonable criterion by which to judge their fitness as teachers. (p. 52)

In other words, "there are competencies in Foundations of Education that teachers must meet in addition to the competencies in those other fields" (Petrovic, 1998, p. 52). Foundations courses thus gain legitimacy through invoking the frame of accountability and resisting external definitions of teacher competency that make absent discussions of democratic character.

(Re)Asserting borders

Even though Foundations, as a field, is in constant redefinition without having been defined in the first place given the consensus discussed previously against laying out hard and fast boundaries, erecting boundaries is, on occasion, a tactic that social Foundations faculty may have to employ. Wendy Kohli, for example, asks, "How do we reinforce our relevance to ourselves and to our peers in education?" (Butin, 2005b, p. 47). Kohli's answer is illustrative here:

> There's a general sense that anybody can teach Foundations. . .When this happens, we are forced to defend (falsely?) disciplinary boundaries, to say, "No, you didn't get a degree in Philosophy of Ed, so, you can't teach that course." I really hate to go down that road, but sometimes it's necessary. (p. 48)

The work of establishing and reproducing disciplinary and/or programmatic boundaries occurs on a daily basis. Indeed, some researchers have argued that this is one of the primary activities of faculty, regardless of discipline (Klein, 1996; Kuntz, 2009; Messer-Davidow, Shumway, & Sylvan, 1993).

Summary

The strategies to replace Foundations outlined in this section all probably fit into the three frames suggested by Butin (2005c) in response to the question of how Foundations matters to teacher education: The liberal arts answer (which notes that good teachers know how schools are linked to society and how teachers learn to think against the grain), the cultural competence answer (which speaks to the "demographic imperative" of being able to deal with an increasingly diverse student body), and the teacher retention answer (which addresses the idea that teachers must be able to analyze schools as institutions such that teachers are better prepared to deal with the lack of support for the increasing responsibility placed upon them while having little authority).

In this section, we have presented examples of the ways some faculty members wish to engage in reframing the social Foundations. From this point onwards, we employ the term "reframe" as a specific synonym for the definition of "replace" as "situate again." The notion of a conceptual frame merges discursive and material realities, recognizing that the (re)placement of Foundations within Education is about more than simply wordplay, invoking material practices as much as linguistic definition. We rely primarily on the cognitive linguistics work of George Lakoff to frame our own work here. A frame is not only a way to look at something but also delimits what we can view by drawing a border.

Cognitive Framing

In order to make better sense of the political strategies utilized by Foundations faculty as they articulate their placement within discourses of education, we now turn to a discussion of the way such strategies are formed and understood within contemporary contexts. Key to such an understanding is George Lakoff's (2008) work on cognitive framing. Within his concept of framing, Lakoff points to an over-emphasis on articulated reason as a means to access reality. This means of determining the real is a historical product of the Enlightenment. As a linguist, Lakoff questions the supposition that language is ever neutral or could ever fully access some reality. Thus, the language of reason never articulates an objective reality, but depicts instead an oriented perspective, a frame.

Such frames assert meanings—renderings of reality—through assigning particular interpretations of key terms and drawing from culturally informed conceptual metaphors. Lakoff (2008) writes, "Our brains and minds work to impose a specific understanding of reality.... Words are defined relative to frames and conceptual metaphors. Language "fits reality" to the extent that it fits our body-and-brain based on understanding of that reality" (pp. 14–15). Within the social world, particular frames win out and are rendered more legitimate than others. In their very placement as reality, such frames colonize interpretations, legitimizing meaning-making and social practices even as they cast alternative frames to the outer boundaries of possibility.

This is perhaps most overtly seen in the political sphere where, for example, the Bush administration asserted a war on terrorism that became a war in Iraq. Both Republicans and Democrats readily accepted the war frame, with few dissenting voices speaking to an alternative frame, for example, the Occupation of Iraq and the ramifications of such a scenario. A war, presumably, has a beginning and an end; an occupation is less distinct. Buying into the war frame legitimized a vast array of practices (e.g., war-time tribunals) and identities (e.g., enemy combatants) not possible in other, delegitimized frames. Such framing may be more subtly known within Education, although it is no less prevalent.

The work of Lakoff and Johnson (1999; 1980/2003)[1] explicates the multiple processes of framing, emphasizing the relational nature of social frames, the ease with which they are accepted as realities-unto-themselves and not simply metaphorical representations of realities-in-production. Importantly, we often fail to see the frames under which we operate. Overlooking the frames, we never understand how our social reality is structured. We position ourselves and our work within existing frames regardless of the consequences of such framing; framing becomes commonsensical, a matter-of-course. Chet Bowers (1987) puts this nicely,

> When used in an unreflective manner, language can subjugate the mind, and it can do this by creating the illusion that we are on the right track when it is actually causing us to mistake abstractions for the actual patterns within which our lives are embedded. (pp. 4–5)

When Bowers' insights are overlayed with Lakoff and Johnson's work on cognitive framing, language is seen to "subjugate the mind" by appealing to legitimized frames, socially reinforced ways of interpreting the world. Without reflection, such frames are invoked without critical attention.

Lakoff and Johnson's classic *Metaphors We Live By* (1980/2003) asserts that our social frames are primarily metaphorical—"what we think, what we experience, and what we do every day is very much a matter of metaphor" (Lakoff & Johnson, 1980/2003, p. 3)—and therefore forever incomplete. In this sense, such incomplete frames cannot simply be invoked; they must be reproduced within multiple contexts through discursive and material repetition. It is through this repetition that particular social frames assume normative status.

Because it is the nature of metaphor to incompletely represent a concept (it cannot completely detail a concept, otherwise it would be that concept) it will necessarily shade or elide other possible meanings. Thus, even as metaphor highlights particular aspects of a concept, it simultaneously removes alternative possibilities. As cognitive frames appeal to metaphorical ways of knowing, they, at the same time, have a disciplining effect on how we understand the world in which we live. For example, metaphors linked with the economic sphere are strong examples of how their repetition enforces a particular interpretation of the world. Indeed, current neoliberal discourse reinforces the value of market-based metaphors, casting aside alternative metaphorical conceptions—those that do not reinscribe the centrality of the economic sphere—as illegitimate and inconceivable. Education has increasingly taken on the governing neoliberal metaphors of efficiency, marking "success" as the efficient progression of student bodies through standardized levels of schooling. Here, "efficiency" means both rapid and inexpensive.

Petrovic (2005) takes up this critique in the arena of language policy noting that neoliberal discourse has forced language pluralists to try to "sell" language diversity. He argues that language pluralists have wrongly (but for the right reasons) framed defenses of progressive language policy (e.g., bilingual education) in neoliberal, economic terms (being multilingual is a personal and national economic resource). Ultimately, language policy framed this way "is doomed to negative reappropriation by capitalist forces" (p. 410). The point here is that this strategy is uncritically derived from and reinscribes neoliberal frames.

A more detailed example of this may be found in Slaughter and Rhoades' (2004) *Academic Capitalism and the New Economy*. In their text, the authors articulate a series of analytical terms or metaphors that draw from the economic frame and are symptomatic of contemporary socio-historical conditions. These economic frames replace previous articulations of education that situate universities as engaged in the pursuit of knowledge for the public good. The frame of education-as-economics replaced education-as-democracy. Contemporary economic frames are, of course, not value free, but instead encourage particular readings of what faculty does specifically and the work of the university more generally.

Slaughter and Rhoades (2004) point to the ease by which contemporary discourses of neoliberalism reinforce market-based metaphors even as they delegitimize alternative educational frames (those that do not reify the economic sphere). Consider the ease with which education is evaluated within a frame of economic efficiency (Cf. Apple, 2006), encouraging neoclassical economic interpretations of production (e.g., the number of FTEs or publications produced by faculty and programs in a given semester, or the number of undergraduate students processed within a standard 4- to 6-year graduation term). This privileging of the economic frame within contemporary educational discourse encourages particular assumptions about the worth of universities and their programs.

Though the economic frame of neoliberalism has proven pervasive throughout many facets of our social world, it overlaps within tertiary education through a border-laden frame that extends from the development and maintenance of academic disciplines and departmental affiliation. In this sense, the (re)placement of Foundations within Colleges of Education plays out in the messy interaction of neoliberalism, disciplinarity, and the interdisciplinary nature of our field.

Building and Policing Disciplinary Borders

The process of maintaining disciplinary affiliation by reproducing the known practices of their field is one way that faculty establishes borders. We recognize someone as a faculty member in sociology, for example, both by the institutionalized assertion of his/her identity (a Professor of Sociology) and the disciplined practices through which they perform their work (the techniques of sociological scholarship). As Burnwood (2006) writes,

> knowing in a discourse, or doing philosophy, history or mathematics, means becoming a philosopher, historian or mathematician. It is to acquire a new identity. . . .. Accordingly, to become a philosopher, historian or mathematician is to acquire a new way of being in the world. (p. 125)

Simply put, "boundary work" consists of a learned set of practices which differentiate one discipline from another along multiple lines (Gieryn, 1983; Klein, 1993) and plays a significant role in the development of faculty identity. Disciplinary boundaries and the identities they mark are never static and are always in the process of (re)inscription. Academic disciplines themselves exist in a state of flux—only given definition through the ongoing reproduction of disciplinary practices. Consequently, incessant boundary work results in disciplinary agreements between competing discourses that, in turn, silence alternative disciplinary discourses even as they legitimate others (Amariglio et al., 1993). Boundary work thus exists as activities that reinforce normative disciplinary practices, displacing and delegitimizing actions and actors deemed outside disciplinary boundaries.

Now, this discussion does not map neatly onto processes in Colleges of Education given the peculiar, multifaceted nature of our work and the historical placement of Educational scholarship as inherently interdisciplinary. A faculty member in Education who, for example, teaches something like secondary Social Studies methods, is both a teacher educator and, hopefully, a historian or a political scientist. In terms of boundaries, there is a slight push-pull operating between the multiple layers of such an identity. Arguably, however, the former, the identity as a teacher educator, is the stronger force, stronger than the pull of the disciplinary identity.[2] This seems to be especially true in the boundary dynamics that we explore between Foundations faculty and other faculty.[3]

Beyond the difficulty in identifying the particulars of boundary work within the field of Education, the discussion also does not map neatly onto Foundations. The question here concerns how boundary work operates within interdisciplinary fields such as Educational Foundations. Not only is Foundations interdisciplinary but it also sets upon us the same push-pull that our methodology colleagues feel. Are we philosophers (historians, sociologists, etc.) first or teacher educators? Of course, we want to identify strongly (or equally) with both, just as we suspect our colleagues want to identify with both of their identities. Nevertheless, the ways that this question and subsequent responses are framed are key, though we may favor duplicity within our professional identities, since the social frames that increasingly define us may not allow for such layered meanings.

Julie Thompson Klein (1996) writes, "The hybridity of interdisciplinary fields is at once their strength and a continuing source of difficulty. Part of the difficulty is the impossibility of doing everything" (p. 58). As Foundations faculty feel the push-pull of interdisciplinary identity we necessarily make what Klein terms "selected cuts" in the techniques and concepts of our field (p. 57). Often, these cuts establish the localized boundaries of our interdisciplinary field even as they are oriented to (or against) larger conversations regarding the place of Foundations within Education. As seen in the section "'Replacing' Foundations in Teacher Education," and to be visited again in the section "Problematized Framings: Embracing a Politics of Survival," these cuts become the political strategies that, in many ways, establish Foundations as a cohesive field unto itself, and/or as a series of practices that nearly all faculty might employ, regardless of programmatic affiliation. As we establish the boundaries that, in part, define our work, we must also consider the idea that discursive frames, as outlined in the previous section, "Cognitive Framing," serve to give these boundaries meaning. We must then consider whose processes of framing are increasingly read as legitimate, perhaps even encountered as common sense within contemporary contexts. These are the considerations that guide our reading of the strategies for survival employed by our colleagues in the field.

In this vein, there are hard questions to ask ourselves. What boundaries do Foundations faculty reproduce in their scholastic practices? Much of the conversation surrounding the role of Foundations within Education questions whether to engage in disciplinary boundary work (thereby asserting Foundations as an entity unto itself) or to situate the practices inherent in Foundations within legitimized and normative disciplinary spaces already in place. Do we align with or work against the normalizing tendencies of disciplinary activity? In many ways, the question of reframing Foundations is one of intentionally working with or countering the dominant frames that constitute contemporary educational discourse.

In the next section, we reexamine the strategies presented in the section "'Replacing' Foundations in Teacher Education," observing the ways such strategies speak to, against, and within contemporary social frames. It is our hope that in problematizing these strategies we also work toward a better understanding of the importance of cognitive frames as a means to inform how Foundations faculty might more intentionally and knowledgeably play an active role in the social processes of framing.

Problematized Framings: Embracing a Politics of Survival

In the preceding sections, we argued that language is an important point of analysis for understanding how conceptual systems govern the ways we interpret and act within multiple social contexts. In short, framing matters. The way in which we frame education—as generating a set of skills useful in the production of work, for example—asserts particular conceptual metaphors (in this example, the metaphor of production). Such metaphors assume particular roles—of teachers, students—and the practices such roles employ. Essentially, the larger discourse of neoliberalism imposes a corporate mentality of measurable inputs and outputs on education. In education, this is articulated in the standards and accountability movement. Consequently, as Foundations of Education programs replace themselves and engage in boundary-work within their respective colleges, they do so by adapting to or reacting against this normative, neoliberal frame of what education is and what it should do.

In the next section, we react against (and with) the arguments in the section "'Replacing' Foundations in Teacher Education." We point out the ways in which some of the arguments directly reflect neoliberalism, intentionally or not. Where the arguments do not directly reflect this, we must recognize that they are still reactions within this particular discourse. Consequently, the arguments invoked in the section "'Replacing' Foundations in Teacher Education" are layered with both possibilities and contradictions.

Minimal Foundations Standards and "A Clockwork Orange" Multiculturalism

Tozer and Miretzky examined particular strategies for framing the work of Foundations in ways that would not lead to its elimination amidst a discourse of improving teacher performance based on outcome assessments. We might recognize the ease with which pivotal terms such as "improved performance" are defined and given credence according to the conceptual frame in which they operate. Furthermore, operating within this frame potentially becomes counterproductive to the extent that we give further credibility to a movement that cannot and increasingly does not want to validate a field that seeks, in part, to undermine that movement.

Given this, earlier we posed two questions in relation to Tozer and Miretzky: To what extent will their strategy of survival affect and continue to redefine the field? How will framing Foundations within the neoliberal language of the standards movement assert particular readings of what Foundations do—enabling and constraining particular practices? A partial response here lies in Tozer and Miretzky's strategy of identifying and claiming quasi-Foundations-friendly standards and in the extent to which that strategy necessarily leads to their second strategy of reframing Foundations as multiculturalism. This is because "diversity" has become one of only two narrow routes available to Foundations, at least as far as the primary accrediting body, NCATE, is concerned. The first route is the fact that, currently, teacher candidates must "understand and [be] able to apply knowledge related to the social, historical, and philosophical foundations of education, professional ethics, law, and policy" (NCATE, p. 22). This is typically handled in a single Foundations course requirement in most programs. In fact, at the University of Alabama, following the enactment of NCLB, two separate courses, educational psychology and social, historical, and philosophical foundations of education, were combined into a single course in the secondary teacher preparation program in order to free up the credit hours necessary to meet NCLB's definition of "highly qualified."

The second route, then, is to appeal to diversity standards and to make the case that Foundations faculty are best prepared to deal with this content. (This argument, by the way, does not tend to appeal to the "real" teacher education faculty, with whom the power lies.) Once having given credibility to standards by claiming those that we can marginally subscribe to, we also give credibility to specific framings of multiculturalism. Framed within performance/assessment, multicultural education increasingly reflects conceptualizations and practices that are, as Garvey (1996) puts it, more akin to "managed care" than being truly educative in a critical sense. Take, for example, the economic imperative in NCATE's reasoning in highlighting diversity:

> Today's society needs a workforce that can apply knowledge, reason analytically, and solve problems. At the same time, American society is becoming more diverse, with students in classrooms drawn from many cultures and ethnic groups. Preparing teachers to teach all students to meet society's demands for high performance has created a new agenda for educators and policymakers." (p. 3)

Within this technocratic, economic rationality, multiculturalism becomes a case of ensuring that teacher candidates can "apply effective methods of teaching students who are at different developmental stages, have different learning styles, and come from diverse backgrounds" and that "[Elementary teachers] understand how elementary students differ in their development and approaches to learning, and create instructional opportunities that are adapted to diverse students" (NCATE, p. 4 and 55, respectively). Multiculturalism, in other words, becomes a technocratized standard by which we can measure a candidate's ability or not "to select or use a broad range of instructional strategies that promote student learning (NCATE, p. 17). While NCATE does pay some lip-service to ideals that might be read more progressively [e.g., "Candidates incorporate multiple perspectives in the subject-matter being taught or services being provided" (NCATE, p. 34)], the neoliberal framing suggests techniques to induce specific measurable outcomes: Multiculturalism as a Clockwork Orange. Thus, the additional cautionary points to Tozer and Miretzky are to not allow our voices in support of engagement with diversity to be appropriated into a discourse of vulgar multiculturalism and to not replace (substitute for) the traditional Foundations with multicultural studies.

Collaboration or Co-option?

Even though, it does not link as directly to the neoliberal framing as, say, Tozer and Miretzky, deMarrais' strategy of reframing teacher education foundationally still must be read as a reaction to the larger neoliberal frame, a healthy reaction, but a reaction nonetheless. In reading the pernicious impact of neoliberalism (which we have no doubt that deMarrais and all of the scholars we react to here do), deMarrais seeks a way to secure the place of Foundations in order to provide students access to other (counter-neoliberal hegemonic) frames. However, this doesn't change the larger frame within which we are teaching. That frame continues to render some content more institutionally legitimate even within the collaborative course deMarrais seeks to develop. To what extent can we control the negative reappropriation of Foundations?

We need also consider the boundary-work enacted here. On the one hand, breaking down the disciplinary walls goes against the neoliberal frame both in the specific, practical sense just described and in the sense that the multidimensionality deMarrais seeks through collaboration is counter to the flattening toward efficiency of neoliberalism more generally. On the other hand, breaking down disciplinary walls also delegitimizes the disciplines such walls defined. In this way, deMarrais' strategy not only disrupts neoliberalism but also Foundations itself.

Politically, of course, this can become perilous given that "anyone can teach Foundations" (as per Kohli's concern). Why shouldn't curriculum and instruction faculty simply do their "own" Foundations content within their own courses? We do not mean to suggest that deMarrais is oblivious to this concern. In fact, in order to counter such a perspective, she notes that the programmatic curriculum is "framed...within the politics of knowledge production" thereby asserting a particular reading of the program that foregrounds the work and study of Foundations. Nevertheless, this does not allay our concern. We will argue in the following section, "Killing Ourselves Softly?" that we are victims of our own success and illustrate through a specific example of how programs and courses get foregrounded in the study of Foundations without us.

Slaughter and Rhoades note, reframing occurs within "the academic heartland not only in terms of what work is done in basic academic departments but also in terms of redefining whether those units are regarded as the center of the academy" (p. 206). Narrowing the academy in this idea to Colleges of Education, the center is comprised of those units that can most efficiently subscribe to efficiency. This inherently defines Foundations as something different. Perhaps Foundations is still part of the work done in basic academic departments, but it is on the fringe, even when (or, perhaps, because) it is integrated.

Good Intentions, Bad Conceptions

At first blush, Bredo's strategy of engaging with or trying to reappropriate the neoliberal language of accountability is a way to address the co-option that deMarrais risks. In this way, both Bredo and Petrovic call for a recognition of accountability but ask as well that such recognition simultaneously redefine the normative processes of accountability. As such, both scholars ask to utilize accountability not only for disciplinary development and refinement, but also to reframe the very notion of accountability, to critically engage with such a rationale.

But this strategy assumes that the frame of neoliberalism can be reconstituted. It may be the case, however, that the logic of neoliberalism will override attempts to reconstitute it since frames operate on the level of conception not intention. As Lakoff and Johnson's (1998/2003) work has shown, frames such as neoliberalism influence the very concepts we use to convey meaning. Frames infuse terminology with their epistemological and ontological assumptions. Consequently, terms such as accountability, however defined, are incessantly reproduced within the neoliberal frame.

In an analysis of the ways that otherwise progressive educators attempt to reappropriate neoliberalism to their purposes in language policy, Petrovic (2005) concludes, "There are several potential outcomes of attaching our hopes, even if only strategically and not sincerely, to the neoliberal language-as-resource strategy and they are all, to my mind, likely to be negative"

(p. 405). Petrovic demonstrates how attempting to operate strategically within a neoliberal frame affects the ways that supporters of progressive language policy end up supporting the status quo instead.

Policing and Reinforcing Borders

Kohli's politics of survival—reasserting disciplinary borders—may just be an inherent feature of academia generally. It is, however, particularly problematic in interdisciplinary fields. As a specific example of exclusionary border-work, at The University of Alabama there exists a "Teacher Education Council" with the purpose of advising the president and provost on matters related to teacher education. When a Foundations faculty member was nominated to fill an empty seat on this council, it was suggested by a faculty member in Curriculum and Instruction that the seat should probably be filled by someone in teacher education instead.

In some cases, then, Foundations is being framed outside of teacher education. We do not want to suggest that this is what Kohli does. On the one hand, asserting the borders of our field is necessitated by the possible appropriation of Foundations into increasingly generalized framings. Foundations can be integrated throughout the curriculum, for example. Or, à la our analysis of Tozer and Miretzky, Foundations can be reduced to multicultural education. It is also necessitated by the need to resist Foundations being co-opted into neoliberal frames demanding measurable products. On the other hand, asserting the borders of our field may have the unintended consequence of distancing us further from teacher education. This is because Foundations faculty generally seek to construct borders that inscribe our duty to disrupt teacher education as it is currently framed by the standards and accountability movement. As a consequence, Foundations runs the risk of existing as mere curricular electives on the educational landscape.

Killing Ourselves Softly?

Dan Butin (2005a) points out, "the history of social Foundations seems to be one of eclecticism. No singular texts, no definitive methodology, no 'best practice' formulations are to be found" (pp. xiii–xiv). In an interesting discussion on a "canon" in social Foundations (see Butin, 2005b), there was a consensus among the participants that there may be important works in Foundations, but that we should not try to identify a canon. There is an overlap of resources that we all draw from, never pulling out the same interpretations or practices according to Eric Bredo. On the one hand, the dialogue, debate, and, indeed, the praxis that such incertitude generates is intellectually and academically sane and a hallmark of the field. On the other hand, it is a political nightmare, especially in this age of standards and accountability.

The politics in the current state of the social Foundations of education operate at both the individual and institutional levels. At the individual level, "No one has a discipline anymore. Everyone does everything," observed educational historian Wayne Urban (personal communication, October 3, 2007). This is not a new observation. William O. Stanley complained in 1968 that "in far too many cases we have senior instructors in the social Foundations area who have had no training in philosophy, history or sociology and very little, if any, in philosophy of education, history of education or sociology of education" (p. 226). Here, Stanley writes not of a systemic move to interdisciplinary scholarship, but a dilution away from the foundational disciplinary perspectives that make up the field.

There are two interpretations of these observations. First, in efforts to keep ourselves relevant within contemporary contexts, Foundations faculty have had to become jacks-of-all-trades. Beyond our disciplinary teaching, we are diversity experts, critical pedagogues, policy gurus, and curriculum theorists. Second, at the level of the institution, many of our graduate programs reflect this turn—often students no longer receive training in the traditional disciplines of Foundations, exposed instead to more generic investigations into questions of diversity, policy, and curriculum studies.

The political strategies increasingly employed by Foundations faculty at the institutional level to secure a place for the field in teacher preparation have necessarily impacted the field itself. This is not a new but an ongoing struggle. R. Freeman Butts, for example, recounts the dilution of Foundations requirements at Teachers College in the late 1940s (see Tozer & Miretzky, 2005). Similarly, Stanley (1968) points out that Foundations courses made up the backbone of the teacher education curriculum at the University of Illinois prior to World War I. Immediately after, he notes, study in the field "went into sharp decline" there and "the emphasis was on 'practical' courses in school administration, methods and curriculum, and upon courses in the science of education" (p. 225).

To our minds, there are several interrelated forces at work that have contributed to the contemporary challenges in Foundations:

1. The emphasis on practical courses is exacerbated in this neoliberal age of accountability.

2. This seems to have pushed the field more strongly along the trajectory (begun by Counts) away from disciplinary expertise to "the social Foundations" and to becoming jacks-of-all trades, as already noted.

3. The art of being a jack-of-all-trades is best captured in "diversity." This explains, in part, current shifts from "the social Foundations" to "cultural studies," for example.

While we view these three forces as running in somewhat linear fashion, there is another force running parallel to and feeding the increasing marginalization of Foundations faculty (as separate creatures in teacher education): Success. Despite the lack of influence in teacher education, the fact is that Foundations has influenced teacher educators. Many, if not most, advanced degree programs in Education have some sort of Foundations requirement. Thus, our colleagues teaching methods courses have typically done coursework in both the methods of their content area as well as other areas (usually educational research and Foundations). On the other hand, advanced degrees in Foundations typically do not require any coursework in methods (although many of us have teaching backgrounds, in particular content areas). Thus, it is often the case that our methods colleagues do, in fact, have sufficient backgrounds in Foundations (writ generically) to teach in the field. Having this background, they also find it important to include some Foundational work within their specific areas. A recent incident at our own institution provides a useful illustration of the many issues we are addressing here.

A faculty member in the department of Curriculum and Instruction (Foundations is housed in a different department) introduced a new course titled "Opportunity to Learn in Secondary Schools." The brief description of the course on the flyer sent out to all faculty read as follows:

In this course, we will explore the concept of opportunity to learn (OTL): the capacity of schools to provide adequate learning opportunities for all students. . . ..We will identify methods for describing, analyzing, and interpreting schooling in grades 6 to 12.

"Key course readings" included Kozol's *Shame of the Nation*, Oakes' *Keeping Track*, Meier's *The Power of Their Ideas*, and Suskind's *A Hope in the Unseen*. Both the description and the reading list struck at least several of the Foundations faculty as, well, Foundational, as opposed to methodological. The following exchange is illustrative of several issues addressed in this chapter so far[4]:

A response to course flyer: I think it's great that you are doing Foundational work. But our students [in Foundations] essentially already take this course as the readings you are using are core to Foundations classes. You might want to check out some of the [Foundations syllabi] to try to avoid some redundancy.

Response from course author: *Just to clear things up—this course is not foundational work, but work directly related to opportunity to learn in literacy—an extension of the research I have been doing since 2002. [This] is a course in our program for the direct study of classroom instructional issues. We will be doing the readings (and/or parts of them) listed so that we can then examine K-12 English language arts classroom issues (tracking, ability grouping, differentiated instruction, critical literacy, the canon vs. contemporary literature, scripted writing vs. process writing, NCTE standards enactment) —all curriculum and instruction issues— through multiple methods.*

This course is in no way to be a "Foundations" course—that is, what you (and nearly everyone you copied on your reply) is here for! Our doctoral students take 12 hours in Foundations courses, sometimes more if I feel necessary, for their PhDs, so I don't think my course will in any way take away from, or replicate, what you do.

I was not aware that [students in some existing Foundations courses] studied opportunity to learn in high school English classes through classroom research. That's interesting. You'll have to share what they learned with me since that is my area of research and publication.

As an aside, to me, no department or program "owns" books or readings, and I have no problem with students re-reading or doing multiple readings of texts key in the field. . .Those that may have read them—or parts of them—before coming to my class can then be great discussion leaders for others. Can you imagine if no one in curriculum and instruction programs around the country [read] Gay's work on culturally relevant pedagogy? Or Oakes' work on tracking in English classes? That would be horrible! Or, if no one in Foundations programs read work by Gutierrez, Moje, or Cochran-Smith?

Hopefully, graduate students will make—and learn to make—connections between and among the courses they have taken, or will take. I would love for CSE graduate students to leave my class more interested in education policy, education research, and/or foundational issues. Any one of these areas could be their second major on the Ph.D. program of study. I think it is absolutely necessary that they see the "big picture." Likewise, if any non-CSE students take the course, I would hope that their backgrounds in educational policy, educational research, and/or Foundations make them leaders in the course for those that might not have taken anything in those areas yet.

The response to the flyer is, à la Kohli, purely political. It is first and foremost a border statement. It is additionally a statement that seems meant to highlight the importance of Foundations—so important that a specialist in English Language Arts who typically teaches courses that are clearly definable as "methods" courses by their titles is compelled to approach this new course from a Foundations perspective.[5]

The rejoinder is similarly political; it too is a border statement. Of course, what are identified as "all curriculum and instruction issues" are all equally Foundational issues. This is one of the dilemmas of an unwillingness or inability (it is both we think) to define Foundations; it often gets defined from without. In this case, Foundations does not include "classroom issues." From the perspective of the author of the response to the flyer, the course belies this contention given that Foundational texts (Meier can be read as philosophy, Kozol as sociology, for example) are used as the points of departure.

So, on the one hand, this is a border dispute that results in border building. On the other hand, the course author's response simultaneously seeks to disrupt the border that has been built. For, in essence, what this Curriculum and Instruction faculty member objects to is the very segmentation that Stanley objected to *in defense of* Foundations. What the response also suggests is that the line drawn by Broudy between applicative and interpretive knowledge is as false as the line between Foundations faculty and teacher education faculty. Applicative knowledge has no meaning, no reason, no motivation without interpretive knowledge. In the end, everything in both responses is correct.

Conclusion

Thus, it is that the work of Foundations might ostensibly be excluded from teacher education (a frame that replaces Foundations to the periphery of such educative work) or asserted to merely contain the issues of diversity and multiculturalism within schools (a complementary frame that replaces Foundations with multiculturalism) or simply inserted without us. Each of these options is, of course, unacceptable and we have reviewed some of the strategies employed or recommended to combat them. We have also argued that in this political struggle (re)framing matters. It matters because it changes the nature of the field and of our work. It matters because it constrains what is seen as possible. It matters because it reveals what may be possible. It matters because it situates us within Colleges of Education and work in teacher preparation in particular, sometimes productively and sometimes reductively, ways. It matters because it affects boundary-work and affects the ways in which such work plays out.

The strategies we have reviewed are, of course, recursively linked. One affects the other. Each is also full of contradiction, constraint, and possibility. For example, in the boundary-work that occurs, as enacted by us and against us, we may be alienated further from teacher education. But this is simultaneously oppressive—the importance of our work is marginalized—and liberatory—healthy spaces of critique from the margins are made possible. Despite the multiplicity of causes and effects ensconced within the contemporary replacing of Foundations it does make sense to bring the way in which Foundations is framed to the fore—to intentionally develop and respond to the positioning of Foundations within the neoliberal order.

This simultaneity can be stifling. How can we (re)frame Foundations outside neoliberalism, liberating ourselves to critique from the margins, and inside neoliberalism, constraining ourselves to survival with the hope of incremental impact from within? The strategies presented by the respected scholars whose thinking we reviewed differ precisely because we must do both simultaneously—a hefty chore to say the least. Reframing Foundations will require intense political work to create the academic culture necessary to support the boundary crossings necessary to sustain, without watering down, disciplinary perspectives.

Notes

1. An interdisciplinary array of scholars has followed Lakoff and Johnson to incorporate the centrality of conceptual metaphor into their work. Gibbs (1994) has examined the role of conceptual metaphor in cognitive psychology, Fauconnier and Sweetser (1996) in cognitive linguistics, and Steven Winter (2001) in law. Lakoff (1987; 1996; 2002) has himself demonstrated the use of conceptual metaphor in the field of politics.
2. The overview of Foundations provided in the first sections of this chapter and the discussions among Foundations faculty outlining some of their struggles for survival are suggestive of this. It is, of course, an empirical question. As our review indicates, extant tensions derive, to some extent, from mandates from state, institutional, and national accreditation bodies.

3. This, too, is an empirical question that requires further investigation. It may be the case, for example, that methodologists who identify primarily with their discipline and those who identify primarily with their craft differ in their relation and attitudes toward Foundations. This might also vary by discipline.
4. This e-mail exchange has been edited to remove names for confidentiality and to avoid in-house nomenclature and course numberings that are obviously unfamiliar to and irrelevant to readers.
5. For the sake of guarding the author's anonymity, we cannot specifically identify the course titles here.

References

Amariglio, J., Resnick, S., & Wolff, R. (1993). Division and difference in the "discipline" of economics. In E. Messer-Davidow, D. Shumway, & D. Sylvan (eds.), *Knowledges: Historical and critical studies in disciplinarity* (pp. 150–184). Charlottesville, VA: University Press of Virginia.
Apple, M. (2006). *Educating the "right" way: Markets, standards, God, and inequality* (2d ed.). New York: Routledge.
Bowers, C. A. (1987). *Elements of a post-liberal theory of education.* New York: Teachers College Press.
Bredo, E. (2005). Addressing the social foundations accountability dilemma. *Educational Studies, 38*(3): 230–241.
Burnwood, S. (2006). Imitation, indwelling and the embodied self. *Educational philosophy and theory,* 118–134.
Butin, D. (2005a). *Teaching social foundations of education: Context, theories, and issues.* Mahwah, NJ: Lawrence Erlbaum.
Butin, D. (2005b). Is there a social foundation canon? An interview with Eric Bredo, Wendy Kohli, Joseph Newman, & Barbara Thayer-Bacon. In D. Butin (ed.). *Teaching social foundations of education: Context, theories, and issues* (pp. 29–55). Mahwah, NJ: Lawrence Erlbaum.
Butin, D. (2005c). How social foundations of education matters to teacher preparation: A policy brief. *Educational Studies, 38*(3): 214–229.
Council for Social Foundations of Education. (1996). Standards for academic and professional instruction in foundations of education, educational studies, and educational policy studies. Retrieved from http://www.uic.edu/educ/csfe/standard.htm.
deMarrais, K. (2005). Reflections on a social foundations approach to teacher education. In D. Butin (ed.), *Teaching social foundations of education: Context, theories, and issues* (pp. 167–188). Mahwah, NJ: Lawrence Erlbaum.
Garvey, J. (1996). My problem with multicultural education. In N. Ignatiev & J. Garvey (eds.), *Race traitors* (pp. 25–31). New York: Routledge.
Gieryn, T. (1983). Boundary-work and the demarcation of science from non-science: Strains and interests in professional ideologies of scientists. *American Sociological Review, 48,* 781–795.
Giroux, H. A. (2005). Academic entrepreneurs: The corporate takeover of higher education. *Tikkun, 20*(2):18–23.
Klein, J. T. (1993). Blurring, cracking, and crossing: Permeation and the fracturing of discipline. In E. Messer-Davidow, D. R. Shumway, & D. J. Sylvan (eds.), *Knowledges: Historical and critical studies in disciplinarity* (185–214). Charlottesville, VA. University Press of Virginia.
Klein, J. (1996). *Crossing boundaries: Knowledge, disciplinarities, and interdisciplinarities.* Charlottesville, VA: University Press of Virginia.
Kuntz, A. (2009). Turning from time to space: Conceptualizing faculty work. In J. Smart (ed.), *Higher education: Handbook of theory and research.* New York: Springer.
Lakoff, G. (2008). *The political mind: Why you can't understand 21st-century American politics with an 18th-century brain.* New York: Viking.
Lakoff, G., & Johnson, M. (1980/2003). *Metaphors we live by.* Chicago: University of Chicago Press.
Lakoff, G., & Johnson, M. (1999). *Philosophy in the flesh: The embodied mind and its challenge to Western thought.* New York: Basic.
Lincoln, Y. & Cabrella, G. (2004). Dangerous discourses: Methodological conservatism and governmental regimes of truth. *Qualitative Inquiry, 10*(5): 5–14.
McLaren, P. (2005). *Capitalists and conquerors: A critical pedagogy against empire.* New York: Rowman & Littlefield.
Messer-Davidow, E., Shumway, D., & Sylvan, D. (1993). Introduction. In E. Messer-Davidow, D. Shumway, & D. Sylvan (eds.), *Knowledges: Historical and critical studies in disciplinarity* (pp. 1–21). Charlottesville, VA: University Press of Virginia.
NCATE (2008). Professional standards for the accreditation of teacher preparation institutions. Retrieved from http://www.ncate.org/public/standards.asp.
Petrovic, J. E. (1998). The democratic sieve in teacher education: Confronting heterosexism. *Educational Foundations, 12*(1): 43–56.
Petrovic, J. E. (2005). The conservative restoration and neoliberal defenses of bilingual education. *Language Policy, 4*(4): 395–416.

Slaughter, S., & Rhoades, G. (2004). *Academic capitalism and the new economy: Markets, state, and higher education.* Baltimore, MD: The Johns Hopkins University Press.

Stanley, W. O. (1968). The social foundations subjects in the professional education of teachers. *Educational Theory, 18*(3): 224–236.

Tozer, S. & Miretzky, D. (2005). Social foundations, teaching standards and the future of teacher preparation. In D. Butin (ed.), *Teaching social foundations of education: Context, theories, and issues* (pp. 3–27). Mahwah, NJ: Lawrence Erlbaum.

Eight

Vocational Education and the Continuing Struggle for Critical Democratic Pedagogy

James H. Adams and Natalie G. Adams

An education that seeks to make a man vocationally efficient must first find a calling in which a given combination of inherited talents most adequately fits, after which systematic training toward efficiency in that calling can be made a dominant purpose. (Snedden, 1977, p. 48)

The principle. . .that the educative process is its own end, and that the only sufficient preparation for later responsibilities comes by making the most of immediately present life, applies full force to the vocational phases of education. The dominant vocation of all human beings at all times is living-intellectual and moral growth. In childhood and youth with their relative freedom from economic stress, this fact is naked and unconcealed. To predetermine some future occupation for which education is to be a strict preparation is to injure the possibilities of present development and thereby to reduce the adequacy of preparation for a future right employment. . .Such training may develop a machine-like skill in routine lines (it is far from being sure to do so since it may develop distaste, aversion, and carelessness), but it will be at the expense of those qualities of alert observation and coherent and ingenious planning which make an occupation intellectually rewarding. (Dewey, cited in Kliebard, 1999, p. 210)

The Smith-Hughes Act of 1917 (which mandated federal aid for vocational training and the large-scale reform of public high schools after the 1918 publication of the *Cardinal Principles of Secondary Education*) firmly institutionalized the idea that the primary purpose of education is to prepare people for work. A century later preparation for work continues to be the primary aim of all levels of education, particularly vocational education.[1] But what exactly is meant by preparing people for work? What kind of work? What kind of curriculum best prepares people for work? Whose interests are most served by this purpose of schooling? These are some of the questions that David Snedden, the commissioner of Education for Massachusetts, and John Dewey, one of the leading school reformers of the day, debated in the early 20th century. Their differences were dramatically highlighted in a 1915 exchange in the *New Republic*. Both were seeking to develop a philosophy of education that would not only guide the future of vocational education but would also articulate a vision of schooling based on their own ideas of democracy and the relationship between schools and work. In this chapter, we revisit that debate to illustrate how notions of democracy, social efficiency, and social progress were used in very different ways to develop a rationale for the integration of school and work. We argue that although Dewey won the rhetorical argument by appealing to philosophical arguments about democratic citizenship and the integration of life and work, Snedden's appeal to efficiency, the practical and early occupational socialization, ultimately prevailed, resulting in a field of study that has struggled for 100 years to find its niche in the educational hierarchy and to escape its association with a singular focus on preparing people for the workforce. We end by highlighting the work of a few contemporary critical vocational educators situated within the new vocationalism who have tried to re-interject a discussion of the importance of philosophy in shaping the goals and future of vocational education.

Progressivism and Vocational Education: The Snedden-Dewey Debate

The National Association of Manufacturers (NAM), which was formed in 1895, was one of the most ardent proponents of schools serving the needs of industry. Their pleas to public schools that their primary goal should be of preparing people for work should sound hauntingly familiar to today's readers: economic competition from a foreign power (then Germany), a dearth of skilled workforce to compete in the new economy (then industrial capitalism), and worries that labor unions had grown too powerful (Kantor, 1986). At the time that NAM was calling for schools to play a more active role in educating students for the workforce, vocational schools to prepare students for work were already in existence in several large cities. In Massachusetts alone there were 24 vocational schools in the first decade of the 20th century (Snedden, 1911). When David Snedden entered the debates about vocational education, he not only had an impressive title to give credence to his arguments, but he also brought with him experience as a teacher, principal, superintendent, and a doctoral degree from Teachers College. His dissertation was an examination of juvenile reform schools, one of the earliest forms of vocational education, and one deemed by Snedden to be a model for public schools to emulate. Snedden was openly disdainful of vocational education being part of the traditional high school and spoke often of the need for separate schools, separate administration, separate curriculum, and a totally different type of teacher (i.e., from the trade itself). In a 1914 address to the National Education Association, he makes clear the distinctions between the aims of a liberal and vocational education as well as differences in curriculum and administration:

> That education which trains him to be a producer is vocational education. That education which trains him to be a good utilizer, in the social sense of that term, is liberal education. (Snedden, 1977, p. 48)

> It is required that when the pupil enters a vocational school he should be able to give it at least six or eight hours per day of undivided attention to the ends of vocational education. Under these conditions, liberal education must be regarded, for such a pupil at this time, as a minor issue. (Snedden, 1977, p. 51)

> It should be governed by or possess an advisory committee containing men who are intimately identified with the occupation for which it trains, both as employers and employees. The vocational school should divest itself as completely as possible of the academic atmosphere, and should reproduce as fully as possible the atmosphere of economic endeavor in the field for which it trains. (Snedden, 1977, pp. 51–52)

Snedden believed that skilled vocational counselors could identify as early as junior high the specific skills a student possessed and direct him to the proper vocation for which the rest of his schooling would concentrate. He proposed that the curriculum could be devised based on the scientific management principles of job analysis:

> It should surely be possible for us, by studying the requirements of recognized callings, such as medicine, teaching, bookkeeping, carpentering, printing, tailoring, cooking, and the like, to derive from each one and to define those specific requirements as to skill, technical knowledge and ideals which persons trained for that vocation should possess. (Snedden, 1977, p. 45)

A proponent of social efficiency, Snedden was part of the Progressive movement in the early 20th century (i.e., Business Efficiency Progressivism) that believed that schools should serve the needs of society. This could best be accomplished through a differentiated curriculum that sorted students into their future occupational roles based on their skills, interests, and innate intelligence. Believing that democracy flourishes when its citizens find their place in the economic order, Snedden insisted that the goal of vocational education was to determine the right occupational fit for pupils and to provide schooling that would prepare them for their role in the workplace. He viewed vocational education as a "means of securing earlier and greater efficiency as wage earners, more self-reliance and self-respect" (Drost, 1977, p. 21). When he addressed audiences, he often pointed out that the elite already had access to higher vocational education in the form of professional schools, such as medical and law schools, normal schools, and colleges. In a 1928 article entitled "Democratic Vocational Education," Snedden passionately wrote: "Dare we shut our eyes, however, to the fact that they [professional schools mentioned above] are schools for the elect only? Can we afford to ignore the fact that for millions of youths of less than superior abilities no correspondingly democratic opportunities exist for induction at public charge into one or another form of superior vocational competency?" (Snedden, 1928, p. 524)

Snedden prided himself on being a realist who understood the imperatives of industrial capitalism built as it is on a rigid division of labor. He made no apologies for his pragmatic solution of preparing the student to fit into those divisions of labor, and it is clear from much of his writing that he believed that the poor and those "who are further handicapped by having only average or less than average able-mindedness" (Snedden, 1928, p. 523) would naturally become working-class workers rather than members of the ruling class. He often referred to his critics as being idealists and romantics for trying to change the system (which, in his opinion, would never happen) rather than prepare students to fit into the system in an economically productive way. Vocational education, he believed, had the ability to match people's inherent intelligence and skills with a trade in which they could be successful, if given the proper technical tools and moral values. Countering those critics who claimed that vocational education only served the needs of industry, Snedden asserted that vocational education would equip students with the skills needed to be competitive in the workplace and, hence, earn a higher wage for more skilled work: "If vocational education does not result in greater productive capacity and if greater productive capacity does not result in a larger share to the laborer, then, indeed, are the times very much out of joint" (*Two Communications*, 1977, p. 37). Clearly, Snedden believed in laissez-faire capitalism in which the market regulates itself and the excesses of capitalism (which had led in the past to disgruntled, unhappy workers) could be controlled through proper educational training.

> To their [Snedden, Prosser, and their protégées) minds, alienation and discontent at work existed not because of the fragmented nature of factory labor but because workers were poorly trained and adapted to the jobs that already existed. If workers were trained for jobs that suited their talents and interests and that matched the economic needs of their communities, they said, the outcome would not only be greater economic efficiency but happier, more contented workers as well. (Kantor, 1986, p. 416)

John Dewey's vocal criticism of Snedden and the type of vocational education he supported played out in a series of articles and exchanges between Snedden and Dewey in 1915. His primary criticism was that Snedden's philosophy of vocational education was anti-democratic in that it placed students in narrowly defined economic roles with no possibility of mobility and, contrary to Snedden's claims, it served the needs of industry while failing miserably to release the individual potential of each student:

> The kind of vocational education in which I am interested in is not one which will "adapt" workers to the existing industrial regime; I am not sufficiently in love with the regime for that. It seems to me that the business of all who would not be educational time-servers is to resist every move in this direction, and to strive for a kind of vocational education which will first alter the existing industrial system, and ultimately transform it. (*Two Communications*, 1977, p. 25)

Snedden seemed surprised at Dewey's vitriolic attack of vocational education since Dewey himself in *The School and Society* (1899) had advocated for a curriculum based on occupations. But Dewey's understanding of incorporating vocations into schooling was not meant as an ends (i.e., specific job training) but as a means to an end (i.e., a way to integrate life and work) as evident in how he utilized the study of occupations in his own Laboratory Schools. As a model of his own thinking about vocational education, he pointed to the progressive schools in Gary, Indiana, in which boys and girls as part of a real-life community participated in all aspects of the running of the school, including helping to prepare lunches, maintaining the electrical system, building school furniture, and printing school materials. Students switched jobs every few months so they could be exposed to a variety of occupations and trades. Dewey explained the distinction between his model of vocational education and the social efficiency model of Snedden: "This is as it should be for pupils are not taking courses to become carpenters or electricians or dressmakers but to find out how the work of the world is done" (cited in Drost, 1977, p. 26).

Dewey's response in the *New Republic* to Snedden's form of vocational education was scathing. He took Snedden to task about the very meaning of the term "vocation" and the incredibly anti-democratic underpinnings of a vocational education which predestined a large number of students to a life void of creativity and individual expression:

> Snedden has himself fallen a victim to the ambiguity of the word vocational. I would go farther than he is apparently willing to go in holding that education should be vocational, but in the name of a genuinely vocational education I object to the identification of vocation with such trades as can be learned from the age of, say, eighteen or twenty; and to the identification of education with acquisition of specialized skill in the management of machines at the expense of an industrial intelligence based on science and knowledge of social problems and conditions. I object to regarding vocational education any training which does not have as its supreme regard the development of such intelligent initiative, ingenuity and executive capacity as shall make workers, as far as may be, the masters of their own industrial fate. . .I am utterly opposed to giving the power of social predestination, by means of narrow trade-training, to any group of fallible men no matter how well-intentioned they may be (*Two Communications*, 1977, p. 38).

Speaking to a class of students, Dewey offered a criticism of capitalism that explains why he was so vehemently opposed to a form of vocational education that led to students' being pigeon-holed into a predestined trade that offered little in terms of financial or emotional remuneration:

> The division of labor is "never complete until the laborer gets his full expression. The kind we now have in factories—one-sided, mechanical—is a case of class interest; i.e., his activity is made a means to benefits others. It can't be complete till he does that for which he is best fitted—in which he finds the most complete expression of himself. (Westbrook, 1992, p. 407)

Dewey was deeply concerned that Snedden's form of vocational education not only made a false distinction between the academic and vocational curriculum, but it also led to students' being prepared for an alienated view of work that failed to make connections between their life and society. An ardent believer in a socialist education, Dewey insisted that all students should be educated to be leaders as well as followers and that preparing a student for a predetermined job in society was detrimental to a democratic nation. Instead schools should be sites for active democratic citizenship that would integrate school, work, life, and leisure (Westbrook, 1992). Dewey explained his vision of how the academic and vocational could be integrated in ways that promote social activism:

> An education which acknowledges the full intellectual and social meaning of a vocation would include instruction in the historic background of present conditions; training in science to give intelligence and initiative in dealing with materials and agencies of production; and study of economics, civics, and politics to bring the future worker into touch with the problems of the day and the various methods proposed for its improvement. Above all, it would give individuals the power of readapting to changing conditions so that future workers would not become blindly subject to a fate imposed upon them. (cited in Braundy, 2004, p. 25)

Contrary to Snedden, Dewey did believe that schools had the capacity to instill in students the skills and knowledge needed to critique capitalism with the hopes of changing it for the better. After all, Dewey was an optimist who had great faith in the capacity for schools to change society.

Interestingly, at the end of the day, neither Snedden's model for vocational education as a separate entity from high schools or Dewey's notion of vocational education as exemplified in his Laboratory School prevailed. Instead, the model for vocational education for most of the 20th century emerged in the form of industrial education for boys and home economics for girls as part of the large comprehensive high schools emanating from the National Education Association's Commission on the Reorganization of Secondary Education. However, the legacy Snedden left on vocational education cannot be overstated in that he relegated the aim of vocational education to a very narrow form of job training: "vocational education is, irreducibly and without unnecessary mystification, education for the pursuit of an occupation" (*Two Communications*, 1977, p. 34). Years after the debates between Snedden and Dewey were over, Julius House succinctly explained in 1921 the long-term negative repercussions of Snedden's narrow view of vocational education. He argued that this type of vocational education leads to a rigid division of labor in which a few have power and the workers have no understanding about the meaning of their work; workers are exploited by those in power; and vocational education has been institutionalized as a means to reproduce an inequitable social order. He further noted than the financial cost of training workers so that businesses profit has now been transferred to the public based on the erroneous "supposition that when business prospers moral values take care of themselves" (p. 223).

House's critique of an instrumental view of vocational education devoid of philosophical discussions of the relationship between school and society, the meaning of work, and how macrostructures shape the micropractices of schooling ought to hit a chord with contemporary vocational educators who are struggling not only to explain their relevancy in the midst of an era of standards and accountability but also to prepare workers for an even more complex economic system defined by globalism, post-industrialism, hyper-capitalism, and a worldwide recession.

Critical Vocational Education and the Resurrection of Dewey

A number of vocational educators, such as Lakes (1994, 1997, 2005), Gregson (1994, 1996), Simon (1983), Kincheloe (1995, 1999), Gaskell (1995), and Simon, Dippo, & Schenke (1991), began advocating in the 1980s and 1990s for a vocational education that returns it to its Deweyan roots. Lakes (1997) defines this movement as new vocationalism "held together by a loose alliance of left-leaning thinkers desiring to keep the ideals of a democratic education alive" (p. 30). Central to new vocationalism is the belief that effective vocational education programs must equip students with both functional and critical empowerment as explained by Lakes (1994):

> Functional empowerment helps individuals learn the technical or applied aspects of a job in order to execute the tasks and duties of their respective or future employment. On the other hand, critical empowerment assists learners in shaping a cultural politics of work, so that by acting together workers may achieve some measure of personal dignity as well as social responsibility for fashioning democratic workplaces and participatory citizenship. (p. 4)

Despite the nod to the functional or technical aspect of vocational education, what clearly emerges as the emphasis of the new vocationalism is the critical empowerment of students as future workers and vocational educators. Harkening back to Dewey in the early 20th century, Kincheloe (1999) argues that "a democratic vocational education struggles to empower future workers by helping them see themselves as living systems within larger living systems" (p. 8).

A series of ethnographies published in the 1970s and 1980s (e.g., Willis, 1977; Valli, 1986; Griffin, 1985; MacLeod, 1987) poignantly demonstrated how contemporary schools sorted different students for different occupational roles. Vocational education particularly came under attack as the dumping ground in schools for poor students to be trained to be low-waged, low-skilled workers. These ethnographies provided ample data for critical vocational educators to revisit Dewey's question of the purpose of vocational education—to prepare workers for the existing and highly flawed economic system or to prepare workers to be critical, active agents of social change. Kincheloe's (1999) differentiation between work, vocation and job is instructive in critical vocational educators' attempts to empower workers. Kincheloe notes that "a job is simply a way of making a living; work involves a sense of completion and fulfillment" (p. 64). Echoing Dewey's challenge to Snedden about the meaning of vocation, Kincheloe asserts that a "vocation is a calling involving meaningful activity" (p. 14). These are important distinctions when shaping the aims and purposes of vocational education based on critical empowerment of workers. In a democratic society, all members—regardless of age, race, class, or gender—should have the opportunity to find purpose and meaning through their work/

vocation. Equally important is the belief that all citizens should have the opportunity to engage in work/vocation that has the potential for both personal and social transformation. Kincheloe (1999) defines the features of "good work" imperative for such a transformation:

1. Workers should be free to self-direct without constant surveillance and supervision.

2. Workers should be active learners who see their jobs as a place of learning.

3. Workers should engage in activities that are free from repetition and boredom.

4. Workers should work in collaboration with others.

5. Workers should contribute to the larger social good.

6. Workers should allow an expression of self and creativity.

7. Workers should participate in their own operation and governance.

8. Play as a virtue must be incorporated into work.

9. The growing disparity in earnings between workers and managers must be reduced (pp. 65–70).

Critical vocational educators advocate a shift from thinking about education to prepare good workers to an education that engenders action toward making all work "good work."

Critical vocational educators have also pointed out the need to change the pedagogical practices of typical vocational education programs. Grubb (1996) aptly notes that there are two dominant approaches in teaching vocational education. The most common approach is a teacher-centered, teacher-directed approach. The second approach seeks to accommodate the changing worksite by offering instruction based on a student-centered, constructivist model of pedagogy. Yet, critical vocational educators have noted that constructivism void of the purpose of social change can perpetuate social inequities and leave taken-for-granted assumptions about work and the relationship between work and schooling intact. Hence, critical vocational education must incorporate a form of pedagogy that combines constructivism and critical inquiry with the basic aim of encouraging learners not only to gain an understanding of the sources of injustice in their own work lives, but more importantly to acquire the analytical tools in which to collectively challenge and act on the origins of their marginalization in the labor market (Lakes, 1994). The work of Brazilian educator Paulo Freire has been instrumental in shaping pedagogical practices in the new vocationalism based on a model of critical dialogue and consciousness raising (Lakes, 1997). Gregson (1994) urges vocational education teachers to be critical pedagogues who create learning environments based on such Freirean tenets as liberatory dialogue, active citizenship, reflective thinking, relevant learning experiences, and participatory, democratic decision-making. Similarly, Herschbach (1994) draws from Freire's problem-posing curriculum to encourage vocational educators to provide students the skills needed to organize collectively for better work and better pay through the adoption of such activities as journal writing, role-playing, case studies, small group work, and collaborative learning groups. Lakes (2005) describes how improvisational theatre based on the teachings of Freire and Augusto Boal has been used in a project with unemployed Turkish and Italian immigrants in Germany as a way for them to explore their own biographies within the larger context of marginalization and exclusion in the workplace. All of these point to the imperative that vocational education must lead to critical consciousness raising and social activism whereby people are empowered to challenge and change existing social and economic structures that continue to marginalize and oppress large numbers of people.

The Need for Philosophy in Shaping the Future of Vocational Education

Certainly vocational education in the last 20 years has moved away from Snedden's narrow definition of its goal (i.e., to prepare people for work) to embrace a more Deweyan perspective of vocational education that integrates the academic and the vocational through hands-on, experiential learning in real-world settings. However, what is far less prevalent in the current discourse of education for work is the more critical aspect of Dewey's understanding of vocational education in which students must be given the skills and knowledge to both critique the existing economic system and to actively work to change it. Reforms in vocational education, like reforms in education in general, continue to be stymied by the propensity to place questions of technique and function over questions of purpose and philosophy. Dewey poignantly affirmed the importance of philosophy over function when he succinctly explained the fundamental aim of the Progressive movement: "to take part in correcting unfair privilege and unfair deprivation not to perpetuate them" (Dewey, 1916, pp. 119–120).

As House pointed out in 1921 and has been made glaringly apparent in the recent corporate scandals, the collapse of the banking and auto industry in the United States and a worldwide economic recession, when business prospers moral values do not necessarily take care of themselves and workers are not the benefactors of corporate prosperity—often quite the opposite is true. The timing is ripe for vocational education to move away from the instrumental technocratic influence of Snedden and return to the democratic ideals of Dewey and his advocacy of vocational education as a form of worker civics in which students are prepared to be actively involved in social and economic reform. The future of democracy, perhaps more so than any time in history, depends on an informed citizenry with a moral compass and a passion for redefining the meaning of work and the workplace.

Note

1. We use the term "vocational education" throughout the chapter for consistency's sake. We recognize that "career and technical education" is the preferred term in 2009.

References

Braundy, M. (2004). Dewey's technological literacy: Past, present, and future. *Journal of Industrial Teacher Education, 41*(2): 20–36.
David, S., & John, D. (1977). Two Communications. *Curriculum Inquiry, 7*(1): 33–39.
Dewey, J. (1916). *Democracy and education*. New York: The Free Press.
Drost, W. (1977). Social efficiency reexamined: The Dewey-Snedden controversy. *Curriculum Inquiry, 7*(1): 19–32.
Gaskell, J. (1992). *Gender matters from school to work*. Toronto, Canada: OISE Press.
Gregson, J. (1996). Continuing the discourse: Problems, politics, and possibilities of vocational curriculum. *Journal of Vocational Education Research, 21*(1): 35–64.

Gregson, J. (1994). From critical theory to critical practice: Transformative vocational classrooms. In R. Lakes (ed.), *Critical Education for Work: Multidisciplinary Approaches* (pp. 161–180). Norwood, NJ: Ablex.
Griffin, C. (1985). *Typical girls?: Young women from school to the job market.* Boston: Routledge & Kegan Paul.
Grubb, W. (1996). *Learning to work: The care of integrating job training and education.* New York: Russell Sage Foundation.
Herschbach, D. (1994). The right to organize: Implications for preparing students for work. In R. Lakes (Ed.), *Critical education for work: Multidisciplinary approaches* (pp. 83–94), Norwood, NJ: Ablex.
House, J. (1921). Two kinds of vocational education. *The American Journal of Sociology, 27*(2): 222–225.
Kantor, H. (1986). Work, education, and vocational reform: The ideological origins of vocational education (pp. 1890–1920). *American Journal of Education, 94*(4): 401–426.
Kincheloe, J.L. (1995). *Toil and trouble: Good work, smart workers, and the integration of academic and vocational education.* New York: Peter Lang.
Kincheloe, J.L. (1999). *How do we tell the workers: The socioeconomic foundations of work and vocational education.* Boulder, CO: Westview.
Kliebard, H. (1999). *Schooled to work: Vocationalism and the new American curriculum* (pp. 1876–1946). New York: Teachers College Press.
Lakes, R. (ed.) (1994). *Critical education for work: Multidisciplinary approaches.* Norwood, NJ: Ablex.
Lakes, R. (1997). *The new vocationalism: Deweyan, Marxist, and Freirean themes.* Columbus, OH: ERIC Clearinghouse on Adult, Career, and Vocational Education.
Lakes, R. (2005). Critical work education and social exclusion: Unemployed youths at the margins in the new economy. *Journal of Industrial Teacher Education, 42*(2): 21–37.
MacLeod, J. (1987). *Ain't no makin' it: Leveled aspirations in a low-income neighborhood.* Boulder, CO: Westview.
Simon, R. (1983). But who will let you do it: Counter-hegemonic approaches to work education. *Journal of Education, 165*(3): 235–256.
Simon, R., Dippo, S., & Schenke, A. (1991). *Learning work: A critical pedagogy of work education.* New York: Bergin & Garvey.
Snedden, D. (1911). Progress of vocational education. *The American Journal of Nursing, 11*(12): 1004–1009.
Snedden, D. (1928). Democratic vocational education. *School Review,* 34(7): 522–527.
Snedden, D. (1977). Fundamental distinctions between liberal and vocational education. *Curriculum Inquiry, 7*(1): 41–52.
Valli, L. (1986). *Becoming clerical workers.* Boston: Routledge & Kegan.
Westbrook, R. (1992). Schools for industrial democrats: The social origins of John Dewey's philosophy of education. *American Journal of Education, 100,* 401–419.
Willis, P. (1977). *Learning to labor: How working class kids get working class jobs.* New York: Columbia University Press.

Nine

Indigenous Knowledge and the Challenge for Rethinking Conventional Educational Philosophy: A Ghanaian Case Study

George J. Sefa Dei and Marlon Simmons

Just what exactly is this thing called philosophy? Where does philosophy reside? How do we come to know philosophy? And which body is accorded the title of philosopher? These are some of the burgeoning questions with which we engage in this piece. With this chapter, we choose to move beyond legitimized geographies of knowledge which constitute themselves as geography. Moreover, we locate philosophy as a hegemonic discursive framework that privilege a particular way of knowing. Of course we recognize philosophy as a canon, one that has, and, continues to make meaningful contributions to ways of knowing and to the different educational systems. We do have a gripe with the dominant epistemic location of philosophy, as it resides within the hallways of academe. We offer a counterinsurgency of knowledge through an indigenous episteme.

Much of the ongoing intellectual discussion on "education" is located in the dominant paradigms of Western thinking. Alternative visions and counter/theoretical perspectives of education struggle to disentangle from the dominance of the Eurocentric paradigm are not encouraged. For example, how much of local cultural resource knowledge base is taught to learners in schools? (see Dei & Asgharzadeh, 2006a; Dei, 2004; Semali & Kincheloe, 1999). This chapter will address the issue of schooling and education in African contexts with a particular focus on the pedagogic and instructional relevance of local cultural resource knowings such as proverbs and folktales. Using Ghanaian (and to some extent Nigerian case studies/material) case studies, this chapter examines how such local cultural resource knowings (as indigenous knowledge and philosophies) inform education and socialization of youth and point to ways for rethinking knowledge, schooling, and education in contemporary times. We argue that contemporary education is mired in the reproduction of colonial hierarchies of power and knowledge and a struggle for local relevance. Such education is cut in the web of reproducing dominant knowledges and not necessarily imagining new possibilities for knowledge production in an academy. Today indigenous and local communities continue to struggle to carve out education that paves the way for new cultural, economic, and political imaginings and imaginaries.

In this burgeoning epoch of globalization and advanced capitalism, schooling and education as populated through the Western body have come to promote a particular ordering of society, one in which the socializing processes for youth today come to be imbued in and through the ebb and flow of compliance and control (see McLaren & Farahmandpur, 2005). From curricula, to pedagogies, epistemologies have been localized to some governing Eurocentric paradigm, well steeped within colonial specificities. But contrapuntal to such standardized knowledge is indigenous epistemes, which have been positioned as operating tangential to the conventional classroom text (see Dei, 2008; Battiste & Youngblood, 2000; Kincheloe & Steinberg, 2008). Yet, education for all must include the multiple ways we come to know and understand our social environment. Education for all must include the local everyday philosophies of students and all learners alike. We cannot continue to buy into the governing neo-liberal ideologies, which profess to be emancipatory and inclusive for all. Education for all must meet the needs of our local communities. Historically, education has produced/reproduced colonial relations within the institutionalized and social settings. Moreover, schooling and education have emerged as commodities of Enlightenment and at the same time proclaimed a particular humanism of Euromodernity, whereby the immanent cultural expressions, attitudes, and ways of behaving help to form the material conditions of the Eurosubject, as reified through the Western text. Education must consider the social environment, the local communities, and the cultural aesthetic; education is not simply out there as some theorized commodity, as positioned by the state, waiting to be consumed by the contemporary subject.

Education ought to be conversant with a holistic conceptualization of the living social beings. School and education are not neutral events, by no means are they apolitical moments as being circumscribed through some ontological neutrality. At the same time we cannot continue to shout *revolution, revolution* and wait for the powers that be, to proceed with haste, to meet the educational needs of the local peoples. If are thinking transformation then, we need to move beyond the shout of resistance and rebellion. We need more to think of a philosophy of education through decolonisation and speak about subversive pedagogies. We need to dialogue with counterinsurgent knowledges that embody the civic will of local peoples and that embody questions of local citizenry, community and environment needs. What does it mean for educational philosophy to reside within conventional classrooms and as being devoid of the lived experiences of the learner? We bring this seemingly simple question to broach some of the limitations and possibilities for schooling and education. Today, immanent within schooling and education all learners alike come to know and understand through a particular mode of alienation. If then we are thinking, dis-alienation, subversive pedagogies, decolonization as oriented dialectically, as particular counterhegemonic processes, then we ought to speak about indigenous philosophies and the link to schooling and education. Indigenous philosophies reside outside the conventional classroom and inculcate different ways of knowing through multiple methods that come to be well-steeped in the social environment through particular moments of self-determination, survival, development, recovery, mobilization, healing, transformation, and decolonization (Smith, 1999, p. 116; Maurial, 1999).

Educational philosophies for social justice ought to embody activist scholarship. Notably, liberation, decolonization, and emancipatory pedagogies have come to be ontologically absent from Enlightenment epistemologies. We are also constantly reminded that philosophy as dwelling within academic corridors reveals itself in a manner that wittingly proclaims an ahistorical phenomenology of racism. Racism in a sense becomes psychologized onto the particular individual body, as differentiated from any historic systemic lineage. Educational philosophy for emancipatory praxis must work with the ontological primacy immanent to the different geo-bodies. With the globalization of education, we ask education for whom and at what cost? What are the perils when we think of "development" through conventional educational philosophies that centre the will of capitalism as its ontological mantra? From global exploitative relations, to the continued production of underdevelopment in the Southern context, to the continued destabilization of racialized geographies, conventional educational philosophies continue to bring sustainability to the Western metropolis. Southern peoples continue to cry for help; in fact, economic inequality has become a way of life for the peoples of the South. Moreover, schooling and education as residing within dominant knowledging produce a set of social practices, in which the organizing principles are steeped within Euro-Enlightenment philosophies (see Abdi, Puplampu, & Dei, 2006; Abdi & Cleghorn, 2006). Pedagogical procedures experienced here engender banking (Freire, 1970) modalities of learning, in which, the expectation being for all learners alike is to reproduce dominant paradigms of knowledge, which then promulgates contemporary schooling. Such educational philosophies often appear as neutral and objective, as not having a politic, as not being biased, as not being racialised, and also, often enough these educational philosophies speak from the location of education for all learners (see Marcuse, 2009a, 2009b). Also ensuing from these philosophies is a particular curriculum that becomes discursively contoured to meet the needs of "development" and modernization from the context of Euromodernity. Today "underdevelopment" is actively deployed through specific measures of governance by overdeveloped countries. From Structural Adjustment Policies (SAPS) to the World Bank to the IMF, Western governments work collectively to ensure the present control of destabilizing relations with Southern geographies are here today and tomorrow (see Langdon, 2009; Dei & Simmons, 2009). If we profess social change, then we ought to seek a critical educational philosophy that ultimately seeks transformation of Western/colonial educational systems through subversive pedagogies. Social change means decolonization. Decolonization is all interwoven with dialectical ways of knowing. So in the African context, educational philosophies for decolonization must consider relevant knowledge that local peoples come to know as their own. At the very least decolonization cannot only be interpreted as another epistemology to be theorized within academic institutions. No, certainly not, if we are talking about decolonization and educational philosophies in the African context then we must speak about the lived experience of Africans on the continent and beyond its boundaries, we must consider the history of Africa in relation to other histories, keeping in mind that all forms of knowledging is political and not independent of consequences and implications, keeping in mind that which is colonial is not simply foreign or alien forces, but also dominating and imposing forces, which might also reside in the local context from within (see Dei, 2006b).

Concerning educational philosophies, the issue of the production and positionality of the different epistemes and how they come to be accorded with power, privilege, and discursive authority within academia need some attention here. In what way do these different moments of power, privilege, and discursive authority come to constitute epistemic violence? (Spivak, 1988) What are the academic perils when an educator speaks through an integrative indigenous discursive framework? What then are the consequences for the different voices of the oppressed when the politics of identification, the politics of representation, the politics of knowledge legitimation, work to dissipate the collective oppressed voice of colonial histories within academic spaces? Many have spoken about Africa before. Many have talked about what Africa is doing and what Africa ought to do. But if we are speaking about "the ought" and Africa, then we have to consider colonial histories, historic specificities and knowledge "for whom." If we are speaking about "the ought" and Africa then we ask: Development/modernization for whom and on whose terms? How long will Africa continue to be represented through the imagination of the colonizer? And what about when the African body his/herself take on this colonial imagination as her/his own? If one of our goals is to counter such colonial imaginations, then schooling and education for Africa must dialogue with educational philosophies imbued through African-centered epistemologies and anti-colonial discursive frameworks (see Asante, 1988, 1991, 2010). But there has to be some type of bridge, that is, to engage with an integrative indigenous discursive framework, which centers the African episteme and at the same time come to broach or to dialogue with conventional forms of knowledging. Today in our classrooms we are saturated with particular Euro-Enlightenment paradigms that work to organize and inscribe classroom curricula, which in turn promote hyper-scientific forms of what it means to be human; put another way it promotes hyper-scientific forms of what it means to be "developed." Hence, all learners alike engage in a form of education where the body engages in certain types of self-regulating practices, beliefs, behavioral patterns and attitudes, and particular expressions, which have historically been cryptically codified through particular colonial Enlightenment moral codes. So the learner comes to be informed through certain permutations of dehumanizing modalities in which the self comes to be known.

We need to conceptualize education *beyond the boundaries* of academic institutions and classrooms and importantly consider the material embodiment of this learning process. With all the *high theorizing* about education, we might forget that education is about doing, education is a lived moment, education is a human experience. By no means is education some empty space. The fact of the matter is that education is filled with bodies as lived through myriad historic-socio-cultural communities. We also need to keep in mind that historically, educational research proclaimed the concept of empiricism as being governed though the humanism of particular geo-bodies as being normate. We are left continually thinking of the ever-shifting consequences for contemporary schooling. Continuously thinking of the implications for learning, continuously thinking of the permutated complexity ongoing for different bodies to come to know, to learn, of coming to make meaning through educational philosophies, which through Euro-Enlightenment beliefs come to be permanently anchored within ethnocentric forms of empiricism, the methodological limitation ensuing here, being Euro-Enlightenment epistemologies as providing the sense for a universalized way of knowing. But knowledge resides with the different indigenous bodies as they come to be grounded through their local histories (see Roberts, 1998). The problem here is that indigenous knowledges have been demarcated and located tangentially to Western philosophy. The challenge for the indigene is to participate in educational research without compromise. If we are speaking here about integrating multiple educational systems of thought, if we are speaking about the different geo-subjects working together in some form of harmony, then the archetype conception of education ought to be re-conceptualized to include these subversive indigenous pedagogies (see Dei, 2000). In a sense then, the task for educational research is to move beyond the positivistic tropes of education and instead genuinely engage in dialogue with holistic, communal forms of knowing and understanding (see Denzin, Lincoln, & Smith, 2008). Yet, as the indigene broach the present lacuna residing within contemporaneous educational philosophies, the caution is to co-exist and not to co-opt indigenous beliefs and historical value systems. On another note concerning the integration of different knowledge systems, that importantly here we are amplifying that with integration while we are concerned about how the resources come to be shared, we feel the need to say we are more concerned with emphasizing which geo-body has the power, the material sense of entitlement to distribute and relocate resources. So, again we return to the ubiquitous question, that, on whose terms do indigenous peoples negotiate their humanism? How long indigenous peoples will have to continue to say, "yes, we too are human and we have the right to live through our ancestral beliefs, customs, language, traditions, spiritual ways of knowing and cultural practices?" And what about the expropriation of indigenous land and raw resources through legitimized juridical procedures of the state? Must this expropriation continue in the name of "development" and globalization despite the constant warnings of the detriment of climate change and global warming?

We know that particularly in the African context, the imposition of European philosophies and theories of knowledge was accompanied by the devaluation of indigenous ways of knowing. This imperial project contributed in no small measure to the epistemological colonization of African indigenous systems of thought. We also know that this imperial project did not go unanswered, in fact a number of indigenous voices have come to the fore with some critical questions (see also Abdi, 2005). Among the current questions being broached are: How do we recover, reclaim and recuperate our indigenous ways of knowing to give full sense of our lives? What are the sites that make such political and intellectual processes for reclamation of local knowledge possible? How do we lay claim to our local/indigenous cultural resource base from an understanding of how rural communities continually reference local proverbs, fables, and tales as part of everyday living and conversations? What are some of the specific teachings highlighted by these indigenous philosophies? And, what are the implications for rethinking philosophy and the philosophy of education? While we do not presume to have answers to all the questions we nonetheless want to draw attention to the various possibilities and challenges of understanding African indigenous philosophies through the study of some of the teachings of local proverbs.

Case Study: Context, Method and Study Findings

Beginning in the 2007–2008 academic year, one of the authors (George Dei) has worked with a team of graduate researchers to examine African proverbs and folktales for the pedagogic and instructional relevance for youth education in the specific areas of character and moral development of the young learner. A major learning objective has been to understand how local cultural resource teachings constitute important knowledge for educating youth in the development of strong character, moral, and civic responsibilities. The study has a specific pedagogic interest in understanding how African proverbs as local indigenous knowings can facilitate school teachings and learning in the academy. In the sociology of knowledge production we believe local cultural resource as indigenous philosophies can serve as important sources of information and/or tool for educational delivery. Throughout the entire research period, 2007–2009, at least a dozen focus group discussions have been organized together with workshop sessions with student-educators, field practitioners, and educationists. There has been a total of over 85 individual interviews conducted with 25 educators, 20 elders/parents, and 40 students drawn from the local universities, secondary schools, and community colleges as well as local communities in Ghana and a college community in Nigeria. The focus on the interviews was understanding the use and meanings of local proverbs and African indigenous philosophies, as well as the instructional, pedagogic, and communicative values and challenges in local teachings using proverbs, fables, folktales, myths, etc. about (in)discipline, and respect for self, peers and authority. The research period has also been a time for George Dei as Principal Investigator (PI) to network with Canadian educators and academic researchers on current directions of undertaking critical investigations concerning research and moral and character education.

In this chapter we highlight local voices as they attest to a particular source of indigenous knowledge and their pedagogic and instructional lessons for learners. We highlight some themes emerging from analysis of the subject voices that not only point to the pedagogic and instructional relevance of African proverbs and folktales but also highlight ways indigenous philosophies can inform the knowledge production and the sociology and philosophy of knowledge.

Proverbs as Indigenous Philosophies: Limits and Possibilities of Knowing

Local communities see proverbs as part of their indigenous philosophies that speak about worldviews and the relations of society, culture, and nature. Proverbs are conceptualized as part of everyday experience. Within cultures proverbs are common but have sophisticated sayings. Nana Bodine is the current assistant headmaster for academics in a local senior high school, and is well known for his use of proverbs in teaching youth. He sees a central place of proverbs in the school system and doubts whether the schools have done enough to promote proverbs in teaching. Teaching local indigenous languages is seen as critical. But while Nana Bodine is enthusiastic about teaching such indigenous knowledges as proverbs in schools, he laments on the question of language and the local contexts for instructing on proverbs:

> No, the schools have not done much. Especially, these days when the local languages are being removed from the schools. You see, just as I said you cannot speak the proverbs in English language to get the impact. [File 09: Text Units 202–220]

Nana Bodine insists proverbs must be about social change and improvement in human lives and asserts there can be some problems attached to some proverbs, which do not instill in youth affirmative solution oriented teachings:

> Yeah, some proverbs that will diminish progress. That will discourage especially the youth. You must avoid them. In our traditional society, they have been using them and do not think about the repercussions but we know that when you say this and you say that you just pull the youth away from being progressive. So if you sit down and you sample some of these things you will know that these ones are not very suitable and appropriate for this time. So you have to do that.

To Nana Bodine there is a responsibility that comes with the knowledge and wisdom that he has on proverbs. He has to ensure that such knowledge is passed on, especially, since he has been made a family head and he sees his role as helping make the person whole in all their knowings. The African learner who has been educated holistically will know about proverbs and their value in society as a powerful medium of communication.

Proverbs have meanings in the languages within which they are uttered. Mastery of local knowledge facilitates an understanding of local proverbs. Lasi, a teacher of Ghanaian languages with a diploma in Akan, discusses his understandings of proverbs and how he came to know about these cultural sayings. When asked how these cultural teachings can be brought back into schools to help educate youth, particularly what exactly needs to be done, Lasi replies:

> What is required is the training of personnel who will handle the subject in the schools. Because during those days, I am talking about something like the Ghanaian language very, very . . . was well taught. Every Ghanaian language was well taught depending upon the society. In the Volta region, they were teaching their Ewe language very effectively. So, if you go to the Akan area too, the same thing. So, by the time the teacher leaves the training college he or she must be well vested in the language and the proverbs. But, these days it is not so. So, if you want to bring back the proverbs then the teaching and learning of Ghanaian language in our training colleges must be reintroduced. [File 22: Text Units 148–149]

> Interviewer: Yeah. . .[and]. . .. beyond the level of comprehension of the proverbs. . ..There is also the question about . . . can some children or some youth say certain kinds of proverbs and at what times or what stage are they considered appropriate or inappropriate?

> Eh proverbs are proverbs. And there are some proverbs whether they are being said by children or adults need caution. That is why we have what we normally say or we have the phrase "sebi ta fra kye." Sebi is more or less the eraser that cleans the dirty aspect of the language. So, if you are a child and you happen to meet up with adults, and it is necessary for you to use a particular proverb there is no limit. You only have to be cautious and use the "sebi" and "Ta fra kye." [File 22: Text Units 236–253]

In the above exchange Lasi recognizes teaching local proverbs in schools call for professional training and local expertise. This is because of the deep meanings often embedded in proverbs. There is also a recognition that proverbs have to be uttered in their appropriate contexts. Some proverbs are said to be for adult usage, in other words, to be appropriately uttered by an adult not a child. While proverbs can become part of everyday conversation in schools, nonetheless, it requires training educators on how to use and teach proverbs to youth. He laments the fact that such training of educators seems to have been lost in the current school system. Lasi notes the culture specificity of proverbs and argues that we have to look at the context in which a proverb is used. When asked if proverbs can "also move from place to place" and prompted with the example of whether a proverb said in the Volta region of Ghana, can have similar meanings in the eastern region, he reasons:

> Oh yes, a lot of them. A lot of them, because there are some proverbs . . . ..No, they cut across because what pertains here also happens there. There are some few examples where what we do here is not done there and therefore proverbs here will not work somewhere else. Generally proverbs cut across but you see there are some proverbs for instance in English, if they are translated word for word may mean nothing to us Akans here. I remember, I was once teaching a class and "Once bitten twice shy." And then a student interpreted it in a very, very. . .and "let sleeping dogs lie." Then he said "ma nkraman a wade da ntwa atoro." (laughs). Look at that. So, you see we have the equivalent here but they may not be in the same wording. [File 22: Text Units 308–340]

He recognizes the wide applicability of proverbs in their pedagogic and instructional value and relevance. But he admits the local contextuality of proverbs and the challenge for the education is to be able to mesh such specificities with the broad lessons for social responsibility, community building, and moral ethic and conduct that proverbs offer learners.

Culture, Schooling, and Indigenous Knowledge

Reclaiming proverbs as indigenous philosophies also is about acknowledging the role of culture in schooling, knowledge production, and education. In a focus group discussion with final-year student teachers specializing in social studies at the University of Education in Ghana the students offered poignant critiques of colonial education and its impact on local culture. The student narratives spoke about the way in which culture, values, and traditions are significant in the schooling of young adults.

> Interviewer: I want to come back to the point about the culture and you said we have lost it, right? Could you speak a bit about it?
>
> Student: We were talking about our culture respect for the elderly is totally not there anymore. When we were kids in the recent past we were told that when you meet an elderly person in a vehicle and you are sitting, you stand up for the elderly person but nowadays it is not there like that. You will be in the vehicle with an old person and this. [File 20: Text Units 2093–2122]

It is interesting that in the foregoing discussion the students highlight respect for the elderly, authority, and school leadership as critical for moulding one's character and perseverance. They point to cultural sanctions that can be applied in local communities to help cultivate in youth, a sense of respect and responsibility to themselves, peers, and authority figures. Teaching African culture is teaching about respect and social responsibility. Respect and culture can be context-bound. They are both part of the socialization process for youth. Socializing a learner is also teaching about respecting oneself, peers and authority. Teaching respect and local culture is also an integrated practice. If one knows about his or her local culture and its values such knowledge cannot be separated from everyday educational practice. Such knowledge is grounded in everything one does. Local cultural knowings can be infused in school/classroom teachings as educators go about their everyday teaching. If socialization and education is to proceed the way African communities have impacted knowledge then it will be seen that local cultural knowings are infused in the various processes of knowledge production, validation, and dissemination. When asked how we bring culture back in education or in school, the final-year student teachers specializing in social studies at the University of Education in Ghana are adamant about noting and understanding the empowering and disempowering aspects of culture and tradition:

> Female student: All of us agree that our culture has been gone and we have integrated. . .but we have forgotten one question. There are some aspects of the culture which was very bad and was very inhuman like the "female genital mutilation,". . . ...Trokosi. . ...and other things which has gone. So as for that I think it is good. But there are some too which we could have retained but those one too are gone. Now looking at our culture as maybe when an older person comes in a bus you stand up and greet; I think that if the bus could have been partitioned.

No culture is immune to criticism. Every culture should be interrogated. The point that is made is very important, because there is a tendency to throw away a lot of an indigenous culture and just adopt some things. So on the question, "how do you bring back culture into the schools?" a student in the focus group responds:

> Student: I said that formerly they had something in school called culture studies. This in particular teaches about culture in the Ghanaian society and teaches both the good aspect and the bad and tells to

show the bad and tells us to maintain the good aspect but as time goes on culture studies has been taken away from the syllabus and has been replaced by other European. . . ..which we are being forced to learn. Because they said the world has become a global village and by so doing we neglect our own culture, so the generations coming forth, their minds are being polluted with the Western European style so they don't normally conform again to that part of the society that we are in. By so doing our culture is lost because it is the youthful generation that replaces the older generation. So until we are able to find that part of culture of our society and inculcate it in the curriculum, from the junior stages so that we can have people to teach and bring resource people from the society to really give examples, then if we do that then it means that we can bring our culture. [File 20: Text Units 1443–1513]

No doubt, the students are lamenting about "lost culture." They also recognize that there are sites of empowerment as well as disempowerment in local cultures and cultural traditions. The students do not bring an unquestioned faith to the reclamation of culture. Every culture is dynamic and culture moves with the times. Their call to "bring back local culture" is grounded in a firm belief that some aspects of traditional cultures have been helpful in socializing learners into responsible adults. No particular culture is an island unto itself. Cultures influence each other but one cannot discard their culture and traditions simply in favor of an alien culture. What learners can be assisted to do is to integrate values and ideas that have proven to work effectively in the socialization and education of youth in their own culture and cultural practices. The critical teaching of culture and cultural studies may be a good starting point. On the relevance of gender and gender values in such discussions concerning schooling, culture and society, final-year student teachers at the local University of Education noted issues of gender bias, disparity and the absence of critical gender analysis in school curriculum:

Female student: It is also very common. . .specially seeing the female being highly marginalized in terms of curriculum in the performance of leadership roles. That is the topic on which I am writing on now. You see them as being sidelined when it comes to the performance of leadership roles in the classroom. Always women are somewhere and that trend has continued.

Female student: When you get out to the field in politics; in all the executive sectors of the economy. We find men throughout. At times too most of them are being ridiculed and the few ones who will like to fight boot to boot with their men counterparts are nicknamed devil, witches and whatnots. I went somewhere and the lady was a carpenter roofing and thousand and one people were gathered looking at her and some calling her names. "Beyiefoo wei" [witches] and what nots. . . all nasty names.

Female student: It all boils down to the values. In our society it is said that even if the woman buys a gun it is the man who is supposed to keep it. It boils down to what the society perceives the woman to be. [File 20: Text Units 755–776]

In reclaiming culture, the place of gender in society must be taken seriously to interrogate social and political structures that marginalize women in society. Schools contribute to the problem by the lack of any critical focus on gender issues to allow learners complete grasp of the complexity of social interactions. If culture is to be claimed then the sites of empowerment as well as disempowerment for certain groups (e.g., women, children and religious, ethnic and sexual minorities) must also be exposed and addressed. Educators must be able to tease out the gender tropes of proverbs in order to teach proverbs critically about gender relations in society. Some proverbs because they are heavily embedded in cultural traditions can be reproducing gender stereotypes of the subordination of women in society. In a patriarchal society proverbs can affirm masculine views and power relations, and the responsibility of an educator is to help learners understand such gender dimensions and to begin to ask critical question about why, how, and when such patriarchal ideologies in society get reproduced in proverbial sayings. Unfortunately not many learners openly acknowledge the problematic aspects of proverbs.

The Question of Language

As already noted one cannot teach proverbs as indigenous knowledge/philosophies without understanding the local language. The connections between language and indigenity are clear. M.Phil. human rights student, Abana, at the university and currently working with the local ministry of management affairs, agrees that language is important in such discussion about proverbs:

> Yeah language is very important because it means that we actually communicate and in communicating language as a tool helps a lot. And, you should be able to understand the language that you are using to convey your message. And, so language is important. [File 07: Text Units 248–253]

Language facilitates communication in local proverbs. Abana's colleague, Amobi expands on the role of language in the teaching of proverbs calling for the integration of local languages and English in the instructing of young learners:

> I think it plays a very important role because language is part of our culture and we can learn best through our own local language. And, if we use our local language in addressing such issues, I think it will have a very good impact on the children. Yes, even though we can still use English language, it is also very important anyway but how they will understand it better is the main thing. So, the local language should be used and we should also add the English language and I think it will help them to move ahead. [File 14: Text Units 165–213]

Arts Design educator Fiifi also argues that language is central or significant to a discussion of proverbs:

> Well, in terms of the language, what I know about language in relation to proverbs; now for instance, the teacher teaching students as I said with the language reference; language you use to teach. Now supposing you are using English in teaching and you have some proverbs to put across, now if you don't have enough to elaborate more on the various tribes because you have different kinds of peoples or students in your class. The best thing a teacher does is if you say a proverb and you think it will be very difficult to explain you just literally translate it in English to make it easier, at least, for every student to understand because that is the language you are noted for to teach with. I think that is far better than to go as being partial to others, I mean to develop hatred between you the teacher and students. [File 15: Text Units 234–278]

Fiifi, however, conversant of the diversity of linguistic groups in the school system would appreciate a more modest approach of using the English language as a starting point to begin conversations around such local cultural knowings as proverbs. Master of Arts in Library studies student who hails from the Upper West region, Danny also links language and proverbs. He points out that to understand the proverbs of the community you must first understand the language of the community:

> The language is necessary because you have to understand the language so that if it is even changed in a certain way, you will be able to know that though this is the direct meaning of this word but in this context it means this. So, it is necessary to understand the language. [File 18: Text Units 123–128]

Focus group discussions with final-year student teachers graduating in social studies at a local Ghanaian university revealed some additional perspectives on indigenous knowledge. In discussing what educators see as their role in the schools, the broader issues of language, culture and indigenous knowledge surfaced:

> Interviewer: . . .. The whole issue about indigenous knowledge; what role do you see the teaching of Indigenous knowledge?
>
> Student: In the school?
>
> Interviewer: Well, in the school, at the college or at the university?
>
> Male student: The teaching of indigenous knowledge, just recently, was the medium of instruction for the lower level of. . .for the lower primary but recently it has changed for the medium of instruction to be the English language. I have a problem with that because. . . if English should be used as the medium of instruction it means that some of the things that we want to teach the children; we cannot do because basically some of these things; you have to say it in the local language for the child to know exactly what you are speaking about. But now we are being told to use the English language to do that and I think it will have a great effect on the students.
>
> Female student: Teaching of indigenous knowledge; to me, I would say to some extent we are doing good in Ghana because we have the teaching of the Ghanaian language in our various schools, through primary school to university level. Even in this university we have a department of Ghanaian languages, where various languages are studied. It is through the study of these languages that other things about our culture will be studied. So for me, to some extent we are doing well in our schools regarding the teaching of indigenous languages. [File 20: Text Units 1551–1593]

The tensions in using the dominant language to convey indigenous perspectives is highlighted in these discussions. Local language is critical to the survival of indigenous ways of knowing. Indigenous language needs to be kept alive in local communities, and schooling and education in Africa has a role to play in such undertaking. Teaching local language then ensures the survival of local indigenous knowledge systems. Language conveys powerful meanings. Language and culture are interconnected. When used inappropriately (as for example outside an appropriate cultural context) such meaning is lost. The language of other peoples cannot be used to teach or convey the full thoughts and ideas as expressed or embedded in such local cultural knowings as proverbs. Mathematics teacher Bafoah speaks about the relevance of teaching proverbs and the question of responsibility. He stresses the importance of meaning and how language is critical to fully comprehending what is contained in the local cultural sayings. He points to some of the things we need to be careful of, when we talk about proverbs, particular how the dominant language (i.e., English) can misrepresent what is being said in a local context:

> . . .I think eh. . .sometimes when we use eh. . .sometimes, the language barrier because sometimes when you want to translate; because sometimes one thing I see is that for the benefit of other students who do not understand the Akan language, it tries to translate it directly into the English language. And, sometimes me being an Akan when he says it in English it does not have the same impulse as it is in the local language. Yeah so that is one of the things. [File 04: Text Units 148–156]

Forty-six-year-old Patiah is a professional teacher with a bachelor's degree in education. He majored in English language and is currently studying to be a human rights advocate at the local university. In his view there is a sense that we need to keep these local proverbs going otherwise they are going to be lost. He sees teaching proverbs also as a way to keep local indigenous languages alive:

> There is the tendency. Even with the present Ministry of Education policy teaching indigenous language at the basic cycle. . . ..Yeah, it is a hot argument. Others are of the view that you start with English language, you know foreign language, even at the nursery. So that, the children will pick on, very early. Other scholars also hold on to the fact that, we should give them, first, the native language so that when they pick the proverbs, other elements and the traditional roles, from that language then they can build upon it when they are in the primary school with the English language. Well, we allow the two things to go on. But I personally feel that the usage of the native language, at the commencement of education, that is the basic level, will help them a lot to imbibe such proverbs. Otherwise, they will get lost. They will die a natural death, so we need to look at that. [File 16: Text Units 166–180]

Patiah's narrative suggests the important place of indigenous language in any attempt to rethink schooling and education to serve local needs and purposes. If we believe proverbs have important pedagogic and instructional relevance when it comes to the education and socialization of the contemporary learner then it is important we cultivate the medium and mode of communication that allows such indigenous cultural knowings be sustained. In fact, Patiah sees the teaching of proverbs as a form of indigenous knowledge and expands on his conception of the term:

> Yes. I see it to be a sequence to uphold the originality of the language. That is the beauty of the language. If you are able to use proverbs they bring about variation. They bring about beauty and it even leads to deep thinking; critical analysis and all those things. So we have to encourage them. There is the necessity that we maintain them. I will even suggest that those who are reading the native languages in the university; they should write more and those on the field should also encourage it so that it remains. [File 16: Text Units 211–220]

Indigenous language, like all languages, is complex and dynamic. Schooling and education must engage in practices that uphold the centrality of indigenous languages. Tamipiah, in speaking about the power and efficacy of traditional knowledge, also points to the dangers, perils and/or limitations in bringing this knowledge into the school system:

> Yes. The. . .challenge that I will still hammer is our indigenous language, our indigenous language that is not being used in schools. Because nowadays it is quite often that we see that teachers use English which is not our mother tongue more often than our local dialect. And, sometimes it is difficult you know to express or give proverbs in English. Sometimes even if you do the literal translation it would not sound as it is. So, it is about time if we want to promote the use of proverbs then it means that our local dialect must also be promoted where students must be made to learn. It will form part of the curriculum to be fixed in there. So, that, when these things are learnt; in delivering it in our local tongues it won't be a problem. But once that thing has not been done, I see it to be a block or impediment for the teaching of the proverbs. And, eh another thing is also understanding the local culture and other things. Now we are looking at somebody who did not stay in the area. He or she went somewhere to stay and is now coming back. Sometimes it will take them more time to be able to let the person know or understand the culture of the area because these proverbs as they are when we say it or when you use it in relation to an expression that you want to say. They try to explain or shorten certain expressions that we want to do. [File 17: Text Units 190–213]

He reiterates that we cannot hope to promote the teaching of proverbs in schools without first ensuring the survival and vitality of our indigenous language system. We cannot also understand local proverbs without a full grounding of local culture. Proverbs are part of the cultural values system. A complete "stranger" cannot teach or fully comprehend local proverbs because she/he hardly knows the indigenous language and culture. They may have an appreciation of such knowledge system but hardly grasp its intellectual intricacies.

Conclusion

Today, one of the challenges facing the academy and indigenous philosophies alike is that indigenous philosophies co-exist through interrelated and interdependent spaces, spaces that might not materialize into some readily available legible text, resulting in a sense, a type of academic gripe for indigenous representation; so, working in tandem with the racial snub from the academy, there exists this epistemological classification, which within conventional knowledge spaces, determines the conditions whereby indigenous oral epistemologies come into being a sum legitimate philosophy. Historically, educational philosophy emerged through the material presence of the written text, consequently forming hegemonic relations with indigenous ways of knowing. Concerning here is the form, the material body of indigenous language, the oral of indigeneity, the flux, the fluidity and the capacity, to come to co-exist in some way with conventional schooling and education. The operative term here being capacity and not compatibility. For as a subversive pedagogy, indigenous philosophy is not seeking some romanticized union with conventional philosophy. At the same time we wish to share with the power resources, so at the same time we are not seeking some segregated space, but to work with conventional knowledging on indigenous terms, acknowledging the multiple ways we learn. Part and parcel of indigenous knowledge, is resistance, survival; it is about operating counter-hegemonic to colonial Western forms of knowledging. Historically, Euro-Enlightenment interpretations of indigenous culture negated personal narratives, life histories, stories, and local proverbs. But these personal accounts were not some narrative to be quickly disposed of by the colonizer, to be deemed suspect knowledge, to be labeled as superstitious, these personal narratives held indigenous culture together.

Educational philosophy ought to be about socializing the learner to be a whole, complete person, a learner who is well aware of her or his surroundings and strives to meet the mutual obligations that go with membership in a thriving community. Proverbs teach about understanding, conduct, and moral behavior. Proverbs motivate one to do healthy deeds. Proverbs offer a course of action to follow in life. The elderly can teach the young. So too can students teach their educators. The critical teacher is not only a listener but someone (who) is prepared to let her or his students teach him/her. In the same vein a critical educator can learn a lot from a traditional elder or cultural custodian well versed in the culture, traditions, and cultural resource knowings of the community. The connection of moral and civic education is significant as it highlights some of the teachings of proverbs that stress social responsibility and the importance of education and socialization in bringing out the community of learners to civic responsibility. To local educators morals address the accepted values of society. It is through education that one begins to learn about the accepted morality and the expectation to govern one's life and experiences accordingly. Values are long-held rules, expectations and codes of conduct of a community. Some values are highly regarded and cherished by all members of the community. Any disrespect for such values is frowned upon and may elicit heavy community sanctions. Children are socialized and educated into the societal values, and it is important for educators to be conversant with a variety of pedagogic and instructional ways to impart societal values to young learners. In other words, values are a way of life. Teaching values is teaching about society in general—culture, traditions, perspectives, expectations, moral standards as well as social relations among groups. Societal values can be found or be expressive in indigenous proverbial sayings.

Note

1. All local names used here are pseudonyms.

Acknowledgments

The fieldwork component of the study was funded by the Ontario Literacy and Numeracy Secretariat (LNS). George Dei would like to acknowledge the assistance of Dr. Meredith Lordan, Munya Kabba, Jaggiet Gill, Camille Logan, Rosina Agyepong, Paul Adjei, Dr. Anthony Kola-Olusanya, and Marlon Simmons all of OISE/UT who at various times worked as graduate researchers on various aspects of the project. Thanks also to Professor Kola Raheem and the staff of the Centre for School and Community Science and Technology Studies (SACOST), University of Education, Winneba, as well as Mr. Paul Akom, former Dean of Students at the University of Education at Winneba for their invaluable assistance on the field research project. Similar thanks to Mr. Tola Olujuwon and the provost, faculty, staff and students of the Adeniran Ogunsanya College of Education, Otto/Ijanikin, Lagos State, Nigeria, where George Dei was a visiting scholar for a short period in the fall of 2007. Special mention to Messrs. Ebenezer Aggrey, Alfred Agyarko, Isaac Owusu-Agyarko, Martin Duodo, Kwaku Nii, Stephen Asenso, and Dickson K. Darko, all who participated as local research assistants. Finally, Marlon Simmons would also like to thank George Dei for the invitation to co-author.

References

Abdi, A. A. (2005). African philosophies of education: Counter-colonial criticisms. In A. Abdi & A. Cleghorn (eds.), *Issues in African education: Sociological perspectives* (pp. 25–42). New York: Palgrave Macmillan.

Abdi, A., & Cleghorn, A. (eds.) (2006). *Issues in African education: Sociological perspectives.* New York: Palgrave Macmillan.

Abdi, A. Puplampu, K., & Dei, G. (eds.) (2006). *African education and globalization: Critical perspectives.* Lanham, MD: Lexington.

Asante, M. K. (1988). *Afrocentricity.* Trenton, NJ: Africa World Press.

Asante, M. K. (1991). The Afrocentric idea in education. *Journal of Negro Education* 60(2): 170–180.

Asante, M. K. (2010). *Maulana Karenga: An intellectual portrait.* Cambridge: Polity.

Battiste, M. & Youngblood, H. J. (2000). "What is indigenous knowledge?" In *Protecting indigenous knowledge and heritage* (pp. 35–56). Saskatoon: Purich.

Cajete, G. (2008). Seven orientations for the development of indigenous science education. In N. Denzin, Y. Lincoln, & L. T. Smith (eds.). *Handbook of critical and indigenous methodologies* (pp. 487–496). Los Angeles, CA: Sage.

Dei, G. J. S. (2000). African development: The relevance and implications of indigenousness. In G. J. S. Dei, B. L. Hall, & G. Rosenberg (eds.). *Indigenous knowledges in global contexts: Multiple readings of our world* (pp. 70–86). Toronto: University of Toronto Press.

Dei, G. J. S. (2004). *Schooling and education in Africa: The case of Ghana.* Trenton, NJ: Africa World Press.

Dei, G. J. S. (2006b). Introduction: Mapping the terrain—towards a new politics of resistance. In G. J. S. Dei & A. Kempf (eds.). *Anti-colonialism and education: The politics of resistance* (pp. 1–23). Rotterdam: Sense.

Dei, G. J. S. (2008). Indigenous knowledge studies and the next generation: Pedagogical possibilities for anti-colonial education. *Australian Journal of Indigenous Education* 37, Supplement: 5–13

Dei, G. J. S. (2011). Introduction: Indigenous philosophies and critical education. In Dei, G. J. S. (ed.). *Indigenous philosophies and critical education.* New York: Peter Lang Publishing.

Dei, G. J. S. & Asgharzadeh, A. (2006a). Indigenous knowledges and globalization: An African perspective. In A. Abdi, K. Puplampu, & G. Dei (eds.). *African education and globalization: Critical perspectives* (pp. 53–78). Lanham, M.D: Lexington.

Indigenous Knowledge and the Challenge for Rethinking Conventional Educational Philosophy

Dei, G. J. S. & Simmons, M. (2009). The indigenous as a site of decolonizing knowledge about conventional development and the link with education: The African case. In Jonathan L. (ed.). *Indigenous knowledge, development and education* (pp. 15–36). Rotterdam: Sense Publishers.

Denzin, N., Lincoln, Y. & Smith, L. T. (2008) (eds.). *Handbook of critical and indigenous methodologies.* Los Angeles: Sage.

Freire, P. (1970). *Pedagogy of the oppressed.* New York: Continuum.

Kincheloe, J.L., & Steinberg, S. (2008). Indigenous knowledges in education: Complexities, dangers and profound benefits. In N. Denzin, Y. Lincoln, & L. T. Smith (eds.), *Handbook of critical and indigenous methodologies* (pp. 135–156). Los Angeles: Sage.

Langdon, J. (2009). Indigenous knowledges, development and education. In J. Langdon (ed.), *Indigenous knowledge, development and education* (pp 1–13). Rotterdam: Sense.

Marcuse, H. (2009a). Lecture on education, Brooklyn College, 1968. In D. Kellner, T. Lewis, C. Pierce, & K. Daniel Cho (eds.), *Marcuse's challenge to education.* New York: Rowman & Littlefield.

Marcuse, H. (2009b). Lecture on higher education and politics, Berkeley, 1975. In D. Kellner, T. Lewis, C. Pierce, & K. Daniel Cho (eds.), *Marcuse's challenge to education.* New York: Rowman & Littlefield.

Maurial, M. (1999). Indigenous knowledge and schooling: A continuum between conflict and dialogue. In L. Semali. & J. Kincheloe (eds.), *What is indigenous knowledge? Voices from the academy* (pp. 59–77). New York: Falmer.

McLaren, P., & Farahmandpur, R. (2005). *Teaching against global capitalism and the New Imperialism.* New York: Rowman & Littlefield.

Richard R. (1989). *Contingency, irony, and solidarity.* Cambridge: Cambridge University Press.

Roberts, H. (1998). Indigenous knowledges and Western science: Perspectives from the Pacific. In D. Hodson (ed.), *Science and technology education and ethnicity: An Aotearoa/New Zealand perspective.* Proceedings of a conference held at the Royal Society of New Zealand, Thorndon, Wellington, May 7–8, 1996. The Royal Society of New Zealand Miscellaneous series #50.

Semali, M. L. & Kincheloe, L. J. (1999). Introduction: What is indigenous knowledge and why should we study it. In M. L. Semali & J. L. Kinchloe (eds.), *What is indigenous knowledge?: Voices from the academy* (pp. 3–57). New York: Falmer.

Smith, L. (1999). *Decolonizing methodologies.* London: Zed.

Spivak, G. C. (1988). Can the subaltern speak? In, C. Nelson & L. Grossberg (eds.), *Marxism and the interpretation of culture* (pp. 271–313). Chicago, Urbana: University of Illinois Press.

Part Two

The Soul: Where Will It Go?

Ten

No Room for Wonder

Clar Doyle and John Hoben

Introduction: The End of Curriculum as the Beginning of Possibility

In this chapter, we intend to explore the relationship between reason and imagination and ask why there is no room to wonder in curriculum and program development in faculties of education. This exploration will be conducted within the nexus of critical pedagogy and philosophy.

As we explore directions toward a curriculum that celebrates philosophical thinking, creativity and wonder, we need to explore the meaning and significance we give to such terms and concepts. If we are to make a claim for creativity and imagination in university curricula, it will be helpful to probe the parameters of these challenging areas. Howard Gardner (1991) insisted that inside every child there is an "unschooled mind" struggling to be liberated from the stereotypes, conceptions, and scripts forced upon children in conventional schooling (p. 119). This claim, we believe, can be made for many students in universities and schools.

And yet, the reality of contemporary schooling is largely one of regimentation and control. Curricular development entails a process of struggle, of negotiation, instead of one of openness and play. Hegemony is played out through the process of curricular development, which too often is powered by those who insist on the need for organization and rigor. In this model, organization and control are virtually synonymous.

What, we ask, is the relationship of the untethered imagination to such sedimented forms of curriculum? As the voice of possibility, the imagination reminds us that control is never complete. Like Gardner, Kieran Egan (2005), writing in *An Imaginative Approach to Teaching*, claims that imagination is at the center of education. "Imagination can be the main workhorse of effective learning if we yoke it to education's tasks" (p. xii). The connection between imitation, memory, and imagination is "crucially important," and theorists have "uncritically" and "with hostility" marginalized the concept of memory to such an extent that within progressive circles the imagination has been "starved" (Egan, 1992, p. 52). Egan sees the imagination as a necessary means to develop a greater understanding of human experience. This ability to reach an understanding of the larger world, both spatially and temporally, is dependent upon the quality of the imagination. For all of us, the powers of the imagination, as an agent for teaching and learning, means not being bound by the conventional ideas and beliefs which people commonly grow up to accept.

In part, this desire to place questions before disciplinary boundaries leads us to consider the ways in which critical pedagogy, aesthetic education and philosophy can create conceptual spaces of imaginative power and critical potential. Even within the conventional constellations of these scholarly spaces, we contend, there is room for the consideration of the sometimes convoluted relationship between freedom, critique, and imaginative desire. For us, wonder is a moment of recognition: an immanent realization of the possibility of encountering ways of knowing and being beyond the taken-for-granted, necessary or mundane.

Seeing wonder as an experience of awakening, of becoming open to the transformative possibility of being different that knowing allows to happen, we want to probe the nature of curriculum as a bureaucratic discourse. Recognizing the cultural and political dimensions of human knowledge, we wish to query the absence of wonder in the university and argue for its necessity. We wish to encourage the democratization of wonder in a fashion that allows it to become a justification for creativity within bureaucratic discourse. We wish to propose a direction that celebrates philosophical thinking, creativity and wonder.

The Play Is Never Finished: Staging Curriculum

A significant challenge for us who work in faculties of education comes from Maxine Greene (1995), who asks of teachers "How else are they to make meaning out of the discrepant things they learn? How else are they to see themselves as practitioners, working to choose, working to teach in an often indecipherable world?" (p. 99).

Part of our struggle to have programs in the arts has as much to do with how we are able to "grade" processes and product of creativity. The struggle to place creativity and the arts toward the center of the curriculum in faculties of education is part of this. If we cannot measure something we are less likely to value it. We have, according to Eisner (2002), the notion that "the arts are somehow intellectually undemanding, emotive rather than reflective operations done with the hand somehow unattached to the head" (p. xi). Eisner goes on to say that in order "to create a form of experience that can be regarded as aesthetic requires a mind that imitates our imaginative capacities and that promotes our ability to undergo emotionally pervaded experience" (p. xii). In terms of seeing creativity and imagination as significant aspects of curriculum for faculties of education, as well as other university sectors, Egan claims, "Engaging the imagination is not a sugar-coated adjunct to learning, it is the very heart of learning. It is what brings meaning and sense and context and understanding to the knowledge we wish to teach" (p. 36). This approach places creativity and imagination at the very center of the work of teaching and learning, way beyond the limitations of "the manageable, the predictable, and the measurable" (Greene, 1995, p. 123).

As we struggle to develop appropriate curricula for faculties of education we can ask ourselves not only about the nexus of philosophy and imagination, but what it means to be educated. Part of what it means to be educated, we believe, has to do with being able "to decide the values and ideas that are embedded in what might be called popular culture as well as what is called the fine arts" (Eisner, 2002, p. 28). Given the muddled mix of culture, this is no easy task. Many of us claim that "what is artistically good is what people value, and what people value is the result of social forces. . .rather than qualities inherent in the work" (Eisner, 2002, p. 30). Where we come down on this claim informs our very approach to teaching and learning and to curriculum development in general. We need to remind ourselves that learning and teaching occur within temporally bounded networks. Flinders and Thornton (2009) start off with the right questions about curriculum: "What do we teach? What should we teach? and Who should decide?"

In curriculum, like many other places, "boundaries are being contested." There is a proliferation of discourses. Part of what we need to realize is that policymakers, and therefore, the people who develop curriculum, have interests in schools, colleges and universities that "are not especially educational; they are instead political and economic" (Pinar, 1998, *Toward New Identities*, p. xiii). In order to begin to come to grips with questions about the place of creativity and imagination as philosophy in relation to curriculum building, we have to draw in so many variables. These variables involve subject/content areas as well as philosophical, social, cultural, economic, and historical issues. This makes for a complex web. We can say that curriculum is about "identification and identity" (p. xviii). The process of identification and the location of identity are at the very core of what we do in education. This is a powerful claim. This means that educators are involved in far more than delivering information or even facilitating knowledge. We also know that one of the primary struggles of curriculum history is the one between a "conventional narrative" (social efficiency) and a "liberation narrative" (social reconstruction).

What part can creativity, imagination, and the possibility of wonder play in such sites? Greene (1995) advocates that "this is where the imagination enters in, as the felt possibility of looking beyond the boundary where the backyard ends or the road narrows, diminishing out of sight" (p. 26). This is where we encourage ourselves and our students to realize that we are in process—that we are in pursuit of our own possibilities. As Augusto Boal would say, the play is never finished.

In advocating for a more secure footing for creativity and imagination in education programs, we need be mindful of the political nature of schooling in general. The curriculum of just one century ago was a form of mental discipline by which learned people committed information to memory. In the ensuing one hundred years, many forces have splintered that conception of schooling. The revolutions in technology, communication, and formatting of knowledge, along with ways of knowing, have given us unlimited options in learning. The massive social transformation of the North American society has demanded new uses and applications from the school, and therefore faculties of education. Our growing understanding of the uniqueness of humans has affected our attempts to develop and deliver curriculum.

However, some things have not changed much in this same period. The basis of our North American curriculum remains, in large part, the sanctioned resources of Western civilization. The delivery of the curriculum continues to occur in a school building that is remarkably unchanging, often resulting in function following form. Finally, the value base of all teachings in a school setting continue to be recognized for what they are—a programming of the next generation. For this reason, curriculum remains a political process with high stakes. As Greene (1995) claims, "the dominant voices are still those of the officials who assume worth of certain kinds of knowledge, who take for granted that the schools' main mission is to meet national economic and technical needs" (p. 9).

Maybe it is wishful thinking, but there seems to be a genuine questioning of what we have been doing with our over-emphasis on test scores and accountability. This focus has often been done in the name of rigor, but at what price? When schools and universities fail to fire the imagination, we do so at our peril. The *Cambridge Primary Review* (2009) points to such peril. When "memorization and recall were valued over understanding and inquiry. . ." there is a blinkered focus on numeracy and literacy, to the exclusion of arts, music, and humanities. As the report claims, "The history of education reform has been superficial change masking underlying inertia. Political calculations have replaced honest appraisal." Eisner (2002) claims there is "a separation of art from intelligence" (p. 43). We are tempted to suggest there is often a separation of creativity and encouragement of imagination from formal curricula in faculties of education, and it is a herculean tussle to get it there. Like Augusto Boal, who broke away from European influenced theatre and created a theatre founded on local experience and sensibilities, we need to help break, even for ourselves, the rigors of the taken-for-granted patterns and find the security in the imagination.

Possibly what we need, sometimes, is to be involved in what Maxine Greene (1978) calls "a move to the imaginary—away from the mundane" (p. 173). In *Reflections from the Heart of Educational Inquiry: Understanding Curriculum and Teaching Through the Arts*, Greene (1991) admits that there have to be disciplines and an acquaintance with the structure of knowledge. She states, however, there have to be the kinds of grounded interpretations possible only for those willing to abandon "already constituted reason, willing to feel and imagine, to open the windows and go in search" (p. 122). This is not the stuff of formula.

As educators, we have differing, and sometimes conflicting, understandings of the terms, creativity and imagination. These understandings range from identifying them with particular subject areas of the curriculum, or having opportunities to be creative in all curriculum areas. We sometimes believe that creativity has to do with an enduring characteristic or talent that is limited to certain people while others believe all people are creative. How we understand creativity and imagination determines how we believe universities and schools promote creativity and imagination and, therefore, how curriculum will be developed. This does not even approach the transformative aspects of creativity and imagination. These observations certainly do not yet leave room for wonder.

> Creative or innovative thinking is the kind of thinking that leads to new insights, novel approaches, fresh perspectives, whole new ways of understanding and conceiving of things. The products of creative thought include some obvious things like music, poetry, dance, dramatic literature, inventions, and technical innovations. But there are some not so obvious examples as well, such as ways of putting a question that expand the horizons of possible solutions, or ways of conceiving of relationships that challenge presuppositions and lead one to see the world in imaginative different ways. (Facione, 2007)

We are not alone in our argument for a place for a philosophy of education that affirms creativity and imagination, and room for wonder, in faculty of education programs. A European report called *Creativity in Higher Education* states, "Creativity has been identified both as a key factor for adequately addressing the challenges caused by these changes as well as a major driving force toward knowledge creation and social and economic advancement through the development of a knowledge society" (EUA, 2007, p. 6). This particular report claims that this interest in creativity, triggered by globalization needs, has not been taken up by academe. It is further claimed that progress toward a knowledge-based society and economy will require that universities, as centers of knowledge creation, need to give creativity their full attention. That particular report goes on to say, "Purely mechanistic approaches geared toward reaching predefined targets will certainly not allow European higher education institutions to contribute adequately toward this ambitious objective" (EUA, 2007, p. 6).

But what, within the confines of contemporary schooling, is the nature of the relationship between the conventional and the "mechanistic"? Is this primarily an issue of content or context? From an educator's perspective, is it enough simply to expand the philosophical content of the curriculum? While we have talked about the importance of the imagination to curriculum, how does the issue of creativity relate to the disciplinary themes and boundaries of conventional philosophy?

Deschooling Philosophy: Imagination and the Curriculum of Everyday Life

These questions, while provocative, are not without precedent. Maxine Greene, who is interested in transformations, openings, and possibilities seeks "ways which we and our students might come to use imagination in a search for openings without which our lives narrow and our pathways become cul-de-sacs" (1995, p. 17). She further claims that "one must have an awareness of leaving something behind while reaching toward something new, and this kind of awareness must be linked to imagination" (p. 20). Greene (2001), in *Variations on a Blue Guitar*, claims that "aesthetics is the term used to single out a particular field in philosophy, one concerned about perception, sensation, imagination, and how they relate to knowing, understanding, and feeling about the world" (p. 5). Later she writes, "Nothing can be predetermined or predicted in the artistic-aesthetic domain. But everything is possible. We have only to free ourselves, to choose" (p. 23).

Taking into account the more recent "linguistic" turn that has animated sometimes-vigorous contemporary philosophical debates, we are reminded that philosophy can also be approached as a form of thinking which reflects upon its own processes, namely those through which knowledge is constructed and disseminated within a human social context. Most importantly, in modernity this broader "context" within which reason is constructed and set to work is both an institutional and a cultural reality.

If, as Deleuze (1994) contends, philosophy is "the art of forming, inventing and fabricating concepts" (p. 2), philosophy can be approached as a corpus of knowledge and a form of discourse that deals with the perennial themes of human emancipation, equality and knowledge and the nature of a society which offers optimal conditions for human fulfillment. This approach represents a kind of thinking that goes beyond the how, why, and when of an empirical calculus of causes. In addition to reason, then, language and imagination, it might be said, are equally at play within the longstanding "discipline" we have come to know and understand as philosophy. And yet, invariably, in the modern world, forms of potentially liberatory thinking are often embedded within a set of institutional and disciplinary practices, which often hinder the birth of naked wonder. Philosophy as a practice of wonder making and amazement, then, can involve systematic reflection on the possibility of transformation, for the individual and society, as that possibility remains immanent in the living conjunction of consciousness, culture and words. As such, philosophy becomes a map of wonder that realizes the impossibility of its own completion. It becomes an analogue or representation of life journeying that requires experience for its very being and fulfillment—the indeterminate curriculum of our own becoming.

Seeing philosophy this way we are able to realize strategic similarities between conventional academic philosophy and critical pedagogy, as both are positioned as disciplines, educational projects and forms of emancipation. Unlike bureaucratic and positivistic forms of means, orientated thinking and critical thinking asks how ends are related to our individual and collective conception of the ends and aims of human practice. Keeping this broader organizational reality in mind, the all too common tendency to equate education with training without questioning the political function of knowledge then means that philosophy and critical pedagogy alike have a role to play as "educators, youth, parents and various cultural workers. . .rethink the meaning of democracy, ethics, and political agency in an increasingly globalized world in which power is being separated from traditional political forms" (Giroux, 2001, p. 53). This propensity to turn the mirror against the institutional and cultural mechanisms of its own production sets critical thinking against the unseen gears and levers of the institutional determinacy machine of ideological production. Untamed and open to wonder it becomes unpredictable, and, hence, dangerous.

Philosophy and critical pedagogy, albeit imperfect, at least provide "even within the watered down version characteristic of liberal democracy, the possibility for both reflecting critically upon its own limitations and implementing the promises of radical democracy" (Giroux, 2001, p. 29). As such, the growing absence of philosophy from educational programs is problematic for critical scholars since, in many respects, critical pedagogy's relationship with philosophy, like critical pedagogy itself, is rooted in the idea of the unfinished nature of human culture and identity. The end of any discourse is not something that can be deduced logically from self-evident first principles, rather, it requires a critical capacity paired with an imaginative empathy to realize the world, both as it is and how it might be.

In the absence of universal epistemological foundations critical pedagogy realizes the necessity of creating forms of cultural work, which utilize both the critical capacity and the imagination in tandem to reveal, "how the other side looks from our own point of view" (Rorty, 1998, p. 365). The imagination as a form of empathetic capability is crucial to coming to the realization that "the understanding of history as possibility rather than determinism. . .would be unintelligible without dreams, just as a deterministic view feels incompatible with them and therefore, negates them" (P. Freire in A.M. Araujo Freire, 2007, p. vii). What promise does thinking hold for us, then, in a history where the specters of Auschwitz, Hiroshima, Dresden and Fallujah loom so large? To what extent does mere philosophical reflection fail to realize, again, in the words of Marcuse, that "within a repressive society, even progressive movements threaten to turn into their opposite to the degree to which they accept the rules of the game" (Marcuse, 1965, p. 97).

Within an age of rampant consumerism and resurgent authoritarianism, underpinning any debate regarding curricula and institutional allocation of resources then are the larger questions of value and power. Clearly what we have seen is distaste by powerful managerial discourses for certain types of questions, including those about the role of democratic schooling and critical thought. Seeing this process of curricular struggle as one which is inevitably political, critical educators must consider not only what is at stake in such conflicts, but, as well, the nature of critical pedagogy's own relationship to what we colloquially call philosophy, as a means of reflexively examining the methodological and ideological underpinnings of its own educational project—one that invariably seeks to expose and confound the hypocrisy of institutions devoted to a curriculum of taming wonder.

In contrast to forms of thought that see philosophy as a form of rational training, we put forward the question of whether contemporary conceptions of a sedimented discipline can be replaced with the simple question of whether human activity, at its most creative and radically reflective, is centered in the critical imagination. Thus, in challenging the conventional boundaries between philosophy, aesthetic criticism, and educational theory we ask simply whether philosophy can become a space of deliberative possibility where we can "link democracy to public action and to ground such a call in defense of militant utopian thinking as a form of educated hope" (Giroux, 2001, p. xiii). A form of educated hope that breaks ranks with the old and facile divisions, which risks outrage to speak against angry voices calling for bloodshed and hatred instead of the careful dialogue required by democratic justice.

In the interests of such a project, we recognize that philosophy is being deinstitutionalized in the sense of being removed from its once revered place in university institutions. However, we also contend that it is necessary to re-imagine philosophy's place within culture rather than only in the classroom, to cross borders in the hopes that by transgressing the divisions of the contemporary academy, new life can be found for critical reflection, creativity, and imagination. How can we mobilize ourselves to chip away the drab uninspiring edifices constructed by the architects of misery, as we seek to reinvent and reinvigorate an academic culture lost in complacency, and the bureaucratic technocracy that is the legacy of a crusading positivism and a militant corporatocracy? Instead we encourage new, eclectic educational spaces that challenge us to create unbroken paths opened up by a pedagogy of wonder.

In this regard, a primary aim of critical pedagogy remains the investigation of the realm of human culture in which theory and philosophy are embedded. Such a project not only requires moving beyond a reductive Marxism, it also entails a rebellion against the utopianism of empirical science and rational positivism alike, as sociological inquiry is combined with radical democratic theory and action.

In contrast to conventional philosophy, critical pedagogy is unashamedly political as it analyzes the interrelationship between the historical and socio-economic parameters of knowledge production. This political focus leads critical pedagogues to the realization that breaking through the "society of the spectacle" requires reaffirming some sense of the real in the wake of philosophy's linguistic turn, which is open to both consequence and the need for wonder to transform image and idea alike. Such a constructivist standpoint is open to the postmodern insight that all we have are stories or "truths," which are context contingent and situationally valid, and yet, opens this insight to a creative, praxis-orientated pragmatism (Rorty, 1998, 2000, 2001).

In this vein, as we seek to assess the strategic possibilities posed by border crossing between critical pedagogy and philosophy we might consider the possibility that questions about "truth" are essentially questions about the justification of particular cultural practices since we reject the argument that "truth is correspondence to reality and that reality has an intrinsic nature" (Rorty, 1991, p. 1). Epistemic issues are ultimately issues of persuasion, whose viability is culturally contingent, as culture determines which arguments resonate with us. Therefore, truth testing is simply a means of identifying contingencies for persuasion, and there are no universalizable means of assessing the validity of propositions independent of particular audiences.

Rorty's idea that rationality can be used to describe a specific set of inherited cultural practices causes us to consider the role of the imagination in promoting tolerance, skill at survival or our ability to evaluate relative social goods. In this sense, what we think of as an innate logical facility is actually contingent upon very specific and historical cultural conditions—many of which are open to redefinition by a process that is essentially dialogical and educative in nature. That is, rationality is a cultural tradition as well as a language of socially conditioned possibility. To say that something isn't rational, then, often simply means that it is not permissible to imagine it as belonging to the everyday realm of the "real." The implications of such a view require us to reconceptualize emancipation as both an imaginative, as well as critical, reworking of the everyday.

More importantly it also implies that if democracy is to realize its radically transformative potential, we must use imaginative new ways of communicating and thinking—that is, "imaginative ability is required if the becoming different that learning involves is actually to take place" (Greene, 1995, p. 22). In part this "becoming different" requires setting apart a curriculum that recognizes, "thinking freely should [not] be reduced to choosing—through some kind of evaluative process, however, reflective it might be—that which is already available. Free and imaginative thinkers, to be considered truly free and imaginative, have to be involved in co-producing new ways of thinking about the world and their place in it" (Weiner, 2007, p. 69).

Of course, as Foucault and Said, among others, have shown us "the real" has its foundations in the hidden grammar of power as it constructs a worldview conducive to its hidden aims and interests. Ideology, despite its obvious destructive tendencies, is also a creative force, meaning that rationality alone, as a means of ascertaining coherence and correspondence to "the real" cannot be a substitute for an imaginative empathy that provides occasion for reflection and dialogue. In the words of Eric Weiner (2007), "[c]onstructing a new critical imaginary is about rejecting the imperatives of realism—rewriting the categories of the real—means, on one hand, questioning the very epistemological foundation upon which our most cherished social and political assumptions rest, while, on the other, developing new categories from which to design new theoretical models of thought and action" (p. 58).

The idea that there might be a kind of artistry to daily living, then, brings a moral and a political dimension to the way narratives provide us with a way to convey meaning to the uncertainty of daily life. They allow us to see difficulties, not as something that are reasoned away, but as experiences that are lived through and that form the raw material of sense making. To be critical in a sense is not to see things as they really are, but, rather to become attuned to this ongoing creative process and to the ways in which it can go awry. Seeing creativity this way, the task of critique is to prevent the moment of transformation presented by wonder from becoming a kind of bewitchment or exile from which there is no return. As Said (1978) puts it, "imaginative geography and history help the mind to intensify its own sense of itself by dramatizing the difference between what is close to it and what is far away" (p. 55).

Recalling Rorty, if we see rationality as being at once skill at survival, a means of setting goals, or weighing relative goods, the distinction between imaginative and rational capacities seems less readily evident. Writing after the linguistic turn of post-structuralism, imagination and re-description seem "fundamental" to the viability and social relevance of philosophy itself. In this way, Rorty's view may share a particular affinity with those of Maxine Greene (1973) who argues that "[p]hilosophy may be regarded as a way of approaching (or looking at or taking a stance with respect to) the knowledge gained by the natural and human sciences, the awarenesses made possible by the arts, and the personal insights into existence each human being accumulates as he lives" (p. 7).

Conclusion: Reimagining Wonder as Awakening

In our quest we need to remind ourselves that creativity needs to be seen as crossing all subjects and domains and not only the domain of the arts. It is important to realize that knowledge and creativity are not opposed to each other but form a needed nexus (Craft, Jeffery, & Leibling, 2001). Part of a transformative education is to be awakened to a kind of thought that enables us to imagine conditions other than those that exist or that have existed. This can be a place for wonder. Vast claims are made for creativity. It has been identified both as a key factor for adequately addressing present day challenges caused by these global changes as well as a major driving force toward knowledge creation and social and economic advancement through the development of a knowledge society.

While creativity has received a high degree of attention from scholars, professionals and policymakers alike, relatively little attention has been paid on how creativity and innovation can be enhanced within and by academe. This does seem strange given the key role assigned to higher education for the development of a knowledge society. Universities, as centres of knowledge creation, and their partners in society and government need to give creativity their full attention. The complex questions of the future will not be solved "by the book," but by creative, forward-looking individuals and groups who are not afraid to question established ideas and are able to cope with the insecurity and uncertainty this entails.

"Reason" says Marcuse, "is the fundamental category of philosophical thought" (Marcuse in Habermas, 1987, p. 381). While Marcuse is right to identify reason as a central organizing theme in the history of philosophy, it is much broader than the rationalistic project that Marcuse describes. As the interminable wrangling about the linguistic turn in philosophy demonstrates, the concerns of contemporary theory are much broader and comprehensive. Such a critique of presence recognizes the hermeneutical nature of human perception: not only can we not know the thing in itself, but, she seems to say, the search for such a thing is itself fundamentally misguided. The modern fetish for certainty (Doyle, 2009) misses the ubiquitous mystery of human thought and linguistic expression that creates as it transcribes the world. As the man on the blue guitar admonishes us to remember, "things just as they are, are changed on the blue guitar" (Wallace in Greene, 1973 p. 19).

A fully human critical faculty—unlike reason—attempts to reflexively encounter principles by understanding their relationship to the imaginative, as well as moral and political, exigencies of experience. What this means is that love and the imagination are needed to transform the cold hard light of pragmatic necessity, which is all too often unthinkingly accepted as inevitable or natural. Encountering the aesthetic and the imaginative allows us to come to terms with the fact that, in the words of Greene, "many want (yet do not want) a song that celebrates the ordinary and the comfortable" (Greene, 1995, p. 19).

Imagination is important to critique since it provides a means of moving beyond the linear conceptions of the analytical to encounter the possibility embodied in the taken-for-granted realm of the everyday. Seeing imagination as a creative process reminds us that abandoning reason's "quest for certainty" is necessary if educators are to unleash the transformative potential of critique and art as we adopt a bricoleur's openness to using philosophy's tools, always ready to adjust them according to the task at hand (Dewey in Greene, 1995, p. 18). If dialogue is to be a social act, it must also be one that is both critical and open to the world of emergent possibility.

As part of this process of reimagining educational dialogue, critical pedagogy is exemplified by a concern with practical politics and theory, as it rejects any simplistic division between thought and action, reflection and response. Recognizing the importance of power and perception in the construction of human knowledge it is characterized by a unique reflexivity and a willingness to modify its means and aims in accordance with the particular "limit-situation" at hand. As such it recognizes that the process of living and learning are profoundly dependent upon an imaginative, emotive human capacity that shapes, and, in turn, is shaped by, a critical facility.

The imagination is, then, a staging ground for the conflicts and struggles of human existence in which identity and ideology contend. Although often characterized as peripheral to the main educational drama, it is the means by which the pedagogical script is composed, re-read, and re-enacted. If critique is a means of fracturing the hegemonic edifice, imagination allows us to enter the vicarious realm made possible by a reinvigorated politics of possibility. The imagination allows us to break with hegemony by making accessible those realms and modes of existence that the monolithic voice of repressive power wishes to hide from our purview.

Seen within such a context curriculum becomes something that is vital, in process, and engaging, since it is, like education itself, attuned to needs and dreams of those whom it seeks to empower. As such, the unfinished nature of curriculum is emblematic of the unfinished nature of the disciplines themselves: that is, the value of philosophy or critical pedagogy is not that they have solved some finite set of problems that can simply be translated or transferred but that they are responsive to the social and cultural context in which they are continually (re)created. Despite the way contemporary curricula are structured, reasoning like imagining, cannot be taught by the transfer of a set of self-contained, discrete units of knowledge or axioms; their utility, their aims and their very conception are determined by the cultural context that they shape and within which they can be said to "function."

Conversely, in many ways, to deny the importance of imaginative ways of seeing and being is to ignore the old dream of universal reason, which is often the impetus for a dark stranger hood of alienation from our very "selves." And yet, old divisions between rationality and imagination, materialism and idealism, theory and practice begin to break down as we learn to see wonder as a phenomenon that is, at the same time, both ideal and embodied, personal and historical. If reason is the tool that sharpens those things that appear within our line of vision, the imagination is the unseen hand that provides the impetus to go in search of new horizons. Quite often wonder startles us with the unexpected beauty of our daily lives, a haunting place where we can hear the lonely song of consciousness, moving outward, seeking, searching through the endless possibilities to be claimed among love, and the as-of-yet-unknown heart of imaginative yearning.

References

Araujo Freire, A.M. (Ed.). (2007). *Daring to Dream: Toward a pedagogy of the unfinished.* A.K. Olivereira (Translator). Boulder, CO: Paradigm Publishers.
Craft, Anna, B. Jeffrey & M. Leibling (Eds.). (2001). *Creativity in education.* London: Continuum.
Dewey, J. (2007). *How we think.* Stilwell, KS: Digireads Publishing.
Doyle, C. (2009). The illusion of certainty. *The Morning Watch.* Vol 37. Nos. 1–2. http://www.mun.ca/educ/faculty/mwatch/fall09.html

Egan, K. (2005). *An imaginative approach to teaching.* San Francisco: Jossey-Bass.
Egan, K. (1992). *Imagination in teaching and learning: The middle school years.* London, Ontario: The Althouse Press.
Eisner, E.W. (2002). *The arts and the creation of mind.* New Haven, CT: Yale University Press.
Eisner, E. (1998). *The enlightened eye: Qualitative inquiry and the enhancement of educational practice.* Upper Saddle Rivier, NJ: Prentice Hall Inc.
EUA, (2007). *Creativity in higher education: Report on the EUA creativity project 2006–2007.* EUA Publications.
Facione, P.A. (2007). *Critical thinking: What it is and why it counts.* Retrieved from http://www.finchpark.com/courses/assess/critical.htm
Flinders, D.J. & Thornton, S.J. (2009). *The curriculum studies reader.* New York: Routledge.
Gardner, H. (1991). *The unschooled mind.* New York: Basic Books.
Gilles, D. & F. Guattari. (1994). *What is philosophy?* London: Verso.
Giroux, H.A. (2001). *Public spaces, private lives: Beyond the culture of cynicism.* Lanham, MD: Rowman & Littlefield.
Greene, M. (2001). *Variations on a blue guitar.* New York: Teachers College Press.
Greene, M. (1995). *Releasing the imagination.* San Francisco: Jossey-Bass.
Greene, M. (1978). *Landscapes of learning.* New York: Teachers College Press.
Greene, M. (1973). *Teacher as stranger: Educational philosophy for the modern age.* Belmont, CA: Wadsworth Publishing.
Habermas, J. (1987). *Theory of communicative action, Vol 2: Lifeworld and system: A critique of functionalist reason.* Boston, MA: Beacon Press.
Habermas, J. (1962). *The structural transformation of the public sphere.* Cambridge: Polity Press.
Marcuse, H. (1969). Repressive tolerance. In R.P. Wolff, B. Moore Jr. & H. Marcuse. *A critique of pure tolerance.* Boston: Beacon Press, pp. 95–137. http://www.marcuse.org/herbert/pubs/60spubs/65repressivetolerance.htm
Pinar, W. (Ed.). (1998). *Curriculum: Toward new identities.* New York: Garland Publishing.
Rorty, R. (1998). *Truth and progress: Philosophical papers, Volume III.* Cambridge: Cambridge University Press.
Rorty, R. (1989). *Contingency, irony, and solidarity.* Cambridge: Cambridge University Press.
Rorty, R. (2001). An imaginative philosopher: The legacy of W.V. Quine. *The Chronicle of Higher Education,* 47(21), 1 – 5.
Rorty, R. (2009). *Universality and truth.* In R. Brandom (Ed.). *Rorty and his critics.* Oxford: Blackwell.
Weiner, E.J. (2007). Critical pedagogy and the crisis of imagination. In *Critical pedagogy: Where are we now?* (pp. 57 – 78). P. Maclaren & J. Kincheloe. (Eds.). New York: Routledge.
Willis, G. & Schubert, W. Ed. (1991). *Reflections from the heart of educational inquiry.* Albany: SUNY Press. http://www.esmeefairbairn.org.uk/docs/CPR-booklet_low-res.pdf

Eleven

Philosophy Applied to Education, Revisited

Barbara J. Thayer-Bacon

Introduction

I started my college career in the early 1970s, as feminist theory was in the midst of a strong second wave of influence (the first wave being women's suffrage and fighting for women's right to full citizenship). The second wave of feminism influenced me as an older child and young adult, in that I was aware that women's "pink-collar" careers included nursing and teaching. I didn't want a typical pink-collar job, doing "women's work" of caring for others. I wanted to do something else and purposely avoided those two fields, instead following my heart and majoring in philosophy. Ironically, the only job I have had as an adult is as an educator, and my research work in philosophy of education has contributed to the development of feminist care theory. It is important to add, right away, that I love the work I do and cannot imagine a more challenging or important job. To be a teacher is to seek a life of continual growth, as good teachers learn as much from their students as they teach, the roles are continually changing (Dewey, 1916). To be a philosopher who continually applies her philosophical skills to the subject of education is to seek to bring theory to bear on real life everyday problems of great significance. Education is how human beings choose to continue their existence and pass on knowledge to the next generation. Many other species have the ability to learn, but human beings are unique in their ability to teach and store what others have taught them (Mead, 1970).

By nature I am a philosopher, I love to think about why things are the way they are, and ponder how they could be otherwise. I think about what our aims and goals are and what will lead us to justice, fairness and equality, beauty and truth, as well as a good, balanced, happy life. These are the kinds of questions philosophers ask, not scientific questions concerning what exists, but normative questions about what should be ideally. We ask questions like: What is the right way to educate children, the just way, that takes into account their marvelous diversity? We do not ask questions like: how do we measure what children are learning in this classroom? I am not saying that one type of question is better, both are important, but it is also important to understand the difference. Causal questions are limited to what exists, philosophical questions try to use what has happened in the past, what exists today, as well as possibilities they can only imagine, to help them make the case for what should be.

In order to be able to answer normative questions, philosophers need to learn how to use many tools at their disposal; their emotions, imagination, intuition, and reason are all important (Thayer-Bacon, 2000). We have to be able to notice problems and concerns and be stirred to care about trying to solve them (felt need is based on our emotions). We also need to be able to critique what is wrong (intuition is vital to helping us understand problems and pull our ideas together, and reason helps us as well to understand and judge the quality of our ideas). We also need our imagination to help us consider various options and think about possible solutions that we may have never experienced. To be a philosopher is to be a poet, prophet, and soothsayer for we must be able to imagine how things could be otherwise, to help make the case for what should be ideally (Dewey, 1922; Rorty, 1989; Greene, 1995).

Philosophers seek reasons to support our claims and ask many questions, trying to understand. We do a lot of clarifying work. We seek to understand what is meant by the concepts people use, for language is very ambiguous and easy to slip and slide on, causing much confusion. We also seek to understand how concepts connect and influence each other, because gaps in reasoning and trying to connect concepts that don't intuitively fit cause much confusion as well. Our data are ideas. Our arguments are theoretical. We use semantic and syntactic criteria to judge arguments for their logical validity. We also judge arguments for their fruitfulness, what benefits they offer society. How will they help us achieve a better life, a more beautiful, truthful, caring and just life?

For a child growing up during the 1960s, there were many troubling problems to draw my attention: the civil rights movement, the women's right movement, the Vietnam war, the cold war, concerns about ecological destruction, apartheid in South Africa, as examples. My attention was not drawn to schools. I couldn't wait to get out of school! Then, I had children. I began to worry about their education, as most parents do. I could critique public schools for their problem, and express my concerns with sending my children. However, I didn't become enthralled with education until I discovered alternative ideas for how to educate children such as Maria Montessori's (1972, 1977) and A. S. Neill's (1960), and I learned about schools such as Summerhill, Montessori, and Waldorf schools, that are very different from what I experienced as a child. Once I discovered these alternative educational ideas, I was hooked. I began to imagine all sorts of possibilities for educating my own and others' children. Without knowing it, I had discovered the world of "philosophy of education." My philosophy degree combined with a Montessori elementary teaching credential and a master's degree in education became a doctorate in philosophy of education, and my path was laid. I have traveled that path with four children in tow, helping to start a Montessori school three of them attended. I served as a consultant for the local Montessori school my fourth child attended. Even though my children are all grown, I still spend time in the schools, missing my elementary classroom and wanting to stay in touch with what life is like for teachers and students. I design research projects that require me to spend time in schools and my partner works in an inner-city high school, thus helping to keep me in tune with conditions in schools.

My overall task in this chapter is to make the case for the value of philosophy of education as a field of study, for educators, whether as parents, teachers in schools, professors in teacher education programs, or researchers in higher education. It is fitting that I write this chapter now, as I find myself having to defend my value and existence on many levels. This is my chance to make my case. I began by way of this introduction, to position myself as a parent, teacher, and scholar. I plan to layout in section one some historical context to the field of philosophy of education. In section two I'll place the field of philosophy of education within the historical context of educational foundations for teacher education programs. In section three I'll turn to a description of current conditions for educational foundations and philosophy of education in particular in America's colleges of education. Throughout, I'll explore ways and reasons to revive the discipline within colleges of education.

Philosophy's Relevance to Education, Historically

Many of us who teach philosophy of education offer a course that explores historical philosophical contributions to current educational practices. At the University of Tennessee that course is titled "Development of Educational Thought." In that course I look at key classical Euro-Western philosophers whose ideas have influenced educational thought and practice in the United States. For me, it's important for educators to understand that philosophy from the past is still relevant. For example, Plato's *Republic* is an important classical work for current teachers to understand for many reasons. Plato's *Republic* is a thought experiment in an effort to define virtue, where he looks at virtue in a large way (by looking at a virtuous nation/state) as his method to understand virtue in a small way (virtuous individuals). Plato tries to describe an ideal, just nation/state and considers in depth what kind of education would be necessary to help such a state exist. He makes the argument that a just state would offer all of its future citizens a free education (paid for by the state). For Plato, this public education would be for girls as well as boys, and for children whose parents were farmers, and merchants, as well as warriors and politicians. The role of the education system is to help the state sift and sort its future citizens and find what they do best, so that they can contribute their talents to the state. Contributing one's talents to the life of the nation/state is what makes one virtuous. The educational system Plato describes helps locate future leaders as well as artists, soldiers, and craftspeople. Thomas Jefferson adopted Plato's plan for the Republic in his own plan for a new, very young country he helped found—the United States of America. Jefferson argued for free, public education, for all children, to help citizens learn the skills they need to be active, participating citizens in a democracy, as well as find our future leaders.

Plato's discussion of the importance of public education is still relevant today. People in the United States have differing opinions of how much commitment the nation/state needs to make to the improvement of our schools, whether the federal government should be involved in the business of running schools, or if the running of schools should be handled at the state level (as the U.S. Constitution describes), or at the local level of school boards and professional educators. In the past three decades, debates have raged concerning the value of charter schools, as a way of offering families choices within the U.S. public school system, versus using school vouchers that families receive to help them send their children to private schools. Plato can help us think through the pros and cons of the role of public education.

In the *Republic* Plato argues for the importance of early childhood education and for the value of censorship in planning a child's curriculum. Plato doesn't want young children exposed to bad influences that will harm them. If they must be exposed to "bad or harmful" things, it should be when they are older and better able to protect themselves. These possible bad influences come in many forms for Plato, in terms of poetry and stories, music and drama, as well as in terms of the human beings who care for the children and serve as their role models. His arguments about curriculum and the need for censorship and guidance are just as relevant today as they were in ancient Greece. Today parents and teachers worry about what possible bad influences children might be exposed to through music, television, movies, and currently the Internet. The case is being made for the importance of early childhood education and for the need to protect children from teachers who might do them harm by requiring finger printing of teachers, for example. Continually we debate what materials should be included in classroom curriculum, including the teaching of sex education or evolution theory, for example. Plato's discussion of censorship and early childhood education can help us think through these issues.

Plato is credited with starting the first university in ancient Greece, and his famous teacher, Socrates, is credited with modeling for us a style of teaching that is still highly regarded, the Socratic method. Plato shows us how Socrates taught through the dialogues Plato wrote, for in those dialogues Socrates is positioned as the teacher who models for us what philosophers do through the questions he asks in his conversations with others and the efforts he makes to clarify ambiguity, order logical reasoning, and justify claims with evidence that will stand up to critical analysis. When I was in college and graduate school, the Socratic method was highly acclaimed as helping students become good critical thinkers, and there were several popular television shows during this time period that modeled Socratic-style teaching in high school classrooms, and law schools, for example. When educators take up the debate about how to become more professionalized with improved working conditions, better salaries, and higher standards, and discussions about how to reward good teaching come to the foreground, concerns about how to make the evaluation process fair for teachers seem to often come back to Socrates, as an example of an excellent teacher who would probably not receive merit pay. He asked too many questions and didn't seem to know the answers to his questions. He pushed and prodded his students, and they didn't like it. He was short on tact, and didn't dress properly. He didn't publish anything. Clearly Socrates would receive poor evaluation scores and would not get a merit raise! Yet, we still know about him today because he was such a good teacher. He serves as an excellent illustration of the problem of how to fairly judge good teachers so we can reward them. Using students' test scores as a way to judge favors teachers who work with higher income children and gifted and talented children, for example, not children with special needs, or children from low-income areas, which in a racist society tends to be minority children. If we rely on test scores, then special education teachers, inner city teachers, or rural teachers will not receive merit raises like their colleagues in wealthier suburban areas. Is that fair? What result will come from such a practice? Who will be helped and who will be harmed? Will these rewards achieve the results hoped for, encouraging less talented teachers to improve and helping excellent teachers to feel appreciated and valued? These are the kinds of questions philosophers of education ask.

Plato influenced another famous philosopher, Aristotle, who was enrolled as a student in his university and then went on to start his own university. In *Development of Educational Thought*, after reading Plato's *Republic*, we move on to read Aristotle's *Politics* and *Nichomachaen Ethics*, for Aristotle had a tremendous influence on American education as well. Aristotle agrees with his teacher, Plato, about the importance of the state offering education to its future citizens, so that those students can grow up to be the kinds of citizens the state needs. However, for Aristotle, public education should only be available to what he considered Greek citizens: property-owning males. In the United States, that same definition of "citizenship" was carried forward in our own constitution, for while the language said, "all people are created equal" and have "certain inalienable rights," the definition of citizenship was meant for property-owning males, not the working class, females, or slaves. It took many years and significant historical events such as a civil war, an industrial revolution and a tremendous influx of immigrants, as well as the women's suffrage movement to make the case for everyone in the United States to have the same rights first granted to property-owning males.

Surely the issue of a free and equitable education is still an important topic for educators, as we are still trying to recover from the exclusionary definition of citizenship upon which the United States was founded. The founders of the country who started with the wealth made off the backs of slave and working-class labor have been able to pass that wealth on to their children for generation after generation, and while their children were attending exclusive private schools or having private tutors, others were fighting for the fundamental right for their children to be taught in schools (Spring, 2009). The United States has a history of high levels of discrepancy in educational quality and opportunities due to the wealth of its citizens, for it has always had a private school and public school educational system, and it has never committed to more than an "adequate" education for its children who can't afford private school tuition rates or tutors or who don't live in areas of the country where the higher property taxes are passed on to the public school systems (Kozol, 1991). We have made progress since this country was first formed, but there is still plenty of room for improvement. Considering Aristotle's position and exploring his philosophy helps us better understand our own past and how we manage to be in our current educational debt situation (Ladson-Billings, 2006).

Taking into consideration his own teacher's influence as well as the influence of the larger Greek society, Aristotle is the philosopher most credited with making a solid argument for the value of a liberal education, meaning for him one that is balanced and harmonious and will lead us to live a free, good life of happiness. For Aristotle, a happy life is one where we use to our fullest capacity the quality that makes us most human, our ability to reason; therefore, a happy life is a contemplative life. In order to live a balanced life, Aristotle argues that our education should include a study of the arts (for him the discussion focuses on music), as well as the study of more academic subjects such as science, mathematics, and language. Aristotle also recommends physical education for our bodies as a balance to the curriculum that develops our minds.

We can see Aristotle's influence today in liberal arts colleges that offer students an opportunity to explore the arts, mathematics, hard sciences, and social sciences, as well as encouraging them to take physical education classes and participate in sports. Many students today choose to attend small liberal arts colleges in order to receive a "well-rounded" education, one that is balanced. Even in large state schools like the one where I teach, all students are required to take general education courses (usually from a list of many possible choices) to give them a balanced base of education, no matter what their major is. At many large state universities, the College of Arts and Sciences is still the most popular college, where students can create a balanced, liberal arts degree, before they go on to a career or graduate level work that is more narrowly focused. Aristotle helps us critique our current loss of balance where, for example, most high school programs across the United States have cut their physical education (PE) requirements and now routinely require no more than 1 year of PE (when I was in high school I had PE every day for four years). At the same time, we complain that our children aren't getting enough exercise and are becoming obese. Aristotle reminds us how important the arts are to a well-rounded education, as today's children are required to take more and more math and science classes just to get their high school diplomas, while arts teachers are laid off and arts programs fight for their continued existence.

Mortimer Adler (1982) used Aristotle's basic argument for the value of liberal education to make the case that we have created "shopping mall" high schools with too many choices where children make poor choices and do not graduate with the same, high quality degree as a result (Powell, Farrar, & Cohen, 1985). In *The Paideia Proposal*, he argues that all students should have to take the same balanced curriculum in order to guarantee that all our children graduate with the same quality education, thus equating sameness with equality. Their only choice is what foreign language they want to take. In contrast to Adler, Nel Noddings (1992), as a former math teacher, writes about the harms caused to children who are all forced into the same mold, for children are not all the same. She argues that it is not only unnecessary, it is unethical to force all children to take three (now in many states it is four) years of mathematics, and cause them to fail or drop out, before they are able to choose an arts program or vocational education program, for example, to fulfill their needs and develop their talents. For Noddings, an equal education is not one that is the same for all children. Aristotle can serve as a source to help all arts and physical education teachers today make the case for their importance in our children's education.

I have only offered two examples here of two very famous philosophers who continue to contribute much to our current thinking about educational issues. In "Development of Educational Thought" we also look at Locke, Rousseau, James, and Dewey's ideas, and consider their significant impacts on American education that are still felt today. One could easily include: Augustine, Aquinas, Calvin, Luther, Kant, Pestalozzi, Montessori, Mccaulay, and Wollstonecraft as famous philosophers from the past who have contributed to our educational thinking today (Cahn, 2009; Martin, 1985; Titone & Maloney, 1999). I have included many of them in earlier versions of my course. Now, I bring women's voices into the conversation right from the start and offer a cultural studies critique to the work of these iconic Euro-Western scholars with the help of Jane Roland Martin (1986), Susan Okin (1979), and Charlene Haddock Seigfried (1996). We read the original writings of the philosophers, not secondary sources discussing their ideas, and students are surprised to find how accessible and relevant the ideas are. Philosophers who have thought deeply about educational issues in the past can still help us to think through issues and how to improve educational conditions for all children.

Philosophy's Position in Relation to Colleges of Education

When I was applying to college in 1970–71, students who wanted to be teachers applied to places that used to be called "normal schools" and became "teachers colleges," described as "professional schools for the training of teachers." It wasn't until the late 1800s and early 1900s that universities began housing departments of education that became schools of education and then colleges of education by the mid-1900s (Allison, 1998). Many attribute the philosopher, John Dewey (1859–1952), with helping to give the field of education enough status, intellectually, that we began to see educational programs in research universities. Dewey had a long, distinguished career as a philosopher who wrote extensively about educational issues, and he is often described as the father of present philosophy of education in the United States. Dewey began his career at the University of Michigan (1884) where he spent ten years before moving in his middle years to the recently founded University of Chicago (1894–1904), where he started and directed an educational laboratory school that became very famous, a school which his own children attended and where his wife, Alice Chipman Dewey, served as principal. Dewey spent his later years at Teachers College and Columbia University, in New York City (1904–1930).

When I started college at Pennsylvania State University in the 1970s there were still many educational lab schools around the country connected to colleges of education, including one at Indiana University. When I went to graduate school at Indiana University, I discovered there were many faculty who still thought of the college of education as an unwanted step-child that had no business being in a research university, even though Indiana University's college of education was ranked among the top ten in the country. Education was viewed by many as a professional degree, similar to business, with a similar status level. I would argue that today business has risen in status in American society, while education still struggles to be taken seriously and still finds it has to defend its own existence in research one level universities. As evidence that this struggle still exists, the last time my university faced an economic slowdown and a budget crisis, the chancellor proposed collapsing the colleges of nursing, social work, human ecology, and education together, even though the college of education has the second highest enrollment numbers of any college at the university, and its students' tuition fees contribute significantly to the cost of educating students in the hard sciences areas. No one proposed collapsing the college of business with any other college, such as the college of communication and information, even though they are smaller in size.

Historically, philosophers who focused on educational issues, like John Dewey or William James, received their graduate degrees in philosophy, not education departments. Programs in colleges of education that offered philosophy of education degrees, like what I earned at Indiana University, used to be housed in philosophy departments only. Philosophy of education programs housed in colleges of education have been developed in the past sixty years or so by such imminent scholars as Israel Scheffler, at Harvard University, and Jonas Soltis and Maxine Greene at Teachers College (Waks, 2008). When Dewey joined the faculty at Columbia in 1904, his position was in the philosophy department, and several biographies I have searched do not even mention that he also had a position as a philosopher with Teachers College, which became affiliated with Columbia University in 1898, prior to Dewey's arrival. Teachers College is located on West 120th Street, directly across the street from Columbia University, and yet it is "the widest street in New York City." The two campuses retain legal and financial independence.

When I joined the Philosophy of Education Society (est. 1942) in 1990 there were still plenty of philosophers arguing about whether they should be located in philosophy departments within colleges of arts and sciences, or in educational foundations departments along with their colleagues in history, sociology, and anthropology of education, in colleges of education. High among philosophers of educations concerns has been a fear of "loss of status" when they step into colleges of education. There are highly regarded programs that offer degrees in philosophy of education, such as the one I attended or the one at University of Illinois, Champaign-Urbana, that are housed in colleges of education. However, when an opening develops for a philosopher of education, at the elite universities there is still a tendency to hire someone with a philosophy degree who specializes in educational issues over someone with a philosophy of education degree. The lesser status from being directly connected to a college of education is still with us.

For many philosophers, a job in a college of education as a philosopher of education is a "fall back" position, if one is unable to get a job in a philosophy department. This is not different from many college students' views, less prevalent today than when I was in college but still existing, that getting a job as a teacher is a "fall back" position, if one is unable to get a job in their chosen field. It hurts the field of education to have people working in it who don't want to be there and only end up there because they don't have a better option. Now that I have been a parent and school-teacher, I feel very strongly that I don't want anyone teaching my children who doesn't care passionately about education. I want only the best and brightest teaching my children, people who love to learn and know how to help keep my children's love of learning alive. I know now that teaching is the most important job one can have, and being a teacher is an incredibly difficult, challenging job with tremendous frustration and reward. Unfortunately, many of my colleagues in philosophy of education have never been teachers in K-12 grade schools and only have teaching experience in higher education. Their lack of experience, and often lack of understanding and respect for the job of K-12 teaching as a result, positions them as outsiders to teacher education programs, even though they have the intellectual skills to make significant contributions to the field. These positions of superiority/inferiority are not recipes for good working relationships between philosophers of education and their colleagues in teacher education programs or for being perceived as important teachers in the lives of the future-teachers they teach about philosophy of education. We, philosophers of education, have hurt ourselves if we have treated the work we do in colleges of education as a consolation prize that is beneath our capacities. With that kind of attitude, we cannot possibly be good teachers who help our students and colleagues understand the important roles philosophy can play for education.

The fault does not lie only on the shoulders of philosophers of education, for I am someone who is also a licensed teacher (licensed as an Montessori elementary teacher, a private school teacher in Pennsylvania, a K-12 teacher in California, and a K-12 teacher in Indiana), with more experience teaching in K-12 schools than many of my colleagues no matter what their field of study (seven years), with four children who have gone through the U.S. school system and a spouse who teaches in an inner-city public high school, yet some of my colleagues want to position me as disconnected from the schools and irrelevant to the education of future teachers. This judgment of my irrelevance and disconnect from educational issues is not based on what my colleagues know about me or my work, for many of them know little about me, but rather more likely based on their own past experiences with professors of philosophy of education. I often feel I am fighting prejudices formed by others who came before me, not formed by anything I have done. So, while I work hard to help my students understand philosophy's relevance to their lives as teachers, I must also work hard to help my colleagues understand the importance of my field of study for building strong teacher education programs and making important contributions to educational research. Let me look more closely from these two different angles at what philosophers of education can and do contribute.

Philosophy's Relevance to Colleges of Education

For nine years I worked for one of the United States's largest teacher education colleges, a former "normal school" for teacher training, Bowling Green State University, in Ohio. At the time I worked there, around 800 new students enrolled in teacher education each year. By the time I arrived in 1991, the university seemed to have forgotten its roots in teacher education, and during the 1990s the college fought hard to maintain lines as faculty retired. I started with a strong educational foundations program of seven faculty, including three philosophers, one of whom was head of a department. By the time I went up for tenure, our department of twenty-one faculty had shrunk to ten tenured faculty able to vote on my case. As people retired, they were often not replaced. Yet, the number of students did not diminish during this time frame. I don't think BGSU was unique in this experience; all across the U.S. colleges and universities used the 1990s as an opportunity to cut faculty lines as professors who were hired to accommodate increases in enrollment retired.

Our college of education and allied professions (what used to be home economics and early childhood education, as well as physical education) had to worry about fighting for faculty lines in competition with other colleges across the campus. The college also experienced pressure from the increase of state and national standards for teacher education during the 1990s. BGSU's teacher education program was an undergraduate degree, held to state standards in terms of how many credits it could require of its students to earn their degree. The state wanted to assure parents their children could graduate in four years, thus BGSU held its required number to 120 credits. At the same time, the state increased requirements teachers must meet to earn their license: for example, one year the state decided all teachers in Ohio should have a phonics reading course. This put the teacher education programs in a vise, as they could not add any courses without dropping some.

When I started teaching at BGSU, I taught "Introduction to Education" to sophomores, and "Teachers, Schools, and Society" to juniors or seniors. My department also housed other "service courses" taught to all education majors, such as "Educational Psychology" and an assessment course titled "Tests and Measurement." The faculty who taught the methods courses for teacher education out-numbered those of us who taught the service courses, and they voted to cut and condense our courses, instead of changing their own. The national board that certifies teacher education programs (NCATE) helped out in this process of cutting educational foundations courses from teacher education, as NCATE used to require all teachers to have a background in educational foundations (history and philosophy of education), through courses taught by a faculty member with a doctoral degree in one of those fields. During the 1990s the educational foundations became more associated with multicultural education and cultural diversity issues as well as ethics, and less with the general knowledge of history and philosophy of education. At the same time, NCATE changed its requirements so they were no longer based on course offerings, but instead were based on teacher candidacy dispositions. Without educational foundations courses being required for teacher certification, it wasn't long before the methods teacher education faculty were deciding they could cut the educational foundations courses from their teacher education programs and claim that they teach about cultural diversity and ethics in their methods courses. Now educational foundations programs are almost entirely gone from colleges of education, and instead we find one or two educational foundations faculty tucked into varying programs such as instructional technology, educational psychology and counseling, curriculum and instruction, or educational leadership and policy studies.

I moved to a research one level college of education in 2000, with the hope of having more time to work on my own research in philosophy of education, as well as have the opportunity to work with masters and doctoral students in my field of study. At the University of Tennessee teacher education is a graduate program, following the Holmes Group (1986) model that requires students to earn a bachelor's degree in their field of study, and then a teaching license as a fifth year. When the students complete their intern year in the schools, they are only twelve credits shy of a master's degree in education. Most of the students go on to complete that master's degree. Once again I have been witness to the shrinking of educational foundations as a field of study during the past eight years, as the college continues to have to address NCATE standards, while also dealing with new social pressures.

Colleges of education have come under national criticism for supposedly not doing a good job of training teachers, as teachers have come under a great deal of criticism for not doing a good job of teaching all of our children. Earlier sociological research such as the Coleman Report (1966) that demonstrated families are much more influential on students' success in schools than teachers, seems to be forgotten. No Child Left Behind (NCLB, Public Law 107–110), passed by Congress in 2001, and signed into law by President George W. Bush in January 2002, places the blame for children not getting a good education in the United States squarely on teachers' shoulders. During Bush's presidency, public schools came under extreme scrutiny and so did teacher education programs. States are offering parents more choices as to where to enroll their children through development of charter schools and offering school vouchers. States are also offering potential teachers alternative routes to teaching licenses, through online licensing programs as well as programs like Teach for America (www.teachforamerica.org). Colleges of education are dealing with economic and social pressures to maintain the quality of their programs, or enhance them, while not having the means to do so, in terms of having the resources to hire more faculty and increase course requirements. In the latest round of NCATE review, our college decided to cut the one 2–credit course students took in educational foundations (remember, I used to teach two 3–credit courses to all future teachers at BGSU), in order to address the students' perceived weaknesses in assessing students and identifying and working with students with special education needs. What is lost to colleges of education with the loss of philosophy of education?

My colleagues at BGSU (Pigge & Marso, 1987; Marso & Pigge, 1997) conducted exit interview surveys with students as they graduated from our teacher education programs and asked students what courses they thought were most valuable and did they have any professors who made a significant impact on their education? I am proud to say there were students who named me as such a professor, but unfortunately our educational foundations courses were not identified as high on their list of "most valuable courses," at the time of their graduation. However, the faculty conducted the same survey five years after the students graduated and had been in the schools teaching, and the educational foundations courses came to the top of former students' list of most valuable courses taken at BGSU. Before they became teachers, they wanted courses that told them, this is what I need to do, tomorrow, to be a good teacher. They wanted "nuts and bolts" courses that gave them specific directions for success. Educational foundations courses helped them place schooling within a larger social context, which they didn't think they needed to know, until they got into the schools.

Our educational foundations courses help teachers understand how the role of teaching has evolved and changed over time. Instead of giving them just a micro view from within the classroom, these courses also give them a macro view that places the current institution of schooling within a larger social, political, and economic context as well as within a larger historical and philosophical context. Educational foundations courses give teachers the tools they need to better understand why teachers' working conditions are what they are, how they have changed over time, and the forces that have brought about those changes. Educational foundations courses help teachers understand the ways that families have changed over time and the kinds of pressures that affect them, such as job changes due to moving from an agrarian society to an industrial society, to now a global society. Educational foundations courses help teachers understand the kind of value, or lack there of, our society places on public education, for example, and how this has changed over time, and continues to do so. Educational foundations courses give teachers the tools they need to know how to research cultural diversity issues and learn more about the diverse cultures their students represent, as well as understand the past schooling experiences their students' parents experienced, that make them hesitant to volunteer in their child's school or distrustful of their child's teacher. They can better understand the discrimination that the parents experienced when they were children in school, when they were punished for having the wrong accent or the wrong skin color, for example. These courses help teachers understand the kinds of pressures their students' parents might be under, due to economic issues and how their economic positions might be tied to histories of racism in the United States.

Courses such as the philosophy of education courses I teach also help teachers in their efforts to become professionals, and treated by our society as professionals. They help them understand the value of theory to support practice, so they are not just apprenticing through internship programs in schools without understanding why certain practices work and others don't. Instead, they are learning about the educational research that exists in support of best practices of teaching in schools. The teachers learn that all fields of study that have developed into professions, such as medicine and business, have done so with the help of extensive research and theory to support daily practice. These theoretical courses help teachers think through their goals for education and develop reasons to support their intended aims. They help teachers learn how to listen generously to parents, colleagues, and administrators, and seek to understand diverse positions on various educational issues, while also learning how to make their case and defend their position, by being able to give good reasons and cite solid research to support their positions.

It has been my continuing position during my career in education that all teachers face philosophical issues on a daily basis. They cannot avoid these. They have to decide what to teach (what to leave in and what to leave out of their curriculum), how to teach (which methods of instruction will they use to support their intended aims?), how to assess their teaching (grading issues), and how to handle discipline issues such as the child who cheats on her test, or the student who bullies another student and calls him "gay." All teachers are philosophers, whether they realize this or not. Maybe the fact that I came to education after already earning a degree in philosophy helped me understand this and be able to name the decisions I had to make for what they were. Decisions about how to discipline children and address their behavior put teachers squarely in the realm of ethics with questions about what is good behavior. Trying to consider my role as a teacher in terms of authority and how I wield it embroils me in issues involving social justice and power. So do questions concerning the role of students, and how to teach them to be future citizens in a way that support aims of fairness and justice, for example. What to leave in and out of curriculum are epistemological concerns about what is important to pass on to our children from the past. These are decisions that no teacher can avoid for we are all limited in terms of how much time we have with our students. Curriculum decisions require judgment calls concerning truth and what counts as knowledge. How do we measure our students' knowledge and judge the correctness of their solutions, based on what criteria? These are epistemological questions as well. Curriculum decisions also involve aesthetics, for teachers must address questions about the kinds of materials they will use, such as Montessori's decision to use attractive teaching materials made from wood or glass beads (her math materials) in order to draw children to the materials and help the children develop an appreciation of beauty, as well as their love of learning. What we take to be our essential, basic categories that help us make sense of our world and guide us in how we relate to each other as well as the living, breathing world in which we live are ontological concerns. The philosophical issues I had to face on a daily basis as an elementary teacher, and continue to face as a professor in higher education, are what keep me fascinated and challenged in the work I do as a philosopher in education.

I seek to help teachers understand that they are philosophers, just like me, and that is a good thing to be, if they want to be professionals in their fields of study (Thayer-Bacon with Bacon, 1998). I encourage and support their efforts to become better philosophers as I work with them to help them see how their daily lives as teachers are full of examples of philosophical questions and concerns. I often feel like my role is to be a translator, someone who makes philosophical texts more accessible to teachers, for even though the language is common it can be obtuse and dense at times. I help to make connections through examples, just as I have demonstrated through this chapter, and I encourage my students to do the same. The more we do this in class through our discussions and in our writing assignments, the better philosophers of education we become. The more we improve our philosophical skills, the better we are able to reason our way through our educational problems, and think about how best to solve them. Yes, we live in a world where we have limited resources and more needs than we can possibly meet in a day, or week, or year. But now we have some tools to help us clear up our confusions and miscommunications and make the case for why we need to use our limited resources this way instead of that, for we know what we are aiming for; we have a vision of where we want to go, and we know why that is the best way to go, the right way, the fair way, the most caring and rational and just way, the way that will lead us toward goodness, growth, beauty, and happiness. These are important contributions philosophy makes to education.

Conclusion

I used to start my philosophy of education classes for future teachers by asking the students to consider why they want to be teachers. (I say "used to" because this course is no longer one that our future teachers take at UT.) I asked them to think about what was the most important thing they wanted to teach their students, so important that even if the students forgot the specific subject matter they taught (what a preposition is, what an algebraic equation is, how to conjugate verbs in Spanish), the teachers hoped their students didn't forget this. How to work well with others and care for each other, how to keep their love of learning alive, how to develop to their full potential, how to be an active, engaged citizen of the world, how to live in a sustainable world, are all examples of strong aims. We spent the semester trying to help them find sources (other philosophers) to help them articulate their own vision. I wanted them to be able to articulate this vision to themselves and any future employer, "This is what I believe in and it is so important to me, that if I am unable to achieve this aim, I don't want to be a teacher at this school." It is not easy to think through and find one's core values, it requires a lot of digging, and stripping away, and bracketing out, to discover what is so important to you, that as long as you can maintain that goal you will be able to keep on working hard to achieve it, no matter what roadblocks are thrown in your way.

Having the opportunity to write this chapter has reminded me how important I think philosophy is to education, and that I must not give up trying to help others understand its importance. I originally went into the field of education hoping to find ways to keep my own children's love of learning alive. I went into teaching future teachers in higher education because I wanted to help them realize they need to ask, why do we do the things we do? What are the pros and cons to how we have structured our schools and classrooms? Are there other ways to teach our children, maybe even better ways? I wanted to help future teachers learn how to look at education as if it could be otherwise. That is my challenge to us all, for philosophy pushes and prods us to continue to critique what is and imagine what should be ideally. It remind us, we can never rest and feel assured that our work is done for there is always room for improvement. That is the definition of an ideal.

References

Adler, M. (1982). *The Paideia proposal: An educational manifesto*. New York: Collier.
Allison, C. (1998). *Teachers for the South: Pedagogy and educationists in the University of Tennessee, 1844–1995*. New York: Peter Lang.
Aristotle. (2009). *Nichomachaen ethics*. In S. Cahn (ed.), *Philosophy of education: The essential texts* (pp. 109–132). New York: Routledge.
Aristotle. (2009). *Politics*. In S. Cahn (ed.), *Philosophy of education: The essential texts* (pp. 133–147). New York: Routledge.
Cahn, S. (ed.). (2009). *Philosophy of education: The essential texts*. New York: Routledge.
Coleman, J. S. (1966). Equality of educational opportunity study (EEOS). ICPSR06389-v3. Washington, DC: U.S. Department of Health, Education, and Welfare.
Dewey, J. (1916, 1944, 1966). *Democracy and education* (3d ed.). New York: Free Press.
Dewey, J. (1922). *Human nature and conduct*. New York: Henry Holt.
Greene, M. (1995). *Releasing the imagination*. San Francisco: Jossey-Bass.
The Holmes Group. (1986). Tomorrow's teachers: A report of The Holmes Group. East Lansing, MI: The Holmes Group.
Kozol, J. (1991). *Savage inequalities*. New York: Crown.
Ladson-Billings, G. (October, 2006). From the achievement gap to the educational debt: Understanding achievement in U. S. schools, *Educational Researcher*, 35(7): 3–12.
Marso, R. N., & Pigge, F. L. (1997). A longitudinal study of persisting and nonpersisting teachers' academic and personal characteristics, *Journal of Experimental Education*, 65: 243–254.
Martin, J. R. (1985). *Reclaiming a conversation*. New Haven, CT: Yale University Press.
Mead, M. (1970). *Culture and commitment*. Garden City, NY: American Museum of Natural History Natural History Press/Doubleday.
Montessori, M. (1972). *The discovery of the child* (2d ed.). (Trans.) M. Josephy Costelloe. New York: Ballantine.
Montessori, M. (1977). *The secret of childhood* (2d ed.). (Trans.) M. Josephy Costelloe. New York: Ballantine.
Neill, A. S. (1960). *Summerhill: A radical approach to child rearing*. New York: Hart.
Noddings, N. (1992). *The challenge to care in schools: An alternative approach to education*. New York: Teachers College Press.
Okin, S. (1979). *Women in Western political thought*. Princeton, NJ: Princeton University Clint Press.
Pigge, F. L., & Marso, R. N. (1987). Relationships between student characteristics and changes in attitudes, concerns, anxieties, and confidence about teaching during teacher preparation. *Journal of Educational Research*, 81(2): 109–115.
Plato. (1979). *Republic* (R. Larson, Ed. & Trans.). Arlington Heights, IL: Harlan Davidson.
Powell, A. G., Farrar, E., & Cohen, D. K. (1985). *The shopping mall high school: Winners and losers in the educational marketplace*. Boston: Houghton Mifflin Co.
Richard, R. (1989). *Contingency, irony, and solidarity*. Cambridge: Cambridge University Press.

Seigfried, C. H. (1996). *Pragmatism and feminism: Reweaving the social fabric*. Chicago: University of Chicago Press.
Spring, J. (2009). *Deculturalization and the struggle for equality: A brief history of the education of dominated cultures in the U.S.* (6th ed.). New York: McGraw Hill.
Steiner, R., school, http://www.steiner.edu/
Teach for America, www.teachforamerica.org.
Thayer-Bacon, B. (2000). *Transforming critical thinking: Thinking constructively*. New York: Teachers College Press.
Thayer-Bacon, B. with Bacon, C. (1998). *Philosophy applied to education: Nurturing a democratic community in the classroom*. Upper Saddle River, NJ: Prentice Hall.
Titone, C., & Maloney, K. (1999). *Women's philosophies of education: Thinking through our mothers*. Upper Saddle River, NJ: Prentice Hall.
Waks, L. (ed.). (2008). *Leaders in philosophy of education: Intellectual self portraits*. Rotterdam, The Netherlands: Sense.
Waldorf Education, http://en.wikipedia.org/wiki/Waldorf_education.

Twelve

Cultivating Unique Potential in Schools: Revisioning Democratic Teacher Education

Craig A. Cunningham

> Democracy cannot flourish where the chief influences in selecting subject matter of instruction are utilitarian ends narrowly conceived for the masses, and, for the higher education of the few, the traditions of a specialized cultivated class. The notion that the "essentials" of elementary education are the three R's mechanically treated, is based upon ignorance of the essentials needed for realization of democratic ideals. Unconsciously it assumes that these ideals are unrealizable; it assumes that in the future, as in the past, getting a livelihood, "making a living," must dignify for most men and women doing things which are not significant, freely chosen, and ennobling to those who do them; doing things which serve ends unrecognized by those engaged in them, carried on under the direction of others for the sake of pecuniary reward.
> —John Dewey, *Democracy and Education* (1916/1890, 200)

The primary purpose of schools in a democratic society is to prepare citizens to participate fully and responsibly in public life. While this includes preparation for a career, this should be secondary to cultivating the knowledge, skills and attitudes that make democratic life possible, including knowledge of the history and purposes of democracy, the skills necessary for deliberation and public consideration of important issues, and attitudes such as tolerance, respect, belief in fairness, and a sense of responsibility. Public schools have an obligation to ensure that each citizen acquires a basic understanding of those responsibilities as well as the capacities necessary to carry them out.

Teacher education ensures that teachers are prepared to structure learning environments so that youngsters achieve these goals. For this to happen, teachers must themselves know the content and possess the skills and attitudes that they are trying to develop in their students. In addition, they must have a sound understanding of learning theory, experience in applying pedagogical methods to particular subject-matter, and tools for continuously improving their practice using local evidence and published evidence. Awareness of historical and contemporary social trends and familiarity with local cultural conditions helps them to maintain a sense of the wider context of their work. These topics and more are covered in required courses in the disciplines, learning psychology, pedagogy, research, and sociology.

However, even if teachers are in possession of all of this content and the attitudes that go with them, they may still lack something critical, which can only be provided through philosophy of education: a sound understanding of how democracy works and why it is desirable, not only for the larger society but for the fullest development of individuals. Democracy's effects on individuals and the individual characteristics that help it flourish are not well understood by most contemporary Americans, including many of those studying to become teachers. This lack of understanding means that schools often become focused primarily on the teaching of particular knowledge and skill as defined by contemporary learning standards, which emphasize only those topics and capacities that can be easily measured with standardized tests. What's more, in an economic context of corporate capitalism, schools are easily diverted into serving the interests that corporations have in securing particular types of workers and consumers. In such an environment, both the public good and personal fulfillment are shoved aside in favor of a purely instrumental education that treats individuals as mere economic instruments rather than as ends in themselves.

To talk about personal fulfillment or the public good these days is to risk being labeled an idealist, a spiritualist, or even a socialist. Contemporary culture—shaped as it is by the popular media with its corporate affiliations—marginalizes idealists, as if they are not in touch with the "real" world. The wider culture emphasizes a kind of materialistic realism, "freedom" of consumer choice, and the allegedly morally valuable dispositions toward entrepreneurship and delayed gratification. "Be real," "let me choose," "achieve the American dream," and "work hard so that you can enjoy your leisure" are the mantras of the age, and these very easily become the mantras of schools and teachers as well, especially if they lack an alternative vision (Schor, 2004).

In this chapter, I want to challenge the notion that schools should primarily serve this corporatized contemporary culture. I want to argue that schools should have as their number one priority the promotion of democracy, even if that means working against contemporary social trends. But the conception of democracy that I will offer here is not the common procedural conception of a democracy as a society in which each individual gets a vote. The democracy I want to describe builds on John Dewey's conception of democracy but goes well beyond that to include the wisdom of the ancient Greeks (supplemented with a bit of Zen Buddhism) and insights gained by a radical transformation currently underway in educational philosophy. This vision of democracy comprehends not only a more compelling sense of the purpose of individual and social life, but a more effective approach to democratic pedagogy as well.

Education for Democracy

Typically, democracy is considered to describe a form of government in which power is held by the people or—more commonly in today's nation-states—by those who represent the people. Democracy is contrasted to oligarchy and monarchy, in which power is held by a small group of elites or by one person. History as taught in schools often describes a struggle for democracy as a struggle for human rights, liberation, and equality for previously marginalized groups. Indeed, because democracies benefit from taking into account not only the views of majorities but of minority groups as well, democracies typically protect the rights of minorities against the potential tyranny of a majority with a binding constitution or statement of human rights. Equality is central to this conception of democracy—at least in its ideal form—for even with a procedural commitment to including every person in decision-making, gross inequality of resources or power will skew decisions toward the interests of the powerful. Democratic decision-making also requires a degree of political freedom, or liberty, so that individuals and groups can express themselves fully in public discourse; otherwise any claim that their perspective has been fairly considered will be a farce.

John Dewey believed that democracy is more than a form of government; it is "primarily a mode of associated living, of conjoint communicated experience" (Dewey, 1916/1980, p. 93) characterized by both freedom of association among groups in the society and with other societies and by a commitment to developing shared interests in the process of decision-making. Participation in shared decision-making requires continual communication among the members of the society so that each person maintains a strong sense of the perspectives of other members as they engage in dialog about mutually beneficial forms of social action. In the process, citizens often refine their private desires as well, while building the capacity for imagination, sensitivity, and self-reflection and subjecting their personal interests to implicit critique by the interests of others (Snauwaert, 1993; Mill, 1861; Rousseau, 1762). For Dewey, a democratic society seeks to utilize "plural, partial, and experimental methods in securing and maintaining an ever-increasing release of the powers of human nature, in service of a freedom which is cooperative and a cooperation which is voluntary" (1939; 187). Participation in this democratic approach to inquiry was, for Dewey, not only central to democratic life but also an effective form of education for democracy, leading him to an abiding commitment to making schools into a form of social life rather than mere preparation for such a life (Johnston, 2006).

The multiple perspectives that one encounters in a democracy cause each person to continually reconstruct their own experiences—to refine their ideas and habits—thus releasing more of their individual potentialities. This release, Dewey writes, is the very function of social institutions:

> All social institutions have a meaning, a purpose. That purpose is to set free and to develop the capacity of human individuals without respect to race, sex, class, or economic status. And this is all one with saying that the test of their value is the extent to which they educate every individual into the full stature of his possibility. Democracy has many meanings, but if it has a moral meaning, it is found in resolving that the supreme test of all political institutions and industrial arrangements shall be the contribution they make to the all-around growth of every member of society. (1920/1988, p. 186)

The connection of democracy and education is clear: a society is democratic to the extent that each member of the society is able to develop themselves fully. While Dewey continued to write about this democratic criterion over his long entire career—and, occasionally, to remark on what it might mean to have an education for democratic participation—his writings about education became gradually abstracted from the demands of actual teaching within schools as institutions, and the task of describing what might be meant by "education for democracy" was largely left to others. For this and other reasons, Dewey's actual influence on American schools was quite limited, leaving them susceptible to the more systematic and apparently scientific methods of educational psychologists, which were more easily adapted to the demands of mass education and more readily co-opted to the perceived needs of corporate interests. In a sense, then, Dewey failed in his most important mission. However, he did leave us with many of the tools necessary to reconstruct education for democracy. For a new Deweyan conception to live, though, it needs to be supplemented with some of his own ideas about imagination as well as some other insights from philosophy, psychology, and cultural studies. It is to those insights that I now turn.

Conceptualizing Each Person's Unique Potential Self

A fairly common traditional conception of individuality is that each person has a "higher self," genius soul, or daimon that represents the fullness of one's potential powers. This daimon, often deemed to be given by God and embodying divine purposes, accompanies each person through life and connects her in some special and personal way to her destiny. This view—common to many cultures and historical periods—holds that each person has a unique set of qualities, interests, talents, or potentials, which demand expression if the person is to find fulfillment in life. Plato (1974) wrote of the daimon at the end of his most well-known work, *The Republic*, and in Aristotle's *Nicomachean Ethics* (1962) one finds this idea in the concept of *eudaimonia*—commonly translated as "happiness" but having a richer etymology as "living in harmony with one's higher self"—which represents the highest reward for living virtuously.

Perhaps the best scholarly source for an understanding of the idea of the daimon as it appears in ancient Greek thought is David Norton (1976). Norton suggests that each person's "unique potential excellence" can serve as a guide to making choices with moral consequences, and that the only way a person "can manifest worth in the world is only by living in accordance with his destiny" (1976, 16). Later, after Norton had spent time in Japan studying this idea in Buddhist thought, he wrote:

> There is a distinctive course of life that is right for each individual, amid countless possibilities. This is the individual's vocation, variously termed his or her "genius," "daimon," "Buddha nature," or "atman." It consists in innate potentialities that predispose persons to a particular direction in life. As distinguished from other possibilities, the actualization by an individual of his or her potentialities affords intrinsic rewards to that person—that is, the activity is personally fulfilling and satisfying. Self-knowledge, then, is knowledge of the activities, situations, and relationships that the individual experiences as intrinsically rewarding. Engaged at these, the individual invests the best of himself or herself and strives continuously to improve, while in the process contributing objective values to others. (1995, p. 165)

In *The Soul's Code: In Search of Character and Calling*, James Hillman (1996) explores the cultural implications of this idea, presenting it as a useful frame for understanding human development. Hillman labels this the "acorn theory" to refer to the notion that the acorn contains or presages the potential mature oak, just as the daimon contains or presages the potential fulfilled human being. Hillman writes:

> Each person enters the world called . . . . The soul of each of us is given a unique daimon before we are born, and it has selected an image or pattern that we live on earth. The soul-companion, the daimon, guides us here; in the process of arrival, however, we forget all that took place and believe we come empty into this world. The daimon remembers what is in your image and belongs to your pattern, and therefore your daimon is the carrier of your destiny. (p. 8)

For Hillman, the daimon has the individual's "interest at heart" (p. 12), preserves him or her from harm, and sometimes provides a "call" to a particular profession or activity that "rings loud and persistent and is as demanding as any scolding voice from the surroundings" (p. 13). This "call" is seen most clearly in the pivotal events in the lives of certain famous people, for example when sixteen-year-old Ella Fitzgerald decided to sing rather than dance (as had been her plan) at Amateur Night at the Harlem Opera House, or when the great violinist Yehudi

Cultivating Unique Potential in Schools: Revisioning Democratic Teacher Education 145

Menuhin refused a toy violin given him by a family friend, insisting upon having the real thing. Hillman's book is based upon an examination of the events of extraordinary lives as a way, Hillman insists, to uncover the extraordinary quality of many ordinary events, "to inspire ordinary lives by displaying their own potentialities" (p. 32). This idea of a "call" can also be seen in the motivation of many people to become a teacher (Hansen, 1995).

On Hillman's view, contemporary psychology, like other modern sciences, has ignored traditional ideas such as that of the daimon (and the "providence" it brings into ordinary lives) and has therefore become blinded to the deeper reasons why some people achieve greatness while others are trapped in meaninglessness or obscurity. By focusing only upon what can be seen or measured, Hillman claims, psychology fails to understand the crucial importance of factors such as destiny, calling, and imaginative vision in the development of fulfilled persons. This failing is especially evident in educational psychology's treatment of exceptional children and their various clinically defined "symptoms" of depression, alienation, hyperactivity, problems of social adjustment, or drug abuse. Rather than seeing such symptoms as clues to the inner genius of these children, they are often "treated" in the attempt to bring their behavior more into line with what is considered "normal." Hillman also criticizes the tendency of educational institutions to judge students according to norm-referenced tests, the desire (whether expressed or implied) of many educators and schools for "order" and compliance with certain norms, the recent fixation in among educational leaders for standards of evaluation and instruction, and the practice of many parents—out of anxiety more than anything else—to compare their children to other children to ascertain, in part, whether they are doing the right things. Most of these tendencies and practices are based upon a very different set of assumptions about human nature.

Suppose that Hillman's thesis is correct, that each of us is gifted with a unique potential (or daimon), which defines a destiny and that successful maturation depends upon finding a way to live life in accordance with this daimon and the destiny it carries. Suppose further that those students who emerge from our educational institutions with a deep understanding of who they are, where they are going in their lives, and what (at least partially) they need to do to get there are more likely to succeed in life than those who have merely learned the academic lessons offered in school or who have shown, by compliance with external rules and expectations, a certain docility of character that leads to success in school but has little to do with the truth of the inner daimon. Suppose still further that students who rebel from parental and institutional expectations—such as those who use illegal drugs or engage in other criminal behavior, or who choose to skip school rather than put up with its common mindlessness—are in fact expressing the lack of fit between their personal destinies and institutional norms. If all these suppositions were true, shouldn't we reconceive the purposes and structures of schools? Instead of aiming to teach certain facts and skills, shouldn't we concentrate on helping each student to find a sense of larger purpose and meaning? Instead of punishing or treating non-compliance, shouldn't we seek to understand the underlying motivations so that we can better provide our youngsters with the guidance they may need to find a fit between their unique potentials and the actual world we live in? Instead of establishing national standards for what teachers should teach and students should learn, shouldn't we encourage educators to develop strong personal relationships with each student so that they can help each to understand their destinies (Noddings, 2003)? Shouldn't it be a primary purpose of teacher education to prepare teachers for the task of helping students to get in touch with their destinies?

Of course, the concept of a daimon "given" to each individual upon his or her birth and providing "providence" in ordinary lives is, as Hillman admits, a myth. In Plato's telling, before each of us is born, our individual soul—"hanging around in a mythical world, having arrived there from previous lives" (Hillman, 1996, p. 44)—chooses a "lot," or portion of fate, which is somehow amenable or attractive to the soul and which thereafter determines the course of its next life. On the basis of the soul's choice, the Fates assign to each person a "genius," or daimon, which is the individual's guardian and fulfiller of the lot chosen by the soul: that is, the guarantor that the individual's life will lead toward the particular chosen destiny. The daimon begins this task at once by playing a part in the first event that affects our lives: the "choice" of who will be our parents. Then, every event that affects the course of a life—or at least the most significant of those events—is affected by the daimon as it leads the person towards his or her destiny. However, because each individual passes before birth over the "plain of Lethe (oblivion, forgetting)" (p. 46), each is born having lost conscious memory of the daimon. But it is nonetheless still accessible, because it is forever located in, or associated with, the individual's "heart," where it can be perceived intuitively during their lifetime. Hillman suggests that we think of the daimon as a "mythic image." "Unpacking the image takes a lifetime. It may be perceived all at once, but understood only slowly. Thus the soul has an image of its fate, which time can show only as 'future'" (Hillman 1996, p.46).

As stated, this myth involves aspects of existence that are transcendent to experience, and thus it is suspect to a scientifically oriented or naturalistic worldview. For example, the notion that our souls exist before we are ever conceived, while may be compatible with much religious understanding, has no evidentiary basis (at least, no scientific evidentiary basis). Indeed, on the current scientific paradigm about life, individuals don't even exist until the random event occurs that unites a specific sperm from the father with a specific ovum from the mother. People do not "choose" who will be their parents; rather, the parent chooses sexual partners, and many seemingly random genetic events "control" how each person is conceived and developed. On this scientific view, destiny—that is, the future—plays no part in the course of events. Rather, the course of life is caused by the confluence of circumstance as it is lived and is only really meaningful in hindsight, when the many random events can be put into historical perspective. But this scientific understanding, whether or not it is accurate, does not force us to believe that the myth has no value. As myths, stories such as this have an important function to play as complements to scientific understandings. Hillman writes:

> These cosmological myths place us in the world and involve us with it. [On the other hand, the] cosmologies of today—big bangs and black holes, antimatter and curved, ever-expanding space going nowhere—leave us in dread and senseless incomprehensibility. Random events, nothing truly necessary. Science's cosmologies say nothing about the soul, about its reason for existence, how it comes to be and where it might be going, and what its tasks could be. The invisibilities that we feel enmeshing our lives with what is beyond our lives have been abstracted by the cosmologies of science into the literal invisibility of remote galaxies or waves. They can't be known or perceived, because they are measured by time, and our lives are mere nanoseconds in the vast panoply of science's myth. What's the purpose of anything? (1996, 47)

Given this sense of purposelessness that inevitably accompanies a strictly scientific account, Hillman believes, myths can reconnect individuals with larger purposes and processes. If it is necessary to "invent" entities beyond experience to explain aspects of lives, which seem unexplainable by science (for example, "gut" feelings that certain choices are wrong or must be made in a certain way), then so be it.

Naturalizing the Daimon

John Dewey, who strove during his middle and later years to naturalize many transcendent elements of traditional thought, can help us to understand what Hillman is after here. Dewey describes imagination as the capacity to visualize things that are not actually present, but may be so potentially. Imagination identifies "the possibilities that are interwoven within the texture of the actual" (1934b, p. 348). "[A]ll possibilities reach us through the imagination. In a definite sense the only meaning that can be assigned the term 'imagination' is that things unrealized in fact come home to us and have power to stir us" (1934b, p. 43). Even "the idea of a whole, whether of the whole personal being or of the world, is an imaginative, not a literal, idea."

> Neither observation, thought, nor practical activity can attain that complete unification of the self which is called a whole. The whole self is an ideal, an imaginative projection. Hence the idea of a thoroughgoing and deep-seated harmonizing of the self with the Universe (as a name for the totality of conditions with which the self is connected) operates only through imagination—which is one reason why this composing of the self is not voluntary in the sense of an act of special volition or resolution. An "adjustment" possesses the will rather than is its express product. Religionists have been right in thinking of it as an influx from sources beyond conscious deliberation and purpose. (1934b, p. 14)

One issue that arises out of the conception of the daimon as an image of the future, or potential self, is the degree to which it is given prior to life, rather than formed during the course of those lives by the accumulation of various choices and experiences. Hillman and Norton were convinced that the image isn't designed by individual imagination or deliberation but rather is in some sense innate and is discovered—rather than created—through continual examination of the intuitive responses that the individual has to ongoing events. John Dewey's distaste for dualisms, especially any alleged dualism between experience and a transcendent realm outside of experience, led him to the idea that these intuitive feelings come not from some pre-existent self but rather from the self as it is progressively formed, during life, by prior experiences and their habitual residues. We can "read" this progressively formed self in our imaginations.

As individuals face choices, they make a "dramatic rehearsal (in imagination) of various competing possible lines of action." One component of the deliberative process is the "experiment" in thought of "finding out what the various lines of possible action are really like" (1922/1988, 132). Dewey later writes:

> [E]very... choice sustains a double relation to the self. It reveals the existing self and it forms the future self. That which is chosen is that which is found congenial to the desires and habits of the self as it already exists. Deliberation has an important function in this process, because each different possibility as it is presented to the imagination appeals to a different element in the constitution of the self, thus giving all sides of character a chance to play their part in the final choice. (1932/1989, pp. 286–287)

By imagining various alternative possibilities, we discern which possibilities are most amenable as our characters have so far developed:

> The reaction of joy and sorrow, elation and depression, is as natural a response to objects presented in imagination as to those presented in sense... We do not think of future losses and expansions. We think, through imagination, of objects into which in the future some course of action will run, and we are now delighted or depressed, pleased or pained at what is presented. This running commentary of likes and

> dislikes, attractions and disdains, joys and sorrows, reveals to any man who is intelligent enough to note them and to study their occasions his own character. It instructs him as to the composition and direction of the activities that make him what he is. To know what jars an activity and what agrees with it is to know something important about that activity and about ourselves. (Dewey 1922/1988, 140)

As a person's experiences change, so too do their preferences—the things that give joy or sorrow, etc. These preferences are equivalent to what Hillman describes, more poetically but perhaps less descriptively, as the "intuitions of the heart." Mark Johnson (1993) puts it more prosaically:

> ...people do not have pre-established, fixed identities on the basis of which they then make choices from among a range of possible goods. Instead, our evolving identity emerges in and through the ends we come to seek, the relationships we establish, and the way others come to regard us. In a sense, we grope around for our identity, which is never a fixed or finished thing. It changes over time, while preserving some degree of continuity with our previous identities. (p. 147)

In choosing this direction or that, each person contributes to the formation of their future selves; that is, to the selves that they will be when we encounter future decisions. Every choice, in addition to expressing the self that exists at the moment of decision,

> ... also shapes the self, making it, in some degree, a new self. This fact is especially marked at critical junctures, but it marks every choice to some extent however slight. Not all are as momentous as the choice of a calling in life, or of a life-partner. But every choice is at the forking of the roads, and the path chosen shuts off certain opportunities and opens others. In committing oneself to a particular course, a person gives a lasting set to his own being. Consequently, it is proper to say that in choosing this object rather than that, one is in reality choosing what kind of person or self one is going to be. Superficially, the deliberation which terminates in choice is concerned with weighing the values of particular ends. Below the surface, it is a process of discovering what sort of being a person most wants to become. (Dewey, 1922/1988, p. 132)

This "discovery," in Dewey's view, is not a process of coming to know a pre-existent or eternal self which is formed in a transcendent realm beyond experience but, rather, a continual process of discovering the directions in which the complete totality of prior experiences, together with genetic impulses and constitutional make-up, point us (Cunningham, 1995).

An ideal, Dewey writes, "projects in securer and wider form some good which has been previously experienced in a precarious, accidental, fleeting way" (1922/1988, 20). It goes beyond the "actual" by concentrating and amplifying some desirable aspect of experience. Ideals are "indications of the possibilities of existences, and are, therefore, to be used as well and enjoyed; used to inspire action to procure and buttress their causal conditions" (Dewey, 1925/1988, p. 311). They are never "final" or complete; rather they are working hypotheses for imagining the future and therefore for planning. Ideals also motivate activity having purposes beyond immediate gratification. The power of ideals is that they can help to form, in imagination, possibilities for the future, which are in some manner "better" or more desirable than other possibilities. For example, a student volunteers at a soup kitchen. What is the motivation? No doubt the student, unless she is being forced to volunteer or has some other ulterior motive, is moved by an ideal of community service. For the student to form an ideal of community service, she must have had some experience, whether personal, social, or vicarious (in stories and myths), of service to the community.

When an individual becomes aware of the ideals that motivate him, he achieves a higher level of self-consciousness and gains "the ability to attend to, and to correct, his conduct in light of his rules and ideals" (Scheffler 1985, p. 25). When all the ideals that affect an individual's activities are combined together, they become an overarching, if often indescribable, ideal for the self. This ideal, Dewey wrote, deserves to be called "soul": "'soul' when freed from all traces of traditional materialistic animism denotes the qualities of psycho-physical activities as far as these are organized into unity" (Dewey, 1925/1988, p. 223). This soul, or ideal of self-unity, constitutes the most basic requirement of morality. As Johnson (1993) writes, "we come to regard a certain course of action as right or wrong, beneficial or harmful, enlightening or deluding, in and through our working out in thought and action just what it is that we are pursuing as an end. Morality defines the arena of commitment, reflection, and engaged exploration of possible actions in which the self-struggles continually both to find and to form its identity within the mass of ends it finds itself pursuing" (p. 147). The mythic, constructed image of a person's daimon of destiny, then, becomes "the means for going beyond ourselves as presently formed, moving transformatively toward imagined ideals of what we might become, how we might relate to others, and how we might address problematic situations" (Johnson, 1993, p. 209). This image serves as an imaginative vision, or ideal, which coordinates the various aspects of a life into a whole. "Through imagination the self is directed beyond itself to an ideal self, and the ideal effects an integration of meaning in life. The ideal at its broadest is an imaginative totality. As ideas function in specific problematic situations, so this ideal functions as a unification of an imaginatively projected totality of conditions and possibilities" (Shea, 1984, pp. 124–125).On this interpretation, it is the capacity to imagine ourselves as a unity—as a unique potential self—that causes us to become moral agents, to have moral characters, and—as I will elaborate below—it is the facilitation of the development of this capacity that is the primary role of moral educators, whether teachers, parents, or other influences on students' development.

It is also important to stress that the construction of one's imaginative sense of their own destiny is not a solitary affair, conducted "inside one's head," so to speak, but involves all sorts of social relationships and the myriad ways in which these relationships serve to constrain and direct our choices and the ways in which we imagine alternative possibilities. Johnson (1993, 151) thus calls the process of self-development a "coauthoring" to stress the communal construction of self-identities. Clearly, such a conception of the process has educational implications. But before we discuss these, there is one more piece of theory that must be put into place.

Toward a Phenomenology of the Coauthoring of Selves

At the height of what is known as the "modern era," when faith in science and in the possibility that experimental methods could ascertain "true" educational methods were at their peak, philosophy of education achieved its highest professional status. As teacher training shifted in the late 19th and early 20th centuries from its traditional locus in so-called normal schools into the universities, philosophy was deployed to help teachers focus on that which was most achievable in mass education: a virtuous, literate society, made up of wise, brave, prudent, and just citizens, each with a rational commitment to the good society, and each operating—unwittingly, in his or her own personal and professional life—to create that good society, which consisted precisely of this collection of autonomous individuals. Modernist philosophy of education questioned neither the achievability of this vision nor its primary method in traditional education and served as a sort of apologetic for mass public education rooted securely in the Western canon, devoted to helping each individual realize his or her potential within the social order.

Dewey's early works on the philosophy of education (including, most notably, *Democracy and Education*) can be seen as embodying this modernist view of the role of philosophy of education, if not entirely its method or contents. However, Dewey's later philosophy—influenced as it was by the new science of cultural anthropology and containing increasingly radical critiques of traditional schooling—eventually contributed to the transformation of the philosophy of education from apologist to critic of modernist education, a shift epitomized by George S. Counts' 1932 *Dare the School Build a New Social Order?* That book was based on the notion that philosophy of education ought to be used to justify the use of schools to reconstruct the wider society, based on the ideals of justice, equality, and humanism. Philosophy of education after Counts would gradually ostracize itself from the mainstream and hence become increasingly irrelevant to teacher education. While some popular leftist critiques such as those of Paul Goodman (1960) and Postman and Weingartner (1969) influenced some teachers, this critical approach to the philosophy of education has served primarily to marginalize the discipline from teacher education, a process accelerated by the move toward outcomes-based (rather than course-based) standards in the 1990s and eventually symbolized by the removal of a commitment to social justice from National Council for the Accreditation of Teacher Education (NCATE) standards in 2007.

Meanwhile, practitioners of the philosophy of education moved away from teacher education as a primary focus, swept up instead into the powerful philosophical movement known as post-modernism, and its primary proponents such as Michel Foucault, Jean-François Lyotard, and Jacques Derrida. These thinkers emphasized the importance of narratives, language, meaning, power, and the social construction of truth, thereby undermining modernism's faith in the possibility of objective knowledge as well as the alleged superiority of science over other approaches to understanding reality. Central to this post-modernist project was its emphasis on human diversity and on the incapacity of modernism and other so-called meta-narratives to capture the full breadth of human experience among different races, ethnicities, cultures, and gender roles. While some elements of this post-modern perspective found their way into mainstream teacher education—most notably in a push toward multicultural curricula in literature and history—post-modern philosophy of education distanced itself from the daily practice of teaching in favor of a trenchant critique of modern culture, replacing belief in any overarching social ideal with a stance of irony and disbelief. In some ways, post-modernism even motivated a turn away from faith in democracy, since in the post-modern view was that there is no escaping unequal power relations, no matter how many procedural safeguards are in place.

However, the story does not end there. Despite its sometimes negative agenda, post-modernism opened the philosophy of education community to the importance of human diversity and the inevitability of pluralism and thus paved the way for a new revolution in thinking about education. While modernist education had sought to overcome human diversity in the effort to create a common culture based on rational virtue, post-modernism raised the possibility that this approach was hegemonic: an imperialistic domination of a particular form of privileged Western European culture at the expense of other, equally valid, modes of life. However, this left many teacher-educators with the following question: if all meta-narratives must be deconstructed in the face of previously marginalized perspectives, then what role—other than spreading ironic detachment—might schools play that could reconnect citizens to the common good?

Fortunately, one branch of post-modernism—phenomenology—has developed an answer to this question. Phenomenology is an approach to philosophy that studies conscious experience rather than objects, ideals, or knowledge. Initiated by Edmund Husserl and Martin Heidegger, it seeks to overcome a purely subjective or personal understanding of consciousness in favor of systematic reflection on lived experience. Like other forms of post-modernism, phenomenology includes a radical critique of the modern ideal of objectivity. However, rather than merely denying the possibility of objectivity, phenomenology replaces it with a new idea: "intersubjectivity." While each person is inherently subjective in the sense that they have a personal perspective that cannot be escaped, intersubjectivity acknowledges that each person can come to a mutual understanding not only of the subjectivity of others but that one's self is an "other" in other people's experience. Each person recognizes that he or she is both a subject of one's own perspective and an other in every other person's perspective. We are all subjective and therefore limited and flawed, but since we all are subjective, we can establish a basis upon which meanings may be communicated and shared even though each other person's perspective is fundamentally irreconcilable with our own.

Emmanuel Levinas (2006), a student of both Husserl's and Heidegger's, took the idea of intersubjectivity further. While a given person or subject may establish effective communication with the "other," the other is never fully knowable and can never be fully assimilated into one's self. The other's otherness, or "alterity," is absolute. This means that any encounter with the other person is potentially life changing. The existence of the other person demands recognition, while at the same time it opens one's own perspective to a potentially violent critique, since the alterity of the other implicitly denies that one's own perspective is completely true or is all that it can or should be. Each encounter with the other therefore demands a response. An ethical person responds to the encounter with the other by both noticing the subjectivity of the other (and thus affirming intersubjectivity) and at the same time acknowledging that the other is of ultimate moral worth, both in the sense that he or she is unique and therefore irreplaceable and also in the sense that he or she offers a unique glimpse of the possibilities for the future growth of one's self. This recognition of the value of the other echoes the notion of George Herbert Mead (1934), Dewey's colleague at the University of Chicago, who believed that one becomes conscious of one's self only by taking on the perspective of the other toward oneself, using the other as a sort of mirror. We become increasingly aware of ourselves only by seeing ourselves from perspectives that are outside of ourselves, that is, through the eyes of the other. Thus, other persons are absolutely essential for development of one's self. What's more, because we cannot possibly know the consequences of becoming other than we are or know how we might see ourselves once we are changed, it is impossible to prejudge any pathway that opens up for our own growth (Deleuze, 1997). Therefore, we cannot ever judge a person as lesser than we are merely because their perspective is different than ours; every perspective is unique, and uniquely valuable, in a way that simply cannot be compared by any objective measure.

In coming to this realization, post-modern philosophers have done more than merely deconstruct the modernist meta-narrative about the purpose of public schools; they have also provided a basis for conceiving of that purpose in a new way. By bringing diverse young members of the community together into a common space, public schools create an ideal arena for each of them to become individuals. Thus, in a democracy, public schools can go beyond preparing students to deal with diversity; their very diversity creates the optimal conditions for developing each student's unique potential.

For this possibility to be fully realized, teachers need a different type of education: as the preparation of teachers for developing the unique potential of their students. How, exactly, should teacher education be revisioned for this purpose?

Revisioning Teacher Education for Democracy

To reinvigorate our democracy, American society desperately needs to recommit itself to the formation of people with a sense of calling, mission, commitment, and vision. Educators must therefore develop not only their students' skills at decoding, figuring, and "critical thinking," but better their students' imaginations as well. Because humans are conscious creatures, they live not just in present realities but in a flow of time in which there are tendencies, hopes, possibilities, and projections into the future. They dream about what might be; these dreams may be to science no more than the seemingly random movement of molecules and electrons in the brain, but they provide a sense of the meaning, or significance, of present realities. Thus, "reality" includes not just the material world but also the mental associations, spiritual longings, and development of personal preferences tat accompany all of experience. Imagination is critical to comprehending this full range of human experience. As Dewey wrote, "Only a personal response involving imagination can possibly procure realization even of pure 'facts.' The imagination is the medium of appreciation in every field. The engagement of the imagination is the only thing that makes any activity more than mechanical. Unfortunately, it is too customary to identify the imaginative with the imaginary, rather than with a warm and intimate taking in of the full scope of a situation" (1916/1985, 244). He goes on:

> An adequate recognition of the play of imagination as the medium of realization of every kind of thing which lies beyond the scope of direct physical response is the sole way of escape from mechanical methods in teaching. . . ..The educative value of manual activities and of laboratory exercises, as well as of play, depends upon the extent in which they aid in bringing about a sensing of the meaning of what is going on. . . ..it is by imagination that symbols are translated over into a direct meaning and integrated with a narrower activity so as to expand and enrich it. (1916/1985, 245–6)

Dewey wrote that the "characteristic human need is for possession and appreciation of the meaning of things" (1925/1988, 272). The meaning of various activities resides in the intelligent connection between those activities and their future consequences. Because these consequences do not currently exist (and because the uncertainty of the future means that we can never be entirely certain what they will be), imagination must come into play: imagination, which realizes the possible directions of events and which provides opportunity for personal preferences to find expression. For this to be realized in schools, students must be given the opportunity to imagine unrealized possibilities, to feel the "stir" that the products of their imaginations may have in light of their personal preferences and then to carry out the implications of these personal preferences. As was mentioned above, only by making such imaginary choices and by learning from how we respond to those choices, can we get better at discerning our actual preferences and taking control of the future development of ourselves.

Mark Johnson (1993) outlines two requirements for learning how to use what he calls "moral imagination." The first is that students need to know more about the ways that imagination works in human experience. This entails a focused attempt by schools and teacher education institutions to offer an alternative to the secular view that "destiny" has no place in rational human discourse. Such an attempt need not threaten the "separation of church and state," because, as I have shown, it is possible to offer this alternative in such a way that basic religious commitments are not brought into question. A suitable curriculum on imagination and destiny needs to be developed that outlines imagination's role in the formation and adjustment of personal narratives. Johnson's book—together with Hillman's more poetic view and Dewey's ruminations on imagination—may serve as the basic theoretical framework for such a curriculum. The second requirement is that students and teachers must cultivate imagination by "sharpening our powers of discrimination, exercising our capacity for envisioning new possibilities, and imaginatively tracing out the implications of our metaphors, prototypes, and narratives" (Johnson, 1993, p. 198). This requires many opportunities for the members of school communities to practice imagination. While this can be done in the context of academic subject-matter, it requires new attention to students' personal life histories, preferences, and imagined futures, not only as these are relevant to academics but as they are relevant to students' present and future lives. Schools must address more than just the various ways that students might earn a living. Life includes so much more: family, playtime, hobbies, morality, spirituality, art, to name a few.

But there's more to the cultivation of the imagination than simply encouraging students to imagine a fulfilling future. That is, while schools should encourage students to imagine the possibilities before them, they should also teach students to be able to distinguish fantasy from reality and to test their imaginings against a realistic assessment of the possibilities afforded by the real world. It is mere romanticism to assume that anyone can "become" anything they want to become. As Dewey wrote, while "the imagination of ideal ends" is the source of all personal initiative and accomplishment, only those ends that are "pertinent to actual conditions" represent "the fruition of a disciplined mind" (1934a/1989, p. 35). This requirement of "pertinence" requires imagination to connect with reality. That is, not all ideals are equally acceptable. As Isaiah Berlin (1991) wrote, the notion that whatever an individual desires, or whatever moves him, is an appropriate ideal because it expresses inner goals, or the "true self," can be destructive of both morality and community. There must be checks on what counts as an appropriate ideal, and I am suggesting that the articulation of ideals, as part of an educational process designed to connect such articulated ideals with realistic plans for their achievement, has the potential to screen out ideals that are repressive of others or in other ways undesirable within the larger community. Far too many 14- and 15–year-olds, for example, claim that they want to be doctors, lawyers, or professional basketball players. A good number of these claims might be unrealistic. As Dewey pointed out repeatedly, ". . . the road to freedom may be found in that knowledge of facts which enables us to employ them in connection with desires and aims" (1922/1988, 209). Without realistic assessment of conditions, ideal ends lead to failure, discouragement, or the conclusion that the world is simply not amenable to idealization, but should be accepted as it is. The latter conclusion, of course, leads to fatalism and cynicism, the primary enemies of social improvement.

Thus, it is important to follow up the age-old question "what do you want to be when you grow up," with a more difficult question, "what do you have to do to get there." This second question, if answered with seriousness, realism, and intelligence, can turn a mere fantasy into a plan. Dewey writes: "What intelligence has to do in the service of impulse is to act not as its obedient servant but as its clarifier and liberator. And this can be accomplished only by a study of the conditions and causes, the workings and consequences of the greatest possible variety of desires and combinations of desire. Intelligence converts desire into plans, systematic plans based on assembling facts, reporting events as they happen, keeping tab on them and analyzing them" (1922/1988, p. 175). Plans require more than just possibilities; they require a knowledge of conditions and of their utilities and obstacles, such that one can formulate a step-by-step method for achieving their ultimate end. Dewey adds:

> [A]cting with an aim is all one with acting intelligently. To foresee a terminus of an act is to have a basis upon which to observe, to select, and to order objects and our own capacities. To do these things means to have a mind—for mind is precisely intentional purposeful activity controlled by perception of facts and their relationships to one another. To have a mind to do a thing is to foresee a future possibility; it is to have a plan for its accomplishment. . ... Mind is capacity to refer present conditions to future results, and future consequences to present conditions. And these traits are just what is meant by having an aim or a purpose. . ... A man is imperfectly intelligent when he contends himself with looser guesses about the outcome than is needful, just taking a chance with his luck, or when he forms plans apart from study of the actual conditions, including his own capacities. (1916/1985, p. 110)

The study of actual conditions connects the training of the imagination to the more traditional academic curriculum. But consciously integrating each student's evolving unique potential into subject-matter—and doing this is a manner that fosters democracy—requires very different teaching than what is common today and involves a much "more difficult kind of planning"; the teacher "must survey the capacities and needs of the particular set of individuals with who he is dealing and must at the same time arrange the conditions which provide the subject-matter or content for experiences that satisfy these needs and develop these capacities. The planning must be flexible enough to permit free play for individuality of experience and yet firm enough to give direction toward continuous development of power" (Dewey, 1938/1991, p. 36).

What's more, students can only learn how to develop their own unique potentials if they see the adults in their lives doing likewise. Teachers therefore have a fundamental professional obligation to engage in a process of continual, public, personal self-improvement. By revealing themselves to be continually struggling to live according to their own unique potentials and by demonstrating a properly open attitude toward the diverse potentials of their students and others, teachers will have a much more profound effect on their students than if they confine themselves to academic subject-matter. Teachers must serve as examples in at least two respects: they must show "exceptional candor and openness" so that students can see the difficulties and the rewards of engaging in self-actualization, and they also must demonstrate understanding of the role of other people in development of the self, that is, "the recognition that outside my personal destiny lies a multitude of truths which, though not my own, are other people's. On this basis [they are] required to foster and encourage destinies different from [their] own" (Norton, 1973, pp. 114–115). Preservice teachers, then, should be expected to go through a well-developed curriculum in imagination and the formation of ideals for themselves before they are deemed to be ready to support the process with their students, the students' parents, and the teacher's colleagues, throughout their career. In this way, the power of the socially constructed mythic image of unique potential, or the daimon, and the important role that every person plays in each other's life, might be progressively realized in schools and in the larger society. But only with a well-developed and articulated philosophy of democratic education will such a radical shift in teacher education be possible.

References

Aristotle, with Martin Ostwald. (1962). *Nicomachean ethics*. Indianapolis, IN: Bobbs-Merrill.
Berlin, I., with Henry Hardy. (1991). *The crooked timber of humanity: Chapters in the history of ideas*. New York: Knopf.
Counts, G. S. (1932). *Dare the school build a new social order?* Carbondale, IL: Southern Illinois University Press.
Cunningham, C. A. (1995). John Dewey's metaphysics and the self. In James W. Garrison (ed.). *The new scholarship on Dewey* (pp. 175–192). Dordrecht: Kluwer.
Deleuze, G. (1997). *Essays critical and clinical*. Minneapolis, MN: University of Minnesota.
Dewey, J. (1916/1985). *Democracy and education*. In J. Boydston (ed.), *John Dewey: The middle works, Volume 9*. Carbondale, IL: Southern Illinois University Press.
Dewey, J. (1920/1988). *Reconstruction in philosophy*. In J. Boydston (ed.), *John Dewey: The middle works, volume 12*, pp. 77–201. Carbondale, IL: Southern Illinois University Press.
Dewey, J. (1922/1988). *Human nature and conduct*. In J. Boydston (ed.), *John Dewey: The middle works, Volume 14*. Carbondale, IL: Southern Illinois University Press.
Dewey, J. (1925/1988). *Experience and nature*. In J. Boydston (ed.), *John Dewey: The later works, Volume 1*. Carbondale, IL: Southern Illinois University Press.
Dewey, J. (1932/1989). *Ethics*. In J. Boydston (ed.), *John Dewey: The later works, Volume 7*. Carbondale, IL: Southern Illinois University Press.
Dewey, J. (1934a/1989). *A common faith*. In J. Boydston (ed.), *The later works, Volume 9*, pp. 1–58. Carbondale, IL: Southern Illinois University Press.
Dewey, J. (1934b/1989). *Art as experience*. In J. Boydston (ed.), *John Dewey: The later works, Volume 10*. Carbondale, IL: Southern Illinois University Press.
Dewey, J. (1938/1991). *Experience and education*. In J. Boydston (ed.), *John Dewey: The later works, Volume 13*, pp. 1–62 Carbondale, IL: Southern Illinois University Press.
Dewey, J. (1939/1991). *Freedom and culture*. In J. Boydston (ed.), *The later works, Volume 13*, pp. 63–188. Carbondale, IL: Southern Illinois University Press.
Goodman, P. (1960). *Growing up absurd: Problems of youth in the organized system*. New York: Random House.
Hansen, D. T. (1995). *The call to teach*. New York: Teachers College Press.
Hillman, J. (1996). *The soul's code: In search of character and calling*. New York: Random House.
Johnson, M. (1993). *Moral imagination: Implications of cognitive science for ethics*. Chicago: University of Chicago Press.
Johnston, J. S. (2006). *Inquiry and education: John Dewey and the quest for democracy*. Albany, NY: State University of New York Press.
Lévinas, E. (2006). *Humanism of the other*. Urbana, IL: University of Illinois Press.
Mead, G. H. (1934). *Mind, self, and society*. In Charles W. Morris (ed.). University of Chicago Press.
Mill, J. S. (1861)[1991]. *Considerations on representative government*, Buffalo, NY: Prometheus.
Noddings, N. (1992). *The challenge to care in schools: An alternative approach to education*. New York: Teachers College Press.
Norton, D. L. (1973, Summer). Social entailments of self-actualization. *Journal of Value Inquiry* 7(2): 106–120.
Norton, D. L. (1976). *Personal destinies: The theory of ethical individualism*. Princeton, NJ: Princeton University Press.
Norton, D. L. (1995). Education for self-knowledge and worthy living. In Howie & Schedler (eds.), *Ethical issues in contemporary society*. Carbondale IL: Southern Illinois University Press.
Plato, with G. M. A. Grube. (1974). *Plato's Republic*. Indianapolis, IN: Hackett.
Postman, N. & Weingartner, C. (1969). *Teaching as a subversive activity*. New York: Delacorte.
Rousseau, Jean-Jacques. (1762). *The social contract*. (Trans.) Charles Frankel, New York: Hafner.
Scheffler, I. (1985). *Of human potential: An essay in the philosophy of education*. Boston: Routledge & Kegan Paul.
Schor, J. (2004). *Born to buy: The commercialized child and the new consumer culture*. New York: Scribner.
Shea, W. M. (1984). *The naturalists and the supernatural: Studies in horizon and an American philosophy of religion*. Macon, GA: Mercer.
Snauwaert, D. T. (1993). *Democracy, education, and governance: A developmental conception*. Albany, NY: State University of New York Press.

Thirteen

Pluralism and Praxis: Philosophy of Education for Teachers

David A. Granger and Jane Fowler Morse

Introduction

A number of scholars have recently expressed concern that philosophy of education is suffering a perceived decline in its relevance both to education and philosophy, particularly as the two domains seem to show little or no interest in each other. We will argue in this chapter, however, that such a decline is not necessarily taking place when examined from the perspective of teacher education.[1] These scholars' concern is, of course, not a new one. Philosophy of education has traditionally been housed within schools and departments of education and in rare instances departments of philosophy and has doubtlessly been marginalized for much of its existence as a single undergraduate course (or two, if teacher education faculty are astute). Such courses are typically based in educational foundations rather than simply philosophy of education. This is significant mainly because the field of educational foundations is a collation of applied interpretive perspectives, including history, sociology, philosophy, and sometimes psychology or anthropology of education. Some purists might, thus, worry that it is easy for philosophy to get watered down or lost in the mix within this sort of interdisciplinary, issues-based arrangement.

Then, too, most teacher education students see themselves as practical-minded people interested in "real world," hands-on methods for helping students learn, not as theoreticians, let alone philosophers. The word "philosophy" lacks appeal to them; in fact, it may be frightening or intimidating, in addition to appearing irrelevant. Nonetheless, we believe that these students will be continually formulating theory (even if they don't think of it as such) as they practice the craft of teaching, if they practice it reflectively, that is, through the mindset of praxis. It might also be argued that such theories, qua theory, before the partitioning of theory into discipline specific concepts, are at bottom philosophical in their underlying presuppositions and perspectives, whether they can be styled as learning theories, social theories, theories based on historical arguments, political theories, psychological theories, or something else. All of these continually evolving ways of interpreting and making sense of human experience are in some way relevant to the practice of teaching. Moreover, the many and diverse tools of understanding such theories provide are interrelated rather than discrete; different tools can sometimes do the same job, though each is, by design, best suited to a particular task (or tasks) and thus offers somewhat different results and degrees of efficacy. A complex, largely public enterprise like education cannot proceed intelligently, nor indeed democratically, without thoughtful, ongoing reflective examination by practitioners using theoretical frameworks. Philosophy of education is, from this perspective, a particularly versatile set of tools for engaging in the ongoing work of praxis.[2]

Philosophy and/as Education

At the most basic level, philosophy of education enables individuals interested in teaching and learning to examine basic philosophical questions and issues underlying education thoughtfully. This often begins with a consideration of the nature and aims of education (as opposed to mere schooling, which in itself is not necessarily educative), and includes analysis of the methods and materials of education, the forms of education, the origins of education, and other aspects of education as a vital human endeavor. Whether educators incorporate Aristotelian, Rousseauian, Durkheimian, Vygotskian, Freirean, Foucauldian, Rawlsian or what-have-you theories, praxis holds that they are continually developing, evaluating, and revising their theoretical perspectives over time as their experience inside and outside the classroom accrues. Although teaching itself may be largely practical, the learning that results from teaching is of the utmost importance philosophically, as John Dewey famously asserted in *Democracy and Education*: "If we are willing to conceive education as the process of forming fundamental dispositions, intellectual and emotional, toward nature and fellow-men [sic], philosophy may even be defined as the general theory of education."[3] As in the practical wisdom (phrōnesis[4]) tradition of Aristotle, philosophy, for Dewey, both begins and ends with ordinary human problems and concerns. Philosophy of education is not so much appending philosophy to education as it is an examination of the problems that surface in the practice of education. One of these problems, of course, is how to teach practical wisdom in its numerous forms, to students, so that they can cultivate their own well-being and, ideally, that of others.[5] Thus, philosophy of education is ultimately inseparable from cultural criticism.

For instance, philosophical questions arise whenever teachers consider the role education plays (or should play) in society. Working within a social justice framework, as teachers in public schools must do, requires teachers to reflect on broader issues of practice as they plan, develop, and evaluate their classroom activities. Today, alas, beginning teachers are often taught to believe that good teaching more or less consists in complying with No Child Left Behind. In our classes, we try to tell them that good teaching, though perhaps more difficult in the current environment, can still coexist with No Child Left Behind, until such legislation is repealed or reformed to promote educative practice.

The values and beliefs that guide the profession of teaching in the relations among teachers, students, and parents are ineluctably philosophical in import. Choosing what is the right action towards others is a subset of ethics; choosing what is worth knowing is a subset of axiology, for the concept of "worth," and epistemology, for the concept of "knowing;" addressing concepts of reality is ontology. Clearly describing or discussing the stated aims of education raises questions pertinent to social and political philosophy, as making schools experientially (intellectually and otherwise) appealing to their inhabitants raises issues of aesthetics. Fostering a sense of self-esteem in students, for example, might raise the questions "Who am I?" "What is my purpose?" and "Who do I want to become?" (which is a subset of ontology) as well as a myriad of psychological/philosophical theories. Such theories might prompt consideration of, among other things, the significance for education of Socrates' self-examined life, Dewey's democratic community, Maslow's hierarchy of needs, or Sartre's existential dilemma of choice (i.e., human beings cannot choose not to choose).[6]

Once again, all of this is to say that philosophy, and issues that call for philosophical examination, are ultimately unavoidable in the profession of teaching. They even appear in the more brick-and-mortar curriculum and methods classes that teacher education students are required to take, although, sadly, these classes are too often separated from their work in foundations, as if there was a clear and inevitable line of demarcation paralleling the artificial theory/practice divide. Yet teachers cannot legitimately base their KWL charts[7] on their students' "knowledge bases" without considering, at some point, what constitutes knowledge. Indeed, if they were to accept uncritically what students think they know as the "K" in a KWL chart, many otherwise well-planned lessons would quickly founder. Similarly, teachers cannot evaluate "research-based teaching methods" or "best practices" without asking philosophical questions about the presuppositions or the validity of that research.

So, despite teacher education students' initial lack of comfort with philosophy, they actually need it and, with the right preparation and support, use it often. We have found that the more informed and purposive we can make their theorizing, the better. Moreover, in our experience many students do, indeed, become interested in "philosophy of education" rather easily, and often enthusiastically, recognizing the value of conceptual analysis—especially when used to examine and critique the educational reforms *du jour*—in courses we teach titled (the title originated when they were originally designed in the early 1970s) "Philosophical and Psychological Theories of Learning" and "The School and Society." In these two master's level courses, students are required to write several papers in which they are asked to explain and demonstrate the relationship to, and relevance for, teaching of some issue or theory addressed in the course, drawing in some way on their own firsthand experiences as teachers, students, or parents. For their culminating experience in the program, these students must undertake an action research project that mines the relationship between theory and practice. Moreover, they are encouraged to situate their projects within their own schools and classrooms, revising a piece of curriculum to include a social justice component, for instance, or modifying their approach to what is commonly called classroom management.[8] Hence we believe that announcements of the death of philosophy of education are premature, although it is still well to remember that philosophy is often mistakenly considered a frill, like art and music, likely to be cut in times of fiscal belt-tightening, an outlook perhaps more evident among our colleagues in teacher education than our students, who, once they are initiated into the mysteries of philosophy of education, find it, after all, not very mysterious. Having attended its wake, however, we are pleased to find it (thus far) alive and well in our own classrooms, like Tom Sawyer, furtively peeking in at his own funeral.[9]

Philosophy of education has at times also been considered redundant. Some years ago, teacher education students were encouraged to think that they already "had" a philosophy of education that would be uncovered by some sort of Rorschach test revealing whether they were essentialists, perennialists, existentialists, behaviorists, constructivists, or unwitting practitioners of various other philosophical "-isms." While we are all shaped intellectually and otherwise by our individual experiences and socio-cultural contexts, there is no doubt something absurd about this regressive project. For it presumes and encourages a non-reflective acceptance of a philosophy of education as something directly and uncritically inherited or somehow innate, belonging to someone *a priori* (assuming that personality is immutable, which we do not believe either).[10]

In addition, these "-isms" regularly occasioned the scorn of mainstream philosophers, who considered philosophy of education—or philosophy *of* anything, for that matter—below them. Philosophy was a "pure" pursuit, only applied to the quotidian world by lower orders of intellectuals. That said, many philosophy departments were driven by the practicality of maintaining enrollments to offer courses in Business or Medical Ethics, and other such applied philosophies as the philosophy of science or mathematics (these more conceptual pursuits being a little more elevated perhaps). Ironically, such courses may have saved academic philosophy from extinction in the eminently practical era of the late twentieth century because of a mistaken and dangerously reductionist idea that theory is both prior and superior to practice. Marx's notion of *praxis* permeates education for good reason; he realized the interdependence of theory and practice in his pronouncement that philosophy must not merely contemplate the world but also seek to alter and enhance it. Without courses in the general education core of major universities, there might not be enough philosophy majors to keep departments of philosophy afloat. This is eminently true at our own institution and surely at many more. Philosophy's value as a form of *praxis* is generally not recognized in our frequently myopic, outcomes-driven society, and there are few employment opportunities for professional philosophers, other than being hired in a philosophy department.[11] This is a sad state of affairs, to be sure, but nonetheless true. The value of solid, clear thinking remains vastly underrated. Yet its value in teaching and the pursuit of education is unquestionable among those who share our view of the nature of the profession. Another pivotal issue, then, is how one thinks about what it means to "do" philosophy in the context of education.

In a recent article bemoaning the paucity of meaningful dialogue between philosophers and educators, René Vincente Arcilla suggests the tradition of skeptical questioning as a general method of philosophy potentially useful in reinvigorating the conversation between philosophers and educators. Importantly, such conversation is, in his view, properly more existential or humanistic than pragmatic or functionalist in orientation. That is to say, it deals more with questions and issues of the human condition and their significance for education and less about purposes related to social melioration and regeneration. Should that humanistic approach fail to take hold, Arcilla allows that philosophers of education might have no choice but to give in to prevailing trends away from philosophy and toward intentional problem-solving, becoming, as he sees it, social scientists, for example, "liberal political-science theorists" or "postmodernist sociological theorists."[12]

While sympathetic to Arcilla's thoughtful petition on behalf of the humanistic dimension of education, which encourages students acquire the necessary wisdom to live with meaning and purpose, we think it is well to remember that the historical function and purpose of skepticism was not first and foremost the stimulation of inquiry regarding the "immortal conversation," as valuable and important as such inquiry surely is from an educational standpoint.

Rather, classic arguments for skepticism, for example the Pyrrhonians, typically reasoned along the following lines. Empirical knowledge is unattainable since sense impressions are often deceptive, but rational knowledge is unreliable when there are two perfectly valid arguments for and against any position. Therefore, the only valid and suitably rigorous philosophical response to claims to know in many cases is suspension of belief, judgment, or action, or, at least, thoughtful action. In the uncertain politics of the Hellenistic world, this basic posture of suspension of belief became the foundation for a whole attitude toward life's exigencies among the so-called Academics. Their principal enemy was dogmatism and its rigid posture of "knowingness," particularly within philosophy itself.[13]

Such a tact may no doubt be useful at times, for instance, when important philosophical positions are in fact suspicious, destructive, or inadequately developed. Yet its limited purview and aims also potentially reduce the function of philosophy to producing its own suspension (or perhaps even annihilation), resulting in a kind of intellectually non-committal, and often ultimately conservative, detachment. This seems to us to be akin to periodic re-examinations of academic philosophy that seek to attack or debunk existing philosophical structures, from Ockham's razor shaving Plato's beard to Hume's Pyrrhonian skepticism about what we can know about causation. Nietzsche announces that he is going to teach us to philosophize with a hammer, but he leaves us alone to do the rebuilding. In the *Tractatus*, Wittgenstein reduces philosophy to a series of true propositions representing "pictures" of "facts" or atomistic truths, which leads him to pronounce the death of philosophy (as we then knew it anyway):

> My propositions are elucidatory in this way: he who understands me finally recognizes them as senseless, when he has climbed out through them, on them, over them. (He must so to speak throw away the ladder, after he has climbed up on it.) He will surmount these propositions; then he sees the world rightly.

He concludes, "Whereof one cannot speak, thereof one must be silent."[14] Later, in *Philosophical Investigations*, philosophy becomes even more anti-systematic through a critique of the improper use of the tools of language, a kind of therapy against meaningless philosophical formulations and the unnecessary problems (e.g., the mind/body problem) that arise "when language *goes on holiday*."[15] Again, this approach can be useful at times. But can there be a more constructive project for philosophy or, more to the point, for philosophy of education?

Pluralist Eclecticism in Philosophy of Education

Rather than the methods of skepticism or other similarly circumscribed views of the nature and purpose of philosophy, we suggest the tools of a pluralist eclecticism. Such eclecticism must be pragmatic, that is, tested in practice. It is pluralist in that it ranges widely over the many and diverse avenues and inquiries of philosophy, broadly conceived, to select concepts and ideas that might in some way illuminate and inform educative practice.[16] We regard this approach as essentially eclectic. The Greek verb "legein" means "to gather, to pick out, to pick out for oneself (med.); to say, tell, command; to wish to say, to mean, to explain more fully."[17] Adding the prefix "ek," "out of," to form the verb "eklegein," augments the sense of choosing something for a particular purpose out of a collection of possibilities: "to pick or single out; to pick out for oneself or choose (med.); to select."[18] Hence, eclecticism, choosing the best elements out of what is available to use for a particular purpose.[19]

Such purposeful choosing is, we think, usefully paired with the pragmatic pluralism of people like John Dewey and William James.[20] For them, our finite human natures and infinite universe mean that there is no single outlook or point of view that can effectively take in and accommodate everything. Newton's achievement of simplifying the explanation of various natural phenomena by discovering the principle of gravity spawned a number of similar attempts at achieving unity in the sciences. But alas, no fixed and final Einsteinian "theory of everything" has appeared.[21] Pragmatism itself is from this perspective fundamentally pluralistic—a continually evolving family of theories of meaning, truth, and inquiry.

What we are calling pluralist electicism cannot, then, simply repeat what others have said or done. That would be mere imitation and, as such, inadequately responsive to the particular demands of our own historical and socio-cultural moment. Rather, pluralist eclecticism embraces the more postmodern motif of creativity as "repetition with a difference."[22] Viewing theories and their various components as tools of creative problem solving, pluralist eclecticism envisions and applies old ideas and materials in new ways that prove illuminating, a process that routinely calls for some degree of retooling as novel situations emerge. In other words, pluralist eclecticism uses our cultural inheritance to enhance our perspectives on issues relating to the unique circumstances of our own time and place—just as every student, every classroom, and every school is, in the last analysis, unique. Like any form of *praxis*, this ultimately requires both practical wisdom (*phrōnesis*) and imagination. It comprises the ability to re-envision solutions to the ever-changing human dilemma, if educators are to avoid shortsighted, single-minded solutions to existing problems in favor of more long-term, ethically responsive approaches that refuse quick-fix instrumentalisms and faddish practices (e.g., "strategies" divorced from theory) that create more problems than they solve. To wit, while it might seem efficacious in the short-term to assess student learning and teacher performance using traditional (read behaviorist) paper-and-pencil tests, we must also consider the long-term consequences of reducing students to mere numbers based on their test scores. One of us has therefore written, scornfully, of the destructively reductionist "paltry empiricism" reflected in the current fascination with test scores as the primary measure of educational success.[23] The other has affirmed the value in the apparently opposing concepts of Marx's idea of dialectical materialism and Mill's view of academic freedom as the (only or chief) vehicles of change in history.[24]

Accordingly, eclecticism has sometimes been accused of erroneously condoning inconsistency or, even worse, incompatibility. As one of us was once asked, "How can you espouse the educational value of both Aristotle's empiricism and Plato's theory of the forms? Are they not contradictory?" In response, we would ask, "Does a philosophical position have to be adopted whole-cloth to be educationally valuable?" Aristotle's empirical philosophy grew out of the very soil thoughtfully tended and prepared by the rationalist, Plato; Kant combined the two when he declared that we need both a rational system of categories for understanding our experience and the empirical experiences themselves.

History suggests that we are in good company in asserting that different philosophies, as different ways of looking at the world and human affairs, can be informative to the educative enterprise in different ways. This is also why, to our way of thinking, philosophers of education would be well served to study the history of philosophy and its various texts carefully and not just embrace one appealing view or system, lest they run the risk of training or inculcating rather than educating.[25] Aristotle did, after all, understand that it matters for our deliberations whether we are moving to or from first principles,[26] a nod to Plato's project of advancing to first principles on the way to knowledge of the Forms, before descending the ladder to apply the Forms to the world of particulars. Aristotle did, after all, write both the *Prior Analytics* and the *Posterior Analytics*. For his part, Dewey did welcome a return (with a difference) to the restless, searching Plato of the *Dialogues* (a "'Back to Plato' movement"), while also embracing the empirical naturalism of Aristotle.[27] And Kant did announce his debt to both an empiricist (Hume) and a rationalist (Descartes) when he acknowledged that he "stood on the shoulders of giants" in uniting the functions of "pure reason" and "empirical intuition" in two of his major works, *Prolegomena to Any Future Metaphysics* and *The Critique of Pure Reason*. Thus Kant's famous declaration, "Concepts without precepts are empty; precepts without concepts are blind."[28] In addition, Kant held that human beings cannot directly know (but only infer) things as things-in-themselves (noumena), but only as they appear to us (phenomena). This echoes a much earlier statement that Boethius puts into the mouth of Lady Philosophy proclaiming that "knowledge is according to the capacity of the knower,"[29] presaging the Copernican Turn in philosophy.[30] For Kant, the vast bulk of our knowledge is "empirical intuition" (sense data), of which we can only "make sense" by sorting it into his twelve categories. From his analysis eventually sprang phenomenology, the genetic epistemology of Piaget, existentialism, the modern insistence on different "ways of knowing," and more. So, out of the ruins of a demolished philosophy springs something new.

Amidst the general destruction, Richard Rorty has insisted that we can do no more Philosophy with a capital P in the postmetaphysical era, no more philosophical edifice building.[31] Many of the old structures are surely in need of razing, but we had better understand them first in order that they fall properly when dynamited. Even Descartes enlisted the metaphor of the destruction of old structures when he analogized philosophy as rebuilding (or remodeling) a house. Rather than doubting everything systematically, however, and embracing as a final position the Pyrrhonian skeptic's programmatic suspension of belief, Descartes used the methodology of doubting to subject his "first principles" to such scrutiny as would reveal which of them could survive scrutiny, thus arriving at his famous pronouncement, "Cogito ergo sum" ("I think therefore I am.").[32] Even Descartes, reviled for his apparent separation of mind and body, used this to assert that we can indeed utilize our senses and do science, a vindication that he hoped would spare him the enmity of the church that Galileo received for daring to contradict the Bible. So even Descartes had something in common with Rorty: out with the old and in with the new, but not without thoughtfully examining, understanding, and learning from the work of our predecessors.

All of this is to recommend that, in our view of what the service philosophy can do for education, we should regard the history of philosophy as largely cumulative in its generation; later philosophies do not so much cancel out earlier ones as use them, revise them (sometimes beyond recognition), and build on them. If parts of them are "wrong," so be it; spotting these errors can be productive of new ideas. Again, this is forcefully evidenced in Dewey's seminal work in the philosophy of education, *Democracy and Education*, which reviews various historical precedents that the resourceful New Englander either accepted or rejected, but nonetheless found illuminating of his own view. Thus, one might argue that, far from being erroneous in its *modus operandi*, eclecticism of some kind is, in the end, the way in which much philosophy itself has developed, even if an Einsteinian "theory of everything" (or metanarrative) was the ultimate goal of many past thinkers. As we will argue in the culminating section of this chapter, that realization, augmented by a pragmatic pluralism, can lend valuable insights to philosophy of education.

Not only do we recommend taking an eclectic view of the value of past philosophy in our assertion that philosophy of education is still alive and relevant to the practice of teaching and teacher education, we additionally note that other creative human responses to the world (art, history, literature, music, etc.) in the 20th century were likewise practicing eclecticism of one kind or another. Bricollage, pastiche, montage, collage, borrowings, and odd juxtapositions abound. While this eclecticism was sometimes "merely" playful in orientation (*jouissance*), resulting, at its worst, in a chaotic and disorienting clashing of styles and cultures, at other times it was more directly purposeful and productive. We believe that this form of eclecticism—especially the more purposeful variety—can likewise prove very informative in offering examples of creative problem solving through the retooling of old forms.[33]

Eclecticism in the Arts

It is often remarked that Gustav Mahler composed his monumental 6th Symphony at the height of his personal and professional life. In this deeply autobiographical work, he freely quotes selections of folk music and rhythms in making a tragic, ironic mockery of the normally cheerful scherzo movement. In this way his brand of eclecticism reshaped (or retooled) the old form, fitting it to a new purpose. As Alma Mahler explains, "In the Scherzo, he represented the unrhythmic games of [his] two children, tottering in zigzags over the sand. Ominously the childish voices become more and more tragic, and at the end die out in a whimper." In addition to this "bizarrely scored" scherzo, the enterprising composer contrasts the sound of cowbells (reminiscent of his happy youth) with a menacing march in the first movement, and in the last movement, adds three hammer blows of fate representing three devastating events in his life. Alma Mahler continues, "In the last movement he describes himself and his downfall; or, as he later said: 'It is the hero, on whom fall three blows of fate, the last of which fells him as a tree is felled.' On him, too, fell three blows of fate, and the last felled him." These three blows refer to the death of his eldest daughter, the loss of his Directorship at the Vienna State Opera, and his diagnosis with life-threatening heart disease. Later, Mahler subtracted one of the hammer blows out of a superstitious dread that it would mark his end for real. In a recent performance one of us attended, a special instrument had to be built for the percussion to give the two remaining blows the right sound: "[not] clangorous and steely, but a non-metallic thud, 'like an axe stroke.'"[34] It was very effective. In its considerable novelty, its ability to express in new ways the inevitable tragedy of the human encounter with the world (not to mention its prophetic accuracy), the creative problem solving utilized in Mahler's 6th Symphony marks both a continuation of the past and a break from it. The conventional formula, the one that made it possible for Franz Joseph Hayden to crank out 104 graceful symphonies, is transfigured almost beyond recognition. Much of the skeleton, however, remains.

Indeed, many composers of classical music invent new forms (or tools) that challenge the old, but at the same time grow out of them. Arnold Schoenberg's twelve-tone music, for instance, depends on the prior existence of the diatonic scale, with its half steps arranged into a pattern of "keys." But he did not conceive the new twelve-tone form from whole-cloth. Schoenberg's predecessor, Hector Berlioz, helped spur these revolutionary compositions through his own works by allowing some of the odd "chromatic" tones to penetrate the modes of the "normal" diatonic scale. In the 20th century, Charles Ives, Lukas Foss, John Corigliano (and numerous others) frequently quoted selected bits and pieces from classical composers (and other musical sources). In doing so, they, too, utilized certain aspects of the old forms but gave them new life through creative retooling. Foss, for example, wrote a set of four two-part inventions, a *Renaissance Concerto for Flute and Orchestra*, and also quotes Bach's *Von Himmel Hoch* in his *Baroque Variations*.[35] Extra-musical experiences and events can spur departures from traditional forms as well.

After seeing the AIDS quilt in 1990, John Corigliano wrote the Grammy Award-winning *Symphony No.1* to memorialize friends and colleagues who had died of the tragic disease. The AIDS quilt itself is deeply eclectic, formed of some 47,000 patches of varied material made by grieving friends and relatives, while also an expression of unity-in-loss. The first movement of Corigliano's symphony uses an offstage piano to represent an absent pianist; in the second, a frenetic tarantella "[pictures] some of the schizophrenic and hallucinatory images that accompany [AIDS dementia]; the third movement uses the traditional form of a chaconne, but allows 'the chords to hazily dissolve into each other'; throughout, Corigliano sets sentences of text [eulogizing his lost friends] to music, then removes the text and inserts them into the symphony as themes, blurring the boundaries between words and music."[36] The result engenders possibilities for still further novel forms and avenues of experimentation beyond convention.

Consider, as well, the "chance operations" of John Cage's "tacit compositions" like *4'33"* (1952), which, like much of his work, was greatly influenced by his diverse interests in the Zen philosophy of D.T. Suzuki, Italian Futurism, and New England transcendentalism—an eclectic array of conceptual tools to be sure. This "fully scored" work in three movements (following conventional form) consists only of incidental and ambient sounds in the performance environment—a particular time and place. In this way, Cage attempted purposefully to interrupt, retrain, and expand listeners' aesthetic sensibilities. In the late 1960s, one of us saw Cage perform a "piece" where he dragged acoustically amplified music stands around an otherwise empty stage. Then there was a lecture he "gave" in which he threw hundreds of sheets of paper from the podium onto the floor, in silence deliberately crumpling them up one by one, presaging or echoing other performance art ("happenings") of the last quarter of the 20th century and into the 21st.

In the graphic and plastic arts we likewise encounter movements that modify the creative tools provided by previous generative models or modes for certain purposes. This is abundantly evident in the very rapid transition from the now-familiar French impressionism of the second half of the 19th century to the 20th century expressionism, cubism, surrealism, minimalism, the "found objects" art (or "readymades") of Marcel Duchamps and others, earthworks art, and the so-called outsider art of the 1970s.[37] As Arthur Danto has persuasively argued, sociocultural context is critical to understanding why something is or is not considered art by the artworld at a given point in time. The artist must know and understand the relevant conventions while, at the same time, teaching her audience how to see and experience them differently (a formidable kind of problem solving itself), and in many cases cross-culturally.[38] With *Les Demoiselles d'Avignon* (1907), for example, Pablo Picasso transformed the graceful, comfortable, chubby nudes of the Baroque Period into angular, glaring, posturing prostitutes, their original faces scraped off the canvas and replaced with Picasso's rendering of African carved masks, which he had seen at a recent exhibit. Considered revolutionary in its own day, this piece would likely not have been accepted by the "artworld" just a half-century before.

In literature, Cesaire Aimee irrevocably changes the (open-minded) reader's view of Shakespeare's *The Tempest*. In his reconstructed version of the play, the post-colonial *A Tempest*, Prospero does not go home and leave Caliban in possession of his mother's land. No European retreat here; Prospero remains to spoil Caliban's potential enjoyment of his possible deliverance from colonialism, as suggested by Shakespeare. Former director of the Boston Shakespeare Company and MacArthur Foundation award winner Peter Sellars has also radically modified the bard's (and others') work through his eclectic stagings of classical operas and plays. These included, early in his career, a production of *Antony and Cleopatra* in a swimming pool at Harvard University (he later did something similar with Handel's opera *Giulio Cesare*); a techno-industrial production of *King Lear*, incorporating a Lincoln Continental and the ambient music of the *Steel Cello Ensemble* to great effect; and, shortly thereafter, a production of *Macbeth* staged in a hallway. At times criticized for straying too far from composers' and writers' intentions, Sellars has also been hailed a great visionary in his successive retooling of old forms and was featured several times on the noted PBS series *Great Performances*.[39]

In architecture, where the notion of postmodern eclecticism was first conceived in the 1940s, we find structures that expressly refuse the popular monolithic concrete and glass construction so prominent in major American cities. The Harold Washington Library in Chicago (1991), to cite a prominent example, features a whole medley of architectural styles and features. The bottom of the exterior utilizes granite blocks and red brick in the Beaux-Arts style, with massive five-story arched windows. The upper portion combines glass, steel, and aluminum, but with green copper ornaments perched on the roof corners, echoing the gargoyles of gothic architecture. Symbolic figures on the building's exterior include the Owl of Minerva, the Greek goddess of wisdom; seed pods and ears of corn, representing the great natural bounty of the Midwest; and the face of Ceres, the Roman goddess of crops. In this way, the Harold Washington Library is able to bring together some of the diverse natural, social, and cultural factors that have shaped and influenced Chicago and the larger region. Numerous other mid- to-late 20th century buildings use similar (post)modern borrowings, with flourishes and ornamentation mimicking different periods of architecture on the same building, and interior and exterior shapes that can be at once surprising and profoundly elegant.[40]

Indeed, the 20th century, with its two horrific world wars, seemed to be looking for a fresh start of some kind. It freely discarded or modified old forms, tried new ones, but was unable to form a new synthesis (the case still), or was unable to let go completely of the old theses and antitheses. Or, more likely, these examples perhaps reveal the inevitable continuity and discontinuity of human endeavors, rather than some sort of failure to forge a new, enduring synthesis. Forces that are philosophical, historical, social, cultural, biological, intellectual, and aesthetic (and more) come together to show a basic humanity with differences. As noted earlier, each mode of philosophy builds in some way on the previous. The different modes address many of the same problems, but from different perspectives and with different intellectual tools. Each goes somewhere new, whether by discarding or modifying the old and building something new or by returning (with a difference) to something older. The real value of going back to the sources is that doing so reminds us that different critics of different ages see different differences. This is why eclecticism thrives on pragmatic pluralism. Merely selecting elements from the possibilities available is not necessarily better; it is better if it is more illuminating, more useful, more stimulating, more productive of some desired result or effect. The human condition is, we believe, shared to a significant degree. Rather than saying, "Oh, they were wrong; now we have something new and different that is right," we ought to affirm that we see the old things in new ways without fear of being retrogressive in a rapidly changing world. In fact, 20th-century philosophy was not exempt from all this, including the occasional nostalgic return to the old forms with a sigh of relief, like the "new Romanticism" in the symphonies of self-taught 20th-century British composer, Havergal Brian.

All of the above is perhaps best summed up in Jean Francoise Lyotard's oft-cited definitions of the modern and the postmodern in *The Postmodern Condition*. The modern, according to Lyotard, seeks a new intellectual foundation of some kind (typically via science), or what he now famously calls a metanarrative, whereas the postmodern is characterized by an "incredulity toward metanarratives."[41] Historically, metanarratives have proven extremely appealing in their tidy simplicity: Plato, "All knowledge is recollection"; Rousseau, "Everything is good as it leaves the hands of the Author of things; everything degenerates in the hands of man"; Marx, "All history is the history of class struggle"; Mill, "All questions of ethics are questions of utility [that is, "what results in the greatest good for the greatest number (of human beings) in the long run[42]]"; Skinner, "All Learning is conditioning"; Sartre, "All men [sic] are condemned to be free"; Rorty, "Everything is characterized by contingency." It is easy to see the great appeal of these sorts of universals as legitimizing or unifying forces in an often precarious and aleatory world such as ours. By that same token, however, metanarratives inevitably reduce this complexity to simplicity by some manner and degree of distortion (which is not to say that they can't also be informative, in limited ways, as tools of understanding). Though Skinner's idea is a very powerful one, all learning, we now believe, cannot simply be explained by behaviorist conditioning: Cage's "lecture" produced a bit of a scandal at the University of Kansas in the 1970s, but it was followed by a general trend in college classes (well, some of them anyway) toward more active forms of learning, more interacting with students and less "talking at" them, which Cage had mocked in his "lecture."

Philosophy of Education and/in the Classroom

As elucidated above, our basic argument is that philosophy of education can be informative, illuminating, or otherwise useful to educators reflectively seeking creative solutions to the problems of educative practice. Moreover, it can do so in a way that both recognizes and responds to the variety and complexity of "real life" situations. Reflective practitioners pursue praxis with the tools of philosophy of education by combining theory-in-practice and practice-in-theory. In addition, pluralist eclecticism, as a form of pragmatic pluralism, improves and enhances praxis by providing a rich fund of diverse materials toward this end. For instance, being able to identify and articulate the flaw(s) in the idea that test scores represent educational excellence can heighten a teacher's sophistication and, we believe, effectiveness in combating or mitigating such "paltry empiricism" as is imposed on their everyday practice by state regulations. Beginning teachers often enter our classes feeling confused, disoriented, and dismayed—at times even angry—by the glaring inconsistency between the way they were taught to teach (by and large constructivist) and the way their students are assessed (by and large behaviorist). Yet they are many times unable to identify and conceptualize, and, insofar as that is true, proactively counter, where possible, the exact source(s) of the inconsistency. For example, by developing and using their own constructivist assessments when and where feasible or advocating effectively for their students who have been mis-assessed by some "official" measurement tool, they could attempt to dissuade students from defining themselves by their test scores.

In their coursework in philosophy of education, teacher education students must then learn to recognize and work intelligently with many critical themes and concepts in teaching and learning so as to be able to address these and similar issues. They might begin with an understanding that the focus on hands-on learning at developmentally appropriate levels arises in part from Locke's insistence on sensory experience as the origin of ideas. Kant adds recognition that our rational capacity helps us to recognize, sort, count, categorize, or what-have-you the experiential material our senses deliver to us, which gives us conceptual learning and opens the door to constructivism. Piaget adds that this capacity develops over time and through stimulation adds developmentally appropriate practice. Vygotsky adds an understanding of the role of the social context (including language) in learning. Skinner adds the role of conditioning. The general view of education emerging from Dewey's pragmatic naturalism provides one possible, and many argue quite useful, creative synthesis of these ideas.

Or to take a more specific example, consider some of the major themes and concepts emerging from classical philosophy in the area of motivation. Here, two philosophical theories tend to stand out. One theory contends that human beings are essentially motivated by pleasure but asks what kind of pleasure. Epicurus, rather than being a rampant hedonist (as many believe), distinguished between katasytematic (lasting) pleasures and kinetic (fleeting) pleasures, pointing out that the former are productive of a good life, but not the latter. Getting drunk, for instance, may feel good temporarily. However it is followed by a hangover, addiction, and maybe even death. Thomas Hobbes, an atomist as well, agreed that pleasure motivates people but also added fear of pain and death as motivators to his well-known duo of cardinal pleasures—desire for power and love of luxury. Subsequently, J.S. Mill, following his father James Mill and fellow utilitarian Jeremy Bentham, concurred that the avoidance of pain and enjoyment of pleasure are prime motivators but asserted that the intrinsic pleasures of Socrates and the life of the mind (higher pleasures) are to be preferred to the more circumstantial pleasures of a pig (lower pleasures), resulting in his own brand of hedonism.

So what does an analysis of this sort have to offer educators? In a nutshell, it equips them with some useful concepts and ideas about how pleasure in the context of learning might be interpreted and understood—a potentially helpful step in the process of learning how better to promote and engage their students in the pleasures of learning. This is still a further expression of the practical wisdom we take to be inseparable from the profession of teaching. Here, once again, we are not overly concerned with the "truth" of the theories we analyze and explore with our teacher education students; with time, experience, and our initial guidance, we have faith (even if it waivers at times) that they will be able to develop the practical wisdom necessary to be good judges of what is adequate and appropriate in what situations and in what way(s). Contrary to much current discourse and policy in education, we maintain that teaching is less a regulated assemblage of knowledge and skills than a complex, multi-faceted mode of problem solving. It is, at its best, an art, a holistic and inclusive idiom that cannot be reduced to a specific set of best practices, prepackaged strategies or other decontextualized formulae. Its goal, like philosophy's, is (or should be) transformational practice, not mere propositional knowledge.[43] Thus, we believe that the fuller our teacher education students' toolboxes are with diverse philosophical tools, the more likely they are to be able to find ones that "work," that illuminate and resolve (if not permanently) the kinds of problematic situations they encounter or create in their efforts to foster and enhance student learning and growth.

What is more, Arcilla reminds us that the endeavor of philosophy of education is ultimately inseparable from the wisdom necessary to live life with significant meaning and purpose, to flourish, with others, as self-actualized human beings. Doubtless for teachers this life can seem a lengthy, even wearying affair when they are standing before a ragtag group of drowsy, uninspired third graders on a cold February morning. Nevertheless, even at such times, living wisely and well requires reflection. The teacher's journey is, consequently, one that must be informed and propelled by a blend of intellectual and moral courage and, just as importantly, humility. Misunderstanding, uncertainty, and failure on the part of either teachers or students is not some accidental risk that can be easily circumvented with "best practices" or "higher standards;" it is a risk that makes education possible in the first place. And so we proceed onward in the activities of negotiating a complex and ever-changing world, with a 21st-century pluralist eclecticism informing an ongoing, engaged *praxis*.

Notes

1. See, for example, René Vincente Arcilla. "Why aren't philosophers and educators speaking to each other?" *Educational Theory* (52:1, Winter 2002), 1–11. For a more recent argument claiming that philosophy of education is both alive and flourishing today as academic subject-matter, see J.J. Chambliss, "Philosophy of Education Today," *Educational Theory* (59:1, 2009), 233–251.
2. For a recent argument on behalf of a broad, transdisciplinary conception of the nature of philosophy of education as practical theory, see Randall Curren, *A Companion to the Philosophy of Education* (Malden, Mass.: Blackwell, 2003).
3. John Dewey, *Democracy and Education* in *The Middle Works of John Dewey, Volume 9*, ed. Jo Ann Boydston (Carbondale: Southern Illinois University Press, 1985/1916), 338.
4. Plato first uses the term phrōnesis in *The Symposium* (209a) and elsewhere under its second meaning as "practical wisdom, prudence in governmental affairs." The term is common in its first meaning, which is listed variously as "purpose," "intention," then "thought," "sense," and "judgment." In the latter capacity it comes to mean "arrogance." The term is common in Greek philosophy and history (Liddell and Scott, *A Greek-English Lexicon*, eds. Henry Stuart Jones and Roderick McKenzie (Oxford: The Clarendon Press, 1940) 1956.
5. For an excellent contemporary discussion of this issue, see Maughn Gregory and Megan Laverty, "Philosophy and Education for Wisdom," in *Teaching Philosophy*, ed., Andrea Kenkmann (London and New York: Continuum Publishing, 2009), 155–173.
6. Jean-Paul Sartre, *Existentialism*, ed., Bernard Frechtman, New York, Philosophical Library, 1947 (56–61).
7. For those unfamiliar with the idea, KWL charts are taught as a method of "hooking into" what students already "know" at the beginning of a new curricular unit. The K stands for "Know," the W for "Want to Know," and the L for "Learned" by the end of the unit. The items proposed as "Ks" by students can astound even experienced teachers. These ideas often must be debunked. This would indeed lead both teachers and students to question the idea of the "knowledge base" if they have not already done so. In addition, the history of philosophy offers many models for debunking false ideas, for instance in the elenchus sections of the early Socratic dialogues of Plato.
8. We do not appreciate this term, which implies that the students' behavior must be "managed" for them by the teacher, preferring instead the notion that students can learn to become self-directing.
9. We have in mind René Vincente Arcilla's much-discussed article, "Why aren't philosophers and educators talking to each other?" *Educational Theory* 53:2 (Winter 2002), 1–11 and the issue in response to it, *Educational Theory* 52:3 (Summer 2002). We will say more on this below.
10. For a recent example of this approach, visit: Beth Lewis, editor, About.com's Guide to Elementary Education, *What Is Your Educational Philosophy?* Available at http://k6educators.about.com/od/helpfornewteachers/qt/edphil.htm, accessed 21 March 2009.
11. For more on this phenomenon as characteristic of American culture, see Richard Hofstadter's classic *Anti-Intellectualism in American Life* (New York: Vintage Books, 1964).
12. Rene Vincente Arcilla "Why aren't philosophers and educators speaking to each other?" in *Educational Theory* 52:1 (Winter 2002) 1–11.
13. See, for example, Sextus Empiricus, *Outlines of Pyrrhonism*, trans. R.G. Bury (Buffalo, New York: Prometheus Books, 1990).
14. Ludwig Wittgenstein, *Tractatus Logico-Philosophicus*, trans. C. K. Ogden (London: Routledge and Kegan Paul, Ltd, 1955) 189.
15. Ludwig Wittgenstein, *Philosophical Investigations*, trans. G.E.M. Anscombe (New York: Macmillan Publishing Co., Inc., 1953) 19.
16. According to the *Columbia Encyclopedia*, sixth edition, "Many Roman philosophers, especially Cicero and the Neoplatonists, were known for eclecticism. Eclecticism among Renaissance humanists, who drew from

Christian and classical doctrines, was followed by a 19th-century revival, particularly with French philosopher Victor Cousin, who coined the term and applied it to his own system. Eclectics are frequently charged with being inconsistent, and the term is sometimes used pejoratively." In "Eclecticism," *The Columbia Encyclopedia, Sixth Edition*, 2008. Retrieved March 09, 2009 from Encyclopedia.com: http://www.encyclopedia.com/doc/1E1-eclctc-phi.html.

17. Henry George Liddell and Robert Scott, *Greek-English Lexicon*, eds. Henry Stuart Jones and Roderick McKenzie (Oxford: Clarendon Press, 1961), 1033–1034.
18. Ibid., 511.
19. The idea of eclecticism in philosophy of education originates from one of us, namely Jane Fowler Morse. It is apparent in her writings applying the philosophy of Plato (Socrates), Aristotle, Epicurus, Kant, Marx and Mill to philosophical problems concerning method, aims, motivation, ethics, and epistemology in education in major articles. This chapter represents a sketch of the idea of eclecticism in philosophy of education be worked on at a later date by this author.
20. This idea is added by the other of us, namely David A. Granger. It is clear to us both that eclecticism requires a broadly conceived pluralism as offering the possibilities out of which the eclectic thinker chooses or which she recombines into new ideas. Combining the two ideas into our concept of "pluralist eclecticism" has led us to some fruitful discussions.
21. James once remarked that, "If we take that whole history of philosophy, the systems reduce themselves to a few main types which under all technical verbiage in which the ingenious intellect of man envelops them, are just so many visions, modes of feeling the whole push, and seeing the whole drift of life, forced on one by one's total character and experience and on the whole *preferred*—there is no other truthful word—as one's best working attitude." See *A Pluralistic Universe* (Cambridge, Mass.: Harvard University Press, 1977/1909), 14–15. We should add that the pluralist eclecticism we are arguing for here is generally (though not exclusively) more purposeful and less playful than so-called postmodern eclecticism.
22. For more on this idea, see David A. Granger, *John Dewey, Robert Pirsig, and the Art of Living: Revisioning Aesthetic Education* (New York: Palgrave Macmillan, 2006), 194–195.
23. David A. Granger, "Positivism, Skepticism, and the Attractions of 'Paltry Empiricism': Stanley Cavell and the Current Standards Movement in Education" in *Philosophy of Education 2003*, ed. Kal Alston (Urbana, Ill.: The Philosophy of Education Society, 2003), 146–154. See also Granger, "No Child Left Behind and the Spectacle of Failing Schools: The Mythology of Contemporary School Reform" in *Educational Studies*, 43:3 (May-June 2008), 206–228.
24. Jane Fowler Morse, "Intellectual Freedom and Economic Sufficiency as Educational Entitlements" in *Studies in Philosophy and Education*, 20:3 (May 2001), 201–211.
25. This issue is provocatively addressed in Dan Liston, Jennie Whitcomb and Hilda Borko, "The End of Education in Teacher Education: Thoughts on Reclaiming the Role of Social Foundations in Teacher Education" in *The Journal of Teacher Education*, 60:2 (March/April, 2009), 107–11.
26. Aristotle, *Nicomachean Ethics, Book VI*, trans. Martin Ostwald (New York: Macmillan Publishing Company, 1962), 146–173.
27. Dewey, "From Absolutism to Experimentalism" in *The Later Works of John Dewey, Volume 5*, ed. Jo Ann Boydston (Carbondale: Southern Illinois University Press, 1988/1930), 155.
28. Kant, *Critique of Pure Reason*, trans. J.M.D. Meiklejohn (Buffalo, New York: Prometheus Books), 170. Kant would later identify the notion of precepts without concepts with the aesthetic.
29. Boethius, *The Consolation of Philosophy*, Book 5, Prose 4, (Macmillan, Library of Liberal Arts: New York and London), 110.
30. The Copernican Turn is the realization that the knowledge of human beings is affected by the perspective of their situations. Copernicus was able to imagine a different stance, which allowed him to hypothesize the heliocentric universe. This imaginative ability is reflected in the plea of Greek scientist Archimedes, who said, "Give me a place to stand and with a lever I will move the whole world." John Tzetzes (12th century AD), *Book of Histories* 2, 129–130. Translated by Francis R. Walton, available at http://www.math.nyu.edu/~crorres/Archimedes/Lever/LeverQuotes.html, accessed 20 March 2009.
31. See *Philosophy and the Mirror of Nature* (Princeton, N.J.: Princeton University Press, 1979).
32. Descartes, *Discourse on Method*, translated by John Veitch (Buffalo, New York: Prometheus Books, 1989/1637), 79.
33. Of course the 20th century was not the only time that artists borrowed or challenged conventions in significant ways. Monteverdi deliberately borrowed the forms of Greek drama to invent opera with dance, dialogue, and music, and the Colosseum in Rome violated the conventions of the day by putting together in one building the three orders of columns—Doric, Ionic, and Corinthian.
34. Some of this material was drawn from the program notes to a recent performance one of us attended. They are available at http://www.rpo.org/s_7/s_118/p_751/Program_Notes_-_Mahler%27s_Sixth/.

35. For many examples, including the work of Lukas Foss, see J. Peter Burkholder, Andreas Giger, and David C. Birchler "Musical Borrowing: An Annotated Bibliography," last updated 4 June 2003, available at http://www.chmtl.indiana.edu/borrowing/, accessed 21 March 2009. For the reference to Foss (and others) from this bibliography, see Glenn Watkins, "Uses of the Past: A Synthesis" in *Soundings: Music in the Twentieth Century* (New York: Schirmer Books, 1988), 640–660. There we read that, "Composers of recent years have had mixed feelings about the use of music of the past, and they have borrowed in a variety of ways. Surges of interest in borrowing arose around certain occasions. For example, the 400th anniversary of Gesualdo's birth inspired a number of new works in 1960, and this helped create interest in using the works of Monteverdi and Cavalli in the 1960s and 1970s. Others have turned to Bach, including Lukas Foss with his innovative use of Bach's Von Himmel Hoch in his Baroque Variations. Beethoven's bicentennial in 1970 inspired composers including Stockhausen and Ginastera to borrow in various ways. Kagel's 'meta-collage' of small quotations from Beethoven's most popular works offers an interesting example. The 20th century has also seen a movement called New Romanticism, consisting of a return to 19th-century tonality. Rochberg's quotation technique led him to a more general stylistic modeling, whereas Berio's use of Mahler was intended to honor him specifically. Eventually, New Romanticism focused more on stylistic modeling than exact references, and with the addition of jazz and ragtime devices, composers achieved a 'polystylistic juxtaposition.'" Many other pieces are mentioned, and the article includes an extensive list of modern works and the works from which they borrowed.
36. The *tarantella* is based on an Italian folk dance in 6/8 time, and a *chaconne* is a baroque era form used as a vehicle for musical variations. Each of these movements was inspired by a particular friend of Corigliano's. See the jacket notes for world premiere of *Symphony No.1*, Chicago Symphony Orchestra, Daniel Barenboim conducting the CSO edition, Meet the Composer Orchestra Residency Series, Erato 2292–45601-2.
37. "Outsider art" refers to art created beyond the boundaries and conventions of the official culture of the "artworld." (The "artworld" is that contingent of institutionally enfranchised persons (e.g., museum curators, art critics, aestheticians) who regulate the criteria used to decide if a given object should be conferred the status of art.) Outsider artists are typically self-taught and their pieces often deal with extreme mental states, offbeat perspectives, or extravagant fantasies.
38. See Arthur C. Danto, *The Transfiguration of the Commonplace* (Cambridge, Mass., and London: Harvard University Press, 1981).
39. Sellars is currently Professor of World Arts and Culture at U.C.L.A.
40. For an excellent discussion of twentieth-century architecture along these lines, see David Harvey, *The Condition of Postmodernity* (Cambridge, Mass., and Oxford, UK: Blackwell, 1989).
41. Lyotard, *The Postmodern Condition: A Report on Knowledge*, trans. Geoff Bennington and Brian Massumi (Minneapolis: University of Minnesota Press, 1984), xxiv.
42. John Stuart Mill, *Utilitarianism* (Buffalo, New York: Prometheus Books, 1987/1863), 16.
43. For more on this very Deweyan idea, see Richard Shusterman, *Practicing Philosophy: Pragmatism and the Philosophical Life* (New York: Routledge, 1997).

Fourteen

Taking Teacher Education into Alien Terrain: The Future of Educational Theorizing

Susan Schramm-Pate

You couldn't swing a dead cat at the end of the twentieth century without hitting a scholarly book or journal article dedicated to improving schooling by taking teacher education into theoretical terrain. Heavy hitters in the field of teacher education argued that the teaching of theory should be inextricably linked to its application (e.g., Britzman, 1991; Bruner, 1977; Carlson, 1992; 1997; Darling Hammond, 1999; Eisner, 1985; Feiman-Nemser, & Remillard, 1995; Giroux, 1997; Goodlad, 1990; 1994; 1997; Greene, 1978; Kneller, 1971; Kincheloe, 1993; Macdonald, 1988; Macdonald; 1995; McLaren, 1989; Zeichner, 1990; 2002). Scholars referenced John Dewey's constructivist theory to learning detailed in his famous book, *Experience and Education* (1938) to remind us that "sound educational experience involves, above all, continuity and interaction between the learner and what is learned" (p. 10). The question of how teacher preparation programs could enable teachers to transfer teacher-knowledge to effective practice, drove the late twentieth-century educational literature. Scholars argued that a background in constructivism, curricular integration, and the rigorous application of critical reflective thinking would enable teacher educators to enter the *living laboratory* of their K–12 classrooms to 'test' the theories and concepts they teach. This knowledge of theory would enable them to examine their own teaching practices while making the necessary revisions and adjustments to their practice. After all, progressives argued, it is during this reflective process of inquiry—thinking, reflecting, and acting on his or her practice (i.e., praxis)—that teacher (and student and school) transformation occurs. The history of American school curricular "reconceptualists" has already been chronicled precisely by Pinar, Reynolds, Slattery, and Taubman (1995) and so the purpose of the present chapter is to ask, "What happened to the emphasis on theory in teacher education?" and "Where do those of us who wish to restore theory into teacher education go from here?"

In the foreword to Pepi Leistyna's book, *Defining and Designing Muticulturalism* (2002), Peter McLaren wrote:

> Readers are not provided with a prefabricated model to be implemented, but with an invitation to engage, to question, and to challenge received orthodoxies, as uncomfortable as this challenge might be for some teachers and for those in the universities who *claim* to be educating them. (p. xvii, italics mine)

In a review of the book for the *Journal of Curriculum Theorizing*, I asked Leistyna if he thought McLaren's comment was rather harsh or fairly accurate of teacher educators in this country. He said:

> My sense of Peter's comment is that he is presenting [my book] as a text for ideas and debate rather than a recipe to be followed to the last grain of salt. . . . .But you're right, there is more to Peter's comment. Are we a society that inspires movement outside the box? I don't think so—the movement towards strict standardization is strong evidence of this. At the same time, I would argue that schools of education do often work to deskill future educators by not encouraging active theorizing. . . .the assault on theorizing is in part connected to ways in which universities traditionally have been working to mold students into uncritical receivers and consumers of existing theory, but rarely viewing them as dynamic and creative participants in the generative process of understanding. (2003, pp. 140–141).

One of the nice things about writing a chapter such as this is that it enables one to reflect on one's own practices and experiences, something that perhaps we often mean to do but do not take the time to do. To frame this chapter, I begin with my personal stories from the 'ivory tower.' I share these in a effort to make sense of why theory is divorced from teacher preparation and to perhaps enable others to reflect on them as well. The first story also serves as a justification for writing this chapter.

The First Story: Dr. X

The first story takes place at a monthly meeting at the beginning of the 2008–2009 school year. Faculty in my department of Instruction and Teacher Education (ITE) within the College of Education (COE) at the University of South Carolina (USC), were shown a PowerPoint presentation on "how to improve teacher preparation programs" by an invited speaker whom my colleagues in ITE almost universally regard as one of the most influential and knowledgeable scholars in the contemporary field of teacher education. The guest speaker, who shall remain anonymous as *Dr. X*, gave what I felt was a very modernist reply to my query. During the question and answer session, I asked (paraphrased):

> I don't teach any undergraduates and I find that by the time students get to my courses, I have to do a lot of remediation of basic theory. In your opinion, Dr. X, what can we do to enable our pre-service and/or undergraduate teacher preparation programs to be better prepared to bridge the theory-practice gap, if indeed one feels there is a gap?

Dr X answered (paraphrased):

> I'd venture to say that if you asked a new teacher what she [sic] felt she needed most, it would be *practical* skills such as classroom management, it certainly wouldn't be theory. They need to be prepared to handle the logistics of the classroom.

I replied (paraphrased):

The literature is rife with concepts of how to 'manage classrooms,' if that is the concern, so it seems to me that the teacher you refer to would benefit from grappling with the various models of classroom management that offer strategies for local and particular situations rather than being told which one classroom management model worked for all students, no?

At this point, Dr. X wanted no more discourse with me and changed the subject. No one followed up and/or expanded on my comments, they simply looked at me in shock. I guess I was not supposed to challenge the great Dr. X.

Later, several of my colleagues approached me and voiced that they too thought there was a need for more theory in our undergraduate programs. When I asked them why they did not challenge Dr. X in the faculty meeting or continue my line of questioning, they simply looked down at the ground. "Interesting," I thought, "no wonder by the time the students get to me they are unfamiliar with the most basic umbrella theories of schooling: progressivism, essentialism, perennialism, and social reconstructionism." Later in December of 2008, when asked by Randy Hewitt and Joe Kincheloe to pen this chapter on teacher preparation and theory, I was not only honored but also felt I was long overdue to write a paper on my critical reflections on this phenomenon.

The Second Story: Exposure to Theory for the First Time

The second story involves a course I teach. As a product of teacher education in the late 1980s, I taught in public schools until receiving a Ph.D. in 1997 from Miami University of Ohio under the influence of major figures such as Dennis Carlson, Peter McLaren, Henry Giroux, and Richard Quantz. As one of two full-time faculty members in the Ed.D. program of Curriculum Studies, I regularly teach a course called, *Principles of Curriculum Construction*. This graduate-level course draws students from diverse program areas such as educational leadership, art education, library science, nursing education, early childhood and elementary education, etc. Some are pre-service and others are seasoned professionals. In many cases this course is the only "curriculum" course many students take within their programs. By curriculum, I am talking about the neighborhood one lives in, the color of one's skin, the slant of one's eye sockets, the clothes on one's back, in addition to the bodies of knowledge and pedagogical and instructional practices. In curriculum studies, we define "curriculum" very broadly and within the diversity of the everyday. For my students this is something totally new.

Within my classroom "laboratory," so to speak, I designed *Principles of Curriculum Construction* into two parts—the theoretical and the practical. Although I teach the course each semester and multiple sections of it in the summer months, I am always stunned at students' responses to part one (theory) of the course. I begin with a discussion of some universal characteristics and the pervasiveness of schooling and educational theory—i.e., its links to anthropology, sociology, etc. To illustrate these links, I cannot say this any better than Donald Vandenberg:

> *Historically*, education is the transmission of the human heritage in order to maintain and enhance the level of civilization a given society has attained. *Anthropologically*, education is the humanization of the young that occurs in the dialogue between generations and that enables the young to attain adulthood and a place in adult society. *Sociologically*, education is the socialization of the young into the societal rules and values believed necessary and desirable for a society's continued existence. *Politically*, education is the preparation for citizenship in the state or nation. *Economically*, education is the acquisition of the knowledge, skills, and values necessary for gainful employment and for training the workforce. *Existentially*,

education is becoming aware of the possibilities of being that enable one to achieve an adult presence to the world as a morally and socially responsible person with one's own value and dignity. *Cosmically*, education is the journey of becoming at home in the universe. (as cited in Goodlad, 1997, p. 1, *italics* mine)

Clearly, we could quibble over some of Vandenberg's words and definitions and the fact that he left out the impact of the field of "psychology," but my point of bringing this up is to illustrate that inevitably my students are amazed (perplexed, concerned) that they have not been exposed to thinking of *educational theory* as linked to sociology, psychology, anthropology, political science, economics, etc. Things become even murkier when we begin to discuss what I refer to as the four major "umbrella" theories of education: 1) *Progressivism* (following John Dewey, 1938); 2) *Essentialism* (following William Bagley, 1934; A *Nation at Risk*, 1983; No Child Left Behind, 2001); 3) *Perennialism* (following Aristotle, 1952; Mortimer Adler, 1982); and 4) *Social Reconstructionism* (following George Counts, 1932; Harold Rugg, 1947). Multiculturalism, in my curriculum course, is not approached as an "umbrella" theory because there are clear differences between *Conservative Multiculturalism* (e.g., Diane Ravitch, 1983; E. D. Hirsch, Jr., 1987), *Liberal Multiculturalism* (e.g., Geneva Gay, 1983; Carl Grant & Christine Sleeter, 1986; James Banks, 1988; 2006), and *Critical Multiculturalism* (e.g., Peter McLaren, 1987; Dennis Carlson, 1992; 1997; Henry Giroux, 1997; Paulo Freire, 1997; Susan Schramm-Pate & Rhonda Jeffries, 2008; Pepi Leistyna, 2002).

What becomes even more problematic to my students is the notion that if they are currently teaching or administering in an American public school, then it is very likely (if not absolutely likely) that they are operating within an *essentialistic* culture. Thus, we go back in time and observe the theoretical pendulum swings. That is to say, by taking a historical approach to the major tenets of the most important American educational philosophies of the past century and current centuries, my students begin their first forays into what some if them refer to as "theory-land." The appendix contains an abbreviated version of my own hand-out of four basic "umbrella theories" (i.e., essentialism, progressivism, perennialism, and social reconstructionism) that I share with them before they delve into the readings. (Note: I include critical multiculturalism in this hand-out to expand upon social reconstructionism).

As students begin the course, *Principles of Curriculum Construction*, they voice concerns regarding how they might make the leap from theoretical generality to 'real world' specificity. Before taking my class, most of the pre-service teachers (in the process of learning to teach) tell me that they are asked and expected to comprehend general information about subject matter (e.g., curriculum models and curriculum mapping) and pedagogy (e.g., classroom management, planning, scope and sequence) and then apply this general knowledge to the particulars of a teaching situation. According to my students, field experiences and student teaching require the ability to recall this information, to interpret it in light of specific context (e.g., student skill and background, particular values and goals), and to design and implement a specific plan for teaching based on those interpretations.

Below are excerpts from student talk-back surveys at mid-semester from *Principles of Curriculum Construction*:

SSP (Susan Schramm-Pate)'s Q1—Within your teacher preparation program, do you feel you read enough theory to be able to write your own platform of beliefs about schooling and learning?

A1—"I recall few theory classes, I learned most of what I know on the job."

A2—"I have a business degree and was certified through PACE [i.e., an acronym for Program of Alternative Certification for Educators], so I haven't had much theory other than our program."

A3—"Theory is important but I always felt I needed more practical application once I got in the classroom."

A4—"I would say that practical application is at least equally important. You can discuss something in theory, but until you apply it, it's just that."

SSP's Q2—Why might a teacher preparation program NOT want pre-service teachers to have a philosophical platform of beliefs about schooling and learning?

A1—"So that pre-service teachers can figure it out on the job or on their own without someone else's theory."

A2—"I wonder if some schools omit the philosophical piece so that they can 'train' new teachers."

A3—"I think a lot of teachers feel helpless when it comes to the demands for accountability and testing; either they comply with the rules or they lose their job."

A4—"Perhaps they have an agenda and they want to 'train' new teachers in that same vein."

A5—"A teacher preparation program wants you to conform to their expectations."

SSP-Q3—What is the "theory" behind the current No Child Left Behind Act?

A1—"I think it's what you said SSP, the NCLB movement is designed to 'deskill' teachers and keep us 'mystified' of the theory behind the practices and all that accountability that is essentialist in nature."

A2—"It is Essentialistic, a lot of accountability in the form of testing and standards."

A3—"It was penned by Teddy Kennedy and Joe Biden, two guys probably born in the 1940s who were exposed to essentialism their whole lives."

A4—"Whatever you call it, it is based on the philosophy that you can pay teachers less and give them less benefits and incentives to do well."

SSP-Q4—If you are public school personnel working in the United States today are you better off not knowing or knowing alternative theories to essentialism?

A1—"Knowing! I think that at least in my school, teachers are afraid to have a voice. Most would rather conform and have their hand held than take a stand."

A2—"I know that knowing theory helps give you a voice; but I am in a district that does not allow for 'voices'."

A3—"Not knowing since they are trying to 'dummy-proof' the curriculum so schools don't have to take the responsibility if a student doesn't do well."

A4—"Many teachers in my school who are forced to use basal readers for literacy instruction say that it feels too scripted. Maybe if they knew some theory behind basal readers they'd have more of a say."

In *Theory as a Prayerful Act*, James B. MacDonald (1995) refers to the phenomenon my students are talking about as a "closed" school where "learning outcomes are synonymous with

178 Susan Schramm-Pate

evaluated performance" (p. 33). In a closed school, or what I call an *essentialistic* school, learning is described as conditioning, reinforcement, problem solving with predetermined answers, factoids that are to be remembered, recognized, and regurgitated. Children are tracked, sorted, and labeled into types and are viewed as 'customers' to be constructed for the 'world of work,' since the purposes of schooling to the essentialist are *cultural indoctrination* and *economic*. That is to say, students are to be prepared for an occupation, citizenship, and literacy within a participatory representative republic and capitalist economic system. Even social relationships are, according to MacDonald,

> [P]rimarily bases of confirmation, sanction, and motivation; and communication is a process of attending to predetermined stimuli with the production of predictable responses. Everything is, in a sense, inside the reality of a restructured relationship. (p. 33)

By contrast, Dewey (1964) said that reflective thinking is the ability to give serious and persistent consideration to a subject in order to act deliberately and intentionally rather than routinely and impulsively. Freire (1971) said that active reflection helps transform pre-service teachers' feelings of doubt, perplexity, and uncertainty, in applying general knowledge to specific teaching circumstances into greater clarity, resolve and understanding. MacDonald (1995) calls this a "reality-centered school" or "open" school, noting,

> Here, learning is seen as the outcome of personal responsiveness to wide varieties of stimulation and wide usages of symbolic media. Children are seen as unities, self-actualizers and creators. The function of the school is to challenge and stimulate the child's creative encounter with reality. (p. 33)

The Third Story:
Who Is Goodlad and What Does He Have to Do with PDS?

The third story involves a meeting of the Professional Development School (PDS) network here at USC. I attended a meeting that was intended to address ways in which the COE could increase the number of PDS school-university partnerships in the Columbia, SC area. The COE decided that it would place as many of its student teachers in PDS schools as possible to work with the cooperating teachers there. Because I had a strong background from Miami University on the philosophical underpinnings of John Goodlad and the PDS network, I naturally assumed that the folks in the room with me who actually worked for PDS were familiar with Goodlad, too. At one point, I asked if Goodlad's famous book, *Educational Renewal* (1994), was given to the teachers (both practicing and pre-service) in the cooperating PDS schools. The chair of the committee glared at me and someone at the table said, "Who is John Goodlad?" At first I thought they were putting me on. Then I realized that they were serious and so I said,

> He's the director and creator of the Center for Educational Renewal at the University of Washington, Seattle and the president of the independent Institute for Educational Inquiry. He and his colleagues started the National Network for Educational Renewal (for school–university partnerships) in 1986 after the publication of the manifesto, *A Nation at Risk*.

Still, they glared at me. So I continued,

Perhaps it might be useful to enable the cooperating teachers and student teachers and other school personnel to know some of Goodlad's theory and ideas for effective partnerships? Perhaps this may help with your mission to increase the numbers of your PDS network here in Columbia?

Some nodded in agreement and seemed to be contemplating the idea. Still I did not get the sense that they were going to run to the library after the meeting to research Goodlad for themselves (especially since I offered to lend them books from my personal library and no one took me up on the offer). I went back to my office and pulled Goodlad's books off my shelves, dusted them off, and typed up a one- or two-page user-friendly hand-out to Goodlad's theory of educational renewal. I thought this way they could share it at PDS meetings with others and perhaps undergird the PDS practice with theory. In retrospect, I should not have been surprised that my hand-out was met with resentment and disdain, even by a department chair who told me it was a "waste of time to burden teachers with theory."

Before moving to South Carolina, I studied with university professionals, both graduate and undergraduate, who stressed understanding the impact of the social, cultural, historical, and political contexts; where theory and theorizing are constantly interwoven into the practice tapestry. At the time I was surprised at the reaction of my colleagues, and I seriously began to consider how different the university culture I now found myself in was from the one I came from.

Over the years, I have gained a fuller understanding about the culture I now live and work in. For example, just last week in an effort to bridle me with a curb bit and chain, a senior faculty member told me, "I'd have a better chance of getting my computer repaired if I would follow 'southern custom' of 'catching more flies with honey than vinegar.'" Excuse me?

Alas, the purpose of this chapter is not a critique of patriarchy and sexism and thus, I digress. However, stereotypes about people and what teacher education is and how pre-service teachers should behave, continue to be perpetuated. Many of us in academe who work with teachers know that teacher preparation removed from theory and theorizing is difficult at best and unethical at worst. There are some major myths about pre-service teachers that persist in all kinds of situations and among all sorts of people, even among the most thoughtful and progressive teacher educators and institutions of higher education. They are so deeply embedded in the culture, that, without our realizing it, they often derail our ability to prepare teachers for twenty-first century classrooms. This chapter concludes with some examples of mythos and logos surrounding some of the reasons why theory and theorizing are readily ignored.

Mythos #1: Teaching is the fallback profession—anyone can do it.

Logos #1

If one is not successful in one's "real" job, one can always teach. How many lay people believe that 'those who can, do; and those who can't, teach?' There is a false sense that teacher education programs are not challenging or rigorous or even that they don't teach one to think. To become a teacher you simply do what was done to you in schools. Clearly, field experiences are needed to enable teachers not only to have experiences in classrooms other than their experiences as students but also to address the disconnect between the image of teaching that is portrayed in university methods courses and the local and particular classroom setting.

The state of South Carolina is in a 'critical needs' situation for teachers and administrators. Many student teachers in SC seek certification through the *Program of Alternative Certification for Educators* (PACE) which

> [W]as established to enable degreed individuals, who otherwise do not meet certification requirements, to gain employment in the public schools in a PACE approved subject area teaching position. (p. 1)

Throughout the website http://www.scteachers.org/cert/pace/PACE.cfm the term "training" is used to refer to teacher preparation. Under eligibility requirements one bulleted item reads:

> Work experience does not have to be teaching experience. An earned masters degree [in any subject] will waive the experience requirement. (p. 1)

Virtually every state has established some alternative route to teacher certification, enabling those who do not hold an undergraduate degree in education to enter the profession. Although people in PACE are generally older and have tried at least one career such as law, banking, or social work, without a strong theoretical background in race, class, and gender theory they may pose a risk in struggling schools with large numbers of poor and minority children no matter how smart they are.

Teacher interns, certified in traditional teacher preparation programs or alternative certification programs, can have difficulty linking theory to practice in field settings. Unlearning as well as learning can be achieved through engaging in professional discourse with practicing teachers, university professors, and the theoretical literature. Transformative teaching begins with understanding and experiencing what it means to be a teacher.

Mythos #2: Theory and practice are like that age-old question: 'What came first the chicken or the egg?'

Logos #2:

Many times we tend to think that theory follows practice and vice versa, but the truth is that theory and practice are inextricably linked. Postmodernism and critical theory reveal the ways in which theory is rendered invisible from its practice, obscuring the fact that practices are always scaffolded by local and particular theoretical perspectives and assumptions. I asked some of my graduate students to read a draft of this chapter and write a response. One seasoned teacher wrote:

> I love the dead cat metaphor . . . my teacher education program was in the 1970s . . . so I missed the whole 'dead cat' era! I think teachers who came through during the same time that I did had a strong practical knowledge of education but since we were missing the theory, maybe we just watched the [curricular] pendulum [swing] and did what we felt comfortable doing but didn't have the theoretical underpinning to say why.

This teacher was not aware of what informed her practice, which is very likely to cause her problems in the future. Leistyna (2002) argues in *Defining and Designing Multiculturalism* that it is key for teachers and administrators to be able to read the existing links between theory and practice—why are we doing what we do and under what conditions? The teacher above said that she felt like she was "doing Dewey" but didn't know it and didn't know why she should know.

Everyone talks about Dewey and no one reads him. His writings are numerous; however, there are some basic writings that are necessary to read in order to understand the relationship between his educational theory and the principles of his general philosophy. Dewey (1964) wrote:

> It is sometimes supposed that it is the business of the philosophy of education to tell what education *should* be. . . . And before we can formulate a philosophy of education we must know how human nature is constituted in the concrete; we must know about the working of actual social forces; we must know about the operations through which basic raw materials are modified into something of greater value. The need for a philosophy of education is thus fundamentally the need for finding out what education really *is*. (pp. 3–4)

Mythos #3: Everything you need to teach is in the textbooks and standards.

Logos#3

Educational theory is how people interpret, critique, and draw generalizations about why schools, as social microcosms, work the way they do. Often teachers feel that if they are 'experts' in their content area then they are fully prepared for the classroom. However, if educators do not understand the background of the community in which they work, the culture of the school in which they teach, or the values and beliefs of the people whom they are entrusted to teach, that content is quite frankly useless. It becomes on more thing to memorize and regurgitate with no connection or relevance to the students' lives or what they value.

One teacher wrote:

> When I came to South Carolina, I truly had a culture shock. Basals were required, middle school students were grouped by ability, desks were in rows, kids weren't supposed to talk. . . . I just closed my door and tried to avoid administrators. One came to my class to see me and noticed that my students were working in small groups. She ordered the desks back in rows and got everyone back into the same book so she could show me how to teach using the basal reader . . . If I had known the theory behind what I was doing earlier, I may not have felt so intimidated.

Dewey (1934/1964) wrote:

> Then essential weakness of the old and traditional education was not just that it emphasized the necessity for definite subject-matter and activities. . . . The weakness and evil was that the imagination of educators did not go beyond provision of a fixed and rigid environment of subject-matter, one drawn moreover from sources altogether too remote from the experiences of the pupil. (p. 9)

He goes on to argue that a teacher should not be a "magistrate set on high and marked by arbitrary authority but. . . a friendly co-partner and guide in a common enterprise" (p. 10). What emerges from Dewey's work is an understanding of education as a conscious, purposeful, and informed activity that involves the aim of the activity [goals and objectives], the agent [teacher] responsible for the activity, the subject [student] of the activity, and the means by which the aim is achieved [curriculum and pedagogy]. In order to accomplish all of this, Dewey maintains that the teacher must be a well-educated professional with a broad knowledge on which to draw in developing units of study and a sound grounding in educational theory so that she or he understands the philosophical, and sociological foundations of education. Dewey insists that a teacher see a reciprocal relationship between theory and practice so that her or his teaching is not reduced to a mere practical activity without grounding in theoretical science or an abstract science that has little relation to practice.

Mythos #4: Theory is ivory tower elitism; it has nothing to do with 'where the rubber hits the road.'

Logos #4

There is no doubt that some educators opt to ignore theory and theorizing because it is often complex, opaque, and seemingly inaccessible. The lexical complexity alone is a major deterrent since it requires virtually learning a new language. As a former public school teacher, I have great respect for people who are 'where the rubber hits the road.' As a university professor, I try to educate teachers and prepare them for what they will face in schools by always trying to ground theory in experience and practice.

Problematizing and decoding the significance of what happens on the ground require linguistic privilege to be sure. Although some in the 'ivory tower' certainly exercise power over teachers by keeping them mystified and marginalized from the critical social theories.

I believe that Dewey (1916) chose to conclude *Democracy and Education* with the chapter, "Theories of Morals," to enable us to see that opening up inner and outer spaces for people to speak and be aware of multiple voices and audiences is to 'do the right thing.'

> The first obstruction which meets us is the currency of moral ideas which split the course of activity into two opposed factors, often named respectively the inner and outer, or the spiritual and the physical. This division is a culmination of the dualism of mind and the physical world, soul and body, ends and means. (p. 346)

When my graduate students complain about the density of critical social theories and critical pedagogy and multiculturalism, I use their complaints as a point of departure for enabling them to think about their sixteen-plus years of formal schooling and why it is that they have not been exposed to such works before. Introductory lectures, texts, teacher-made hand-outs, and a glossary of key words, enable them to scaffold into ongoing discussions and debates around complex economic, political, sociocultural, psychological, and pedagogical issues. The point is to try to get teachers to make meaning of the complex sociopolitical issues they face in schools, not to necessarily agree with the conclusions that I draw. Discrimination, racism, sexism, classism, tracking, violence in schools, all of these things are political in nature, and the goal should be to theorize why these things exist and begin to fight the good ideological fight. As professionals, teachers need input. It is unethical to hand them scripted classroom materials based on someone else's vision of good schooling. Disregarding the specificities that real people work in every day at best forces teachers to become objects of someone else's theory and practice and, at worst, deskills, objectifies, and marginalizes them.

Conclusion

Following Dewey (1964), I believe that it is impossible to separate theory and practice. He says it best:

> On one hand, we may carry on the practical work with the object of giving teachers in training working command of the necessary tools of their profession; control of the technique of class instruction and

management; skill and proficiency in the work of teaching. . . . On the other hand, we may propose to use practice work as an instrument in making real and vital theoretical instruction; the knowledge of subject-matter and of principles of education.

This quote illustrates the embrace of *both/and* thinking and the rejection of *either/or* thinking that IS classic Deweyian pragmatism. It is not *either* an apprenticeship (e.g., teacher in training) *or* a laboratory (e.g., classroom practice), but involves *both* working to master levels *and* continually reconstructing (to use one of Dewey's favorite terms) practices. Setting up dualisms, contrasts between the two serves to limit our worldview, our profession, and our students. For example, students can enter the "hermeneutic circle" in which they may strive to uncover the meaning of both others' actions and one's own actions in relation to others'. Theory, research, and practice will merge as both parties continue on the road of shared discovering and understanding that leads to transformational growth (McDonald, 1988).

Other professional development schools such as engineering, law, medicine, architecture, etc. may be in the business of training professionals, but schools of education should have "nothing to do with the training of teachers" (Dewey, 1904/1964, p. 329). Schools of education should recognize the need to enable teachers to conduct their practical work *both* "for the sake of vitalizing *and* illuminating intellectual methods" (p. 316, italics mine). If teaching is a "calling" as so many of my students tell me it is, let's heed the call for holding teacher preparation programs responsible for deskilling teachers by promoting standardization, ignoring theory and theorizing, stifling dialogue, keeping students mystified with oversimplification and de-contextualization of the field. Let's insist instead on transformative praxis (Freire, 1997).

Appendix: Theories of Curriculum and Schooling

PROGRESSIVISM

AIMS: To promote democratic social living, to foster creative self-learning;

KNOWLEDGE: Focus on growth and development; a living-learning process; active and relevant learning;

TEACHER'S ROLE: Teachers are guides for problem solving and scientific inquiry;

CURRICULUM: Curriculum centers on student interests; involves the application of human problems; subject matter is interdisciplinary.

ESSENTIALISM

AIMS: To promote the intellectual growth of the individual; to educate the competent person for the benefit of humanity.

KNOWLEDGE: Focus on essential skills and academic subjects; mastery of concepts and principles of subject matter.

TEACHER'S ROLE: Teachers should act as authority figures who have expertise in subject field or content areas.

CURRICULUM: Curriculum centers on essential skills (three Rs) and major content subjects such as English, Science, History, Mathematics, and Foreign Language).

PERENNIALISM

AIMS: To educate the rational person; to cultivate the intellect through transmitting worthwhile knowledge that has been gathered, organized, and systematized.

KNOWLEDGE: Focus on past and permanent studies, mastery of facts and universal truths (from the Western canon).

TEACHER'S ROLE: Teachers should help students think rationally; based on Socratic Method, oral exposition; explicitly teach traditional values (i.e., Western, hetero-, patriarchal, middle-class).

CURRICULUM: Curriculum centers on classical subjects, literary analysis. It is constant.

SOCIAL RECONSTRUCTIONISM

AIMS: To improve and reconstruct society; education for change.

KNOWLEDGE: Focus on skills and subjects needed to identify and ameliorate problems of society; active concern with contemporary and future society.

TEACHER'S ROLE: Teachers serve as change agents for reform; they help students become aware of problems confronting humankind.

CURRICULUM: Curriculum centers on examining social, economic, and political problems, present and future, on a national as well as an international (global) level.

CRITICAL MULTICULTURALISM

AIMS: Global educational reform where monoculture Eurocentric hegemonic discourses are challenged to include pluralism, diversity, and multiplicity. The aim is to empower students to look at the human condition globally.

KNOWLEDGE: Focus on the West's struggle for self-understanding including self-reflection and enabling students to understand the experiences of historically marginalized groups such as women and people of color.

TEACHER'S ROLE: Teachers are critical intellectuals who develop critical strategies for a meaningful praxis that challenges essentialist notions of culture now being generated within capitalist globalization (in other words, challenging the homogenization of "other" cultures such as Asian-Americans, African-American, Hispanic Americans and so forth).

CURRICULUM: Curriculum shifts from simply "learning about 'other' cultures," to broader issues of race, class, and gender politics. The pedagogical task is getting students to critically examine stereotypes.

References

Adler, M. J. (1982). *The Paideia proposal: An educational manifesto*. New York: Macmillan.
Archambault, R. D. (1964). (Ed.). *John Dewey on education: Selected writings*. Chicago: University of Chicago Press.
Aristotle (1952). Politics, great books of the Western world. *Encyclopedia Britannica*, p. 544.
Bagley, W. C. (1934). *Education and emergent man*. New York: Nelson.
Banks, J. A. (2006). *Cultural diversity and education: Foundations, curriculum, and teaching*. (5th ed). Boston: Pearson.
Banks, J. A. (1988). *Multiethnic education: Theory and practice* (2nd ed). Boston: Allyn and Bacon, Inc.
Britzman, D. (1991). *Practice makes practice*. Albany, NY: State University of New York Press.

Bruner, J. (1977). *The process of education.* Cambridge, MA: Harvard University Press.
Burbules, N. C., & Rice, S. (1991). Dialogue across differences: Continuing the conversation. *Harvard Educational Review,* 61(4), 393–416.
Carlson, D. (1997). *Making progress. Education and culture in new times.* New York: Teachers College Press.
Carlson, D. (1992). *Teachers and crisis: Urban school reform and teachers' work culture.* New York: Routledge.
Counts, G. S. (1932). *Dare the schools build a new social order?* New York: John Day.
Darling Hammond, L. (1999). Educating teachers for the next century: Rethinking practice and policy. In G. Griffin (Ed.), *The Education of Teachers.* Chicago: The University of Chicago Press.
Dewey, J. (1964). *John Dewey on education: Selected writings.* Chicago: The University of Chicago Press.
Dewey, J. (1938). *Experience and education.* New York: Macmillan.
Dewey, J. (1916). *Democracy and education.* New York: Macmillan.
Eisner, E. W. (1985). *The educational imagination.* New York: Macmillan.
Feiman-Nemser, S., & Remillard, J. (1995). Perspectives on learning to teach. In F. Murray (Ed.). *The teacher educator's handbook.* San Francisco: Jossey-Bass.
Freire, P. (1971). *Pedagogy of the oppressed.* New York: Continuum.
Gay, G. (1983). Multiethnic education: Historical developments and future prospects. *Phi Delta Kappan,* 560–563.
Giroux, H. A. (1997). *Pedagogy and the politics of hope: Theory culture and schooling.* Boulder, CO: Westview Press.
Goodlad, J. I. (1997). *In praise of education.* New York: Teachers College Press.
Goodlad, J. I. (1994). *Educational renewal: Better teachers, better schools.* San Francisco: Jossey-Bass.
Goodlad, J. I. (1990). *Teachers for our nation's schools.* San Francisco: Jossey-Bass.
Grant, C. A., & Sleeter, C. E. (1986). Race, class, and gender in educational research: An argument for integrative analysis. Review of Educational Research, 56, 195–211.
Greene, M. (1978). *Landscapes of learning.* New York: Teachers College Press.
Hirsch, E. D. (1987). *Cultural literacy.* New York: Vintage, Random House.
Kincheloe, J. L. (1993). *Toward a critical politics of teacher thinking: Mapping the postmodern.* Westport, CT: Bergin & Garvey.
Kneller, G. F. (1971). *Foundations of education.* New York: Wiley.
Leistyna, P. (2002). *Defining and designing multiculturalism: One school system's efforts.* Albany: State University of New York Press.
Macdonald, B. J. (1995) (Ed.). *Theory as a prayerful act: The collected essays of James B. Macdonald.* New York: Peter Lang.
Macdonald, J. B. (1988). Theory, practice, and the hermeneutic circle. In W. F. Pinar (Ed) *Contemporary Curriculum Discourses.* 101–113. Scottsdale, AZ: Gorsuch, Scarisbrick.
McLaren, P. (1989). *Life in schools: An introduction to critical pedagogy in the foundations of education.* New York: Longman.
National Commission on Excellence in Education. (1983). *A nation at risk: The imperative for educational reform.* Washington, D.C.: U.S. Department of Education.
No Child Left Behind (2001). Pub.L. 107-110, 115 Stat. 1425, enacted January 8, 2002.
Pinar, W. F., Reynolds, W. M., Slattery, P., & Taubman, P. M. (1995). *Understanding curriculum: An introduction to the study of historical and contemporary curriculum discourses.* New York: Peter Lang.
Program of Alternative Certification for Educator (PACE). http://www.scteachers.org/cert/pace/PACE.cfm Retrieved 6/20/2009.
Ravitch, D. (1983). *The troubled crusade: American education 1945–1980.* New York: Basic Books.
Rugg, H. O. (1947). *Foundations for American education.* Yonkers-on-Hudson, NY: World Book.
Schramm-Pate, S. L. , & Jeffries, R. B. (2008). (Eds) *Grappling with diversity: Readings on civil rights pedagogy and critical multiculturalism.* New York: SUNY Press.
Zeichner, K. (2002). Beyond traditional structures of student teaching. *Teacher Education Quarterly,* 29(2), 59–64.
Zeichner, K. (1990). Changing directions in the practicum: Looking ahead to the 1990s. *Journal of Education for Teaching,* 16(2), 105–132.

Fifteen

On the Importance of Philosophy to the Study of Teachers

Greg Seals

Philosophers will have already identified several crucial but rich sources of ambiguity in the title of this chapter. For example, the very idea of philosophy is manifold in its meanings. "Philosophy" can refer to a set of academic subject matters, a theory or orientation within a given field of study, or most generally a worldview. Similarly, "teacher" has at least a double meaning depending on whether it is taken in its functional sense as describing a person who successfully imparts learning or in its occupational sense in which a teacher is understood to be a faculty member at a school whether or not he or she has ever successfully fulfilled the function of a teacher. "Importance," too, has a variety of connotations. Perhaps chief among them are the seemingly quite different ideas of value commitment and methodological requirement. Finally, "study," as used in the phrase "study of teachers," may refer to what teachers apply themselves when learning and/or plying their trade or what is of use to learn about teachers when seeking to understand or assess them in their functional capacity.

Other interpretations of these key concepts are no doubt available and I don't presume to have explicated them all in a single paragraph. However, I have attempted to list meanings of interest when it comes to answering two related questions: "What has contributed to the diminished role philosophy of education now seems to play in teacher education?" and "What can bring philosophy into a more central place in the teacher education curriculum?" To get at answers to these questions I will develop an argument that holds a constant meaning of "philosophy" in an effort to use a particular theory of teaching—one eminently at odds with most mainstream philosophy of education nowadays—to explore and unify the ambiguities that surround the terms "importance," "study," and "teachers."

The general strategy of the argument is to put forward a philosophy of education able to draw together issues surrounding ideals and realities of teaching as both a functional and occupational endeavor by prescribing patterns of preparation and professionalism for teachers. The argument given, it becomes possible to propose further that philosophies of education incapable of or unconcerned with providing unity to an understanding of teaching remain largely irrelevant to the work and the work lives of faculty members. It is because philosophy of education tends to abstract itself from the places where processes of education actually occur, that it continues to lose cachet and suffer diminished influence in the teacher education curriculum. Philosophic focus on understanding the educative process promises to bring philosophy into prominence in the field of teacher education.

Therefore, in what follows, I will discuss John Dewey's attempt at a science of education in *Experience and Education* in terms of a causal theory of teaching. Dewey's causal theory of teaching has as its major implications a program about what is important for teachers to study both in the pre-service and in-service phases of their careers and a description of what is of importance to know about the practices of teachers in order to correctly assess their capacity to carry out the functional demands of their profession. In turn, these implications of Dewey's scientific approach to teaching will be shown to help to unify understanding of the functional and occupational notions of "teacher" by unifying ideological and methodological ideas about teaching. Finally, I will suggest that it is the ability to offer a theory that does these things that is the central challenge any philosophy of education must meet to protect itself from the perceptions of irrelevancy from which the field currently suffers.

A Causal Theory of Teaching

Ask a philosopher the question, "What is knowledge?" and you are likely to get an analysis of the concept. However, the question is subject to a metaphysical interpretation, as well. That is, the question, "What is knowledge?" may also be taken to ask what sort of thing knowledge is. I will explore the thesis that for John Dewey knowledge is the effect of experience. More specifically I will argue that, for Dewey, knowledge is the causal result of experiences had under certain conditions. Specification of the causal conditions of knowledge, in terms of what Dewey calls universal formulae and propositions of kinds, promises to create a perspective from which teaching may be seen as a scientific endeavor.

In order to advance the argument it is necessary to discuss Dewey's theory of causation and his theory of coming-to-know. According to Georges Dicker, Dewey's "thesis with respect to coming-to-know is that the entire temporal process of inquiry is itself the 'act of knowing'" (Dicker, p. 197, emphasis in original). The stages in that process of inquiry, Dicker suggests, are laid out by Dewey in Chap. 6 of *How We Think*. There Dewey lists five logically distinct steps in the process of inquiry or coming-to-know. These, famously, are (i) a felt difficulty; (ii) its location and definition; (iii) suggestion of possible solution; (iv) development by reasoning of the bearings of the suggestion; and (v) further observation and experiment leading to its acceptance or rejection; that is, the conclusion of belief or disbelief (Dewey, 1910, p. 72).

The difference between coming-to-know and knowledge consists for Dewey, according to Dicker, in the consistency of the correctness with which we anticipate consequences. The more consistently we anticipate correctly, the more properly we are said to know (Dicker, 1973). Like any causal theory of knowledge this one is beset by problems of iterative skepticism it cannot solve on its own (Collier, 1973). However, we may stipulate that the theory of coming-to-know fails as an adequate analysis of the concept of knowledge, and still find value in the theory. By taking "coming-to-know" to mean "learning," this theory suggests a causal connection between inquiry and learning. Thus, it seems a useful approach to take in discussion of education when education is understood generically as the process by which we come to know.

George Stone (1994) has made an attempt to articulate instructional practice along the lines suggested by the theory of coming-to-know. As Stone interprets the theory of coming-to-know, knowledge occurs whenever students and teachers work together to solve real life problems in terms of causal processes. Unfortunately, this reading renders the theory of coming-to-know a *non sequitur* for a causal theory of teaching. Stone, that is to say, mentions causal processes in his theory of instructional practice but does not use them. Students learn by exploring and coming to understand causal processes, Stone tells us, but he never explores in any detail the causal processes involved in such student explorations. His theory never explains pedagogy as a causal process, precisely what we had reasonably hoped to learn from Stone.

What forces Stone's theory to swerve around the issue of teaching as a causal process in its own right is the unacceptable level of generality with which he discusses the issue. Stone, in pedagogy, like Dicker, in epistemology, makes the error of discussing causal processes at the level of what Dewey calls "gross events." Resting at this level of analysis is what Dewey says led David Hume to declare of causes that they were among the most obscure ideas in all of metaphysics (Hume, 1740/1936). Considered as a cause, Dewey continues, "the gross event directly perceived can be understood only through its resolution into minuter events (interactions) so that some of the minuter events become constituent elements of a spatial-temporal continuum" (Dewey, 1938, p. 449). For Dewey, explanatory adequacy is the crucial element in causality (Reuter, 1993). Causality is a logical rather than a metaphysical idea. Nonetheless, as Jim Garrison has argued, "Instrumental logic has ontological implications because it is a powerful tool for the event of human nature to alter the historical process of other historical events" (Garrison, 1994, p. 10).

Dewey suggests two ways to begin the process of resolving gross events into constituent elements. One is the creation of universal formulae and the other is development of propositions of kinds. A universal formula is, George Stone suggests, "a nonexistential and therefore nontemporal relationship of characters, preferably written in the form of a mathematical equation that can be employed as a formula by which a particular form of generalization or law can be made, namely, a *universal proposition*" (Stone, 1994, p. 422). A proposition of kinds is, Stone goes on to say, "an existential proposition that refers to actual conditions determined by experimental observation" (Stone, 1994, p. 423). Together these two ways of resolving gross events into causal explanation, again using Stone's words, "form the content of the scientific account of what happened in the singular case" (Stone, 1994, p. 423).

What Stone's theory of instructional practice and Dicker's theory of coming-to-know fail to give us is any universal formula or any proposition of kinds. Their analyses rest at the level of gross events. Yet Dewey's theory of causation clearly requires more. In Dewey's view, problems of pedagogical practice need to become amenable to resolution in causal terms because insight into the processes of causation involved in teaching "represent the goal of educational procedure on its intellectual side" (Dewey, 1910, 275). This request is not unreasonable because Dewey suggests that the most compelling reason to believe in the principle of causation is the human capacity for labor. What is true of the work of craftswomen, tradesmen, and business people is surely true of the labor of the teacher. In the spirit of Dewey's attempt to take truth making to be a workaday affair I will attempt to develop a more adequate causal account of the teacher's work (Garrison, 1994). I will state Dewey's views on pedagogy as a universal formula and then suggest a set of propositions of kinds implicit in that formula.

If we ask what sort of inquiry characterizes teachers' work an answer that springs to mind is the education of their students. Getting a grip on the nature of this problem is central to further development of a causal theory of teaching. Perhaps Dewey's most general attempt to do so is found in *Experience and Education* in his discussion in Chapter 3 of "Criteria of Experience" (Dewey, 1938/1963). His job there is to present the principles that are most significant in framing a theory of experience that informs educational practice. This philosophy of educative experience looks to factors of control inherent in experience to discover and put into operation a principle of order and organization that follows from understanding what educative experience signifies. Dewey argues that the educative force of an experience is dependent upon the quality of an experience as assessed in terms of two criteria, both universal features of experience, continuity and interaction.

Dewey defines interaction as the transaction of the external (physical and social) environment encompassed in an experience with the internal state (needs, desires, capacities, purposes, and so on) of the person having that experience. Suitability of external environment to inner state enhances interaction. This principle of interaction, moreover, influences continuity, the other chief variable constituting the educative force of an experience. Because events and things continue only over time, continuity implicitly makes reference to the past, the present, and the future. Thus, full assessment of the continuous quality of an experience must include evaluation of what the person having the experience brings to the experience, how internally coherent the present experience is, and how the experience will affect future experience. When continuity is influenced in a good way by interaction the result is enhancement of the potential for continued growth of the learner, described by Dewey as a widening of the possibilities of having richer experiences in the future. When interaction influences continuity in a bad way the result is limitation of the learner's potential for continued control of future experiences and diminishment of the learner's power of judgment and capacity to act intelligently in new situations.

The ideas explored in *Experience and Education* admit of an interpretation on which continuity and interaction may be said to stand to each other as elements in an equation purportedly descriptive of the educative force of any experience. A formula fitting this description, attentive to Dewey's desire for a science of education, and inclusive of Dewey's comments in *Experience and Education* about the relation of educative force to the continuous and interactive qualities of experience, takes the following form:

$$e \approx p \frac{c_1 c_2}{i^2}$$

where e is the educative force of an experience, p the relation of past experience to present experience, c_1 the salience of present experience, c_2 the coherence of present experience with future experience, and i^2 the distance between external and internal environments in an experiential situation (Seals, 2004; Ericson & Ellett, 1987). Applied to education in schools the formula states that the educative force of any school lesson depends primarily upon relations among the experiences brought by students to the lesson, the coherence of the lesson, the congruity of the lesson with subsequent experiences had by students outside the context of the lesson, and the involvement of students in the external, that is, physical and social, environment of the classroom.

What Teachers Need to Study

Universal description of the causal conditions of knowing helps to legitimate discussion of education as a science. However, it does not by itself provide a proposition of kinds. Importantly, though, the formula ties educative force to the personal experience of some learner(s) or other. The universal statement substitutes a certain kind and quality of personal experience for education. The emphasis on personal experience in the variables of the formula suggests a connection between Dewey's views on pedagogy and phenomenological analysis. Because continuity and interaction are qualities of personal experience, the science of education is a phenomenological science (Husserl, 1917/1981). Elements of the phenomenology of the educative act provide a basis from which to make concrete recommendations to teachers as to how to think about their work in ways that promise to improve the educative effects of their pedagogical efforts. In short, for its successful completion teaching, considered as a causal process, requires observation of and response to the life-worlds of students (Garrison & Shargel, 1988).

Phenomenological sociologist Alfred Schutz suggests that the life-world or the world of everyday reality is the world as encountered with a certain attitude. The life-world is the world taken as "something that we have to modify by our actions or that modifies our actions" (Schutz, 1970, p. 73). Elements of the life-world, as parsed by Schutz, are: (1) a stock of previous experiences had by our predecessors, (2) our own experiences, and (3) the pragmatic tasks before us. Together for each individual they form a biographically determined situation or as Schutz describes it, a "stock of knowledge at hand that serves him as a scheme of interpretation of his past and present experiences, and also determines his anticipations of things to come" (Schutz, 1970, p. 74).

The life-world maps onto the universal formula of Dewey's views on pedagogy. The educative force of any lesson depends on teacher's ability to insert curriculum into student's life-world. Teachers succeed in their educational efforts when curriculum makes sense to students in terms of the stock of knowledge students bring to class, when the curriculum serves students in solving the pragmatic tasks set for them in their everyday worlds of action, and when the environment in which students experience the lesson is one in which they are able to adopt the natural attitude of being modified by the world and, by their actions, being able to modify the world. Thus, the universal formula of Dewey's views on pedagogy receives interpretation in a proposition of kinds by matching elements of the life-world to variables in the formula.

In this way, law-like statement of Dewey's views on pedagogy provides teachers with some ideas to test out and some information to gather.[1] Dewey's causal theory of teaching gives somewhat detailed advice in this regard. At any rate it gives advice sound and articulate enough to accommodate description of the educative act via gross events, a universal proposition, and propositions of kinds. What's left for the theory to do is find some examples that show it working, that make it an acceptable explanation of success or failure in pedagogical practice. Only inquiry into this suggestion will serve to certify it as false or true. That is, only inquiry into actual processes of the pedagogical encounter as bearing out or doing in Dewey's law will demonstrate its level of usefulness to education practice and determine the wisdom of foregoing the theory altogether or refining it through continued use. The best place to begin that process is assessing quality of teaching in terms of Dewey's view.

Accountability by Process

Recent complaint about measuring teacher accountability in terms of adherence to performance standards and student performance on standardized tests has been accompanied by recommendation that teacher responsibility be assessed in terms of pedagogical effectiveness and educational responsiveness to student need (Sion, 2004). A problem with this recommendation that proponents of it candidly admit is that assessment in terms of teacher responsibility ". . . is more resistant to procedural description than behaviors generally associated with product-process research" (Sherman, 2004, p. 122). However, this dark assessment of the relation between accountability and responsibility may be brightened when put in light of John Dewey's views on a science of education. Teacher responsibility, on this view, consists in ability to manipulate the variables of the theory in ways that effect student learning for the better. By tying teacher responsibility directly to pedagogical effectiveness Dewey can argue that standards-based and standardized conceptions of teacher accountability may indirectly measure teacher responsibility.

However, Deweyan solution to the problem of teacher accountability via a causal theory of teaching is faced by the serious objection that Dewey's scientific theory of teaching separates talk of teacher accountability from talk of teacher responsibility. That is, extending a factual description of teacher accountability to a moral account of teacher responsibility commits the is/ought fallacy as described by David Hume in *A Treatise of Human Nature*. Recall that Hume complains moral reasoning has an annoying tendency to move from descriptive statements to normative ones without pausing to explain how the transition took place (Hume, 1740/1969). However, Dewey's solution is not compromised by Hume's objection. Hume admits two conditions under which reason can play a role in moral judgment: "either when it excites a passion by informing us of the existence of something which is a proper object of it; or when it discovers the connexion of causes and effects, so as to afford us means of exerting any passion" (Hume, 1740/1969, p. 469). Dewey's view meets both conditions.

First, development of an explanatory principle is precisely what Hume has been taken to mean by discovering cause and effect connections (Beck, 1974; Callicott, 1982; McBeth, 1992; Roma, 1970). Science lays claim to a quite legitimate influence on our human psychological processes. That is, the discovery of new facts is very likely to change what we value. For example, assuming a person's interest in her or his own health, discovery, say, that cigarettes are harmful to one's health is a sufficient reason (although unfortunately not a sufficient motive) to stop smoking. Similarly, discovery that the educative force of lessons is enhanced by intelligent manipulation of four key variables provides direct moral status to intelligent manipulation of those variables.

Second, consistently successful enhancement of educative force is a matter of what may quite legitimately be called natural self-interest to teachers. Success as a teacher is virtually defined by the learning a teacher accomplishes among students during progression of the educative act. In this way Dewey's view meets Hume's second condition. That is, Dewey's view, using Hume's parlance slightly altered to fit the case of education, "excites a [professional] passion by informing us [teachers] of the existence of something [methods of enhancing educative force] which is a proper object of it [the professional passion]." Thus, Dewey is safe from commission of Hume's is/ought fallacy and his view may be correctly characterized with equal accuracy as a moral theory of teacher accountability or a scientific theory of teacher responsibility. As such, Dewey fulfills the desire of teacher responsibility theorists to combine canons of teacher effectiveness with criteria of teacher responsibility (Oser, Dick, & Patry, 1992).

Moreover, by connecting explanation of educative force to his account of teacher responsibility Dewey enjoys an advantage over more purely normative statements of teacher responsibility. Standard treatment of teacher responsibility eschews, even spurns any talk of a science of education for fear of sliding into product-process accountability talk (Sherman, 2004). But by distancing itself from any understanding of a science of education teacher responsibility theory also estranges itself from description of how exactly teachers are to fulfill their responsibilities, especially under current conditions of classroom instruction. This puts teacher responsibility theory in the embarrassing position of failing the rule of "ought" implies "can" typically held to govern the development of moral principles (Kant, 1793/1934). Excuse for failure becomes more the rule than does attempt at success when moral agents believe there is no real way to accomplish moral ends (Heinz, 1975). Dewey, on the other hand, by articulating his view of teacher responsibility in scientific terms, expresses quite clearly the processes by which teachers are to accomplish that which they ought to do. In doing so, Dewey expands rather than contracts the possibility of teachers becoming responsible professionals and certifies the propriety of teachers being held accountable for expertly fulfilling their responsibilities.

A Bread and Butter Issue for Philosophers of Education

The relation between Dewey's scientific musings about education and the loss of face and place of philosophy of education in the teacher education curriculum may be seen by contrasting his approach to the moralist perspective of Maxine Greene. In *Releasing the Imagination* Greene's focus is on the ethical in education. Referring to the title the collection of her essays bears, Greene comments that "I am reaching toward an idea of imagination that brings an ethical concern to the fore, a concern that, again, has to do with the community that ought to be in the making and the values that give it color and significance" (Greene, 1995, p. 35). But in pushing moral concerns to the front of her thinking Greene seems at the same time to shove scientific or technical concerns to the back of it. According to Greene, "the role of imagination is not to resolve, not to point the way, not to improve. It is to awaken, to disclose the ordinarily unseen, unheard, and unexpected" (Greene, p. 28). Starting from that proposition, Greene says she hopes for the following: "If I can make present the shapes and structures of a perceived world, even though they have been layered over with many rational meanings over time, I believe my own past will appear in altered ways and that my present lived life—and, I would like to say, teaching—will become more grounded, more pungent, and less susceptible to logical rationalization, not to speak of rational instrumentality" (Greene, pp. 77–78).

Her interest in pursuing the ethical over the scientific in education is the commendable one of softening administrative languages of dominance that negatively affect schooling so that the voices of teachers and students may be more clearly heard. On these points Greene says, in regards to students

> Surely, education today must be conceived as a mode of opening the world to critical judgments by the young and to their imaginative projections and, in time, to their transformative actions. . . . We must acknowledge the fixities and corruptions of our consumer-based and technized culture. We must take into account the languages of technology and violence, even as we do the miseducation in much that is done in schools. They are, after all, largely hierarchical, bureaucratic institutions with their own internal de-

mands for self-perpetuation and equilibrium. By their very nature, they make it extraordinarily difficult for openings to be explored and critical thinking to take place (Greene, p. 56).

And in regards to teacher voice:

Traditional notions of ways to achieve efficiency feed into claims that schools can be manipulated from without to meet predetermined goals. The implication often is that for their own benefit, teachers and their students are to comply and to serve. How can teachers intervene and say how they believe things ought to be? What can they do to affect restructuring? What can they do to transform their classrooms? (Greene, p. 56)

However, Greene describes in dichotomous terms the difference between the theory she develops in *Releasing the Imagination* and traditional patterns of schooling by contrasting the two types of theories as oppositional types of vision. "When applied to schooling," Greene explains, "the vision that sees things big [Greene's theory] brings us in close contact with details and with particulars that cannot be reduced to statistics or even to the measurable. The vision that sees things small looks at schooling through the lenses of a system—a vantage point of power or existing ideologies—taking a primarily technical point of view" (Greene, pp. 10–11).

According to Greene, "Local knowledge and local coming together ought to counter the tendency toward abstraction, as should a conscious concern for the particular, the everyday, the concrete" (Greene, p. 69). She buttresses this point by saying, "[w]ith traditional rationality now in question, more and more people have come to view philosophy as a mode of social critique. That is, philosophy is seen as a way of posing questions about inequities and unmasking the ways in which communication is distorted by technicizing and by confusing types of inquiry useful in the social as opposed to the natural sciences" (Greene, p. 60).

Now Greene's dualistic approach runs two risks. First, by turning attention away from technical issues of teaching Greene threatens to imbue her theory with an inability to advise teachers in any empirically meaningful way as to how to achieve success in their work with students. Second, by turning away from scientific thinking about schooling Greene weakens her position relative to any competing theory that claims scientific justification for its tenets. And, indeed, the theory seems not only to run these risks but also to run aground upon them.

Greene seems sure as to the goal of teaching when she asserts that because "Individual identity takes form in the contexts of relationship and dialogue; our concern must be to create the kinds of contexts that nurture—for all children—the sense of worthiness and agency" (Greene, p. 41). Moreover, she seems equally sure about the means of achieving that goal when she says: "The difficult task for the teacher is to devise situations in which the young will move from the habitual and the ordinary and consciously undertake a search" (Greene, p. 24), but she never specifies in any concrete way how these means are to be employed to attain the end to which they are suited. She claims "the arts have a unique power to release the imagination" (Greene, p. 27) but also gives the clear impression that the presence of the arts in the curriculum is neither a necessary nor a sufficient condition for that release. Several comments bear this reading out: "Apathy and indifference are likely to give way as images of what might arise" (Greene, p. 5); "When teaching, responding to the grasping consciousness of a young student in her or his distinctiveness, we can only continually combat life's anaesthetics, moving individuals to reach out toward that horizon line" (Greene, p. 30); and "Trying, yes, and the pursuit of freedom and critical understanding and a transformation (if we are lucky) of lived worlds" (Greene, p. 59).

In addition, an interesting personal account of how Greene's own acquaintance with the arts affected her education, which she offers to shed light on "curriculum exigencies today" (Greene, p. 90), is essentially undone by the appearance in some of the essays in *Releasing the Imagination* of what may be called "somehow clauses." Says Greene: "We have somehow to understand this world and provoke others to understand it if we are in some fashion to transform it" (Greene, pp. 44–45). She opines further by saying: "I also think we have to hold in mind that the modern world is an administered world structured by all sorts of official languages. More often than not, they are the languages of domination, entitlement, and there are terrible silences where ordinary human speech ought to be audible, silences our pedagogy ought somehow to repair" (Greene, p. 47). And, as part of a discussion about the usefulness of a problem-posing curriculum for improving learning she notes, "Somehow, we have to enable them [students] to transmute these problems into shocks to be explained and to develop the shock-receiving capacity in each one" (Greene, p. 108).

Even the strategy Greene offers for closing the gap between big vision and small vision in education leaves teachers without sound advice as to a positive program of action. Greene suggests, "The challenge may be to learn how to move back and forth to comprehend the domains of policy and long-term planning while also attending to particular children, situation-specific undertakings, the unmeasurable, and the unique. Surely, at least part of the challenge is to refuse artificial separations of the school from the surrounding environment, to refuse the decontextualizations that falsify so much" (Greene, p. 12). Worse, Greene's own attempts to meet this challenge of moving back and forth between the universal and the particular, planning and practice, big and small vision in education involve oxymoronic combinations of positionalities: "All we can do, I believe, is cultivate multiple ways of seeing and multiple dialogues in a world where nothing stays the same" (Greene, 1995, p. 16). And "justice, regard for human rights, freedom, respect for others. . .are standards that every intelligent individual in the community ought to be expected to heed, or so many of us believe" (Greene, p. 66). In both of these quotes the transsubjective positionality expressed in the word "all" and the word "every" is immediately undercut by the unisubjective and intersubjective uses, respectively, of "believe."

A source of this irony in Greene is her commitment to postmodernism. "My interpretations are provisional" Greene asserts. "I have partaken in the postmodern rejection of inclusive rational frameworks in which all problems, all uncertainties can be resolved" (Greene, p. 16). Relying on advice she attributes to Richard Rorty, Greene suggests that "the best we can do is to describe the familiar procedures of justification in our society rather than reaching for some fixed truth. Like Rorty's pragmatist, I would suggest that we not seek out a theory of truth but affirm an ethical base for our accounts of the value of cooperative human inquiry. All we can do is articulate as clearly as possible what we believe and what we share" (Greene, p. 69).

Following this advice makes it easy enough for Greene to share her beliefs, but it puts obstacles in the way of her attempts to gain converts to her beliefs. There is a great difference between sharing one's beliefs and getting others to share one's beliefs. That is, Greene is clear as to what she wants teachers to do: "The young can be empowered," she urges," to view themselves as conscious, reflective namers and speakers if their particular standpoints are acknowledged, if interpretive dialogues are encouraged, if interrogation is kept alive" (Greene, p. 57), but she is without a convincing reason for teachers and schools to follow her imperative to inquiry. This puts her in an embarrassing, "big if" position. She knows what she wants from teachers and from education but cannot say how she can achieve it. Greene offers an imperative to guide the actions of teachers but fails to specify how those actions may be successfully undertaken. As Kant scholar Lewis White Beck notes in a discussion of the logic of imperatives, "For there to be any imperative which is not merely an unreasoned ejaculation in the imperative mood, there must be a law. The imperative expresses the necessitation of an action, the necessity (either conditional or unconditional) of which is expressed in a natural law. Unless there were such a law, imperatives would be mere prayers or persuasions or ejaculations for which no reason could be given" (Beck, 1969, p. 146). It is just such a law that is missing from Greene's account.

While the absence of a law or principle of justification from Greene's theory of teaching may be acceptable as a limit on her theory alone, it is just this absence of an operational principle that has prevented progressive ideas in education from wide implementation in schools. It has become a commonplace that Dewey and the other pedagogical progressives lost and Thorndike, Hall, and other administrative progressives, so-called, won the education research and policy wars waged over U.S. schools during the early 20th century (Lagemann, 2000). One of the main reasons the war went the way it did, according to Michael Glassman in his "Running in Circles: Chasing Dewey," was that the progressives were never able to come up with measurable theories of key educational concepts (Glassman, 2004). Continued failure to state its views in appropriately scientific terms has kept progressivism on the margins of educational policy formation. As Glassman argues the case, "the reason many of the 'alternative' theoretical models that enter into our discourse initially gain traction is because they once again raise critical issues about subjects such as context and reapproximation of ends. But ultimately each of these theoretical models is doomed to live out its existence on the margins for many for the same reasons that Dewey left the field and was left behind by it" (Glassman, 2004, p. 341).

Glassman's broad point supports the present analysis of Greene's outlook on education. Seen through the lens of Glassman Greene appears as yet another in a long line of progressive educators unable to articulate or uninterested in articulating measurable theories. However, Glassman is wrong about Dewey. While Dewey may not have articulated an appropriately scientific theory of education in time or with sufficient clarity to help win the war for control of schooling, he did attempt to state just such a view in the 1938 Kappa Delta Pi lecture expanded and published as *Experience and Education*. So, if a scientific theory of progressive education will help make schools look more like the ideal institutions Greene describes in the prayerful abstract, it seems worthwhile to take a run at a scientific reading of Dewey.

While there is ample substantive agreement between Dewey and Greene the primary methodological difference between Greene and Dewey on this issue is that Dewey grounds his belief in something sturdier than his belief. Dewey sums up this difference in an article written in the same year that *Experience and Education* was published by saying "philosophical and scientific discourse differ fundamentally. What is implied in the constructive ideas of philosophy is that they have authority over activity to impel it to bring possible values into existence, not, as in the case of science, that they have authoritative claim to acknowledgement because they are already part of the order of nature" (Dewey, 1938/1987, pp. 263–264).

Bringing Philosophy Back In

The possibility that education may to some degree be able to function autonomously as a science remains broadly neglected by philosophers of education. René Vincente Arcilla points out that Dewey's call for a philosophy of education able to generate solutions to problems of education practice has failed for the simple reason that social sciences now perform that function. In this situation, on Arcilla's view, philosophers of education are left with only two options. First, we may take up theoretical issues appropriate to some social science or set of social sciences. On this option we become, to use Arcilla's list of evolutionary intellectual adaptations already transforming some philosophers of education, feminist anthropological theorists, liberal political science theorists, or postmodern sociological theorists. Second, we may become the gadflies of education practice and take up the search for ways to make skepticism, especially about the socially reproductive aspects of schooling, of use to educators and to education (Arcilla, 2002).

Law-like statement of Dewey's views on pedagogy offers an alternative neglected in Arcilla's analysis and provides a tool with which to examine the possibility that education is itself a social science. Clearing conceptual ground to begin the work of constructing a science of education is a positive, as opposed to a skeptical, task unique to the office of the philosopher of education. Further, work toward an autonomous science of education promises to free practitioners to generate their own responses to challenges they face in carrying out their work. Dewey's law opens a window of opportunity for philosophy of education to inform school practice in ways that empower education practitioners to take charge of their own circumstances.

Whatever the fate of the theoretical and practical suggestions made here under the presumption that teaching is a causal process, universal formula and propositions of kinds analyses of the commonsense or gross event suggestion that education arises out of experience advance the idea that teaching may be usefully articulated as, in large part, a causal activity. Considerations put forward here, as sketchy as they may be at present, demonstrate that gross event analyses of coming-to-know and inquiry-as-education are not the final word on a science of teaching. That is, they make possible closer inquiry into and interrogation of that most fundamental, student-centered, causal question facing educators: "How do we get them to learn?" To the extent that philosophers of education can find a way to contribute to understanding of this question and make useful attempts at formulating answers to it their relevance to the teacher education curriculum becomes less easily contested.

Notes

1. I note only in passing that, sadly, information about students' life-worlds, the sort of information Dewey's causal theory of teaching says teachers need at their disposal to improve pedagogy, is just the sort of information that schools tend to be slow in collecting, dull in analyzing, and clumsy in utilizing.

References

Arcilla, R. V. (2002). Why aren't philosophers and educators speaking to each other? *Educational Theory*, 52, (1), 1–11.
Beck, L. W. (1974). 'Was-Must Be' and 'is-ought' in Hume," *Philosophical Studies*, 26, 219–228.
Beck, L. W. (1969). Apodictic imperatives, 134–162 (L. W. Beck, Trans.) (R. P. Wolff, Ed.), *Immanuel Kant: Foundations of the metaphysics of morals*. New York: Bobbs-Merrill.
Callicott, J. B. (1982). Hume's *is/ought* dichotomy and the relation of ecology to Leopold's land ethic. *Environmental Ethics*, 4, 163174.
Collier, K. W. (1973). Contra the causal theory of knowledge. *Philosophical Studies*, 24, 350–351.
Dewey, J. (1910). *How we think*. Lexington, MA: D. C. Heath.
Dewey, J. (1938). *Logic: The theory of inquiry*. New York: Holt, Rinehart & Winston.
Dewey, J. (1938/1963). *Experience and education*. New York: Collier.
Dewey, J. (1938/1987). The determination of ultimate values or aims through antecedent or a priori speculation or empirical inquiry, 255–270. (J. A, Boydston, Ed.) *John Dewey: The later works, volume 13*. Carbondale: Southern Illinois University Press.

Dicker, G. (1973). Knowing and coming-to-know in John Dewey's theory of knowledge. *The Monist*, 57 (2), 191–219.
Ericson, D. P. & Ellett, F. S., Jr. (1987). Teacher accountability and the causal theory of teaching. *Educational Theory*, 37, (3), 277–293.
Garrison, J. (1994). Realism, Deweyan pragmatism, and educational research. *Educational Researcher*, 23 (1), 5–14.
Garrison, J. W. & Shargel, E. I. (1988). Dewey and Husserl: A surprising convergence of themes. *Educational Theory*, 38, (3), 239–247.
Glassman, M. (2004). Running in circles: Chasing Dewey. *Educational Theory*, 54, (3), 315–341.
Greene, M. (1995). *Releasing the imagination: Essays on education, the arts, and social change*. San Francisco: Jossey-Bass.
Heinz, L. L. (1975). Excuses and "ought" implies "can," *Canadian Journal of Philosophy*, 5, (3), 449–462.
Hume, D. (1740/1936). *Enquiries concerning the understanding and concerning the principles of morals*. (2nd ed.) (L. A. Selby-Bigge, Ed.) Oxford: Clarendon Press.
Hume, D. (1739/1969). *A treatise of human nature*, (L. A. Selby-Bigge, Ed.) Oxford: The Clarendon Press.
Husserl, E. (1917/1981). Pure phenomenology, its method and its field of investigation, 1–10. (R. W. Jordan, Trans.) (P. McCormick and F. A. Elliston, Eds.) *Husserl: Shorter works*. Notre Dame, IN: University of Notre Dame Press.
Kant, I. (1793/1934). *Religion within the limits of reason alone*. (Theodore M. Greene and Hoyt H. Hudson, Trans.) Chicago: Open Court.
Lagemann, E. C. (2000). *An elusive science: The troubling history of education research*. Chicago: University of Chicago Press.
McBeth, M. (1992). 'Is' and 'ought" in context: MacIntyre's mistake," *Hume Studies*, 18, (1), 41–50.
Oser, F. K., Dick, A., & Patry, J-L. (1992). Responsibility, effectiveness, and the domains of educational research, 3–13. (F. K. Oser, A. Dick, and J.-L. Patry, Eds.), *Effective and responsible teaching: The new synthesis*. San Francisco: Jossey-Bass.
Reuter, R. (1993). The radical agent: A Deweyan theory of causation. *Transactions of the Charles S. Pierce Society*, 29, (2), 239–257.
Roma, E., III. (1970). 'Ought' and 'is' and the demand for explanatory completeness. *Journal of Value Inquiry*, 4, 302–307.
Schutz, A. (1970). *On phenomenology and social relations*. (H. R. Wagner, Ed.) Chicago: University of Chicago Press.
Seals, G. (2004). Conceptualizing teaching as a science: John Dewey in dialogue with the National Research Council. *Educational Theory*, 54, (1), 1–26.
Sherman, S. (2004). Responsiveness in teaching: Responsibility in its most particular sense. *The Educational Forum*, 68, (2), 115–124.
Sion, R. T. (2004). A standards obsession: What happened to pedagogy? *Kappa Delta Pi Record*, 40, (3), 100–103.
Stone, G. C. (1994). Dewey on causation in social science. *Educational Theory*, 44 (4), 417–428.
Stone, G. C. (1996). John Dewey's concept of causation in instructional practice. *Journal of Thought*, 31 (2), 73–84.

Sixteen

Philosophy of Education: Looking Back to the Crossroads and Forward to the Possibilities

Douglas J. Simpson and Lee S. Duemer

Introduction

Our title, much like the title of the book—*What Happened to Soul?: The Eradication of Philosophy in Education*—may seem to imply that philosophy and education as a field of inquiry has already passed the place of decision-making regarding whether it will survive much less thrive in colleges of education. Indeed, the term *eradication* appears to ominously announce that the long existing journey of philosophy and education for a place of respect in teacher education has come to an end. Clearly, at least from one perspective, the soul of educator preparation programs—philosophy and education—has been intentionally eliminated by a variety of people or entities—or, by, stated more accurately, groups of loosely knit people whose primary element of solidarity is the wish to purge an unwanted contributor from educator preparation units, perhaps because of its perceived and actual hegemonic tendencies (for example, we may see our field as the soul of colleges of education). These people or entities have been successful. The assassination and, perhaps, betrayal of the field have occurred. We are now left with the task of describing the field's demise.

Other pictures of where the field of philosophy and education is today exist, including those offered in this chapter. Indeed, part of our title—"Forward to the Possibilities"—suggests at least another perspective. Our depiction overlaps with and draws on prior and current understandings of the question but offers somewhat different if not unique hermeneutical elements. We include these elements in the form of three overly simplified hypotheses for critique and, when merited, further investigation and action. First, we suggest that the evolution of educator preparation is a major factor in the perceived death of philosophy and education. Second, we speculate that the altercations in the field of philosophical inquiry are contributors to the offering of eulogies for the death of philosophy and education. Third, we propose that the field of philosophy and education has been, is, and will continue to be in the process of transformation rather than having experienced a termination. We analyze these three themes below. Before doing so, we wish to suggest that the sheer fact that this work exists indicates that philosophy and education has not been totally eradicated from colleges of education. Indeed, it seems to be oxymoronic to claim that it has been exorcized given the contributors to the volume.

The Evolution of Educator Preparation

Philosophy, of course, is considered one of the long-standing disciplines of the so-called liberal arts. These have evolved and grown since their origins in a variety of settings, including, among others, the ancient scholars of Egypt, Greece, India, Mexico, and China. Some people, mostly within the field, have considered philosophy to be the pinnacle of the disciplines. But like many other disciplines, philosophy has often been understood as a field of study intended to transmit knowledge, foster rational thought and critical inquiry, and contribute to one's overall well-being. Likewise, philosophy has frequently been seen as providing students with a particular kind of foundational knowledge base that serves as an underpinning for lifelong inquiry, critique, and construction. At various times in history and in particular countries, philosophy has been seen as a conveyor of metanarratives that provides an explanation for all of life and thought. Conversely, the aforementioned conclusions have been challenged, rejected, re-envisioned, and reconstructed by alternatively thinking philosophers, including educational philosophers.

We may wonder, given the diverse if not conflictual history of philosophy, how it, an ancient and contemporary form of inquiry, found its way into the preparation of future and practicing educators. The influence of the inquiry genre is probably nearly as old as teaching and learning, understood in both formal and informal ways. Philosophical questions (e.g., Who should be educated?), assumptions (e.g., Are not the sciences the most important subjects to study?), themes (e.g., Which types of effective pedagogy are to be rejected on ethical grounds?), arguments (e.g., If we have a limited amount of time and resources, we have a cogent reason for excluding certain content from the curriculum, don't we?), topics (e.g., How do we know when our students have adequate reasons for their educational and political beliefs?), and controversies (e.g., Why should we spend so much money on certain populations who will contribute so little to society?) have seldom been absent from educational discussions—or at least the minds of those educating and those providing for it.

As formal settings and institutions for educator preparation gradually evolved in scattered locales of the world, "philosophy of education" as a phrase was infrequently used although variations of such phrases as educational aims, principles, and values were. When normal schools—institutions designed largely for the preparation of future and aspiring teachers—started emerging in France, the United States, Mexico, and many other countries, the term, while not necessarily the concept, was still missing in many cases. Naturally, most normal schools were considered chiefly practical institutions that were designed to help teachers learn how and what to teach students, not emphasize how educators might or should think about broader professional questions and responsibilities, for instance philosophical, political, curricular, theoretical, scientific, or fiscal matters. But embedded in their pedagogy courses, in many cases, were the philosophical questions, assumptions, and themes noted heretofore. In time, both the phrase "philosophy of education" and related subject-matter were made explicit in many normal schools and their descendants—for example, normal colleges, teacher colleges, state universities—as well as in educational literature. For instance, Barnes (1920, p. 144) complained that "obfuscated philosophy in education" was responsible for much of the lack of progress in schooling. The subtitle of the magazine *Education* in which Barnes published his article indicates that philosophy had a voice in educator preparation programs—*A monthly magazine devoted to the Science, Art, Philosophy and Literature of Education*—but was not, apparently, deemed the dominant one or the soul of preparation programs.

In the middle and late 20th century, "philosophy of education" and "philosophy and education" as terms and courses appeared more frequently, especially in the middle two quarters of the century in English-speaking countries. But there was competing content from other academic standpoints in those quarters, too. By way of illustration, education courses were sometimes labeled to convey the fact that more than one discipline was a contributor to the study, for example, school and society, foundations of education, history and philosophy of education, culture and education, and introduction to education. As the century moved closer to the 21st, philosophy of education as a distinct course was less frequently found in many public universities although private, especially religiously oriented ones, were more inclined to retain the course because of their founding principles and their view of the subject, sometimes deemed to be equivalent to educational theory. During this time, studies in philosophy and education seem to have shifted in large part to the graduate level where the form of inquiry may or may not have been welcomed. Actually, its welcome may have depended basically on traditional, contextual and personnel considerations, not exclusively or even mainly on academic and professional considerations.

In the last quarter of the 20th and the early part of the 21st centuries, the field of educator preparation has experienced an ongoing evolution in at least two major directions, ways that we label for convenience as (a) disciplinary and interdisciplinary and (b) structural and accountability. The disciplinary and interdisciplinary evolution is manifest and influential. In part, the disciplinary evolution has been fueled by the maturing inquiry of other disciplines such as history, sociology, psychology, and anthropology into questions of how we can and should prepare future teachers to teach P–12 students. In addition, the development of the field has been nudged by realms of inquiry that focus on the practical sciences and arts of teaching mathematics, science, language arts, and social studies. School law also injected its right to be heard into the curriculum, especially in undergraduate teacher preparation programs and in graduate administrator education programs. Moreover, the emergence of feminist, multicultural, and diversity studies and their relevance to educator preparation have caused colleges of education to reconsider their offerings. Likewise, the appearance and flourishing of critical theory, critical pedagogy, and related subjects in many colleges of education have moved discussions and curriculum development in still other directions. Additionally, the paradigm shifts that are evidenced by the controversies connected to modernism, postmodernism, and post-postmodernism have unsettled the canonical views of teacher and administrator preparation.

The structural and accountability evolution of educator preparation programs is no less important. Indeed, a strong argument can be made that this evolution or, perhaps, revolution, has outweighed the influence of disciplinary and interdisciplinary developments. The creation of state requirements for teacher and administrator certification or licensure and national accreditation agencies—for example, National Council for the Accreditation of Teacher Education (NCATE), The Teacher Education Accreditation Council (TEAC), and Council for

Accreditation of Counseling and Related Educational Programs (CACREP)—injected voices that now and again led away from philosophy and education or transformed a subfield of philosophy such as ethics into specific professional preparation programs, for example, ethics and counseling, ethics and educational leadership, ethics and school psychology, ethics and teaching, and so forth. Critiques of educator preparation programs also impinged upon curricular offerings by demanding that competency and outcome-based questions be raised and answered. Some institutional program developers used these new guidelines to eliminate nearly any subject that could not be readily transformed into a measurable, observable, and behavioral performance. Others assumed that the guidelines were both prescriptive and definitive even when they were not. Combined with restrictions on the length of degree programs by higher education governing bodies, these critiques and accountability steps led to less emphasis on education coursework and more study in teaching fields. Hence, performance—skills, dispositions, understandings, and attitudes—as a philosophically thinking future educator often disappeared from the legislative and policy literature in any explicit sense.

The Altercations in the Field of Inquiry

While the previously mentioned developments were emerging and growing, the well-documented debates in philosophy and education regarding (a) the nature of philosophy, (b) the roles of philosophers of education, (c) the expected relationships between philosophers of education and schools, and (d) the connections between philosophy of education, educational theory, and educational practice were thriving. Briefly, if also simplistically, these altercations raised meta-questions that were rarely of interest to large numbers of practicing teachers, principals, and superintendents or to legislators, policy makers, and school board members. Much of our attention and energy was directed toward asking questions about, proposing answers regarding, and delineating how educational philosophers could help in significant and immediate ways for both aspiring and practicing educators. We were often asking ourselves, among other questions, the following ones: What is philosophy of education? Should there be an expectation for educational philosophers to examine in accessible ways "practical" P-12 issues? What should philosophers' contributions be to the field of educational theory? How should philosophy and education adjust their agenda in a postmodern setting? With some exceptions, our search for clarity about what we were well advised to do in our courses for future and practicing educators excluded understanding their perceptions and feedback.

The significant debates between loosely and often pejoratively labeled analytic and continental groups of philosophers and among educational philosophers at least drew considerable attention away from what some considered burning issues in education even when the ideas debated were worthwhile issues. Plus, neither arguments about historicism, romanticism, scientism, nihilism, and post-structuralism (Glendinning, 2006) nor summaries of debates between realism, idealism, existentialism, and pragmatism (O'Neill, 1981) seem to have convinced many teachers, administrators, teacher educators, and policymakers that we had much to offer the profession. If scarce programmatic space was to be devoted to questions of diverse cultures, language and mathematics literacies, or classroom management, or to ontology, aesthetics, epistemology, or logic, there were few who chose to support the later cadre of studies. Endless conceptual analyses seemed to have garnered little, if any, more support. Rightly and wrongly, possibly, we were critiqued and, worse, stereotyped as twiddling our "concepts and arguments while schools and society . . . [went] up in flames" (Simpson, 1994, p. 135).

Altercations within philosophy and education circles and within colleges of education also took other forms. These altercations were in part related to what was claimed regarding philosophers in colleges of education and those in departments of philosophy although there has never been a strict dichotomy between the two spheres. To begin with, the partial split between the two academic domains and related ways of thinking seems tied to whether we saw ourselves primarily as philosophers or largely as teacher educators. Philosophy, of course, has its roots in the liberal arts, and education has its roots in a professional field. A professional program is not a liberal art but is rather contributed to by the liberal arts and sciences in varying proportions. Education, as a professional area of study, is most heavily influenced by disciplines such as psychology, sociology, philosophy, politics, and economics. The purpose of educator preparation, as a professional program, is to develop skills, understandings, attitudes, and dispositions by those who plan to be teachers and administrators and to enable them to function reflectively, pedagogically, and ethically in classrooms and schools.

As such, professional education programs have traditionally placed more emphasis on practice rather than theory. Theory has usually been considered less important than application and practice. The purpose of theory is more often than not seen as the handmaid of practice. In other words, theory has to justify itself, in the minds of many if not most, by showing how it is relevant in terms of explaining and suggesting ideas regarding practice. The weight of this tradition is still felt today although it is more common to hear discussions of theory in particular, realms of teacher and administrator preparation programs, for example, reading, learning, and leadership theories. But theories of education, including the contributions of philosophy, have been seriously neglected. As a consequence, we may often feel like we live on an island of unsolved and unsolvable questions, surrounded by a sea of practitioners who seem to need only answers, not more questions.

Philosophy and education as a field is also distinct from many other professional education studies in that it frequently identifies the unknown, uncertain, or undecided rather than the known or well substantiated. Thus, many future and current educators—who have a need and bent for knowing how and knowing that—find philosophical reflection tedious if not worthless. The question "What should be the form and purpose of education in society?" probably has much less appeal than "How can I address the needs of an autistic student?" As Bredo and Feinberg (1982) have pointed out, education focuses on practice and tends to be cautious of abstraction, while philosophy focuses on the abstract and has generally little interest in practice. The fundamental differences between these fields make it inherently difficult for the two groups of scholars to communicate with each other. Or, stated differently, the purposes of philosophers and teacher educators are frequently so different that neither teacher educators nor would-be educators see the value of philosophy of education. Such breakdowns in communication easily result in misperceptions and, eventually, disvaluing philosophy and education. This reality places those of us who are committed to educational philosophy, or the intersection of any of the disciplines with professional education studies, at a distinct disadvantage. But educator preparation programs are not completely unlike other professional preparation programs in this regard. Perhaps we might be able to learn from these other professional preparation programs how they treat philosophical issues or concerns. Conversely, they might have much to gain by our history and practices.

The emphasis educational scholars have placed on practice has regularly resulted in their looking to the social sciences for guidance, rather than to philosophy. We should not be surprised that those who prepare and who are practitioners look to fields of study such as psychology or sociology, as these disciplines, though they do have a strong theoretical component, are equally interested in the practical. It is only logical that our colleagues in colleges of education should turn to these disciplines for affinity. The social sciences have, after all, focused on bridging theoretical understanding with societal application through the development of both qualitative and quantitative research. We might ask ourselves if philosophers of education have much to learn from educational psychologists, sociologists, and anthropologists.

In addition to the core differences between philosophy and education, there exists another factor that creates tension between the two. Scholars refer to this as the provincialism of time. This term refers to the idea that newer scholarship and ideas are generally considered better or more valuable than what preceded them, for no other reason than the fact that they are new. While we do not impugn the credibility of recent scholarship, the idea that it may be better because of its newness is problematic.

That provincialism of time is accepted by so many people is partly our own fault. Like much of the academy, we have regularly placed too much emphasis on writing for each other rather than for a more general audience in education. Nearly all of our most prestigious journals are published primarily for specialists in educational philosophy, and emerging scholars in our field are encouraged to read and publish them because they carry the most weight in the tenure and promotion process. Journals that appeal to the broad spectrum of educational researchers are often devalued. A second problem concerns the claim that we have allowed philosophy and education to focus on topics of little relevance to educational studies. The growth in the attention that is given to epistemological controversies as an area of study within educational philosophy is an example of this problem. Emphasizing the notion that we can claim to know very little if anything and that the unknown, uncertain, and undecided reign supreme in educator preparation, schooling, and life offers exciting intellectual possibilities but few suggestions for dealing with an angry parent, an abused student, or an irate board member. While these topics are worthy of study and have important implications for evaluating knowledge claims in classrooms and qualitative research in education, the value of such an overcrowded preparation program probably does not generate much support for its inclusion in many colleges of education. For a variety of reasons, then, philosophy and education have undergone a transformation.

The Transformation of Philosophy and Education

For good and ill, philosophy and education have been and continue to be transformed. We could not expect less of a dynamic and controversial form of inquiry although we may wisely or unwisely mourn certain permutations. Nevertheless, understanding that there is an unending transformation of the field of philosophy and education may be helpful in realizing that the perceived crossroad that split into two roads—a boulevard to the revitalization of philosophy and education and a highway to the eradication of philosophy and education—for colleges of education was, perhaps, a misperception. Perhaps the perceived crossroad was a roundabout or rotary that offered multiple options for re-envisioning possibilities for philosophers of education. Perhaps it was an opportunity for philosophers to enter different highways in educational circles and to see emerging freeways to unexamined educational communities and issues. Perhaps it was a narrowing but not a closing of what may have been some regularly travelled routes.

Examples of transformation are plentiful. For example, Schiro (2008, p. xiii) noted in his curriculum theory volume that it is "intended to help both experienced and pre-service educators understand the educational philosophies [emphasis added] . . . they are likely to encounter in their everyday lives." But there are many other examples. That is to say, philosophers of education are examining numerous issues related to education, such as academic freedom (Simon, 1994), administration and ethics (Wagner & Simpson, 2009), constructivism in the science curriculum (Matthews, 1998), learning theory (Phillips & Solitis, 2003), moral education (Noddings, 2002), politics and education (Gutmann, 1999), school choice (Dwyer, 2002), sex education (Archard, 1998), teaching and ethics (Strike & Soltis, 2004), and teaching mathematics (Steiner, 1998). In one sense, the aforementioned studies are neither new nor surprising. Philosophers of education have long inquired into nearly any realm that is in need of examination. Raising questions, seeking clarification, and searching for justifications are a part of engaging in philosophical inquiry, historically, and presently.

Whether or not these and other (Curren, 2007; Kohli, 1995) alleged and actual shifts or adjustments in philosophical inquiry into education are reaching diverse audiences such as teachers, administrators, and teacher educators is an empirical question. Whether they ought to address these and other audiences raises philosophical and ethical questions, too. Whether we as philosophers of education want a future in colleges of education is an issue that no doubt will be debated for years to come, unless of course our courses are eradicated from the halls of academy. Our immediate wish is merely to suggest that the teaching of philosophy and education courses in colleges of education has been transformed in many cases, and, therefore, the strength of the field in colleges of education cannot be determined by a cursory search for courses that are labeled with explicit philosophical terminology.

Conclusion

In spite of the aforementioned complex and, often, uncontrollable considerations, there are those of us who appear to wish to return to a rather straightforward argument that we think should convince any reasonable person that a course in philosophy and education should be required of all aspiring and/or practicing educators. We, much like Rescher (2001, p. 10) who echoed Aristotle's notion that we must philosophize whether we wish to or not, may believe that arguments and programmatic offerings should and can be settled by rational discourse. Hence, we might argue that our profession ". . . can abandon philosophy, but . . . cannot advocate its abandonment through rational argumentation without philosophizing." We may note the inconsistency between philosophizing in order to abandon philosophy and education courses in colleges of education and, worse, the lack of philosophizing and still eradicating educational philosophy course offerings. But if we take this approach, we seem to overlook at a minimum the differences between understanding the rational desirability of studying in a field of inquiry and the existential realities that preclude acting on ever desirable course of action. This is not to say that we should cease offering, we hope, cogent arguments for the inclusion of philosophy and education courses in colleges of education. We think such courses are needed today as they have sometimes been in prior times. It is to say, that we should consider being more creative and comprehensive in our view of philosophy and education. Taking fundamentalist and essentialist views of the field of inquiry may be academically satisfying but professionally unsatisfactory.

What does this say for those of us who work in colleges of education whether we are in departments or programs of educational leadership, curriculum and instruction, educational foundations, or educational policy? At the moment in many institutions, our field seems to have become less important than it has been in decades, perhaps in the last century. Partly we have ourselves to blame. That we have spent too much of our time writing and examining questions only of importance to other educational philosophers has resulted in comments by colleagues that our course content is antiquated, obsolete, or irrelevant. There is, of course, a vital difference between philosophical and educational content that is antiquated and taught in pedagogically traditional ways and philosophically and educationally important content that is taught in pedagogically stimulating ways. So, we may need to ask ourselves: "Have we done the best we can to make clear to our students and peers these differences?" Colleagues can continue to judge us and our courses by what they experienced a decade or two or three ago unless they have at least anecdotal and environmental evidence for thinking otherwise. They can continue to misjudge our courses because they know neither us nor our field. At a minimum, then, a case can be made for our being better at publicizing and clarifying what it is we do as philosophers and why what we do and teach is pertinent to either beginning or practicing educators. On the other hand, if our major contribution to educational discussions is to create doubt about every educational policy, protocol, and pronouncement, then we need not wonder why our colleagues and students doubt our professional practicality.

In addition, we seem well advised to look for other inroads into educator, especially teacher and administrator, preparation programs. We mention just two potential inroads we can make as educational philosophers to develop connections with our educational colleagues and to help make our field better understood and valued in the profession. The first of these is to reconnect with and update some of the philosophical ideas and thinkers that have done much to link philosophy and practice. While there are many possibilities, we mention just one person: John Dewey. Dewey (1915, 1916, 1948) was likely one of the most effective voices in demonstrating how educational philosophy can inform and shape practice. But in doing so, he saw the necessity of an ongoing reconstruction of our views of philosophy, society, education, and schools. The fact that he is widely admired and criticized today makes him an even better choice for some of us. But we should not stop with him. The search for ideas and educational philosophers who connect in accessible ways with the concerns of practitioners is too important to stop with him.

Second, we may be well advised to reexamine the way we view and interact with people in other education preparation fields. Standing on the outside of the worlds and work of our colleagues and criticizing them appears largely unfruitful. Entering into their realms of professional perception and activity and joining with them in their research and teaching may be challenging but such also holds the promise of greater influence in colleges of education and improved contributions to the fields of educator preparation and P-12 teaching. For instance, rather than standing alone to critique, say, certain policies implemented by administrators, specific kinds of diversity discourse, questionable claims of some critical theorists, particular feminist dichotomies, and individual learning theories, we might be better advised to see issues through their eyes, understand their paradigms, appreciate their findings, and collaborate with them on projects that are mutually informative.

An example of entering into the worlds of our colleagues may be found in the field of educational research. Think for a moment about the contributions an educational philosopher could—and actually do—make if she or he taught in the area of qualitative research. With the increasing sophistication of qualitative research, questions about the nature of meaning and scholarship and the requirements for knowledge discovery and construction have become important discussions for social science researchers. This change opens the opportunity for us to examine epistemological questions in a way that is relevant to educational research and practice of aspiring and practicing classroom teachers, district administrators, and education professors.

Of course, there can be a distinct cost to pay for tying philosophy to other fields of study. If we are to claim that philosophy, or even philosophy of education, is a distinct field of study we must be able to demonstrate a knowledge base and form of inquiry of intrinsic value, rather than basing the justification of our existence entirely on providing assistant to other fields. This dilemma requires a careful balancing act for us to follow, to make ourselves relevant, without losing our own identities and unique contributions. In order to retain credibility in educational philosophy circles and, perhaps, with general philosophers, we must continue to embrace and expand our knowledge base. This unending reflective balancing process calls for us to claim a standard of inquiry that is both philosophy and education. Some argue, perhaps correctly, that this is an impossible demand to place on philosophers of education. We differ in that we think doing philosophy of education is adding to the knowledge base of philosophy as well as contributing to the knowledge base of education just as doing philosophy of science adds to both domains. In closing, we wish to note a comment by a former colleague that is only partially recalled: "Philosophers have it relatively easy if they limit their inquiries and teaching largely to theoretical matters which seldom influence the everyday lives of people. Educational philosophers seldom if ever have this luxury." We might add that educational philosophers who claim this luxury frequently contribute to the demise of philosophy and education in colleges of education.

References

Archard, D. (2000). *Sex education*. London: Philosophy of Education Society of Great Britain.
Barnes, W. (September 1920). Culture and efficiency: Their relation to English subjects. *Education, 12*(3): 135–147.
Bredo, E. & Feinberg, W. (1982). The positivistic approach to social and educational research. In E. Bredo & W. Feinberg (Eds.), *Knowledge and values in social and educational research* (pp. 13–27). Philadelphia: Temple University Press.
Dewey, J. (1915/1976). *The school and society*. Carbondale: Southern Illinois University Press.
Dewey, J. (1916). *Democracy and education*. New York: Macmillan.
Dewey, J. (1948). *Reconstruction in philosophy*. (Enlarged edition). Boston: Beacon Press.
Dwyer, J. (2002). *Vouchers within reason*. Ithaca, NY: Cornell University Press.
Glendinning, S. (2006). *The idea of continental philosophy*. Edinburgh: Edinburgh University Press.
Gutmann, A. (1999). *Democratic education*. Princeton, NJ: Princeton University Press.
Matthews, M. (ed.) (1998). *Constructivism and science education: A philosophical examination*. Dordrecht: Kluwer.
Noddings, N. (2002). *Educating moral people: A caring alternative to character education*. New York: Teachers College Press.
O'Neill, W. (1982). *Educational ideologies: Contemporary expressions of educational philosophy*. Santa Monica, CA: Goodyear.
Phillips, D., & Soltis, J. (2003). *Perspectives on learning* (4th ed.). New York: Teachers College Press.
Rescher, N. (2001). *Philosophical reasoning: A study in the methodology of philosophizing*. Oxford: Wiley-Blackwell.
Schiro, M. (2008). *Curriculum theory: Conflicting visions and enduring concerns*. Los Angeles: Sage.
Simon, R. (1994). *Neutrality and the academic ethic*. Lanham, MD: Rowman & Littlefield.
Simpson, D. (1994). *The pedagodfathers: The lords of education*. Calgary, AB: Detselig.
Steiner, M. (1998). *The application of mathematics as a philosophical problem*. Cambridge, MA: Harvard University Press.

Strike, K., & Soltis, J. (2004). *The ethics of teaching* (4th ed.). New York: Teachers College Press.
Wagner, P., and & Simpson, D. (2009). *Ethical decision making and school administration: Leadership as moral architecture.* Los Angeles: Sage.

Seventeen

Education, Philosophy, and the Cultivation of Humanity

William B. Stanley

In this chapter, I provide a brief summary of the current educational context in terms of its hostility to philosophical study. The reasons why a lack of emphasis on philosophy makes a difference are then explored. I follow this exploration with two examples of practical reasoning and curriculum as Bildung to illustrate the inextricable relationship between education and philosophy. Finally, I offer some suggestions for how we might address this issue in professional education programs.

Structural Context

As this chapter makes clear, the low esteem for philosophical study in our culture is increasingly evident in our K–12 curriculum and impoverishes how we design and implement programs for teacher and other professional education programs. On those occasions where philosophy is an explicit component of teacher education programs, it is generally subsumed within educational foundations (or introduction to education) courses, and educational foundations itself is a shrinking component of teacher education. The attention to philosophy is even less in current graduate programs in educational leadership, literacy, school counseling, or special education. In the midst of the current bipartisan No Child Left Behind reform climate, there is little to no support for expanding an emphasis on philosophy in professional education programs. What if anything can (or should) be done?

To do nothing would be an abdication of professional responsibility. As I will argue below, education is an intrinsically philosophical process, and candidates unaware or unable to understand this dimension of education are condemned to get it wrong in practice (Blake et al., 2003). That said, the realistic options for change are limited. Under the constraints of the various national and state accountability and standards reform policies, most states have reduced or capped the number of education credits in undergraduate teacher education programs. State and national teacher education standards have also been raised significantly over the past 40 years. While some of the new requirements are well intentioned and related to an expanded conception of student rights, educational research, and technological developments (e.g., "Title I legislation" requiring an inclusive learning environment for all students, training in culturally and linguistically appropriate methods for English-language learners and an increasingly diverse student population, utilizing instructional technology, classroom management, and a strong emphasis on content knowledge). Of course, the accountability/standards movement also reflects an oppressive ideology and corporatist conception of schooling that deskills teachers and treats students as empty vessels to be filled with the knowledge required to maintain the social order (Ross, 2001; Vinson & Ross, 2001; Pinar, 2004, 2006).

Whatever the motivation, the net effect of the dominant education reform movement is a need to fit a great deal more prescribed information into a static or shrinking conception of professional education programs. In short, the expansion of standards-driven program requirements combined with reductions or caps on education credits has led to eliminating some content and experiences to make room for others that address the new standards. Educational foundations courses (excepting educational psychology) have low status in the competition for program space. Many programs have eliminated foundations courses dealing with educational philosophy (or history and sociology for that matter). The foundations courses that do survive are generally diluted to justify their existence by incorporating elements of the expanding state and national standards. Exacerbating the problem, educational foundations courses are often taught by faculty with little or no training in philosophy. In many respects, the problem is worse in graduate professional education programs. Any attempt to inject philosophy into any of these programs is not a significant concern of national or state accreditation bodies.

Except for post-certification graduate programs in education, required courses in educational philosophy are rare and dependent on the interests of particular faculty, who often move to another institution or retire, leaving a philosophical vacuum in the program abandoned. In those undergraduate certification programs where an introduction to a philosophy course is included as a general education requirement or elective, the potential impact of the course is limited, as courses in philosophy departments are almost always taught without any relation to or dialogue with campus teacher education programs. While there are exceptions to the claims made above, the summary provides a good sense of the structural curriculum challenges faced by proponents of educational philosophy as an essential component of teacher education.

The challenge, however, is not merely a question of whether of not we include more philosophy in professional education programs, but how we conceive of philosophy's role in education. The Greek origin of the word philosophy (*philosophia*) refers to the love and pursuit of wisdom. Philosophy's low esteem in our culture aside, most education reformers across the political spectrum would acknowledge an allegiance to a philosophical orientation. For example, there are frequent references to critical thinking in the dominant discourse on school reform, and even ardent proponents of No Child Left Behind (NCLB) might agree wisdom is one goal of education. The important point is that how one conceives the relevance of philosophical wisdom to education. The dominant discourse on education reform treats philosophy as something external to educational practice, something imported into the curriculum passed on to teachers and educational leaders and orienting the standards to be implemented and assessed.

On the other hand, even those advocating an explicit inclusion of philosophy in professional education programs are divided as to philosophy's purpose. In the current debates over education, there are three influential approaches to answering this question (Hogan & Smith, 2003). The first perspective views philosophy as providing foundational "truths" or principles to orient education and teacher education, in particular (Plato, 1955; Hirst, 1974). This approach seeks to socialize students to certain dominant cultural narratives and is often expressed in arguments for "core knowledge," universal values, objective foundations for knowledge, and a rejection of any form of perspectivism, relativism, or skepticism. The proponents of national standards and NCLB either explicitly or tacitly espouse this sort of epistemology.

A second approach, the postmodern approach to pragmatism reflected in the work of philosophers like Richard Rorty (1979, 1982, 1989, 1990a, 1990b), holds that there is no truth and objectivity anywhere. The best we can hope for is the solidarity provided by community to orient our praxis. Rorty questions philosophy's potential to contribute anything of value to education. At best, the study of philosophy might serve a therapeutic function, helping undergraduate students break free of outmoded ideas and "the crust of convention" (Rorty, 1990, p. 41). At the graduate level, philosophy might help students "reinvent themselves," although Rorty provides no guidelines for what might constitute a preferred rediscription of the individual. The irony is that Rorty's work, despite his apparent indifference to philosophy's relevance to education, is of more value than he acknowledges.

The philosophical rejection of foundationalism, rather than arguing for the irrelevance of philosophy to education, can lead to a different conception of education as philosophy. This third alternative to how philosophy and education are related was recognized by John Dewey in the late 19th and early 20th centuries (Dewey, 1916, 1917). Dewey (1929), responding to the impact of modernism, saw the human preoccupation with the "quest for certainty" in response to lost foundations as misguided and counterproductive. He believed that philosophy should abandon metaphysical search for foundations (the problems of philosophers) and focus on methods for dealing with the concrete and practical problems of men (Dewey, 1917). Dewey's conception of education understood knowledge not as something apart to be acquired but the product of human experience with the world. Education, by placing students in lifelike problematic situations, could develop a method of intelligence (inquiry) with individual and social growth as the ever-evolving "end-in-view." Indeed, education was essential to the revival and preservation of democracy (Dewey, 1927, p. 324).

What Difference Does It Make?

For those who succumb to the prevailing accountability/standards movement rhetoric, philosophy must seem far removed from the day-to-day world of teaching and curriculum. Indeed, the current reform movement, for the most part, conceives of teaching as an essentially technical profession, one in which teachers and educational leaders see their task as implementing curriculum established by groups external to the schools. This narrow technical conception of education badly underestimates the complexity and nature of human growth, curriculum development, and teaching. The current accountability and standards movement is one more phase in a long-term effort to deprofessionalize teaching and design educational materials that are "teacher and educational leader proof," rejecting the teacher's role as public intellectual (Apple, 1996, 2001; Pinar, 2004, 2006). Curriculum today is characterized by an overemphasis on teaching techniques, standardized testing, and outcomes-based education linked to a narrow, vocational, and corporate model. This pernicious approach to curriculum institutionalized by No Child Left Behind miseducates our youth and helps perpetuate a dysfunctional and anti-democratic social order, a situation Pinar (2004, 2006) calls our current "nightmare" in education.

Pinar et al. (1995, 1996) attributes the shift away from the progressive view of educators as public intellectuals in the early 20th century to the gradual exclusion of curriculum theorists from curriculum development in the public debates over education policy after 1969. As curriculum theorists lost what limited influence they had over schooling, they were replaced by a variety of stakeholders including representatives of the academic disciplines, psychologists, textbook publishers, corporate interests, conservative scholars and think tanks, and state and federal policy. It is these stakeholders that now control the public school curriculum, and the current educational power structure is unlikely to extend curriculum theorists any meaningful respect or role in curriculum development in the near future (Pinar, 1999, pp. 14–15, 2006). To paraphrase Orwell, those who control the K–12 curriculum control the curriculum of professional education.

Practical Reasoning

It is not that knowledge assessed by standardized tests has no place in education. The problem is the limited conception of education assumed by such methods of assessment. Conceived this way, curriculum is reduced to technical knowledge (akin to the Greek techne), that is, knowledge to accomplish specific predetermined ends separate from the interests of students. Cultural and technical knowledge is undoubtedly an important component in any culture. We could all generate a long list of cultural and technical knowledge essential to the survival of any society (e.g., foundation myths, core metaphors, medical tests, automobile repair, navigation, computer programming, spelling, and so on). As important as cultural and technical knowledge is, it does not encompass the full range of individual and cultural development.

In contrast, teaching and education more generally involve more complex, practical forms of knowledge related to the need for cultural change and individual growth (Schon, 1987; Schwab, 1984). Think of the multitude of decisions a teacher must make day-to-day in classrooms throughout the nation: Should I intervene or ignore what just happened? If I intervene, should I reprimand or counsel the student? On what basis should I abandon a lesson plan and take advantage of a "teachable moment?" When designing lessons, how should I deal with controversial issues that have no predetermined "right" outcomes? These are not decisions one can make in accordance with any a priori technical algorithm or decision-rule. The ancient Greeks describe a form of knowledge distinct from techne, that is, phronesis (praxis), which refers to the practical human competence to make decisions in situations that do not have predetermined best outcomes. Phronesis is at the core of education and something essential to our human being-in-the-world (Stanley & Whitson, 1990, 1992, p. 4). I use the term "practical" (or pragmatic) to refer to the character of the essential interpretive competency characteristic of our human being in the world (1990, p. 5). The difference between phronesis and techne can be expressed "as the difference between 'action' or 'doing' (praxis) and 'production' or 'making' (poiesis) (p. 5). Thus, techne and poiesis involve the skill to produce something that can be defined or conceived in advance so as to provide the specific rules and standards to determine completion of the task.

Phronesis, in contrast, refers to the competence necessary for praxis, that is, "human action for the sake of doing what is really good for people" (Whitson & Stanley, 1990, p. 6). *Phronesis* is employed for "the realization of human well-being, which, by its nature, must be open to continual reinterpretation" (p. 6). This does not deny that human praxis might be directed toward more immediate goals, but these should not be seen as ends but as intermediate objectives perceived as necessary for the general end of human well-being. As such, intermediate or proximate goals must constantly be reformulated as we constantly reconceptualize our view of human betterment. In other words, phronesis simultaneously involves both the competence to reformulate goals as well as the ability to determine goals and the actions necessary to achieve them. This process is antithetical to technical or instrumental action toward predetermined ends. In other words,

> Practical activity differs from the technical not simply because outcomes are unspecified, but because the activity itself is related to the outcomes in more than just an instrumental way, and it is for this reason that the objectives cannot be fully specified in advance of the practical activity. . . ..Praxis is inherently a mode of activity in which progressive development in understanding the purposes being pursued emerges within the activity itself. (Whitson & Stanley, 1990, p. 7)

In this way, the possible progressive reconceptualization of human well-being is contained within those practical activities wherein we pursue well-being itself. In other words, we formulate provisional conceptions of the good pursued, and this activity involves, in turn, a provisional interpretation of ourselves as human beings.

Beyond differentiating phronesis from technical competence, we should also understand phronesis as both the basic competence for interpretive activity, which is at the heart of curriculum development, teaching, social relations, and citizenship. To be human is to exist as an interpreting being (Gadamer, 1975; Habermas, 1971; Beiner, 1983; Bernstein, 1983). Interpretation or the competence for judgment is not merely something humans do; rather it is constitutive of our humanness, our being-in-the-world. This human competence for judgment involves all dimensions of human activity including the aesthetic, linguistic, political, and social. While practical judgment is critical in the public sphere, it is no less so in our private or other social activity. Indeed, as we come to understand the centrality of phronesis, the boundary between public and private begins to blur. Since phronesis involves practices and habits that are intellectual, moral, and aesthetic, we cannot consign practical competence to any distinct domain such as the cognitive or affective categories that pervade mainstream educational discourse (Whitson & Stanley, 1990, p. 9).

Put another way, phronesis represents a fundamental human interest, which includes all dimensions of human thought and action, particularly an ethical dimension involving a quest for the good or human betterment. A definitive conception of human good cannot be specified a priori but will evolve through the quest for this end in sight. Nevertheless, provisional and contingent human values are always already at the heart of this basic human project, since any individual's use of phronesis is already grounded in a preexisting shared culture. In other words, we do not develop practical competence in a values vacuum but always find ourselves acting within a multicultural context, at a particular historical juncture, and particular value context.

It is evident, as noted earlier, that the current structure of schooling and dominant school reform discourse largely ignore this critical element of curriculum. A related, but easily missed, problem is the tendency to reduce practical reasoning, when allegedly employed, to a set of critical thinking skills, leaving out the necessary emphasis on discernment, emotion, and imagination (Dunne & Pendlebury, 2003). Obviously, some adequate level of philosophical awareness is required for professional educators to understand and support genuine practical reasoning in the schools. We turn now to a conception of curriculum that incorporates human growth and the cultivation of practical reason for human betterment.

Education as Bildung

The Latin origins of the word "curriculum" (currere) can be understood as the course of experience in which a human being is formed. This idea is also captured in the German term "Bildung," as cultivation or coming to form (growth). In the Bildung tradition, philosophy and education are essentially synonymous terms designating the ongoing process of personal and social maturation. The Bildung concept was adopted in America by the St. Louis Hegelians and influenced Dewey's philosophical development in the late 19th century (Garrison, 2007; Good, 2007). Dewey was also influenced strongly by the emergence of philosophical pragmatism (Menand, 2001). Within the philosophical framework of pragmatism, it is the task of teachers to enable students to "come to form" in terms of their individual and social potential. The contours of coming to form are not something we can determine with precision in advance, as they evolve within the course of educational experience. Practical reasoning is a critical competence required for developing curriculum as Bildung. During this process, the end-means distinction proves to be an illusion, as any end is contingent on the consequences it generates and therefore a means to further ends, evolving and changing as we continually develop new sets of evolving means in response to our reconstruction of knowledge. This conception of the means/end relationship is consistent with Dewey's (1916) "end-in-view" approach to the purpose of education, as noted earlier. Dewey, of course, became the leading (although frequently misunderstood) proponent of this pragmatic/progressive approach to education in the 20th century.

Contrast the pragmatic conception of education with the dominant discourse on education reform, which sees curriculum (a set of content and objectives) as distinct from pedagogy (a means to achieving the objectives). Education as Bildung rejects the attempt to differentiate curriculum and pedagogy as a specific example of the confusion between means and ends mentioned earlier. To enable students to come to form—realize their full individual and social potential—requires a planned set of experiences (including exposure to content) relevant to that purpose. Determining what to teach and when to teach it are what Whitson (2008) describes as elements of the "topical facet" of curriculum. Beyond topics, curriculum also includes a wide range of interests, identities, relationships, practices, and contexts that shape how we form curriculum and, in turn, are formed by it individually and socially. This practice is always shaped by the practical decisions one needs to make in specific teaching contexts.

Whitson understands curriculum as textual reality. He does not use "text" as mere metaphor but a description of the human creation and experience of curriculum as a basic feature of our world. Much as a textile does not exist before the materials are interwoven, the school curriculum's existence requires the complex interweaving of human reality, including cultural, economic, gendered, historical, political, racial, sexual, etc. The school curriculum, however, central to those of us in education, is only a component drawn from what we might call the wider life curriculum in which we are continually being formed as we go about the process of curriculum formation itself.

Like practical reasoning, we can develop impoverished views of Bildung as a prescribed course to be run (set of experiences) with a predetermined end. This is not how Dewey understood the metaphor, and Whitson's (2008) nuanced conception of curriculum both complements and extends Dewey's ideas. Whitson argues we need to move away from "What knowledge is of most worth?" as the fundamental curriculum question. While acknowledging this question remains important and has oriented much of the work done in curriculum history and foundations, the more fundamental concern for educators involves questions like: "What is going on?" (in the current context of schooling) and "What should we be doing to facilitate individual and social growth for human betterment?" Absent the consciousness that can result from engaging in a sort of reflection, curriculum development and practice is blind. From Whitson's perspective (much like Dewey's), curriculum as Bildung then is a profoundly moral project, as teachers accept a professional responsibility to create educational experiences that help form students individually and socially consistent with an evolving conception of human betterment—the "end-in-sight." Within this conception of education, the question of philosophy's role in teacher education takes on new meaning and importance.

Where Do We Go from Here?

All things being equal, it would be better to have more opportunities to engage in philosophical reflection in professional education programs. It should be apparent, however, that merely adding philosophy courses or required units of study to foundations courses in professional education programs is unlikely to transform practice to focus on curriculum as Bildung. The problem is akin to one faced by other professions (e.g., business, law, medicine) that are periodically criticized for not giving sufficient attention to ethics in their respective programs. The most typical response to such criticism is to create a three-credit course in ethics required for all candidates in the program. Inoculation is the metaphor that comes to mind as programs attempt to inculcate ethical behavior by "vaccinating" each candidate with a three-credit dose of ethics. The effect, while well intentioned, is to cast ethics as a separate element that can be grafted onto a program to provide guidelines for professional action. Paradoxically, the inoculation model tends to marginalize ethics, reinforcing the view that it is peripheral, not central to the profession. Instead, professions at their core should have an ethical orientation (e.g., the "first do no harm" injunction in medicine) infused throughout the curriculum. The same might be said about human growth and betterment as professional education's "end-in-sight."

Obviously teacher educators must study some philosophy to enable them to understand practical reasoning and appreciate the nature of education as Bildung. Although Dewey was not an advocate of adding philosophy courses to professional education programs, providing more space in the teacher education curriculum to consider philosophical approaches to education is probably a necessary if not sufficient condition for progress. We must remain alert to the tendency for philosophy to be reduced to providing recipes (merely a set of values, principles, or more logical forms of thinking to apply when we practice education). Curriculum as Bildung does not add philosophy as an element external to education; education in action is philosophical in practice.

What then can be done? As Pinar (2004, 2006), Whitson (2008) and others have argued, we need a reconceptualized approach to education. Pinar makes a complex, nuanced argument for an intellectualized approach to curriculum as "complicated conversation," with an emphasis on education more grounded in a revised conception of the interdisciplinary synoptic text and individual "study" rather than instruction as a technical method to realize predetermined objectives and academic disciplinary knowledge (Pinar et al., 1995; Pinar, 2004, 2006). Curriculum theorists, and teacher educators in general, should develop an educational "counterculture" to help reconstruct individual and social awareness (2004, pp. 161–162).

Pinar, however, has little faith that schools of education are up to this task. Pinar (2004) even wonders if it might not be the time to consider closing schools of education and decoupling teacher certification from education courses so that those who continue to study education will do so out of intellectual interest. "The field would suffer a cataclysmic contraction—education schools would become small, perhaps reorganized as small departments in Colleges of Arts and Sciences—but the field that survived (if one survived at all) would be an academic, intellectual field, worthy of the name" (Pinar 2004, p. 220). Pinar's question is jarring but necessary to a relevant radical analysis of the problem, and our present structure for professional education is too often saturated with anti-intellectual elements, including a general contempt for philosophy. On the other hand, Pinar's attack on schools of education is music to the ears of critics on the right who seek to privatize education. Pinar takes pains to distance his ideas regarding teacher education from reactionary forces (with very different motives) who seek to privatize public education (pp. 220–222). He seems aware that privatization would eliminate the crucial role of the state in providing an education to sustain a democratic culture. However poorly this task is performed by the state in the present, abandonment of public education would ensure the elimination of a major source of the oxygen essential to democratic life.

There are good reasons for Pinar's pessimism. However, his attack on schools of education and call for curriculum theorists to distance themselves from schooling in their quest to produce the necessary counterculture leaves practitioners—teachers and administrators—in the lurch. I have raised my own concerns regarding teacher education and schooling to develop the sort of adults who are motivated and competent to participate in the strong form of deliberative democracy envisioned by most educators on the left (Stanley, 2007). Whatever the challenges, and they are indeed formidable, to abandon education as *Bildung* would be an act of nihilism. I find Whitson's (2008) approach to curriculum development and study more relevant, practical, and hopeful.

References

Apple, M. W. (1996). *Cultural politics and education*. New York: Teachers College Press.
Apple, M. W. (2001). *Education the "Right" way: Markets, standards, and inequality*. New York: Routledge Falmer.
Beiner, R. (1983). *Political judgment*. Chicago: University of Chicago Press.
Bernstein, R. J. (1983). *Beyond objectivism and relativism: Science, hermeneutics, and praxis*. Philadelphia: University of Pennsylvania Press.
Blake, N., Smeyers, P., Smith, R., & Standish, P. (2003). *The Blackwell guide to philosophy of education*. Oxford, UK: Blackwell.
Dewey, J. (1916). *Democracy and education: An introduction to the philosophy of education*. New York: Macmillan.
Dewey, J. (1917). The need for a recovery of philosophy (10th ed.). In J. A. Boydston (ed.), *The middle works, 1899–1924, Volumes 1–10*, Carbondale. IL: Southern Illinois University Press, 1969–1991.
Dewey, J. (1929). *The quest for certainty: A study of the relation between knowledge and action*. New York: Minton, Balch..
Dewey, J. (1933b). The underlying philosophy of education. In W. H. Kilpatrick (ed.), *The educational frontier* (pp. 287–320). New York: D. Appleton Century.
Dewey, J. (1935c). The need for orientation. *Forum* 93(6): 333–335.

Dewey, J. (1962). *The school and society*. Chicago: The University of Chicago Press.
Dunne, J., & Pendlebury, S. (2003). *Practical reason*. In N. Blake, P. Smeyers, R. Smith, & P. Standish (eds.), *The Blackwell guide to philosophy of education*. Oxford, UK: Blackwell, Chapter 11: 194–211.
Gadamer, H. G. (1975). *Truth and method*. London: Sheed & Ward.
Garrison, J. (2007). Identifying traces of *Bildung* in Dewey's philosophical system. Paper presented at the 34th annual conference of *The Society for the Advancement of American Philosophy*, Columbia, South Carolina, 3/8–3/10, 2007.
Good, J. A. (2007). The German *Bildung* tradition, Paper presented at the 34th annual conference of *The Society for the Advancement of American Philosophy*, Columbia, South Carolina, 3/8–3/10, 2007.
Habermas, J. (1971). *Knowledge and human interests*. Boston: Beacon.
Hirst, P. H. (1974). *Knowledge and curriculum: A collection of philosophical papers*. London: Routledge & Kegan Paul.
Hogan, P., & Smith, R. (2003). The activity of philosophy and the practice of education. In N. Blake, P. Smeyers, R. Smith, & P. Standish, (eds.), *The Blackwell guide to the philosophy of education*, Oxford, UK: Blackwell, Chapter 9: 165–180.
Menand, L. (2001). *The metaphysical club: A story of ideas in America*. New York: Farrar, Straus, & Giroux.
Pinar, W. F. (1999). Gracious submission. *Educational Researcher, 28*(1):14–15.
Pinar, W. F. (2004). *What is curriculum theory?* Mahwah, NJ: Lawrence Erlbaum.
Pinar, W. F. (2006). *The synoptic text today: Curriculum development after the reconceptualization*. New York: Peter Lang.
Pinar, W. F., Reynolds, W. M., Slattery, P., & Taubman, P. M. (1995). *Understanding curriculum*. New York: Peter Lang.
Plato. (1955). *The republic*, trans. H.D.P. Lee. Harmondsworth, England: Penguin Books.
Rorty, R. (1979). *Philosophy and the mirror of nature*. Princeton, NJ: Princeton University Press.
Rorty, R. (1982). *The consequences of pragmatism*. Minneapolis, MN: University of Minnesota Press.
Rorty, R. (1990a). The dangers of over-philosophication: Reply to Arcilla and Nicholson, *Educational Theory, 40*:,41–44.
Rorty, R. (1990b). Education without dogma. *Dialogue, 2*:44–47.
Schon, D. A. (1987). *Educating the reflective practitioner*. San Francisco: Jossey Bass.
Schwab, J. J. (1983). The practical 4: Something for curriculum professors to do. *Curriculum Inquiry, 13*(3): 239–256.
Stanley, W. B. (2007). Critical pedagogy: Democratic realism, neoliberalism, conservatism, and a tragic sense of education. In J. L. Kincheloe (ed.), *Critical pedagogy: Where are we now?* New York: Peter Lang.
Stanley, W. B., & Whitson, J. A. (1992). Citizenship as practical competence: A response to the new reform movement in social education. *International Journal of Social Education, 7*(2): 57–66.
Ross, E. W. (2001). *The social studies curriculum* (revised edition). Albany, NY: State University of New York Press.
Vinson, K. D., & Ross, E. W. (2001). In search of the social studies curriculum: Standardization, diversity, and a conflict of appearances. In William B. Stanley (ed.), *Critical issues for social studies research in the 21st Century: Research, problems, and prospects* (pp. 39–71). Greenwich, CT: Information Age.
Whitson, T. (2008). Decomposing curriculum, vs. curriculum–as–text. *The Journal of Curriculum and Pedagogy, 5*(1): 111–137.
Whitson, J. A., & Stanley, W. B. (1990, November). *Developing practical competence in social studies education*. Paper presented at the College and University Faculty Assembly, National Council for the Social Studies, Anaheim, California.

Eighteen

A Critical Complex Epistemology of Practice

Joe L. Kincheloe

In the 1980s, questions began to emerge in a variety of fields about how one learns to engage in the practice of a profession. Profound questions were raised about the role of professional knowledge and how it is used in the process of educating practitioners in a variety of domains. Teacher educators have learned from researchers studying situated cognition and reflective practice that practitioner ways of knowing are unique, quite different from the technical ways of knowing traditionally associated with professional expertise. Indeed, professional expertise is an uncertain enterprise as it confronts constantly changing, unique, and unstable conditions in social situations, cultural interchange, sci-tech contexts, and, of course, in classrooms.

The expert practitioners studied by socio-cognitivists and scholars of reflective practice relinquished the certainty that attends to professional expertise conceived as the repetitive administration of techniques to similar types of problems. Advocates of rigorous complex modes of professional practice insist that practitioners can develop higher-order forms of cognition and action, in the process becoming researchers of practice who explore the intricacies of educational purpose and its relation to everyday life in the classroom. This chapter explores what exactly such higher-order forms of cognition and action might look like in relation to the process of learning to teach.

Two Cultures: Researchers and Practitioners—the Complex Relationship between Research and Practice

Grounded on the assumption that traditional scientific notions of the relationship between knowledge produced about education and practice, the paper calls for more research on the complex nature of this relationship. At present a culture gap often exists between practitioners and researchers. Many teachers have come to believe that educational researchers have little to say that would be helpful to their everyday lives. In this context research and practice are separate entities—educational researchers are captives of their epistemologies and their professional culture's own agenda. They are captives in the sense that they have tended to ask only those questions answerable by the empirical methods of physical science. One discipline or paradigm is not adequate to the task of understanding the network of the intricate and ambiguous human relationships making up a classroom or a school. Researchers need a multidimensional set of research strategies to help understand such school/classroom interactions and their relationship to deep social, cultural, and economic structures. In the technical rationality of much educational research, the attempt to translate such intricate relationships into pedagogical knowledge often renders the data gathered meaningless in the eyes of practitioners. Until researchers gain a deeper understanding of the relationship between knowledge and practice—the epistemology of practice—the gulf between researchers and practitioners will remain.

Many educational research studies depend on observations within strictly controlled teaching situations that have little to do with everyday classrooms. What teachers perceive as the irrelevance of such research often relates to what Lee Shulman labeled "task validity," that is, the degree to which the environment in a laboratory is analogous to the complex environment of the classroom. Informed by the practical knowledge, many teachers have intuitively questioned the generalizability of laboratory research findings to the natural setting of the classroom. Teachers have suspected the inapplicability, but too often the social science, psychological, and educational research establishment was not so insightful. The "normal science" of the dominant paradigm assumed that laboratory research findings were the source of solution applicable in every classroom setting. Such a technical science has failed to understand that every classroom possesses a culture of its own with particular problems and their solutions.

A more complex educational science accounts for knowledge of what has happened previously in a classroom—how classroom meanings, codes, and conventions have been negotiated. An educational researcher simply cannot walk into a classroom without an understanding of the previously negotiated meanings and expect it to make sense. Indeed, it is even more unrealistic for the researcher to expect that generalizations applicable to other classrooms can be made from this incomplete and often misleading snapshot of a classroom. To understand the complexity of the classroom, more multidimensional, multiperspectival methods must be employed.

A more complex understanding of both the research process in general, and research methodology in particular, helps educational researchers appreciate that the space between teaching and the outcomes of learning is shaped by a cornucopia of variables. Because of this complexity, the attempt to explain divergence in student performance by reference to a few generalizable dimensions of teacher action is reductionistic and misleading. Central to this paper is the need for recognition of the complex and multidimensional relationship between research and practice. Our goal is not simply to research education but to explore new and more rigorous ways of engaging in such inquiry, to develop modes of research that lead to the development of practical forms of knowledge with a profound use value for educators.

Educating Reflective, Scholarly Practitioners Who Consume and Produce Educational Research

Teaching prospective teachers how to teach may be one of the most difficult pedagogical tasks a university assumes. Too often, however, it is assumed to be a mere technical act with little connection to philosophical purposes, politics, social and cultural questions or epistemological perceptions of what constitutes knowledge. Many teaching methods courses and textbooks that are based on traditional forms of empirical research reduce teaching to step-by-step recipes removed from any consideration of pedagogical purpose that transcends the mechanical transfer of data from teacher to student. Our theme of complexity emerges once again, as we consider that all performative activities from being a standup comic to teaching an algebra class are consistently interrupted by unexpected circumstances. In such a surprising situation initiates a form of reflection-in-action (Schon, 1995) that helps the entertainer or the teacher reconsider her understanding of the circumstance and the strategies she has been employing to accomplish particular goals. In many situations reflection in light of such surprises may lead to a reconceptualization of the goals themselves.

A scholarly, rigorously educated, reflective practitioner possesses the ability to restructure her conceptual framing of a situation—not only at the micro-level as it involves rethinking a technique but also at the meso- and macro-level as it involves school policy or socio-cultural understanding. In these contexts the practitioner has developed a professional expertise that allows her to improvise a new course of action that can be tested and interpreted on the spot. A teacher may employ such a form of professional cognition when she encounters a student whose learning style does not fit particular textbook archetypes. The teacher's ability to diagnose a learning problem resulting in such a circumstance involves a wide variety of social, cultural, psychological, cognitive, and pedagogical insights as well as the ability to conduct research in the immediacy of the classroom experience. Such reflection-in-action involves these activities and the questioning of the efficacy of particular assumptions, strategies, or beliefs involving one's own educational work.

Thus, the knowledges of professional education and educators are of a different variety than the propositional knowledge of science. Such propositional knowledge—for example, more time on task improves test scores—is not especially helpful to teachers who have to deal with the ever-changing dynamics of everyday life in schools. When researchers assume that teachers simply apply this propositional knowledge to their *technologies* of teaching, they make an epistemological mistake. Such application assumes an unproblematic relationship between research and practice. A complex understanding of educational research appreciates the multidimensional interaction between knowledge of education and educational practice. Educational research as it is conceptualized here is not produced for practitioner application but for the more interactive and complex purpose of cultivating educational insight. A complex articulation of educational research *informs* practitioners, it does not *direct* them. Indeed, it respects the interpretive ability of teachers and educational leaders to discern what, if anything, such research helps them understand about the context(s) in which they operate.

The assumption on which a more complex form of teacher education research rests is that teachers are reflective, scholarly professionals not technicians who merely follow the directives of superiors. More reductionistic modes of educational research support a classroom-based model of teacher education that inculcates teacher education students with empirical knowledge about teaching, subsequently placing them in field experiences where they implement such findings. The relationship between such knowledges and educational practice are often insufficiently discussed. Indeed, analysis of the types of educational knowledges studied and the diverse types of knowledges that exist in the universe of educational research are typically ignored.

In the reductionistic model there is no need for "mere practitioners" to waste their time with such questions. Moreover, the reductionistic model assumes that the empirical research produced by experts is of a universal variety—that it is true and applicable in all times and all places. A more complex view maintains that knowledge derived from such research must always be viewed in light of the unique circumstances of particular cases. Thus, teachers must view such knowledge within the social, cultural, economic, linguistic, and philosophical contexts of their own experiences. Thus, the complex view of research, practice, and their relationship transcends an epistemological model that promotes an evidence-based set of technical teaching skills for universal adoption by the teaching profession. A teacher education program based on the reductionistic model simply operates to *deliver* the certified technical teaching skills to students. Questions of conceptual frameworks and overall philosophies of professional education are irrelevant in the reductionistic context (Munby & Russell, 1996; Vavrus & Archibald, 1998; Ferreira & Alexandre, 2000).

A central dimension of what we are exploring here involves the positioning of teachers in the larger understanding of educational research and its relation to practice. In addition to its epistemological and scientific flaws the reductionistic orientation to research and practice contributes to the deskilling of teachers. As referenced above, teachers in this model are not viewed as professional knowledge consumers and producers or expert interpreters of educational research and its relationship to the contexts in which they are operating. Teachers in the reductionistic context are deprofessionalized, molded into functionaries who are not trusted to use their professional judgment. In this context the sanctity of the entire democratic educational process is compromised, as teachers are induced to adhere to standardized techniques mandated from above, from external entities.

We are dedicated to a philosophy of research and practice that respects teachers and their professional prerogative to diagnose and assess their students. In this process such teachers not only have the right but are also encouraged to develop curricular and pedagogical strategies to address specific classroom problems. Expert developed systems never function as well as rigorously educated individuals with an understanding of systemic purpose and the multiple contexts that shape the system, its stated and unstated goals, and professional practice within it. Obviously, such rigorously educated practitioners do not operate by applying an externally produced set of rules but on the insight gained from understanding the system from many angles combined with their professional experience. These insights are central to our complex epistemology of practice.

Epistemological Mismatch: Scientific Theories and Problems of Practice

The epistemological problems outlined above are not exclusive to teacher education but represent a long history of problems with knowledge and practice in the professions. The diverse professions bought into an epistemology of practice that assigned researchers to the task of applying systematic knowledge to the problems of practice. A form of technical rationality emerged in these higher educational contexts that viewed practice as primarily a process of adjusting the techniques of practitioners to clear and measurable system goals (Schon, 1995). Thus, educational research in such an epistemological context involves finding out what practitioner techniques will most efficiently raise test scores.

Thus, the complications of a complex enterprise such as teacher education are solved: teacher educators simply pass along the findings of research to the empty minds of passive students. The role of the teacher education researcher here involves creating a "correct" knowledge base for teaching. In our complex epistemology of practice the concept of practice itself is problematized. In this conceptual context, educational researchers explore not only diverse forms of educational knowledge but also their utility (Munby & Russell, 1996; Geeland & Taylor, 2000). What is the practitioner able to do via her encounter with this particular set of understandings? What does the knowledge we are producing look like when encountered and conceptualized in diverse contexts of practice?

Contemporary forms of epistemology of practice emerging out of initiatives such as the No Child Left Behind (NCLB) legislation are in many ways a recovery of epistemologies dominant in mid-twentieth century scholarship. Such modus operandi was especially common in post-World War II schools of business. Business educators of the era maintained that there existed a discrete set of managerial tasks in all organizational settings. Business researchers would produce research on the most effective way to perform such tasks and formal university educational programs would be established to *train* managers how to operate on the job (Whitley, 1995). Of course, what such managers encountered when they graduated from such programs is that standardized managerial skills are not very helpful in the diverse and multidimensional situations encountered in everyday commerce. The world of business is much too complex to employ standardized strategies designed for ideal situations quite different than the messy ones encountered on a daily basis. Being a manager, like being a teacher, requires a synthesis of multiple knowledges, ad hoc thinking and action, and a facility for an informed improvisational ability. The universal knowledges of reductionistic science do not deal with such complexity.

Of course, one way of dealing with the relationship between research and practice has been to ignore academic knowledges about practice and focus instead on trading stories of "real-world experience" with student practitioners. Obviously, such a strategy is ill advised, but one can understand the frustrations that lead to such a professional curriculum. Such stories *are* important and have a place in professional education simply because much of knowledge of practice resides in the context in which professional activities take place. This situated nature of professional knowledge, this knowing-in-action is an epistemological form that helps teachers deal with the ambiguous, mercurial, value-laden, and interpersonal dimensions of practice. Indeed, the problems of such practice are not merely technical but moral, philosophical, social, political, ad infinitum in character. Knowing-in-action subverts the reductionistic epistemology of practice with its notion that theory precedes practice. In this positivist context, professional education students get the theory—the correct way to teach—in classroom courses that they put into practice in the school setting (Hoban & Erickson, 1998; Munby & Russell, 1996).

Obviously, we are profoundly concerned with the failures of the technical-rational model of teacher education. Central to this failure is the positivist model's lack of concern with questioning the meaning of theory and concurrent devaluing of the need for analyzing the complex, multidimensional relationship between theory and practice. As noted above, this concern with positivist theory and its relationship to practice should not be interpreted as a rejection of theory and a retreat to an undertheorized notion of professional practice. Understanding these dynamics, we are interested in developing and studying complex forms of teacher education that don't simply *apply* the knowledges produced by various disciplines but instead interpret the insights produced by various academic disciplines in relation to the purposes, ethics, political and socio-cultural dimensions, and technical problems of educational practice. This is a different task, than the one delineated in the technical-rational model (Ferreira & Alexandre, 2000).

In this context, we are deeply interested in exploring the relationship between science and experience, especially, of course, as this interaction relates to the domain of learning to teach. Technical science is much more successful when it operates in domains where the bifurcation of knowledge and experience is possible—for example, "pure research" settings. Once knowledge production is situated in a context where the separation of knowledge and experience is not possible—for example, professional schools and professional education—numerous problems emerge. These professional settings with their unique demands of science have not been granted sufficient attention by the academy. The problems and enigmas encountered in such contexts have many times not been deemed worthy of extensive research. Thus, the insights needed to improve the quality of professional knowledge production and professional education have been neglected. In this important domain there is a profound need for rigorous research informed by the epistemological insights delineated here.

With these concepts in mind, professional educators begin to discern that rigorous educational practice transcends the simple application of scientific knowledge to the act of teaching. With this understanding in place the teacher education and the professional practice we envision involve much more than prospective teachers simply learning proscribed curriculum knowledge, replicating certified classroom management and motivation skills, and implementing practices designed to raise student test scores. Indeed, our complex vision involves studying the ways that teachers can develop the multidisciplinary-informed wisdom to understand the impact of particular social, cultural, political, economic, and ideological contexts on the functions of schools and the performances of diverse students, to appreciate the educational effects of specific forms of educational/school organization, to discern the consequences of certain cognitive theories on the nature of the teaching and learning that takes place in a school or a system, to uncover the assumptions about the role of teachers embedded in particular pedagogical strategies, and to gain the ability to imagine diverse ways of organizing educational experiences when professional diagnoses reveal problems with the status quo (Webb, 1995; Crebbin, 2001).

Lessons Derived from Practice in a Complex Epistemology

The adept practitioner envisioned in a complex epistemology of practice is a teacher who contextually frames the ill-defined problems she faces. In such a situation the practitioner uses her wide set of understandings to examine the vicissitudes of the educational act. Such forms of practitioner cognition empower the teacher to change her practice by making reasoned interpretations of the situation she faces. Such ways of operating allow the teacher to attack the sticky, ambiguous problems of the briar patch called everyday practice. Technical-rational knowledge of practice tends to ignore the highly important but messy problems of everyday institutional life while focusing on relatively insignificant but well-defined problems. Such well-defined problems tend to be technical—for example, the five steps to constructing a classroom bulletin board—not ethical or normative.

Thus, the confusing problems of lived practice do not lend themselves to one simple solution that is final. Depending on practitioners' values or normative assumptions, the solution to a problem shared by several practitioners may be acceptable to some but not to others. Values and their contradictions inform educational knowledge and answers to pedagogical questions.

Solutions to educational problems will vary from context to context, as a strategy appropriate in an upper-middle class, predominately white school may not be appropriate in a poor school in a heavily Latino area. Such complexity demands different forms of knowledge and practitioner thinking than the ones represented in a rational-technical model. An important question emerges in this context: What are the characteristics of professional knowledge that make it useful for practitioners?

The answers to such a question are central to our study of professional education and research. Instead of understanding the dynamic complexity of such a question and the need for rigorous research and analysis, higher education has often retreated to the safehouse of "pure research." In this conceptually truncated and epistemologically naïve domain, professional education is positioned as an "immature discipline" (Ferreira & Alexandre, 2000) because of its immunity to universally valid pronouncements about its practice. Instead of demeaning the discipline because of its complexity, higher education is promoting the study of the relationship connecting research, knowledge and practice. All domains of higher education have much to learn in such study. Indeed, it might be argued that the future of higher education and educationally informed action may reside in this interrelationship. In this context, knowledge is viewed less an abstract entity that can be stored in the computer folders of a mechanistic model of the brain and more as a living entity embedded in diverse situations and in practice (Hatton & Smith, 1995; Schon, 1995; Whitley, 1995; Lomax & Parker, 1996).

Raised in a technical-rational culture, practitioners involved in professional education ache for professional educators to tell them what to do. Responding to their students' pleas to "give us something we can use," they often succumb to the simplicity of step-by-step procedures—for example, the five ways to teach phonics to first graders. Here one can easily discern the way practice is abstracted from context, from a sense of purpose, or a social vision. When denizens of the modern research university observe such practice-based pedagogies, they reel with disdain and condescension. From their exalted positions in the research university the very integrity of higher education is compromised by such low-level activity.

The only alternative, however, they can offer in lieu of such vulgarly practical practices involves passing along particular forms of disciplinary knowledge that is, of course, completely disassociated from the perils of professional practice. Again, questions concerning the relationship connecting research, knowledge and indeterminate zones of practice are erased as they are deemed unfit for serious academic exploration. The idiosyncratic dynamics of situational ambiguity, conflict, confusion, chaos, and complexity are epistemologically estranged from dominant forms of research in many disciplines. A complex epistemology of practice offers an escape from both vulgar practicality and knowledge abstracted from practice. Such an escape employs a variety of research methodological and theoretical discourses—I have referred to this process elsewhere as the bricolage (Kincheloe, 2001; Kincheloe & Berry, 2004). Using the bricolage in a complex epistemology of practice, professional educators explore the disjunctions and the stresses of the interaction of the triad of research, knowledge, and practice. In these zones of interaction, researchers of the complex epistemology of practice can begin to understand how to deal with the research problems presented by these messy domains of ambiguity.

Acting on such understanding, educational researchers/professional educators begin to validate the insights and concerns of practitioners and to take seriously the lived conditions of teaching. Teachers have been telling educational researchers and professional educators for a long time that empirical generalizations about practice have little use in their teaching. This is why it is so important to think carefully about the types of knowledges that exist in the domain of practice. As we understand the different types of educational knowledges, we can become better equipped to understand how they are best produced, where they fit in a teacher education program, and how we might teach them. Professional education in numerous domains has never devoted sufficient attention to such questions. These inquiries are central to the type of research we propose to do.

Solving a problem or finding all the pieces of a jigsaw puzzle are not the end goals of research constructed within the framework of a complex epistemology of practice. This is not to argue that practitioners need to solve problems they encounter in practice. A key characteristic of the rigorously educated and well-prepared scholar teacher we seek to graduate, however, involves the ability to identify problems in schools and in practice that have not traditionally been viewed as problems. In this domain of scholarly practice, teachers learn to ask questions that are normative and philosophical and answer them in relation to larger contextual insights. Such abilities are both scholarly and practical—and that is the recipe for good teaching for which we are always searching. Those practitioners capable of such scholarly and practical skills surely have reached a level of practice that could be labeled rigorous. Indeed, in rigorous practice the scholarly and the practical cannot be separated.

This merging of the scholarly and the practical in a framework grounded on a complex epistemology of practice would help professional educators and practitioners in all domains begin a new conversation with one another. It would also help professional educators begin a new conversation with the university community in which they are housed. A central dimension of these conversations revolves around epistemology and epistemological analysis. Unfortunately, epistemology has not been viewed as especially important in teacher education, teaching practice, or in higher education. Even a few philosophers I have spoken with about these matters find the *applied* use of epistemology strange in "practical" contexts. Calls for scholar-practitioners to construct their own knowledges in both curricular and practice-based domains still seem out of step with the dominant impulses of professional education and the academy in general (Noone & Cartwright, 1996; Munby & Russell, 1996; Goodson, 1999). It is central to our understanding of the research, knowledge, and practice triad that these dominant impulses be addressed in our research.

The Move to Critical Complexity

At this point it is important to argue for a more rigorous epistemology of practice, one that understands the complications of lived reality and educational practice. The epistemological concept of critical complexity helps us move in such a direction. On one level, the notion of the web of reality is merely a metaphorical way to describe the importance of context in the construction of knowledge, human consciousness, and not just action. The more we understand the various contexts in which teaching and learning take place, the more we appreciate the complexity of the processes. The more of these contexts with which educators are familiar, the more rigorous the teaching and learning becomes. I am not arguing here for rigor for rigor's sake. The problems of teacher education and teaching are multidimensional and are always embedded in a context. The more work critical scholars studying cognition produce, the more it becomes apparent that a large percentage of student difficulties in school result not as much from cognitive inadequacy as from social contextual factors. Teachers need a rich understanding of the social backgrounds of students, the scholarly context in which disciplinary and counter-disciplinary knowledges are produced and transformed into subject matter, and the political context that helps shape educational purpose.

In the neo-positivistic schools of the contemporary era, learners' lives are decontextualized. When we examine the contexts and relationships connecting learner, culture, teaching, knowledge production and curriculum, teachers begin to move into a more complex paradigm. In this "zone of complexity," learning is viewed more as a dynamic and unpredictable process. As a complex, changing, unstable system, it resists generalized pronouncements and universal steps detailing "how to do it." Complex systems interact with multiple contexts and possess the capacity for self-organization and creative innovation. Each teaching and learning context has its unique dimensions that must be dealt with idiosyncratically. Our understanding of educational purpose is also shaped by the complexity of these contextual appreciations. Teacher educators and teachers who are aware of this complexity embrace an evolving notion of purpose always informed and modified by encounters with new contexts. This act rids teachers of the burden laid on them by a positivistic epistemology of practice.

Teachers informed by this critical complex epistemology act on these contextual insights to not only help understand a variety of educational knowledges but to grasp the needs of their students. In the critical complex orientation, such concerns can never be separated from the socio-political context—macro in the sense of the prevailing *Zeitgeist*, and micro as it refers to the context immediately surrounding any school. Critical teachers listen to marginalized voices and learn about their struggles with their environments. With these insights in mind, teacher educators and teachers delineate the effects of the contemporary political context shaped by corporations and economic interests; they build deep relationships with local communities, community organizations and concerned individuals in these settings. In this setting, students gain new opportunities to learn in not only classrooms but in unique community learning environments. Here they can often address particular socio-political dynamics and learn about them in very personal and compelling ways.

Teachers informed by a critical complex epistemology of practice place great emphasis on the notion of context and the act of contextualization in every aspect of their work. When problems in their teaching arise, they stand ready to connect the difficulty to a wider frame of reference with a broad array of possible causes. When pedagogical problems fail to meet the criteria of an archetype, these teachers research unused sources and employ the information acquired to develop a larger understanding of the interaction of the various systems involved with the difficulty. When teachers fail to perform such an act of contextualization, students get hurt.

For example, a student who is doing poorly in school may be viewed as lacking intelligence. Upon contextualization, teachers may find that the student is disturbed by a problem at home or by an undiagnosed illness. His or her lack of academic success may have nothing to do with the question of ability. When teachers do not contextualize, they tend to isolate various parts of a pedagogical circumstance and call each a problem. They tinker with components of the problem but never approach its holistic nature. Educational data, for example, derive meaning only in the context created by another data. Context may be more important than content. These insights change the way educational professionals approach their work.

As is often the case, John Dewey wrote decades ago of these contextual dynamics. In the second decade of the twentieth century, Dewey observed that many thinkers see knowledge as self-contained, as complete in itself. Knowledge, he contended, could never be viewed outside the context of its relationship to other information. We only have to call to mind, Dewey suggested, what passes in our schools as acquisition of knowledge to understand how it is decontextualized and lacks any meaningful connection to the experience of students. Anticipating the notion of a critical complex epistemology and a postformal (Kincheloe & Steinberg, 1993) cognition, Dewey concluded that an individual is a sophisticated thinker to the degree to which he or she sees an event not as something isolated "but in its connection with the common experience of mankind" (Dewey, 1916, pp. 342–343). To overcome the reductionism that has plagued education and allowed for its technicalization and hyper-rationalization, critical educators must take Dewey's insights into account.

What we label knowledge, the ways it is arranged and presented, the ways it is taught and learned, and what is considered an appropriate display of having learned it is inseparable from the way we view the world, the purposes of education, the nature of good society, and the workings of the human mind. Such issues are connected to issues of power and questions of who is entitled to promote his or her view of the world. Thus, the contemporary effort to hold educators accountable—a key feature of current discourse on educational reform—is not some simple process where experts merely decree the proper instrument to measure the quality of teaching. Instead, it is part of a larger struggle between proponents' various worldviews, social visions, and conceptions of what it means to be human. A critical complex pedagogy maintains that in order to contribute to the effort to improve education, teachers, students, parents, politicians, and community members must gain a more textured understanding of the momentous issues being discussed here.

The worldview and epistemology that support standardization reforms assume that absolute forms of measurement can be applied to human endeavors such as education. The teaching and learning processes, advocates of standardization believe, are sufficiently consistent and stable to allow for precise measurability. The strategies that educators use and the factors that produce good and bad student performance can be isolated and even expressed in mathematical terms. Therefore, because questions based on students' acquisition of selected bits of knowledge can be easily devised and we can determine a student's and a teacher's competence with little difficulty because such measurements can be accurately made, advocates of reductionist standardization see little complexity in the effort to hold teachers accountable. Critical educators aware of a complex epistemology of practice want to move beyond this simplified model, to help all parties understand the multiple contexts that shape in diverse and sometimes conflicting ways of what is going on in such a process. Despite the pronouncements of many experts, the evaluation process is more complicated than simply designating the mastery of a fragment of content as an objective and then determining if it has been achieved.

Regardless of a critical complex pedagogy's recognition of the complications and loaded assumptions of this evaluation process, standardized reform movements continue to hold sway in the public conversation about education. One reason for this may involve the simplification process referenced here—they are easy for everyone to understand. Simplicity sells, complexity doesn't. "We can keep close tabs on student performance at the school level," the proponents of educational standardization tell the public. Using our mathematical measurement of student acquisition of content, they continue, we can compare the performance of schools, school districts, states/provinces, and nations regardless of the contextual differences that make them unique. All of these measurements and comparisons are guided by a *faith* in the value of standardized, content-based tests and the knowledge they produce. The faith in the meaning of what is measured by such tests is not grounded in some form of rigorous empirical evaluation. Indeed, such a process is the quintessence of reductionism.

The idea that such tests measure student achievement or ability and teacher effectiveness is an interpretation—nothing more, nothing less. Obviously, those of us who embrace a critical complex pedagogy have no trouble with interpretations—all knowledge is produced by an interpretive process. The problem here is that advocates of standardization do not reveal the interpretive aspects of the testing process; they present the data and its meaning as scientifically validated truth. A rigorous analysis of how such truth is produced reveals many interpretive (subjective) steps in the process. A critical understanding of knowledge induces us to ask that the reasons for particular ascriptions of test meaning be provided. Concurrently, such a critical stance moves us to abandon claims of objectivity in such an accountability process, such an epistemology of practice.

Guided by a leap of faith in what tests tell us about the educational process—Is the district wealthy? Are there many formally educated parents? Does every child come from a family whose first language is English? ad infinitum—advocates of standardized reforms have unleashed a process where students and teachers will be ranked and ordered to an unprecedented degree. Once students are placed in the low rankings, it becomes extremely difficult to get them out. Thus, reductionist educational reforms along with the testing and the ranking that accompany them are willing to construct an entire educational system including its purposes, rewards, and punishment structures on a faith in the worthiness of an unexamined mode of knowledge production and standardized testing process. In the norm-referenced measurements used in this context there must be winners and losers.

The fact that there are losers "proves" the system's rigor. Students are pitted against one another in a fierce competition for restricted rewards. As teaching and learning are reduced to knowing what, meaning is lost. Tragically, particular patterns begin to emerge involving which demographic groups tend to succeed when schools are arranged in this manner. Often students who come from lower socio-economic and non-white homes do not have the benefit of a parent who has a college degree. In homes where parents perform low-skill jobs, families may not see schoolwork in the same way as upper-middle class, white, English-speaking families. Studies of the social context of schooling point out that poor and racially marginalized students have learned to view academic work and the testing of technical standards as unreal, as a series of short-term tasks rather than activities with long-term significance for their lives.

Without such compensation or long-term justifications, such students may display little interest in academic work. Their poor performance on the tests and subsequent low ranking is viewed in the context of standardization as a lack of ability and academic failure. Their faith in the testing process moves educators to issue a scientifically validated assessment of cognitive inferiority to such students. Such a decontextualized, reductionistic view of the complex process of schooling and students' performance is unacceptable—indeed, it is socially dangerous as it contributes to an unfair, unjustifiable sorting of the haves and the have-nots. Teaching is simplified, teachers are deskilled, and students who fall outside particular "mainstream" demographics are severely punished. Even students from the mainstream are subjected to an inferior, simplified education. Even despite the fact that many of them may succeed in the system of rewards, their scholarly abilities are undermined and their view of themselves and the world obstructed. A critical complex pedagogy that understands these epistemological dynamics takes on an urgent importance in this social context, as it attempts to rectify the human damage caused by an uncritical view of knowledge—this is positivist epistemology of practice.

References

Crebbin, W. (2001). The critically reflective practitioner. Retrieved from http://www.ballarat.edu.au/~wcrebbin/tb780.critreflect.html

Dewey, J. (1916). *Democracy and education*. New York:The Free Press.

Ferreira, M., & Alexandre, F. (2000). Education for citizenship: The challenge of teacher education in postmodernity. Retrieved from http://www.ioe.ac.uk/ccs/conference2000/papers/epsd/ferreiraandalexandre.html

Geeland, D., & Taylor, P. (2000). Writing our lived experience: Beyond the (pale) hermeneutic. *Electronic Journal of Science Education*, 5. Retrieved from http://unr.edu/homepage/crowther/ejse/geelanetal.html

Goodson, I. (1999). The educational researcher as public intellectual. *British Educational Research Journal, 25*(3): 277–297.

Hatton, N. & Smith, D. (1995). Reflection in teacher education: Towards definition and implementation. Retrieved from http://www2.edfac.usyd.edu.au/localresource/study1/hattonart.html

Hoban, G., & Erickson, G. (1998). *Frameworks for sustaining professional learning*. Paper presented at the Australiasian Science Education Research Association. Darwin, Australia.

Kincheloe, J.L., & Steinberg, S. (1993). A tentative description of post-formal thinking: The critical confrontation with cognitive theory. *Harvard Educational Review, 63*(3): 296–320.

Kincheloe, J.L. (2001). Describing the bricolage: Conceptualizing a new rigor in qualitative research. *Qualitative Inquiry*, 7(6): 679–692.

Kincheloe, J.L. & Berry, K. (2004). *Rigour and complexity in educational research: Conceptualizing the bricolage*. London: Open University Press.

Lomax, P. & Parker, Z. (1996). Representing a dialectical form of knowledge within a new epistemology for teaching and teacher education. Paper presented at the American Educational Research Association, New York.

Munby, H., & Russell, T. (1996). Theory follows practice in learning to teach and in research on teaching. Paper presented to American Educational Research Association, New York.

Noone, L., & Cartwright, P. (1996). Doing a critical literacy pedagogy: Transforming teachers in a teacher education course. Retrieved from http://www.atea.schools.net.au/ATEA/96conf/noone.html

Schon, D. (1995). The new scholarship requires a new epistemology. *Change, 27*(6): 26–29.

Vavrus, M., & Archibald, O. (1998). Teacher education practices supporting social justice: Approaching an individual self-study inquiry into institutional self-study process. Paper presented to the Second International Conference on Self-Study of Teacher Education Practice, Herstmonceux Castle, UK.

Webb, J. (1995). Extending the theory-practice spiral: Action research as a mechanism for crossing the academic/professional divide. *Web Journal of Current Legal Issues*, 2.

Whitley, R. (1995). Academic knowledge and work justification in management. *Organization Studies, 16*(1): 81–105.

Appendix 1

The Southern Epistemology[1]

Joe L. Kincheloe

The exploration of place in a southern context highlights the value that place sensitivity brings to educational theorizing. An understanding of southern place involves the history, literature, and sociology of the South for sure, but it also involves a more textured understanding of the southern mind—the southern epistemology. Not only does the South find itself inhabited by the living presence of a unique history, a peculiar literary tradition, and an unusual set of social relationships; Southerners also possess a distinctive way of knowing, an epistemology of place.

Southerners are suspicious of deterministic ideas, centering themselves on the notion of individual will. In their politics, religion, and literature Southerners have seen themselves as free moral agents. Exterior or interior forces of which they were not aware or over which they had no control did not, they have believed, determine behavior. Social or psychological theory smelled like determinism to the Southerner and was dismissed, often with great hostility. Positive thinking, religious fundamental, Zig Ziglar of Yazoo, Mississippi writes in *See You at the Top* (his textbook used in thousands of schools across the South to "promote patriotism, loyalty, and self-concept") that the two men who have caused the greatest harm in world history are Freud and Marx. Both men, Ziglar maintains, promoted ideas that claim that men are slaves to forces beyond their control. Reject Freud and Marx he urges students, accept Jesus Christ, and control your own destiny.

Men and women are responsible for their actions and even for the actions of their ancestors, most Southerners believe. In a region with such a tortured past with its evil and suffering, Southerners have been beset by guilt. This notion of responsibility has driven Southerners to extreme denials of the past or to painful struggles for atonement (Lawson, 15). The southern way to deal with the sins has been to tell stories about them rather than proposing abstract explanations. Southerners have consistently rejected the tendency of continental or for that matter Yankee intellectuals to value abstraction as reality (Montgomery, 176–77).

Such a mind set promotes a political conservatism in Southerners, which moves them to reject utopian visions based upon theoretical speculations (Havard, 40). Social programs that are not grounded on a recognition of the ambiguities of the concrete social world are not to be supported by many Southerners. Reform based on theoretical generalization will not work, they argue, and serves merely to hide a form of domination from the top down. Reform is only possible in the realm of the particular, they insist, for the individual is separate from his environment. The southern conception of justice is thus very personal and is illustrated by a suspicion of those who talk about and claim to act on the basis of "a social conscience."

Indeed, because of southern epistemological predisposition sociological ways of thinking have not come easily to Southerners. At its essence sociology is a generalizing discipline requiring, at least to begin with, that one disregard differences between individuals and between groups. The sociologist concentrates on their commonalities. When it is doing its job sociology applies abstract theoretical categories to diverse social phenomena in order to disclose the similarities between dissimilar empirical situations. Idiosyncrasy is often of little interest— hell, it's a nuisance that is often viewed by the larger model as an error. Sociology examines the forest; individual trees are not its primary concern. Southerners are raised to demand the very type of detail that social theorists have often instructed practitioners to ignore. Thus, the sense of place takes on a special importance to Southerners. Similar things are not seen as interchangeable and as a result the Southerner is a locally oriented entity (not necessarily parochial) with an emotional attachment to specific places.

Southerners have come to know their world through their respect for particularity and place. Such a way of knowing finds itself much more at home with philosophical, historical, and artistic modes of understanding human affairs than with the analytical modes of the mathematical sciences. Scientism, the Southerner suspects, reduces nature to fact; the entire process is then mystified by statistical manipulation. This is why Southerners have consistently held fill-in-the-blank questionnaires suspect. Statistics, they scoff, can be used to prove anything. This disdain of the late twentieth-century obsession with the quantifiable has made southerners dangerous to the progress of industrial capitalism with its instrumentally rational separation of means from ends (Wilson, 2). The modern era with its ever-spreading industrialization of the South and its conquest of more and more southern schools with its technocratic education is attempting to squash this "anachronistic" southernism.

The southern sense of place implies a historical awareness, which expresses itself in an attachment to the extended family—a localism of the Gemeinshaft variety. This southern localism involves a tendency to think of communities as distinct from one another and to prefer one's own in the process. At its best this predisposition is closely related to sense of place as it sensitizes one to those things that make a community unique: its natural setting with those places, for example, that one likes to be when the sun sets, the webs of friendship, and those kinship ties that would be impossible to reproduce elsewhere (Reed, 136). Such sensitivities often translate into a preference for the concrete over the abstract, which places concern with personal, family, and community relations on a higher level of priority than legal, contractual, and formal bureaucratic conventions. Southern life often centers around the family. Modern image makers in southern politics can promote no thirty-second TV impression of a candidate that succeeds better than "he's a solid family man."

The southern epistemology of place holds scores of implications for understanding the "mind of the South," as W. J. Cash put it. Truth, the southerner believes, is more easily discovered in a particular locale at a particular time. Essences are revealed to people close to the soil as they associate with their neighbors in proximity to the hills, valleys, and streams known intimately by all (Montgomery, 180). This was the argument of the Nashville Agrarians in the early 1930s when they objected to industrialization on the grounds that it destroyed this sacred quality of southern existence. Implicit in the Agrarian position and the southern ethos of localism is a rejection of secularism and its tendency to destroy the epistemology of place. Placelessness is the great southern phobia. Southerners are wary of individuals without place. In the southern oral tradition the traveling salesman is an exemplar of placelessness, and, as such, he is viewed with suspicion.

The "obdurant particularity" of the southern mind hangs on precariously. It is a particularity that intuitively rejects the ravages of late twentieth-century industrial alienation with its standardization, anonymity, and distrust of feeling (Wilson, 10). Intuition plays a major role in the southern epistemology. Understanding and insight often come to the Southerner in an immediate and spontaneous way—principles on which life are based are derived from shared emotion rather than a rational process (Havard, 35). The southern mentality, unlike other forms of Western rationality, has often escaped a dehumanizing logocentrism. In the last decade of the twentieth century the questions become: how much longer can the Southerner hold out? and has the logocentrism posse finally captured the southern renegade?

The southern epistemology holds an intrinsic suspicion of the attempt of social and educational science to generalize. The same southern mentality that sees reform possible only in the realm of the particular is uncomfortable with a grand scheme such as my own use of critical theoretical analysis. When history is subjected to secular theorizing a la Hegel, Marx, or the New Humanists, southern scholar Marion Montgomery writes, "humanity" emerges as shibboleth that may be employed as a tool for manipulation. "The reality of human life," he continues, "is 'deconstruct ed' by whatever selfproclaimed lords of existence have declared the world a mechanism in need of repair." This is what happened to the children of the 1980s, Montgomery concludes, as "some of them turned to Marcuse in desperation and with violent consequences." Montgomery's comments illustrate the paradox of southern epistemology (Montgomery, 180, 183).

To read Montgomery's work is to gain an appreciation of the aesthetics of southern particularity and the sense of place that accompanies it. At the same time, however, it confronts us with the underside of particularity conceived in isolation from the insight of more general analytical devices. The consequences of this underside of southern epistemology have haunted the region for decades. Even though Montgomery represents only one small portion of this underside, he is—through his rejection of what he calls secular theorizing—party to the perpetuation of its consequences. The southern fury against social theoretical generalization, which emerges from a radical particularity, often encourages an idea-related xenophobia (if not an outright xenophobia), a discomfort with the intellectual, an aversion to analysis, and a reluctance to embrace reform and social change (Hobson, 53).

This opposition to social reform that emerges from the epistemology of particularity finds its expression in the southern perception of the public and private domains. In their particularity Southerners fail to perceive the existence of a defined public sphere. The familial space, the private, expands far beyond its literal dimensions to engulf what is typically understood as public space. Racial integration was initially met with such hostility in the south because Southerners, immersed in their racism and their lack of public sense, saw the desegregation of public facilities as an invasion of their parlors.

The public/private question in southern life well illustrates the paradox of the southern epistemology. While radical particularity has slowed the necessary legal correction of institutionalized racism in the region, it has concurrently postponed the evolution (or is it devolution?) of the South into that alienated mass society where individuals are objectified into machine parts supervised by faceless bureaucrats. This is one manifestation of the reaction against modernity that W. J. Cash labels the "savage ideal" of the South (Cash, 327). The southern perception of the private sphere implies that a face-to-face relationship is a better mode for mediating both individual and social conflicts than is abstract and legally institutionalized arrangement (Havard, 41–42). The Southerner has traditionally preferred the informal chat to the office memo.

The southern epistemology of particularity exhibits itself in the region's institutions—especially in southern fundamentalism. The discomfort with theoretical generalization is revealed on the religious terrain in the form of a literal mindedness. Epistemological particularity and fundamentalism find themselves in a reflexive relationship; the impulse of particularity helps determine what aspects of the Christian theological tradition are emphasized; the fundamentalist disposition, in turn validates providentially the implicit particularistic, socially atheoretical outlook of the southern believer.

The southern evangelist has not been the prophet of sociological theory. Southern congregations are accustomed to sermons that are tailor-made for their particular sins (Sentelle, 152). Fingers are pointed, toes are stepped on, and in some cases individuals are singled out for condemnation. The code of southern fundamentalist behavior revolves around a litany of Thou Shalt Nots. Such a code evokes a concern for individual behavior that eventuates in mutual surveillance. The concern of fundamentalist parishioners with one another's "goings-on" is reminiscent of Theodor Adorno's description of authoritarian aggression in his work on the authoritarian personality. Southern fundamentalism, thus, has emphasized the action and feeling portions of Christianity while neglecting thorough and theological analysis. Such an emphasis leads fundamentalist preachers to exhort their congregations to give their hearts to Jesus without a serious examination of just who Jesus is.

Southern fundamentalist believers see individual salvation as the one way to social amelioration. The critical notion of the interrelationship between individual and society is incomprehensible to the southern fundamentalist. Humans are independent individuals, bestowed with the power of free will, to choose Jesus or to choose hell. The idea of a socially formed individual is not only theoretically incorrect in the eyes of the southern fundamentalist, it is unchristian. The particularistic nature of southern political conservatism is, from the fundamentalist perspective, validated by God Himself. In this conservative framework the individual inhabits a terrain where the social construction of personality is not important to a man or a woman concerned with a particularistic God who determines their eternal destiny in a socially atheoretical manner on Judgment Day.

A true believer raised in a fundamentalist tradition with its denial of the role of social theory in the process of understanding an individual's destiny has learned more than a mere theological position. The particularistic, socially atheoretical training influences the believer to view texts in general as literal documents. As literal documents they do not necessitate analysis and theoretical interpretation—they simply need to be mastered, i.e., committed to memory. A critically oriented teacher who values text deconstruction will experience great frustration with fundamentalist students who have been raised to view texts as literal. The attempt to expose the implicit political assumptions of a curriculum will often be met with a literal-minded resistance. Influenced by such an epistemological orientation southern education has suffered for decades from an acceptance of surface meanings.

Fundamentalist theology is an obvious place to look for the underside of the southern epistemology of particularity, but examples can be found elsewhere. The reaction of some contemporary southern illuminati to fellow southerners who have chosen to criticize the malformations of the homeland is quite revealing. The widespread condemnation of Mississippi journalist, novelist, and editor Willie Morris has been especially strident. In his books and essays on the South Morris has attempted to explain the nature of the region's racism and conservatism. Ever mindful of the southern sense of place and the insight it may provide, Morris writes of his boyhood home and of contemporary Mississippi life. His portrayal of the changing nature of southern race relations in *The Courting of Marcus Dupree* is an insightful and sensitive portrayal of the modern South.

Morris' work has evoked accusations of treason against the "southern nation." He has told the northern liberals what they want to hear, George Garrett writes. By denouncing southern life Morris and other "traitors" have ingratiated themselves to their northern "oppressors." Morris and his friends, like slaves of the Old South, pull wool over the eyes of the Yankee liberals by

> acting out with gusto and enthusiasm the part already assigned to them. This example is not likely to be followed by many southern writers, if only because there is no room for more than a few "house Southerners" in the North at one time. (Garrett, 145)

Garrett's brand of conservatism is grounded on a localism turned sour—a localism which has lapsed into provincialism. Those southerners who criticized Willie Morris on this level offer merely a chauvinistic defense of one's locale, which ignores the larger social questions demanded by social theorizing. Epistemological particularism becomes in this case a means for protecting unjust power relations. The social wounds of southern racism, sexism, and class bias will never be healed by mass amnesia.

Thus, the paradox of the southern epistemology of particularity reflects the larger enigma of the South: Mardi Gras and Jimmy Swaggart, Elvis Presley and Tennessee Ernie Ford, moonshine and Baptist punch, Hunter S. Thompson and James J. Kilpatrick, Andy Griffith as sheriff of Mayberry and Bull Conner. Faced with such paradox Southerners often find generalization too vexing. As a result, they have sought an anecdotal mode of particularity—an orientation that has helped produce the southern raconteur. The southern storyteller as cultural figure transcends classification as mere entertainer, for the storytelling becomes a means of comprehending reality, a method of reasoning. Cultural forms in the South often grew up around the storytelling impulse. Only the American South with its epistemology of particularity could have produced country music. Indeed, country music symbolized the anecdote as an epistemological form.

The lyrics of country music tell stories that are loaded with details—the journalistic who, what, when, where, and why (Reed, 50). Country singers are not dealing with Everyman but with particular people (most often southern folks) from particular southern places: Blue Ridge

Mountain Boy, Louisiana Woman, Mississippi Man, Blue Kentucky Girl, etc. . . . The stories of Johnny Cash and Tom T. Hall tell us of the locales, the predispositions, the appearances, the "mud, the blood, and the beer" of their subjects. When Johnny Paycheck sings "Take This Job and Shove It" we do not listen to a treatise on worker-management conflict but a story about a particular worker and a particular foreman with a flattop haircut. In "Wreck on the Highway" Roy Acuff sings of a car crash in such detail that his descriptions of whiskey and blood running together invite satire of the song as camp comedy. Whatever our reactions the songs share the emphasis on the particular so characteristic of the South. The emphasis on the individual, the concern with locale, the literary sense of place are all manifestations of the southern epistemology of place and particularity. To understand the south, its history, and its schools, to deconstruct the codes of the region, to develop a southern curriculum one must be familiar with this peculiar and paradoxical view of the world.

Note

1. Delivered as the Presidential Address at the 1990 meeting of the Southwestern Philosophy of Education Society and published in the *Proceedings of the Southwestern Philosophy of Education Society*, volume XLI, 1991.

References

Cash, W. J. (1941). *The mind of the South*. New York: Vintage Books.
Garrett, G. (1981). "Southernliterature here and now." In *Fifteen Southerners, Why the south will survive*. Athens, GA: Universityof Georgia Press.
Havard, W. C. (1981). "The distinctiveness of the South: Fading or reviving." In *Fifteen Southerners, Why the South will survive*. Athens, GA: University of Georgia Press.
Hobson, F. (1981). "A South too busy to hate." In *Fifteen Southerners, Whv the South will survive*. Athens, GA: University of Georgia Press.
Lawson, L. A. (1984). *Another generation: Southern fiction since world war II*. Jackson, MS: University of Mississippi Press.
Montgomery, M. (1981). "Solzhenitsyn as southerner." In *Fifteen Southerners, Why the South will survive*. Athens, GA: University of Georgia Press.
Reed, J. S. (1982). One South: An ethnic approach to regional culture. Baton Rouge: LSU Press.
Sentelle, D. B. (1981). "Listen and remember." In *Fifteen Southerners, Why the South will survive*. Athens, GA: University of Georgia Press.
Wilson, C. N. (1981). "Introduction: Should the South survive?" In *Fifteen Southerners, Why the South will survive*. Athens, GA: University of Georgia Press. (a version of this essay is included in William Pinar and Joe Kincheloe, Curriculum as social psychoanalysis: Essays on the significance of place. Albany, New York: State University of New York Press, 1991.

Appendix II

Soul

Lyrics by Joe L. Kincheloe

I'm not too happy 'bout the way things're going
I'm unimpressed with the seeds they've been sowing
My face is burning from the cold wind blowing
In cosmic poker I do think I'm folding

Chorus
But I wanna know, I wanna know, I wanna know
What happened to soul?
Where did it go?
What happened to soul?

I wanna tell you bout the history of soul
From out of the Delta it rocked and it rolled
Moved to the city where it really took hold
All that followed was cast in its mold

It smoldered deeply like a fire in the night
It laid the soundtrack for the Civil Rights fight
Warmongers quivered in the light of its might
We all were inspired by its power to incite

Bridge
It's the most American thing that I know
But the purveyors of power could not let it grow
They crucified it, buried it deep in a hole
But you just can't kill the power of the soul

Putting out a call across the land
To every child, every woman and man
Resurrect the soul, you know you can
Heed the call, make your stand

©2008 by Joe L. Kincheloe (http://www.youtube.com/watch?v=GEDy657ahd8)

Contributors

James H. Adams
James Adams is an Associate Professor in Instructional Systems and Workforce Development at Mississippi State University. He originated and teaches Issues of Diversity in Work and Educational Environments, and his research interests include the meaning of work in a diverse society and contradictions in job readiness programs. JAdams@colled.msstate.edu

Natalie G. Adams
Natalie Adams is a Professor in the Social Foundations of Education at The University of Alabama. She is the co-author of several books, including *Learning to Teach: A Critical Approach to Field Experiences*, *Cheerleader! An American Icon*, and *Geographies of Girlhood*.

Robert V. Bullough, Jr.
Robert V. Bullough, Jr. is Professor of Teacher Education and Associate Director of the Center for the Improvement of Teacher Education and Schooling (CITES), Brigham Young University, Provo, Utah, as well as Emeritus Professor of Educational Studies, University of Utah. His most recent books include (with Craig Kridel), *Stories of the Eight-Year Study: Reexamining Secondary Education in America* (SUNY Press, 2007), selected AERA, Division B, Outstanding Book for 2008, and *Counternarratives: Studies of Teacher Education and Becoming and Being a Teacher* (SUNY Press, 2008). His professional interests are wide ranging, from studies of the history of education and teacher education to mentoring, beginning teacher development, and self-study. Most recently he has completed a book addressing the various issues associated with traumatic brain injury and recovery.

Dennis Carlson

Dennis Carlson is a Professor of Curriculum and Cultural Studies in the Department of Educational Leadership at Miami University. He is the author of *Teachers and Crisis: Urban School Reform and Teachers' Work Culture*, *Making Progress: Education and Culture in New Times*, and *Leaving Save Harbors: Toward a New Progressivism in American Education and Public Life*. He has also co-edited a number of books in education, including *Keeping the Promise: Essays on Leadership, Democracy, and Education* (with C. P. Gause) and *Promises to Keep: Cultural Studies, Democratic Education and Public Life* (with Greg Dimitriadis). He has also published chapters in many edited volumes and articles in major educational journals. carlsodl@muohio.edu

Craig Cunningham

Craig A. Cunningham is Associate Professor in the department of Integrated Studies of Teaching, Technology, and Inquiry at National-Louis University in Chicago, where he teaches the history and philosophy of education as well as technology in education courses. Among Craig's specific research interests are the impact of Web 2.0 tools on learning in and out of school, the history of moral education in the United States, and John Dewey's theory of inquiry. Currently, Craig is working on a book about the teaching of systems thinking and modeling in K-12 classrooms. craig.cunningham@nl.edu

George J. Sefa Dei

George J. Sefa Dei is Professor [and immediate past Chair] of the Department of Sociology and Equity Studies, Ontario Institute for Studies in Education of the University of Toronto (OISE/UT). His teaching and research interests are in the areas of anti-racism, minority schooling, international development and anti-colonial thought, and he has published extensively in these areas as well as on minority youth schooling. In 2008 he published *Racists Beware: Uncovering Racial Politics in Contemporary Society* (Sense) and '*Crash' Politics and Anti-Racism: Interrogating Liberal Race Discourse* (Peter Lang) [co-edited with Philip Howard]. His forthcoming book is: *Teaching Africa: Toward a Transgressive Pedagogy* (Springer).

Clar Doyle

Clar Doyle has worked as a high school teacher, school district supervisor and coordinator, and is presently Professor Emeritus at Memorial University. He holds degrees in English and Education from Memorial University, Newfoundland; Religious Studies from Providence College, Rhode Island; and Curriculum Studies from Boston University, Massachusetts. He is on the Founding Members Advisory Board of The Freire Project at McGill University. He has published internationally and is the author of *Raising Curtains on Education* (1993). He has co-authored, with Amarjit Singh, *Reading and Teaching Henry Giroux* (2006) and has published widely with his colleagues on critical pedagogy and reflection in teacher education. He is the author of twenty produced plays. cdoyle@mun.ca

Lee S. Duemer

Lee S. Duemer is Professor of Educational Psychology in the College of Education at Texas Tech University. He did his graduate work at the University of Pittsburgh. He teaches history and philosophy of education, and qualitative research. His research focuses on history of higher education in the United States, and philosophical foundations of qualitative research.

Contributors 241

David Granger
David A. Granger is Professor of Education at SUNY Geneseo, where he currently serves as the Coordinator of the Foundations and Childhood Education Division. He is the author of *John Dewey, Robert Pirsig, and the Art of Living: Revisioning Aesthetic Education* (Palgrave Macmillan, 2006), and has published numerous articles on Dewey in journals including *Educational Theory, Studies in Philosophy and Education*, the *Journal of Aesthetic Education*, the *Journal of Curriculum Studies, Teachers College Record, Educational Studies*, and *Educational Change*. Most recently, Granger became editor of the John Dewey Society journal *Education and Culture*. granger@geneseo.edu

Randy Hewitt
Originally from Greer, South Carolina, Randy Hewitt has been at the University of Central Florida since 2001 and was promoted to Associate Professor in the spring of 2007. Hewitt's current research focuses on the critical sense of the American pragmatist and social reconstructionist traditions and on the art of democratic pedagogy. He is the author of *Dewey and Power: Renewing the Democratic Faith* (SENSE).

John Hoben
A former lawyer, as well as a teacher and poet, John Hoben is a Ph.D. candidate in Memorial University's Faculty of Education. John's teaching in the classroom is centered around creating spaces where students can bring imagination and personal experience to their academic work. In 2007 he was awarded a Canada Graduate Doctoral Scholarship from the Social Sciences and Humanities Council of Canada for a study on teachers and free speech. He, his wife, Sylvia, and their wonderful daughter, Sophia, live in Torbay.

David Kennedy
David Kennedy is Professor in the Department of Educational Foundations at Montclair State University. He is author of *The Well of Being: Childhood, Subjectivity, and Education* (SUNY Press 2006), *Changing Conceptions of Childhood: Images of Childhood from Renaissance to Post-Modernity* (Mellen, 2006), and *Philosophical Inquiry with Children: Essays on Theory and Practice* (Mellen, forthcoming), as well as numerous journal articles on philosophy of childhood and community of philosophical inquiry with children. kennedyd@mail.montclair.edu

Joe Kincheloe
Joe L. Kincheloe (1950–2008) was a philosopher's philosopher, a researcher's researcher, a teacher's teacher, and the quintessential embodiment of critical pedagogy. A tireless champion for socially-just pedagogy, he authored and edited over 60 books and hundreds of articles underpinned by his commitment to engagement, authenticity, and cultural work. His notions of teacher as researcher, critical constructivism, research bricolage, post-formal thinking, and critical cultural studies are internationally recognized. Joe was the supervisor and chair for scores of doctoral students from Pennsylvania State University, CUNY Graduate Center, and McGill University. His work and legacy continue to make a difference in faculties, schools, and communities from Barcelona, Spain, to Utrecht, Netherlands, to Daejong, Korea, to Melbourne, Australia, to Winnipeg, Manitoba, and back to where his work was grounded, Sao

Paulo, Brazil. Joe was a father, a husband, a musician, a teacher, a friend, and a researcher; his life was a bricolage of hyperreality, Tennessee Volunteers football, epistemological quandaries, his grandkids, and radical love. His curiosity and wonder informed his work and he filled his life with questioning the unquestioned and naming the unnamed. His collaboration with Randy Hewitt was his final book, fittingly with Randy, who was his undergraduate student in Clemson, South Carolina. Randy was the kid brother Joe always wanted, and Kelley, Sadie, Moey, and Althea/Doris were family.

Craig Kridel
Craig Kridel is the E. S. Gambrell Professor of Education and Curator of the Museum of Education, University of South Carolina. His research interests include progressive education, documentary editing, and educational biography. He has recently edited *The Sage Encyclopedia of Curriculum Studies* (2010) and *Classic Edition Sources: Education* (2009). He is currently completing a study of black progressive high schools from the 1940s (funded by the Spencer Foundation) and, in 2011, will serve as Scholar-in-Residence at the Rockefeller Archive Center, continuing his research into 1930s–1940s educational film. craig@sc.edu

Aaron M. Kuntz
Aaron M. Kuntz is Assistant Professor of Qualitative Research Methods at the University of Alabama. His research interests include: critical geography, academic citizenship and activism, materialist methodologies, and critical inquiry. He received his doctorate in Education from the University of Massachusetts Amherst.

Jane Fowler Morse
Jane Fowler Morse graduated from the University of Chicago with a degree in Classical Literatures and Languages and earned her doctorate in Educational Foundations at the University of Kansas. She taught high school in Topeka, Kansas, before moving to the State University of New York at Geneseo to teach the philosophy and foundations of education and humanities. Dr. Morse is the author of *A Level Playing Field: School Finance in the Northeast* (SUNY Press, 2007) and articles on the philosophy of education.

John E. Petrovic
John E. Petrovic is Associate Professor of Educational Foundations and Policy Studies at The University of Alabama. He teaches in the areas of philosophy of education, multicultural education, and policy studies. His recent research has focused on developing a post-liberal philosophy of language policy. He is editor of and contributor to *International Perspectives on Bilingual Education: Policy, Practice, and Controversy*. petrovic@bamaed.ua.edu

Greg Seals
Greg Seals is Associate Professor in Social Foundations and Philosophy of Education at the College of Staten Island/CUNY. His primary areas of scholarly interest are John Dewey, the metaphysics of education, school desegregation and philosophy for children. seals@mail.csi.cuny.edu

Susan Shramm-Pate

Susan Schramm-Pate is Associate Professor of Curriculum Studies at the University of South Carolina and coauthor (with Katherine C. Reynolds) of *A Separate Sisterhood: Women Who Shaped Southern Education in the Progressive Era* and coeditor (with Rhonda B. Jeffries) of *Grappling with Diversity: Readings on Civil Rights Pedagogy and Critical Multiculturalism*. sschramm@gwm.sc.edu

Marlon Simmons

Marlon Simmons is a Ph.D. candidate in the Department of Sociology and Equity Studies at the Ontario Institute for Studies in Education, University of Toronto. His current research interests include anti-colonial thought, issues of governance and self in the context of schooling, and educational reform. The focus of his thesis is on modernity and colonialism, with a particular attention to Diasporic experiences and the interplay in the context of the West. He recently co-authored *The Indigenous as a Site of Decolonizing Knowledge for Conventional Development and the Link with Education: The African Case* (Sense, 2009), with George J. Sefa Dei, edited by Jonathan Langdon.

Doug Simpson

Douglas J. Simpson is a Professor and the Helen DeVitt Jones Chair in Teacher Education, Texas Tech University. His research explores the normative grounds of educational and curriculum theory by examining questions of ethical, epistemological, conceptual, and theoretical adequacy. doug.simpson@ttu.edu

William B. Stanley

William B. Stanley is Professor of Social Studies, Educational Foundations, and Curriculum Theory at Monmouth University, Long Branch, New Jersey. He is the author of *Curriculum for Utopia* (SUNY Press, 1992) and *Critical Issues in Social Studies Education* (Information Age, 2001), as well as author or coauthor of numerous book chapters and publications in a variety of journals including *Educational Theory, Educational Leadership, Social Education, Journal of Cognitive Science*, and *Theory and Research in Social Education*. Professor Stanley was a secondary social studies teacher for fourteen years and served as Department Chair at the University of Delaware, and Dean of Education at the University of Colorado-Boulder, the University of Redlands, and Monmouth University. wstanley@monmouth.edu

Shirley R. Steinberg

Shirley R. Steinberg is the incoming Chair and Director of the Werklund Foundation Centre for Youth Leadership Education, and Professor of Youth Studies in Education at the University of Calgary. Formerly a Research Professor at the University of Barcelona, she is the co-founder (with Joe Kincheloe) of The Paulo and Nita Freire International Project for Critical Pedagogy. She is the author and editor of many books in critical pedagogy, urban and youth culture, and cultural studies. Her most recent books include: *Teaching Against Islamophobia* (2010); *19 Urban Questions: Teaching in the City* (2010); *Christotainment: Selling Jesus Through Popular Culture* (2009); *Diversity and Multiculturalism: A Reader* (2009); *Media Literacy: A Reader* (2007); the award winning *Contemporary Youth Culture: An International Encyclopedia*; *Kinderculture: The Corporate Construction of Childhood* (2010, 2004); and *The Miseducation of the West: How*

Schools and Media Distort Our Understanding of the Islamic World (2004). She is currently finishing two books: *Writing and Publishing* and *The Bricolage and Qualitative Research*. She is also the founding editor of *Taboo: The Journal of Culture and Education*, and the Managing Editor of *The International Journal of Critical Pedagogy*. A regular columnist for CTV and CBC Radio Montreal, she is the author of many articles and chapters for books, sits on the board of several journals and speaks internationally on issues of pedagogy, diversity, social justice, and youth.

Clifton S. Tanabe
Clifton S. Tanabe has a Ph.D. in Educational Policy Studies and a law degree both from the University of Wisconsin—Madison. His scholarly interests include educational law and policy, educational/political philosophy and multiculturalism. Dr. Tanabe is the founder and former Co-Director of the Research Center for Cultural Diversity and Community Renewal at the University of Wisconsin—La Crosse. Currently, he is an Assistant Professor in the College of Education and an Adjunct Professor in the William S. Richardson School of Law at the University of Hawaii at Manoa, where he also serves as the Director of the Leaders for the Next Generation Program and Co-Director of the Hawaii Education Policy Center. His most challenging and rewarding position, however, is as a father of three (two well-behaved daughters ages 13 and 2 and one hilariously rambunctious 5-year-old son). cstanabe@hawaii.edu.

Barbara J. Thayer-Bacon teaches graduate courses on philosophy and history of education, social philosophy and cultural diversity at Indiana University, Bloomington. Her primary research areas are: philosophy of education, pragmatism, feminist theory and pedagogy, and cultural studies in education. She is an active member of numerous professional organizations, such as American Educational Research Association, American Educational Studies Association, and Philosophy of Education Society, and presents papers regularly at their annual conferences. She is the author of over a dozen chapters in essay collections and over fifty journal articles, published in professional journals such as *The Journal of Thought, Educational Theory, Studies in Philosophy and Education, Inquiry, Educational Foundations,* and *Educational Studies*. She has written four books, *Philosophy Applied to Education: Nurturing a Democratic Community in the Classroom*, with Dr. Charles S. Bacon as contributing author (Merrill, 1998); *Transforming Critical Thinking: Constructive Thinking* (Teachers College Press, 2000); *Relational "(e)pistemologies"* (Peter Lang, 2003), and *Beyond Liberal Democracy in Schools: The Power of Pluralism* (Teachers College Press, 2008). bthayer@utk.edu

Paul Theobald
Paul Theobald holds the Woods-Beals Chair in Urban and Rural Education at Buffalo State College in Buffalo, New York. He has published widely in the area of community-based and place-based education and is probably best known as one of the nation's leading authorities on the history of rural education. His most recent book is titled *Education Now: How Re-thinking America's Past Can Change Its Future* (Paradigm, 2009). theobapg@buffalostate.edu

Paul Thomas
An Associate Professor of Education at Furman University since 2002, P. L. Thomas taught high school English for 18 years at Woodruff High along with teaching as an adjunct at a number of upstate colleges. He has published fiction, poetry, and numerous scholarly works since the early 1980s. Currently, he works closely with the National Council of Teachers of

English (NCTE) as a column editor for *English Journal*, *Challenging Text*, and the SC Council of Teachers of English (SCCTE) as coeditor of *South Carolina English Teacher*. His major publications include a critique of American education, *Numbers Games* (Peter Lang, 2004); a text on the teaching of writing, *Teaching Writing Primer* (Peter Lang, 2005). He also edits a book series for Peter Lang Confronting the Text, Confronting the World—the most recent volume in which is *Reading, Learning, Teaching Ralph Ellison* (Peter Lang, 2008). He has also coauthored works with Joe Kincheloe, *Reading, Writing, and Thinking: The Postformal Basics* (Sense, 2006), and Renita Schmidt, *21st Century Literacy: If We Are Scripted Are We Literate?* (2009, Springer). His next books include *Parental Choice?* (Information Age, 2010) and the first volume in a new series he edits, *Challenging Genres: Comics and Graphic Novels* (forthcoming, Sense). His scholarship and teaching deal primarily with critical literacy and social justice. paul.thomas@furman.edu

Ed Welchel

Ed Welchel is an Associate Professor of Education at Wofford College in Spartanburg, S.C. Ed entered the world of higher education after 23 years teaching secondary social studies, particularly Advanced Placement U.S. history, in the public schools of South Carolina. His most recent book-length publication is *Reading, Learning, Teaching Howard Zinn* (Peter Lang, 2009). Ed's areas of research include the history of American education, educational biography, critical pedagogy, social class and education, and secondary social studies instruction. His doctoral dissertation was a biography of William Van Til, and he earned his Ed.D. in curriculum studies from the University of South Carolina.

COUNTERPOINTS

Studies in the Postmodern Theory of Education

General Editor
Shirley R. Steinberg

Counterpoints publishes the most compelling and imaginative books being written in education today. Grounded on the theoretical advances in criticalism, feminism, and postmodernism in the last two decades of the twentieth century, Counterpoints engages the meaning of these innovations in various forms of educational expression. Committed to the proposition that theoretical literature should be accessible to a variety of audiences, the series insists that its authors avoid esoteric and jargonistic languages that transform educational scholarship into an elite discourse for the initiated. Scholarly work matters only to the degree it affects consciousness and practice at multiple sites. Counterpoints' editorial policy is based on these principles and the ability of scholars to break new ground, to open new conversations, to go where educators have never gone before.

For additional information about this series or for the submission of manuscripts, please contact:

> Shirley R. Steinberg
> c/o Peter Lang Publishing, Inc.
> 29 Broadway, 18th floor
> New York, New York 10006

To order other books in this series, please contact our Customer Service Department:
> (800) 770-LANG (within the U.S.)
> (212) 647-7706 (outside the U.S.)
> (212) 647-7707 FAX

Or browse online by series:
> www.peterlang.com